William Joseph O'Neill Daunt

Eighty-Five Years of Irish History, 1800-1885

William Joseph O'Neill Daunt

Eighty-Five Years of Irish History, 1800-1885

ISBN/EAN: 9783744730747

Printed in Europe, USA, Canada, Australia, Japan

Cover: Foto ©ninafisch / pixelio.de

More available books at **www.hansebooks.com**

EIGHTY-FIVE YEARS OF IRISH HISTORY

"We know our duty to our Sovereign, and are loyal: we also know our duty to ourselves, and are resolved to be free."—*Declaration of Dungannon Volunteers*, 1782.

"You may make the Union binding as a law, but you can never make it obligatory on conscience. It will be obeyed as long as England is strong; but resistance to it will be in the abstract a duty, and the exhibition of that resistance will be merely a question of prudence."—RIGHT HON. WILLIAM SAURIN.

"Union is Irish alienation."—RIGHT HON. HENRY GRATTAN.

"Union is not unity. Heterogeneous and repugnant things may be arbitrarily tied together, but this is not unity. Closer contact elicits the repugnances which rend all external bonds asunder."—CARDINAL MANNING.

"Independence sends life through all the veins of a nation."—GOLDWIN SMITH.

EIGHTY-FIVE YEARS

OF

IRISH HISTORY.

1800—1885.

BY

WILLIAM JOSEPH O'NEILL DAUNT.

New Edition.

TO WHICH A SUPPLEMENTARY CHAPTER IS ADDED,
BRINGING DOWN THE NARRATIVE TO 1887.

LONDON:

WARD AND DOWNEY,

12, YORK STREET, COVENT GARDEN, W.C.

1888.

CHARLES DICKENS AND EVANS,
CRYSTAL PALACE PRESS.

PREFACE TO FIRST EDITION.

THE enactment of the Legislative Union in 1800 has been followed by almost incessant agitation to obtain its repeal. The desire of the Irish people to recover their right of domestic legislation is as natural as a sick man's desire for restoration to health. Ireland's vital need is Self-Government; the exclusive control and development of her own resources. "Placed," says the late Robert Holmes, "on the western skirt of Europe, with three-fourths of her shores washed by the Atlantic, after the discovery of a new world had opened to European enterprise new objects of adventure and new sources of aggrandisement, Ireland seemed destined to be an important connecting link in the intercourse between the Eastern and Western Hemispheres. Independent of the discovery of America, and the new field thereby opened for commercial enterprise, the situation of Ireland seemed peculiarly fitted for maritime pre-eminence. . . . Ireland, too, had before her many glorious examples of what free States, very inferior to her in extent of territory and other natural advantages, could achieve by commercial daring. The powers of independent existence seemed to be marked in her structure in such bold characters by nature, that it required the unceasing efforts of an active and malignant policy to defeat the obvious purposes of Creation." *

That active and malignant policy was never more perniciously exercised than in its efforts, first to corrupt, and

* "The Case of Ireland Stated." By Robert Holmes, Esq. 1847.

then to suppress, the Irish Legislature. To emancipate our country from its deadly influence is the purpose which has never been absent from the Irish mind for eighty-five years. It is a purpose consistent with the most devoted loyalty to the Crown. Its achievement would give strength and stability to Irish Constitutional loyalty by removing that fruitful source of discontent—the denial to Ireland of her indefeasible right of Self-Government.

In the following pages I have traced our exertions to recover that right—exertions in which I have been an humble but zealous participator.

During the recent debates that have followed Mr. Gladstone's introduction of the Government of Ireland Bill, an effervescent Orange member referred to the rebellion of 1798 as the result of Grattan's Constitution. "It was Pitt who did it," exclaimed Mr. Gladstone. This utterance of the Premier is extremely valuable. There is in England a nearly universal unacquaintance with the real character of the Union, as well as of the sanguinary means employed to achieve it. Therefore it is important that the English people should learn, on the high authority of the Premier, that the Act of Union is not only leprous with corruption but encrusted with blood—with the blood of the multitudes who, on both sides, fell in the rebellion which was deliberately provoked and fomented by Pitt and his agents as an indispensable preliminary to the destruction of the Irish Parliament. It was indeed Pitt who did it.

It is inspiriting to hear Mr. Gladstone sympathetically quoting from Grattan such a sentence as this : "I demand the continued severance of the Parliaments with a view to the continued and everlasting unity of the Empire."

"Was that," continued Mr. Gladstone, "a flight of rhetoric, an audacious paradox ? No, it was the statement of a problem which other countries have solved, and under circumstances much more difficult than ours."

Mr. Stansfeld is equally explicit in his recognition of the just claim of Ireland to autonomy. "Ireland," says the right hon. gentleman, "is a nation, and the denial of her nationality is an insult to her people." And again: "I believe in nationality—I believe in Irish nationality."

Such a declaration from a Cabinet Minister shows a vast change from the time when Lord John Russell coldly spoke of substituting what he called "Imperial nationality" for Irish nationality; or when Sir Robert Peel styled the legislative Union a "compact" too deeply rooted in the Constitution to suffer disturbance.

Our cause has many elements of strength. The first is its plain justice. The second is the great and rapid progress of English opinion in our favour, which progress has been accelerated by the Parnellite organisation in and out of the House of Commons. A third omen of our strength is, I think, the hostility of the Orange party; for it is a simple fact that their hostility has been usually followed by the triumph of whatever measure they opposed. They tried to prevent Her Majesty's accession to the Throne, and to make the Duke of Cumberland King. The traitorous plot fell through, and Her Majesty reigns. They declared that they never would permit the Emancipation of the Catholics—the Catholics were, of course, emancipated. They would not tolerate Municipal Reform. Orange opposition had its usual result—Municipal Reform was triumphantly carried. Then came Disestablishment of the State Church—Orange thunder shook the firmament. "No surrender" was shouted from every Orange platform. As on all previous occasions, Orange hostility was followed by the exhibition of Orange impotence —the State Church was disestablished. They now assail Home Rule with the menaces to which we are accustomed; they are to shake the torch of civil war all over Ireland with terrific glare; ditches are to be lined with heroes bearing rifles and Bibles—in short, Orange opposition is to be as formidable to Home Rule as it has been to the Queen's accession, and to all the other measures unpalatable to Orange prejudice. Mr. Gladstone accurately appreciates the value of their threats. "If," he says, "upon any occasion, by any individual or section, violent measures have been threatened in certain emergencies, I think the best compliment

I can pay to those who have threatened us is to take no notice whatever of the threats, but to treat them as momentary ebullitions."

It is especially interesting at the present juncture to look back at the time of the Union, at the acts and objects of its promoters and of their opponents, and at the successive agitations to shake off an unnatural and irritating yoke— a yoke as repulsive to the feelings of the great majority of the Irish nation as it is injurious to their material interests.

NOTE.

A REVIEWER in *Blackwood* notices that the present work is substantially an enlarged reproduction of "Ireland and her Agitators," originally published in 1845, and suggests that I should state that this is the case. I accept the suggestion of my critic; the more readily as it gives me an opportunity of mentioning that the aforesaid work, and also my "Personal Recollections of O'Connell," have been extensively plagiarised by Mr. C. M. O'Keeffe, in his "Life and Times of O'Connell."

CONTENTS.

CHAPTER I.
RECORDS OF THE UNION PERIOD 1   *PAGE*

CHAPTER II.
HOW THE REBELLION OF 1798 WAS PROVOKED . . 9

CHAPTER III.
PARLIAMENTARY CORRUPTION IN ENGLAND AND IRELAND 29

CHAPTER IV.
HOW IRISH DISCONTENT IS VIEWED BY SOME ENGLISH WRITERS 40

CHAPTER V.
THE DIPLOMACY OF MARQUIS CORNWALLIS . . . 44

CHAPTER VI.
REPEAL ACTION—SECTARIAN OBSTRUCTION . . . 53

CHAPTER VII.
THE EMANCIPATION STRUGGLE 66

CHAPTER VIII.
THE ZEAL OF A PACIFICATOR 81

CHAPTER IX.
ANTI-TITHE AGITATION OF 1831-2 90

CHAPTER X.
THE DISESTABLISHMENT CAMPAIGN 98

CHAPTER XI.
STATE CHURCH ARGUMENTS EXAMINED . . . 102

CHAPTER XII.
PROGRESS OF THE ANTI-TITHE MOVEMENT . . . 120

CHAPTER XIII.
THE REPEAL CAMPAIGN OF 1832 130

CHAPTER XIV.
ELECTIONEERING AGITATION IN 1832 144

CHAPTER XV.
NATIONAL COUNCIL CONVENED BY O'CONNELL IN 1833 . 154

CHAPTER XVI.
IRISH POLICY OF THE FIRST REFORMED PARLIAMENT . 162

CHAPTER XVII.
RESULTS OF THE COERCION ACT OF 1833 . . . 166

CHAPTER XVIII.
THE REPEAL DEBATE OF 1834 177

CHAPTER XIX.
O'CONNELL'S FINAL EFFORT FOR REPEAL . . . 192

CHAPTER XX.
GRADUAL PROGRESS OF THE REPEAL ASSOCIATION . 199

CHAPTER XXI.
PROPAGATION OF REPEAL BY MISSIONS . . . 205

CHAPTER XXII.
THE YOUNG IRELANDERS COME PROMINENTLY FORWARD 219

CHAPTER XXIII.
REPEAL DEBATED IN THE DUBLIN CORPORATION . . 228

CHAPTER XXIV.
THE MONSTER MEETINGS OF 1843 234

CHAPTER XXV.
MILITARY PREPARATIONS TO OPPOSE THE REPEALERS . 241

CHAPTER XXVI.
IMPRISONMENT OF O'CONNELL AND HIS FRIENDS IN 1844 247

CHAPTER XXVII.
CAREER OF A ROMANTIC AGITATOR 260

CHAPTER XXVIII.
CONDITION OF THE REPEAL MOVEMENT AFTER THE LIBERATION OF THE PRISONERS 269

CHAPTER XXIX.
ENGLISH POLITICIANS ON NATIONAL CLAIMS TO SELF-GOVERNMENT 280

CHAPTER XXX.
SUCCESSIVE AGITATIONS AGAINST POPULAR GRIEVANCES . 290

CHAPTER XXXI.
FORMATION OF BUTT'S HOME GOVERNMENT ASSOCIATION 298

CHAPTER XXXII.
PUBLIC CONFERENCE ON HOME GOVERNMENT . . 304

CHAPTER XXXIII.
THE GENERAL ELECTION OF 1874 308

CHAPTER XXXIV.
MR. PARNELL'S QUALIFICATIONS FOR LEADERSHIP . . 312

CHAPTER XXXV.
THE QUESTION OF REPEAL EXAMINED 319

CHAPTER XXXVI.
THE GLADSTONIAN FRANCHISE—HOME RULE PROPOSED 356

MISCELLANEOUS APPENDIX.
THE FINANCIAL GRIEVANCES OF IRELAND . . . 369

A LETTER TO HIS HOLINESS POPE LEO XIII. . . 391

EIGHTY-FIVE YEARS

OF

IRISH HISTORY, 1800—1885.

CHAPTER I.

RECORDS OF THE UNION PERIOD.

AMONG the traditionary anecdotes of the Union struggle, it is told that when Lord Castlereagh visited Mr. Shapland Carew, the Member for the County Wexford, in order to offer him a peerage and some other more substantial advantages, as inducements to vote for the Legislative Union, Mr. Carew indignantly exclaimed: "I will expose your insolent offer in the House of Commons to-night; I will get up in my place and charge you with the barefaced attempt to corrupt a legislator."

Castlereagh coolly replied: "Do so, if you will. But if you do, I will immediately get up and contradict you in presence of the House. I will declare, upon my honour, that you have uttered a falsehood; and I shall follow up that declaration by demanding satisfaction as soon as we are beyond the reach of the Serjeant-at-Arms."

Mr. Carew, it is said, desired the noble Secretary of State to get out of his house with all possible expedition, on pain of being kicked down the hall-door steps by his footman. Castlereagh accordingly withdrew; but Carew did not execute his threat of exposing the transaction to the House. It were idle to speculate on the motives which induced him to practise that forbearance. The incident vividly illustrates the desperate and unprincipled determination with which the Government and its tool pursued their object.

The Irish aristocracy and gentry of that period were a race of men who lived high, drank hard, fought duels, and often pursued a career of reckless extravagance. These habits were generated by their situation, which rendered them, to a very considerable extent, the irresponsible monopolists of local power. They largely partook of the national taste for splendour and magnificence—a taste which, duly regulated, tends to adorn the land and to refine and civilise the people; but which, in the circumstances then affecting the upper classes in Ireland, ensnared its votaries into that wasteful and ruinous expenditure which threw so many of their number upon the worst expedients of political corruption to retrieve their shattered fortunes.

The penal laws had wrought a most disastrous separation of the people from the gentry. The dominant Protestant party—the jovial, fox-hunting, claret-drinking squirearchy—all looked down on their Catholic countrymen as a totally inferior race of beings, intended by God Almighty for the inheritance of serfdom, and with whom it would be a degradation to suppose they could have the least community of interest. They were trained from the cradle to look thus scornfully on the Catholics. Contempt was a doctrine of their political Bible.

On the part of the Catholics, the moral consequences of the penal gulf that divided them from their more favoured countrymen were various, according to the varying dispositions of men. There was, amongst some, the reaction of deep and deadly hate. Others were awed into a social idolatry of Protestants. I knew one most respectable and very wealthy Catholic merchant who declared that when a boy at school, about the year 1780, he felt overwhelmed and bewildered at the honour of being permitted to play marbles with a Protestant schoolfellow. Every Protestant cobbler and tinker conceived himself superior to the Catholic of ancient lineage and ample inheritance. No wonder that there should have been offensive assumption on the one side, and rankling animosity as well as degrading servility on the other, when the law placed all the good things of the State in the hands of the few, and excluded the many from all participation in place, power, and emolument.

The Protestant aristocracy of Ireland wanted that wholesome check, that strong guarantee of political honesty, which would have arisen from contact with and representative dependence on the people. A whole people never can be bribed. But the people—the Catholic masses of Ireland—were a political nonentity for nearly the whole century. They formed no element of power, no ingredient in the speculating politician's calculations; a Lord Chancellor announced that the law of the land assumed their non-existence. And even after some of the restrictions on Catholics had been removed, the sentiment of Protestant contempt survived in full force, preventing that cordial coalition, that thorough mutual understanding between the two classes, which alone could have availed to defeat the ministerial assault on Irish legislative independence.

The Protestant nobility and squirearchy, half fearing and entirely despising their disfranchised countrymen, had for a long time looked upon themselves rather in the light of an English garrison occupying the country than as the legitimate aristocracy of Ireland. The notorious Doctor Patrick Duigenan, in a speech against the Catholic claims delivered in the House of Commons, 4th February, 1793, said: "In truth the Protestants in Ireland are but a British garrison in an enemy's country."* Yet, despite the colossal power of corruption, and the pernicious influence of religious bigotry, the very circumstance of their residing in, and making laws for, Ireland, had begun to produce its natural results on the minds of her domestic rulers about the time of the American war. The spark of patriotism had ignited the Protestant heart, and blazed up with dazzling brilliancy in the memorable and successful struggle of the Irish volunteers for Free Trade in 1779, and for constitutional independence in 1782.

But—fatal error!—the Catholics were not incorporated into the Constitution. Glorious and imposing was the superstructure; but it was fated to perish, because its foundations were too narrow to sustain its weight. It did not rest on the broad basis of the people. Yet the Catholics had done their best to assist in achieving the triumph of that period. Doctor Duigenan, in the speech already cited,† bears the following testimony: "The Catholics," he says, "not only mixed with Protestants in most of the volunteer corps throughout the kingdom, were regimented, carried arms publicly, and learned military tactics, but they formed themselves into large and numerous corps, well armed, accoutred, and instructed in military exercise, and marched, and

* Speech, p. 51. I possess the Doctor's oration in the shape of a pamphlet published at the time.
† Pages 23, 24.

appeared in military array on all occasions as other volunteers. I saw myself a corps of Dublin volunteers, called the Irish Brigade, nineteen in twenty of which were Catholics, march through the city of Dublin, and close to the gates of the Castle, the residence of His Majesty's Lieutenant, along with other volunteers, to be reviewed in His Majesty's Phœnix Park."

Elsewhere, in the same speech, the Doctor says: "Thousands of Irish Catholics carried arms during the season of volunteering without having procured any license whatever."*

This evidence of the active part borne by the Catholics in the national struggle to recover the Irish Constitution occurs in a speech directed against the admission of the Catholics to any of the privileges of the Constitution they had helped to establish. Sir Jonah Barrington, in recording the activity of the Catholics in the volunteer organisation, adds that they placed themselves under the command of Protestant officers.†

The Protestant patriotism of 1782 was a gallant and a goodly display; yet it presented some anomalous features. There was in it a great deal real, and something illusory. It was a curious sight, that of men in arms to enfranchise their country, yet resolved to perpetuate the disfranchisement of the great body of its inhabitants; men in arms to assert the honour and dignity of Ireland, yet entertaining a cordial contempt for five out of every six of its people. In truth, the Protestants had been so long accustomed to omit the Catholics from their political arithmetic that they had learned to look upon themselves—being then about one-sixth—as forming the sum total of the Irish nation. The thunder of Grattan had not yet shaken the strongholds of their bigotry. Their ambition culminated in the establishment of a free Constitution, of whose political benefits they were to be the monopolists.

Another anomaly was to be found in the fact that the bitterest enemies of Catholic Emancipation were sometimes the most strenuous champions of theoretic Irish independence. At a meeting of some of the friends of the volunteer movement, held in their house in Grafton Street, which Flood, Grattan, and Bartholomew Hoare attended, Flood, whose hostility to the Catholic claims was inflexible, proposed to

* Page 49.   † "Rise and Fall of the Irish Nation," chap. xvi.

his *confrères* a plan of total separation from England. Grattan said : "If you persevere in your proposition, I certainly shall not oppose it here; but I shall quit this room, and proceed at once to the Castle—to my Sovereign's Castle—and there disclose the treason, and denounce the traitor."

Yet Flood, the separatist, could not tolerate the notion of emancipating the Catholics; whilst Grattan, the zealous friend of the Catholics, and the champion of a free Irish Parliament in connection with the British Crown, denounced the ultra patriotism of the Protestant ascendency statesman, as treason. Flood, I need not add, withdrew his proposition.*

Emancipation, under an Irish Parliament, would have speedily blended all classes of religionists in one political mass. But the Catholics continued unemancipated; the Protestants remained a separate and exclusive band, distinct from, and rarely sympathising with, their fellow-countrymen. Thus placed far aloof from the people, there was little to countervail the corrupting influence of a profligate Court with which they were brought into close contact, and which derived immense facilities of corruption from the number of pocket-boroughs in the Irish House of Commons. With an unreformed Parliament and an unemancipated people, the distributors of place and pension enjoyed an easy sway. The pension list was swollen to an enormous magnitude; the number of sinecures incessantly augmented; and parliamentary profligacy came at last to be so general, that men lost all sense of its shame through the force of its prevalence.

Whilst the Government thus practised corruption on the largest scale, there were social vices peculiar to the period which extensively prevailed among the upper ranks. Of these practices the principal were duelling and drinking, which were carried to an excess happily now almost incredible. Take, for a specimen, Mr. Bagenal of Dunleckny, in the County Carlow—*King* Bagenal, as he was called throughout his extensive territories; and within their bounds no monarch was ever more absolute. Of high Norman lineage, of manners elegant, fascinating, polished by extensive intercourse with the great world, of princely income and of boundless hospitality, Mr. Bagenal possessed all the qualities and attributes calculated to procure for him popularity with every class. A terrestrial paradise was Dunleckny for all lovers of good wine,

* This anecdote was told me by O'Connell, to whom it had been narrated by Bartholomew Hoare, one of the persons present on the occasion referred to.

good horses, good dogs, and good society. His stud was magnificent, and he had a large number of capital hunters at the service of visitors who were not provided with steeds of their own. He derived great delight from encouraging the young men who frequented his house to hunt, drink, and solve points of honour at twelve paces. His politics were popular; he was mover of the grant of £50,000 to Grattan in 1782. He was at that time Member for the County Carlow.

Enthroned at Dunleckny, he gathered round him a host of spirits congenial to his own. He had a tender affection for pistols; a brace of which implements, loaded, were often laid before him on the dinner-table. After dinner the claret was produced in an unbroached cask; Bagenal's practice was to tap the cask with a bullet from one of his pistols, whilst he kept the other pistol *in terrorem* for any of the *convives* who should fail in doing ample justice to the wine.

Nothing could be more impressive than the bland, fatherly, affectionate air with which the old gentleman used to impart to his junior guests the results of his own experience, and the moral lessons which should regulate their conduct through life.

"In truth, my young friends, it behoves a youth entering the world to make a character for himself. Respect will only be accorded to character. A young man must show his proofs. I am not a quarrelsome person—I never was—I hate your mere duellist; but experience of the world tells me there are knotty points of which the only solution is the saw-handle. Rest upon your pistols, my boys! Occasions will arise in which the use of them is absolutely indispensable to character. A man, I repeat, must show his proofs—in this world courage will never be taken upon trust. I protest to heaven, my dear young friends, that I advise you exactly as I should advise my own son."

And having thus discharged his conscience, he would look blandly round upon his guests with the most patriarchal air imaginable.

His practice accorded with his precept. Some pigs, the property of a gentleman who had recently settled near Dunleckny, strayed into an enclosure of King Bagenal's and rooted up a flower-knot. The incensed monarch ordered that the porcine trespassers should be shorn of their ears and tails; and he transmitted the severed appendages to the owner of the swine with an intimation that he, too, deserved to have his ears docked; and that only that he had not got a tail, he (King Bagenal) would sever the caudal member from his dorsal extremity. "Now," quoth Bagenal, "if he's a gentleman he must burn powder after such a message as that."

Nor was he disappointed. A challenge was given by the owner of the pigs. Bagenal accepted it with alacrity, only stipulating that as he was old and feeble, being then in his seventy-ninth year, he should fight sitting in his armchair; and that as his infirmities prevented early rising, the meeting should take place in the afternoon. "Time was," said the old man with a sigh, "that I would have risen before daylight to fight at sunrise, but we cannot do these things at seventy-eight. Well, heaven's will be done."

They fought at twelve paces. Bagenal wounded his antagonist severely; the arm of the chair in which he sat was shattered, but he escaped unhurt; and he ended the day with a glorious carouse, tapping the claret, we may presume, as usual, by firing a pistol at the cask.

The traditions of Dunleckny allege that when Bagenal, in the course of his tour through Europe, visited the petty Court of Mecklenburg Strelitz, the Grand Duke, charmed with his magnificence and the reputation of his wealth, made him an offer of the hand of the fair Charlotte, who, being politely rejected by King Bagenal, was afterwards accepted by King George III.

Such was the lord of Dunleckny, and such was many an Irish squire of the day. Recklessness characterised the time. And yet there was a polished courtesy, a high-bred grace in the manners of men who imagined that to shoot, or to be shot at, on "the sod," was an indispensable ingredient in the character of a gentleman. Look at Bagenal, nearly fourscore, seated at the head of his table. You observe the refined urbanity of his manner, and the dignified air which is enhanced, not impaired, by the weight of years. You draw near to participate in the instructions of this ancient moralist. What a shock—half ludicrous, half horrible—to find that he inculcates the necessity of practice with the hair-triggers as the grand primary virtue which forms the gentleman!

At a somewhat later period the same extravagant ideas prevailed. At a contested election for the County of Cork, the well-known "Bully Egan" fought fourteen duels. Pugnacious barristers, whose knowledge of law was not very profound, sometimes made large sums of money at elections where fighting counsel were required. Elections in those days often lasted a fortnight or three weeks. Indeed they occasionally lasted longer. It is stated that Lord Castlereagh's first elections for the County Down lasted for forty-two days, and cost £60,000. Contests thus protracted might average, if party or personal animosity ran high, from one to two duels a day. It accordingly was the policy of the candidates to select good shots for their counsel. Within the present century Mr. Thomas O'Meara was agent at a Clare election, where he conducted the business of his client in a style so pacific as to excite the astonishment of a friend who was aware of his fire-eating propensities. "Why, Tom," said his friend, "you are marvellously quiet. How does it happen that you haven't got into any rumpus?" "Because my client does not pay me fighting price," replied Tom, with the most business-like air in the world. The tariff included two scales of payment for election counsel, the talking price and the fighting price.

These delirious notions were undoubtedly the indirect results of the anomalous position of the "Protestant garrison" in Ireland; of their immense and irresponsible social power, and of the lax, devil-may-care morality systematically acted on in the government of the country by successive administrations.

At an election for the County of Wexford in 1810, when Messrs. Alcock and Colclough were rival candidates, some tenants of a friend of Alcock declared their intention of voting for Colclough. "Receive their votes at your peril!" exclaimed Alcock. Colclough replied that he had not asked their votes, and that he certainly would not be bullied into rejecting them. Alcock thereupon challenged Colclough to fight. They met on the next day; the crowd who assembled on the ground included many magistrates; Colclough was shot through the heart, and Alcock, having thus got rid of his opponent, was duly returned for the county. He was tried at the next assizes for the murder of Colclough. Baron Smith publicly protested against finding him guilty, and the jury unanimously acquitted him.

CHAPTER II.

HOW THE REBELLION OF 1798 WAS PROVOKED.

"Of that system of coercion which preceded the late insurrection in Ireland, of the burning of villages, hanging their inhabitants, transporting persons suspected without trial, strangling and whipping to extort confession, and billeting the military at free quarters in districts in which individuals had been disorderly, his lordship (Charlemont) has been uniformly the declared enemy."—*Memoir of Lord Charlemont in "Public Characters of 1798."* Dublin, 1799.

THE motto I have prefixed to this chapter describes the mode taken by the agents of Pitt's Government to lash Ireland into that rebellion which was used as one of the arguments against our legislative independence. The rebellion, which the authorities "made to explode" (the words are Lord Castlereagh's), was deliberately provoked, in order to give England a pretext for filling Ireland with troops to crush out popular opposition to the Union. While military force was thus employed to destroy our Constitution, bribery on a scale of unprecedented magnitude was employed to purchase votes for the Union in the Houses of Parliament.

It is sometimes weakly urged that the venality of the last Irish Parliament is a perpetual disqualifier of the Irish people from the right of self-legislation. It might as well be said that the owner of an estate was disqualified from the rights of possession by the rascality of his agent. The Irish people had nothing to do with the venality of their legislators. The sin was not theirs, nor should its punishment be visited on them. And in the last grand struggle, the men who really were their representatives—the men who were returned for open, popular constituencies—nearly all voted against the ministerial project, and for the preservation of the Irish Parliament.

In glancing, however rapidly, at the Repeal agitation, we should not lose sight of that which is ever uppermost in the mind of every Irish Repealer—namely, that the Union is the offspring of conjoined fraud and force; that the means by which it was achieved were such as would inevitably vitiate any private transaction between two individuals. That Lord Castlereagh found many nominees for pocket-boroughs, many placemen, and every staff officer* in a

* Except Colonel O'Donnell.

Parliament which had been dexterously packed for the question, who were not so impracticable as Mr. Shapland Carew, was by no means the worst feature in the case. The machinery of crime which was to effectuate the Union had been long in preparation. With respect to the turbulent condition of Ireland for some years prior to the Union—with respect to the share the Government had in producing that turbulence, I shall not enter into lengthened details.

The following brief statements must suffice :

The Government goaded the people to rebellion, in order that the popular strength might be paralysed by civil war and its attendant horrors, so as to enable Mr. Pitt to force the Legislative Union on a prostrate and divided people. So far back as 1792, Edmund Burke had used these remarkable words : "By what I learn, the Castle considers the outlawry (or at least what I look upon as such) of the great mass of the people of Ireland as an unalterable maxim in the government of Ireland."

The Presbyterian population, principally fixed in Ulster, demanded a Reform of the House of Commons. The Catholics, outnumbering all the other bodies of religionists, demanded the full rights of citizenship. The Nationalists of all creeds who composed the confederation of United Irishmen would at the outset have been perfectly satisfied by the concession of these just demands. It appears from Tone's autobiography that the Irish public did not ask for separation from England; for he tells us that when he published a pamphlet in which separation was propounded, he found that the public mind had not advanced to that point; "and my pamphlet," he adds, "made not the smallest impression." *

The efficacy of a thorough reform in allaying discontent is stated also by Arthur O'Connor to the secret committees of the Lords and Commons by whom he was examined in 1798. His words are these :

"Restore the vital principle of the Constitution which you have destroyed, by restoring to the people the choice of representatives who shall control the executive by frugal grants of the public money, and by exacting a rigid account of the expenditure. Let the people have representatives they can call friends—men in whom they can place confidence— men they have really chosen—men chosen for such a time that if they should attempt to betray them they may speedily

* "Life and Writings of Theobald Wolfe Tone," p. 33. McCormick's edition.

have an opportunity of discarding them. Give them such a House of Commons, and I will answer for the tranquillity of the country."

But the tranquillity of the country just then would not have suited Pitt's designs against Ireland.

"Pitt," says Thorold Rogers, "permitted in Ireland a reign of terror hardly less atrocious, though better concerted, than the massacres of September, and the fusillade at Lyons."

The reign of terror, the intolerable persecution of the people, was indispensable to create and intensify the mutual distrust of the Catholic and Protestant communities, whose combination was essentially necessary to defeat the machinations of their common enemy. For in the confusion of a popular outbreak, nothing could be easier than to give the appearance of a war of religion to the inevitable outrages on either side. England could then take advantage of the dissensions her manœuvres had inflamed. She could assume the position of a coercive mediator, and say, "As you Irish are maddened by your religious hatreds, we must take you in hand and protect you from each other."

To extinguish sectarian animosity was one of the leading objects of "The United Irishmen." "All we wanted," says Arthur O'Connor, "was to create a House of Commons which should represent the whole people of Ireland; and for that purpose we strove to dispel all religious distinctions from our political union." *

To exasperate the friends of Reform, not only by an insolent rejection of their claims, but also by a shameless perseverance in the practice of parliamentary corruption, became a settled part of the policy of the Government. It was likewise resolved to exasperate the Catholics, who, according to Tone, required nothing more than equal justice to render them thoroughly peaceable and loyal. I quote the words of Tone, who, the reader will remember, was a Protestant:

"The Dissenters," he says, "from the early character of their sect, were mostly Republicans from principle. The great mass of the Catholics only became so from oppression and persecution. Had they not been goaded by tyranny in every hour and in every act of their lives, had they been

* "Memoir: being a Report of the Examinations of Messrs. Emmett, O'Connor, and MacNevin, before the Secret Committees of the Lords and Commons." Published by themselves; p. 62.

freely admitted to an equal share in the benefits of the Irish Constitution, they would have become, by the very spirit of their religion, the most peaceable, obedient, orderly, and well-affectioned subjects of the empire. Their proud and old gentry, and their clergy, inclined even rather to feudal and chivalrous, and somewhat to Tory principles, than to Democracy. But common sufferings now united them in a common hatred of the Government, and desire for its subversion."*

Opposed to the just demands of Reform and Catholic Emancipation were the powerful parties who enjoyed the great pecuniary profits of parliamentary corruption, and the monopoly of office and of political influence which Reform and Emancipation would necessarily terminate. The monopolists and bigots were supported by the whole power of the English Government against the great majority of their fellow-countrymen. In such a state of things it was not difficult for an able and unscrupulous Minister to embroil this kingdom in a civil war, the results of which might facilitate his favourite scheme of a Union. By encouraging political profligacy in the Irish Parliament, he might hope to render that body unpopular with the Irish nation. By playing off contending parties against each other, and inflaming their mutual hostility, he might make the Catholics look upon the rule of an English Parliament as a smaller evil than the Orange brutality to which he took good care they should be subjected at home.

The Report of the Secret Committee of the Irish House of Commons, printed "by authority" in 1798, affirms that by the original papers seized at Belfast in the month of April, 1797, the numbers of United Irishmen in the province of Ulster alone were stated to amount to nearly 100,000. Throughout the writings of Wolfe Tone we find Ulster invariably named as the first and best-prepared province in the revolutionary movement, of which the nucleus was in Belfast. It seems to have been considered by the English Cabinet that the Catholics would be more effectually stimulated to unite with the Northern conspirators, by alternating their "outlawry" with promises of speedy and complete emancipation; by then suddenly dispelling the hopes thus excited, and recurring to a system of barbarous persecution.

This game was adroitly played. On the 15th of October, 1794, the illustrious Grattan had an interview with Pitt on

* " Life of Tone," *ut supra*, p. 90.

Irish affairs. "Mr. Grattan," says his son, "stated to him what his party desired, and mentioned the measures that he thought Ireland required. The essential one was the Catholic question." With regard to the Catholic question, Mr. Pitt used these words : " Not to bring it forward as a Government measure; but if Government were pressed, to yield it." * Mr. Grattan observes that this was unquestionably a concession of the Catholic question, for Pitt well knew the question would be pressed. We have Earl Fitzwilliam's authority for the fact that Pitt and his Cabinet empowered his lordship, when accepting the Viceroyalty of Ireland, to support the claims of the Catholics. In his letter to the Earl of Carlisle he says : " It was at the same time resolved that if the Catholics should appear determined to stir the business, and to bring it before Parliament, I was to give it a handsome support on the part of the G[overnmen]t."† Pitt, in fact, included the full emancipation of the Catholics in the programme settled between the King's Ministry and Earl Fitzwilliam, previously to that nobleman's departure from London to assume the reins of government in Ireland. And Earl Fitzwilliam tells us that on no other terms would he have accepted the office of Viceroy. How completely he fell into the trap laid by Pitt, how thoroughly he credited the sincerity of Pitt's insincere declarations in favour of the Catholics, can best be learned from his lordship's own words. He says : " From a full consideration of the real merits of the case, as well as from every information I had been able to collect of the state and temper of Ireland from the year 1793, I was decidedly of opinion that not only sound policy, but justice, required on the part of Great Britain, that the work which was left imperfect at that period ought to be completed, and the Catholics relieved from every remaining disqualification. In this opinion the Duke of P[ortlan]d uniformly concurred with me; and when this question came under discussion previous to my departure for Ireland, I found the Cabinet, with Mr. P[itt] at their head, strongly impressed with the same conviction. Had I found it otherwise, I never would have undertaken the g[overnmen]t." ‡

* "Life of Grattan," by his Son, vol. iv. p. 177.
† Earl Fitzwilliam's "Letter to the Earl of Carlisle," p. 4. Dublin, 1795.
‡ Letter, pp. 2, 3. The Duke of Portland was then principal Secretary of State for the Home Department; Mr. Pitt was Chancellor of the Exchequer.

It is quite clear that Earl Fitzwilliam considered himself the authorised herald of Emancipation to the Irish Catholics. But Pitt had no other intention than driving the Catholics to desperation by disappointing the hopes thus treacherously excited. On the 8th of February, 1795, the Duke of Portland wrote to the Viceroy that Emancipation was to be postponed, and that its postponement would be "the means of doing a greater service to the British Empire than it has been capable of receiving since the Revolution, or, at least, since the [Scotch] Union." * The "greater service" thus indicated was the destruction of the Irish Parliament.

The reader will remember that, in 1792, Mr. Burke said that the treatment received by the Catholics amounted, in his judgment, to outlawry. In 1795 Lord Fitzwilliam, during his short Viceroyalty, warned Pitt's Cabinet, in a letter to the Duke of Portland, that the course pursued by Pitt would, if persevered in, "raise a flame in the country that nothing short of arms would be able to keep down;"† and in his Letter, already cited, to the Earl of Carlisle, he asks, in reference to the ministerial policy, "must the Minister of England boldly face, I had almost said the *certainty* of driving this kingdom into a rebellion, and open another breach for ruin and destruction to break in upon us?" ‡

Lord Fitzwilliam's remonstrances do honour to his heart and to his statesmanship. He might, however, have spared them. A rebellion was just what Pitt wanted. The mutual atrocities it would produce were certain to inflame the reciprocal animosities of the belligerents to a pitch of fury, and furnish a convenient pretext for introducing martial law, and overwhelming the kingdom with troops. Under the reign of terror thus established the task of destroying the Irish Parliament would be comparatively easy.

Pitt calculated that if Emancipation were persistently denied to the Catholics in the Irish Legislature, their support of a Union might be purchased by holding out a hope that the Imperial Parliament would enfranchise them. Reports of this project having got into circulation, an aggregate meeting of Catholics, held in Dublin on the 9th of April, 1795, passed the following resolution :

* "Letter to the Earl of Carlisle," p. 14.
† In Earl Fitzwilliam's Letter to Lord Carlisle, he states that he addressed that warning to the Duke of Portland.
‡ "Letter to the Earl of Carlisle," p. 24. The word "*certainty*" is italicised by his lordship.

"Resolved unanimously, That we are sincerely and unalterably attached to the rights, liberties, and independence of our native country; and we pledge ourselves, collectively and individually, *to resist even our own emancipation*, if proposed to be conceded on the ignominious terms of acquiescence in the fatal measure of an Union with the sister kingdom."

Of the pretended assent of the English Cabinet to Catholic Emancipation, and the disastrous result of retracting that assent, Sir Laurence Parsons thus expressed himself in the Irish House of Commons on the 2nd of March, 1795:

"If the British Cabinet had held out an assent and had afterwards retracted, if the demon of darkness should come from the infernal regions upon earth and throw a firebrand among the people, he could not do more to promote mischief. The hopes of the public were raised, and in one instant they were blasted. . . . . He protested to God that in all the history he had read, he had never met with a parallel of such infatuation as that by which he (Mr. Pitt) appeared to be led. Let him persevere, and you must increase your army to myriads; every man must have five or six dragoons in his house."

It was not infatuation, except so far as infatuation consists in deliberate and systematic wickedness. To provoke rebellion was the object of Pitt's policy; and the exasperation of the Catholics, excited by political disappointment, contributed to the success of that policy.

On the 29th of January, 1799, when the ministerial scheme of Union had sufficiently ripened, the Duke of Portland wrote to Lord Castlereagh: "Catholic Emancipation must not be granted but through the medium of an Union, and by means of an united Parliament."* Next day (30th) the Duke wrote more strongly to the same effect. The Viceroy (Marquis Cornwallis) had previously written to the Duke of Portland, "Were the Catholic question to be now carried, the great argument for an Union would be lost, at least so far as the Catholics are concerned." †

Here we have the key to the "service" which Pitt's Cabinet expected to derive from postponing the concession of the Catholic claims which Lord Fitzwilliam was instructed to support in 1795, and which Pitt, in 1794, had directly led Grattan to expect.

---

* "Cornwallis Correspondence," vol. iii. p. 59.   † *Ibid.*

A rebellion was deemed a useful means of laying waste the strength of this kingdom. But the desired outbreak was not to be left to the chance of mere political exasperation. Stronger provocatives than the breach of ministerial promises were to be applied to the Catholics.

Lord Fitzwilliam, a man of high honour, could not act on Pitt's infernal policy. He was of course recalled. Of the effects of that recall upon the public mind, a contemporary writer says:

"The nation again seemed to sink into despondency. The houses, shops, etc., in every street through which he passed, were all shut upon the memorable day on which he sailed for England; and at noonday a solemn silence and melancholy mourning marked the metropolis, and seemed to indicate the sad catastrophe which has since befallen that ill-fated country."*

Discontent was fearfully increased by the system of torture put in practice against the people in various districts. The following evidence, given by Lord Gosford, describes that system as it existed in 1795 and 1796:

"A persecution," says his lordship,† "accompanied with all the circumstances of ferocious cruelty, is now raging in this country. Neither age, nor sex, nor even acknowledged innocence can excite mercy. The only crime which the wretched objects are charged with is the profession of the Roman Catholic faith. A lawless banditti have constituted themselves judges of this new delinquency, and the sentence they pronounce is equally concise and terrible; it is nothing less than confiscation of property and immediate banishment. It would be painful to detail the horrors of this proscription —a proscription that exceeds, in the number of its victims, every example of ancient and modern history. For, when have we heard or read of more than half the inhabitants of a populous country being deprived of the fruits of their industry, and driven to seek shelter for themselves and their families where chance may guide them? *These horrors are now acting with impunity.* The spirit of justice, without which law is tyranny, has disappeared in this country."

The persecution Lord Gosford describes took place in 1795.

* Memoir of Earl Fitzwilliam in " Public Characters of 1799 and 1800," p. 272.
† Address of Lord Gosford to the Magistracy of Armagh, printed in the *Dublin Journal*, 5th January, 1796.

So far Pitt's policy had borne its intended fruit.

The late Lord Holland, speaking of the recall of Earl Fitzwilliam from the Viceroyalty, says:

"His recall was hailed as a triumph by the Orange faction, and they contrived about the same time to get rid of Mr. Secretary Pelham, who, though somewhat time-serving, was a good-natured and a prudent man. Indeed, surrounded as they were with burning cottages, tortured backs, and frequent executions, they were yet full of their sneers at what they whimsically termed 'the clemency' of the Government, and the weak character of their Viceroy, Lord Camden. . . . The fact is incontrovertible that the people of Ireland were driven to resistance, which possibly they meditated before, by the free quarters and excesses of the soldiery, which were such as are not permitted in civilised warfare, even in an enemy's country." *

The evidence of the Protestant Bishop of Down (Right Rev. Doctor Dickson) illustrative of some of the particular features of the system, is thus given by Lord Holland in the work now quoted:

"Dr. Dickson assured me that he had seen families, returning peaceably from mass, assailed without provocation by drunken troops and yeomanry, and the wives and daughters exposed to every species of indignity, brutality, and outrage, from which neither his remonstrances, nor those of other Protestant gentlemen, could rescue them. The subsequent Indemnity Acts deprived of redress the victims of this wide-spread cruelty."

Of particular outrages committed on the people by the armed agents of power, the following quotation from Lord Moira will furnish illustrative specimens:

"I have," says Lord Moira, "known a man, in order to extort confession of a supposed crime, or of that of some neighbour, picketed till he actually fainted; picketed a second time till he fainted again; and when he came to himself, picketed a third time till he once more fainted; and all this upon mere suspicion. Men had been taken and hung up till they were half dead, and afterwards threatened with a repetition of this treatment unless they made a confession of their imputed guilt." †

---

* "Memoirs of the Whig Party during my Time," by Lord Holland, edited by his Son. Longmans, 1852.

† Speech of Lord Moira in the British House of Lords, 22nd November, 1797.

The picketing mode of torture consisted in suspending the victim by his arms, while his foot had nothing to rest on but the point of a sharpened stake. Horrible as was the tyranny described by Lord Moira, yet it seems that he did not tell the worst cases, for on the 2nd of December, 1797, he wrote as follows to the Hon. Valentine Lawless : *

"You have truly observed that in my recital I suppressed many of the grossest instances of outrage, with the details of which I could not but be acquainted."

Lord Moira took care to state that the crimes he described were not isolated outrages. "These," said he, "were not particular acts of cruelty, but formed part of the new system."

The object of that system was to carry the Union.

The late General Cockburn gives, in his "Letters" (p. 47), an account of the documents prepared to enable Lord Moira to substantiate his statements, and he adds : "They (the documents) contained details of the most horrible outrages on the people, of cruelty and foul deeds, that perhaps, after all, it may be as well to have now effaced from Irish records of violence ; and though the people in many cases were driven to retaliation, it was not before murder, burning, destruction of property (often on suspicion of being suspected) and flogging, drove them to desperation."

I add the testimony of Henry Grattan. On the 26th of February, 1796, he said in the Irish House of Commons that it was "a persecution conceived in the bitterness of bigotry, carried on with the most ferocious barbarity by a banditti, who, being of the religion of the State, had committed with greater audacity and confidence the most horrid murders, and had proceeded from robbery and massacre to extermination."

The outrages referred to in the above passage were chiefly committed in the County Armagh. Grattan, in an address to his fellow-citizens in 1797, enumerates among the crimes with which he charges Government, "the order to the military to act without waiting for the civil power; the imprisonment of the middle orders without law ; the detaining them in prison without bringing them to trial ; the transporting them without law; burning their houses; burning their villages; murdering them ; crimes many of which are public, and many are committed which are concealed by the suppression of a free press by military force . . .

* Fitzpatrick's "Life of Lord Cloncurry," p. 150.

finally, the introduction of practices not only unknown to law, but unknown to civilised and Christian countries."

Plowden tells us in his "History of Ireland," that in the beginning of 1796, "it was generally believed that 7,000 Catholics had been forced or burned out of the county of Armagh, and that the ferocious banditti who had expelled them had been encouraged, connived at, and protected by the Government." *

In the examination of the United Irishmen by the Secret Committees of the Lords and Commons the Lord Chancellor asks Emmett, "What caused the late rebellion?" To which question Emmett answers, "The free quarters, the house-burnings, the tortures, and the military executions, in the counties of Kildare, Carlow, and Wicklow." †

Arthur O'Connor, in his examination before the Secret Committees of the Lords and Commons in 1798, complains of "the uniform system of coercion and opposition which had been pursued from 1793 by the Irish Government against the Irish people;" and on being asked to state the object contemplated by the United Irishmen in organising their society, he answers in the following words: "We saw with sorrow that the cruelties practised by the Irish Government had raised a dreadful spirit of revenge in the hearts of the people; we saw with horror that to answer their immediate views, the Irish Government had revived the old religious feuds; we were most anxious to have such authority as the organisation afforded, constituted to prevent the dreadful transports of popular fury."

A member of the Committee (apparently Lord Castlereagh) remarks that "Government had nothing to do with the Orange system, or their oath of extermination." To which O'Connor thus replies: "You, my lord (Castlereagh), from the station you fill, must be sensible that the executive of any country has it in its power to collect a vast mass of information, and you must know from the secret nature, and the zeal of the Union, that its executive must have had the most minute information of every act of the Irish Government. As one of the executive, it came to my knowledge that considerable sums of money were expended throughout the nation in endeavouring to extend the Orange system, and that the Orange oath of extermination was administered. When these facts are coupled, not only with the general

* Plowden's "History of Ireland," vol. ii. p. 377.
† See Madden's "United Irishmen," First Series, p. 111.

impunity that has been uniformly extended towards all the acts of this infernal association, but [with] the marked encouragement its members have received from Government, I find it impossible to exculpate the Government from being the parent and protector of these sworn extirpators."*

O'Connor's reasoning on this point is irresistible. The Government were merely carrying out Pitt's policy. Of that policy Lord Holland's opinion may be learned from the following passage in the work already quoted: "My approbation," says his lordship, "of Lord Edward Fitzgerald's actions remains unaltered and unshaken. His country was bleeding under one of the hardest tyrannies that our times have witnessed."

As to the administration of the law, it was not very easy for the people to repose confidence in its justice when such an incident as the following could occur. In the spring of 1797, Solicitor-General Toler, afterwards Lord Norbury, presided during the illness of one of the judges in the criminal court at the assizes for the County Kildare. Captain Frazer, a Scotchman, was prosecuted for the murder of a peasant named Christopher Dixon, under the following circumstances: Part of the County of Kildare, near Carberry, was at that time proclaimed. Other parts were exempt from proclamation. There was a flying camp in the proclaimed part, consisting of the Frazer Fencibles, under the command of Captain Frazer. One night, on his return through Cloncurry to the camp from a jovial dinner-party at Maynooth, Frazer saw Dixon repairing a cart by the roadside. Thinking that he was in his own proclaimed district, he seized Dixon for being out after sunset, and made him mount behind the orderly dragoon in attendance, with the purpose of taking him to the camp to flog. Passing a turnpike-gate, Dixon asserted that the proclamation did not extend to the district in which he had been found, at the same time appealing to the gatekeeper to confirm his assertion. The gatekeeper said that the district in question had not been proclaimed; upon which Dixon descended from the crupper of the orderly's horse and went towards home. Frazer and the dragoon furiously pursued him, and gave him sixteen wounds, of which seven or eight were mortal. A coroner's jury returned a verdict of "Wilful Murder" against the homicides. A neighbouring magistrate, Mr. Thomas Ryan, endeavoured to

* Madden's "United Irishmen," Second Series, 8vo, pp. 318, 319.

take Frazer, but his soldiers resisted. Mr. Ryan reported the facts to Lord Cloncurry, who was then in Dublin, and who directed his son, the Hon. Valentine Lawless, to visit the Commander of the Forces, Lord Carhampton, in order to demand the body of Frazer in pursuance of the provisions of the Mutiny Act. Mr. Lawless made the demand in presence of Mr. Ryan, and of Colonel (afterwards General Sir George) Cockburn. Lord Carhampton refused to give up Frazer. Mr. Lawless thereupon told his lordship that Frazer was *ipso facto* cashiered.

At the assizes Frazer went voluntarily to be tried. His approach to the Court House was a sort of ovation, for he was attended by a military band playing "Croppies, lie down."

Mr. Toler presided. On the bench beside him sat the Duke of Leinster and the unfortunate Lord Edward Fitzgerald. The facts of the case were distinctly proved by unexceptionable witnesses. There were many persons examined who deposed to the good and peaceful character of the deceased, his exemption from all "treasonable" machinations, and his general habits of morality and industry. There were also witnesses upon the other side who testified to the admirable character of Captain Frazer and the orderly dragoon, investing them especially with the military virtues.

Mr. Toler charged home for an acquittal. He regretted the homicide—it was very unfortunate—good, respectable man—worthy character, and so forth—witnesses of unimpeachable credit had said so. "There had, however, been witnesses who gave a most admirable character to the gallant captain in the dock, which the jury could by no means overlook—he was a brave and faithful soldier to his King—loyal—devoted—in a word, the sort of person needed in this unhappy country at the present time. The occurrence for which he was tried was most deeply to be deplored; he would not disparage the deceased; he would only say that if he had been as good as the witnesses for the prosecution had represented him, he was well out of a wicked world. If, on the contrary, he were a firebrand" (here Toler looked significantly at Mr. Lawless), "the world was well rid of him."

A judicial dilemma well worthy of record. The jury acquitted Captain Frazer.*

* I possess the above narrative in the handwriting of Valentine, second Lord Cloncurry, by whom it was kindly given to me with the purpose of being used in the first edition of "Ireland and Her

I shall add a few incidents—the results of the Governmental policy of the period—recorded in the narrative of Miles Byrne, a native of the County Wexford; one of those men who were goaded by intolerable persecution to join the insurgents. He subsequently went to France, and ended his days as *chef-de-bataillon* in the French service. I give the title of Miles Byrne's work below.*

" Flogging, half-hanging, picketing," says Colonel Byrne, 'were mild tortures in comparison of the pitch-caps that were applied to those who happened to wear their hair short, called croppies. The head being completely singed, a cap made of strong linen well imbued with boiling pitch was so closely put on that it could not be taken off without bringing off a part of the skin and flesh from the head. In many instances the tortured victim had one of his ears cut off." †

" In short, the state of the country previous to the insurrection is not to be imagined, except by those who witnessed the atrocities of every description committed by the military and the Orangemen who were let loose on the unfortunate, defenceless, and unarmed population." ‡

Byrne mentions that among the " Loyalists " most active in applying the pitch-cap was a clergyman named Owens. This reverend gentleman was afterwards seized at Gorey by the rebels, who applied the pitch-cap to himself.

Among the more zealous and prominent Orangemen whose deeds are recorded by Byrne, Mr. Hunter Gowan of Mount Nebo, and Captain Beaumont of Hyde Park, hold a principal place. Of the former Byrne gives the following anecdote : " Hunter Gowan, Justice of the Peace, captain of a corps of yeoman cavalry, knowing that Patrick Bruslaun, a near neighbour of his, and with whom he had always lived on the most friendly terms, was confined to bed with a wound, rode to Bruslaun's house, knocked at the door, and asked Mrs. Bruslaun in the kindest manner respecting her husband's health. ' You see,' said he, pointing to his troops drawn up at a distance from the house, ' I would not let my men approach lest they might do any mischief. Conduct me to your husband's room ; I want to have a chat with

Agitators." For the infamous character of Lord Carhampton, see Fitzgerald's " Sham Squire," and the sequel to that work.
* " Memoirs of Miles Byrne," *Chef-de-bataillon* in the service of France, Officer of the Legion of Honour, Knight of St. Louis, etc. Edited by his Widow. Paris : Gustave Bossange et Compagnie, 25, Quai Voltaire, 1863. The work is in three volumes.
† *Ibid.*, vol. i. p. 32.   ‡ *Ibid.*, p. 34.

poor Pat.' She, not having the least suspicion of what was to follow, ushered Gowan to her husband's bedside. He put out his hand, and after exchanging some words with poor Bruslaun, deliberately took out his pistol and shot him through the heart. Turning round on his heel, he said to the unfortunate woman, 'You will now be saved the trouble of nursing your damned rebel Popish husband.' These details I had from Mrs. Bruslaun's lips; and how many more of the same kind could I not add to them, were it of any use now to look back to that awful epoch of English tyranny and slaughter in Ireland."*

Of Captain Beaumont's loyal zeal we are given the following instance; the victims upon this occasion were the writer's uncle and cousin, Mr. Breen of Castletown and his son. "Captain Beaumont of Hyde Park had both him and his son murdered in the presence of my aunt Breen and her four daughters, on the lawn before the hall door. Beaumont, who was escorted by a detachment of cavalry, knocked at the door and asked to see my uncle, with whom he was on the most friendly terms. As soon as Mr. Breen came out, Beaumont's first question was: 'Are your sons Pat and Miles at home?' 'Certainly; where should they be?' was the answer of the poor father. 'Well, let them appear, or those men who accompany me won't believe it.' When they came out, the father, and the eldest son Pat, were placed on their knees and immediately shot. Miles, who was only sixteen years of age, was sent prisoner to Arklow, and from thence aboard a guard-ship in the Bay of Dublin. No pen can describe the state of my unfortunate aunt and her four daughters at this awful moment. To add to their misery, one of the assassins had the brutality to tell the eldest daughter, Mrs. Kinsla, who had been married but a year or two before, that she would find something else to weep over when she returned home. She had come but half-an-hour before to visit her family, her own place being but a short mile from her father's house. As the monster told her, when she went home she found her husband lying dead in the courtyard, and a young child of a few months old in his arms. The unfortunate man had taken it out of its cradle, thinking that the sight of the poor infant might soften Beaumont's heart and incline him to mercy. But this stanch supporter of the Protestant ascendency could not let so good

* "Memoirs of Miles Byrne," vol. i. pp. 236, 237.

an opportunity pass of proving his loyalty to his king by thus exterminating a Catholic neighbour." *

Most persons who know anything of the rebellion of 1798 have heard of Father John Murphy, parish priest of Monageer and Boulevogue, who held a command among the Wexford insurgents.†

Colonel Byrne tells us that Father Murphy, like many other priests, had seriously advised the people to surrender their weapons to the Government. But on the 26th of May, 1798, a party of yeomanry scoured the parish, burning and destroying all before them. When Father Murphy saw his chapel and his house in flames, as well as many other houses in the parish, his patience was exhausted, and in reply to the crowd who gathered round him for advice, " he answered abruptly that they had better die courageously in the field than be butchered in their houses ; that for his own part, if he had any brave men to join him, he was resolved to sell his life dearly." ‡

In addition to these testimonies, we have the Marquis Cornwallis's direct and positive assertion (which I shall quote at length in a future chapter of this work) that the country had been driven into rebellion by violence and cruelty.§ His Excellency had previously described the violence as displaying itself in the burning of houses, the murder of the inhabitants, the infliction of torture by flogging, and universal rape and robbery.||

Those who brand with every epithet of ignominy the names and principles of the insurgents of 1798, should ask themselves whether such elaborate pains had ever been taken in any other country to goad a reluctant people into insurrection? With the cup of hope held brimful to the lips, to be rudely dashed aside the next moment; with a regularly organised system of torture, with a social condition of frightful insecurity ; without any protection from the

---

* " Memoirs of Miles Byrne," vol. i. p. 254, et seq.
† This is the Father Murphy of whom the editor of the "Cornwallis Correspondence" gives the following character: "A thorough ruffian—the worst possible specimen of a reckless demagogue. He persuaded his infuriated followers that he was invulnerable, and used to show them bullets which he said he had caught in his hands."
‡ " Cornwallis Correspondence," vol. i. p. 46.
§ His Excellency wrote this on the 16th November, 1799. "Correspondence," vol. iii. pp. 144, 145.
|| Ibid., iii. 89.

established tribunals of the law—whither were the people to turn for succour? To the so-called tribunals of justice? A sanguinary buffoon upon the Bench might openly recommend the impunity of their murderers in a harangue of solemn banter. Should they turn to the Government for help? The Government had a direct interest in their sufferings and turbulence. Where, then, were the people to look for the removal of their grievances? They were absolutely driven to their own rude, undisciplined, and inefficient warfare. The blazing cottage—the tortured peasant—the violated wife or daughter—the familiar outrages on property and life—the demoniac license of which they were the victims, literally left them no alternative but rebellion. Instead of their outbreak in 1798 being a subject of astonishment, the real wonder would have been, if, with such intolerable provocation, they had not resorted to arms. Good men may now regard their struggles with the feeling expressed in the celebrated lines of a Protestant Fellow of Trinity College:

>   Who fears to speak of ninety-eight?
>   Who blushes at the name?
>   When cowards mock the patriot's fate,
>   Who hangs his head for shame?

No. The true shame and sin were with the Government, whose oppressive crimes compelled a peace-loving people to take the field in their own defence.

The country at length became embroiled enough to satisfy the most ardent aspirations of Pitt, Clare, and Castlereagh. Troops were poured in, to the number of 137,590.* Among other proofs of the complicity of the Government is the damning fact that they might have prevented the rebellion by arresting its leaders at any moment during thirteen months immediately preceding the outbreak. The Appendix marked No. XIV. of the Report of the Secret Committee of the House of Commons, printed by the authority of Government in 1798, is prefaced with the following words:

"The information contained in this number of the Appendix was received from Nicholas Maguan, of Saintfield, in the county of Down, who was himself a member of the Provincial and County Committees, and also a colonel in the military system of United Irishmen. He was present at each

---

* These figures are taken from a speech delivered by Lord Castlereagh on the 18th of February, 1799, prefacing a motion on military Estimates.

of the meetings of which an account is here given ; and from time to time, immediately after each meeting, communicated what passed thereat to the Rev. John Clelland, a magistrate of said county."*

Mr. Clelland was land-agent to Lord Castlereagh's family, and through him the Government received the fullest information respecting the machinery of the impending insurrection, the names of its leaders, and their plans and movements. He is shown to have received communications from Maguan immediately after each meeting. Now, the meeting, of which an account is first given in Appendix No. XIV., was held on the 14th of April, 1797, or about thirteen months before the Rebellion broke out. It is clear that at any time during that period the Government could have prevented the explosion by the simple act of taking the leaders into custody. But the reader has seen that the quiet prevention of an outbreak was inconsistent with their guilty policy. Their plan was to convulse the frame of society to its centre; to create mutual hatred and terror between the Protestant and Catholic inhabitants of the land ; to paralyse both into a total incapacity to resist the Union ; to promote the burnings, the murders, the unspeakable atrocities which forced the people to rebel; to coerce both Protestants and Catholics with an irresistible army of occupation ; and then, by means of gigantic and unprecedented bribery, to corrupt the Parliament (which had been dexterously packed for the occasion) to vote its own extinction.

They must have been short-sighted statesmen who calculated that an Union thus produced by force and bribery could ever be maintained by any other means than force and bribery. They must have known but little of human nature if they imagined that a people whose legislature had been made the subject of a regular purchase and sale could ever acquiesce in that traffic. They must have known nothing of the Irish nature if they expected that the series of demoniac crimes which culminated in the destruction of the Irish Parliament could ever be effaced from the national memory ; or that the recollection would ever be unaccompanied with the resolve

---

* " Report of the Secret Committees," printed by authority. It should be observed that the examinations of Arthur O'Connor, Samuel Neilson, and Thomas Addis Emmett were so greatly abridged in the Government publication, that those gentlemen took means to publish them in full. I possess both their publication and that of the Government.

to recover, whenever God should send us the means, the Constitution of which we were wickedly plundered.

And it was an Union thus achieved that Mr. Pitt described as a compact voluntarily entered into on the part of Ireland. Mr. Under-Secretary Cooke did not venture to deny that Ireland was dissatisfied with the hateful measure; but then he predicted that when once fast clutched in the embraces of England, "dissatisfaction would sink into acquiescence, and acquiescence soften into content."

The fallacy of this prediction has been shown by the incessant agitation for Home Government from 1800 to the present day.

Amongst the Irish Parliamentary Unionists the most prominent leader was Lord Chancellor Clare. His only motive was the hope of personal aggrandisement. He had, by his commanding talents and great strength of character, acquired a dictatorship in the Irish House of Lords. Over the imbecile puppets who formed the majority of that assembly he domineered with the most insolent tyranny; and he indulged in visions of the vastly enlarged power with which a dictatorship in the British Parliament would invest him. It never occurred to him that he should not be equally dominant there as he was in the Upper House of the Irish Legislature.

Clare had a species of intellect not uncommon amongst the leaders of the French Revolution, of which the leading trait was its strong but ill-directed energy. His bigotry against the Catholics was intense. In private society he seldom named them without some contemptuous epithet. He threw all his abilities into the struggle for the Union. In order to give the reader some idea of the habitual insolence with which he bullied the Irish peers, I shall quote the following audacious attack made by him on the Earl of Charlemont, the Marquis of Downshire, and some other lords, who ventured to oppose the Union :

"If loud and confident report," said Lord Clare, "is to have credit, a consular exchequer has been opened for foul and undisguised bribery. I know that subscriptions are openly solicited in the streets of the metropolis to a fund for defeating the measure of Union. I will not believe that the persons to whom I have been obliged to allude can be parties to it. One of them, a noble earl" (Charlemont) "I see in his place; he is a very young man, and I call upon him as he fears to have his entry into public life marked with dishonour ; I call upon him as he fears to live with the broad mark of infamy on his forehead and to transmit it indelibly to his posterity, to stand up in his place and acquit himself before his peers of this foul imputation. I call upon him publicly to disavow all knowledge of the existence of such a fund ; or if he cannot disavow it, to state explicitly any honest purpose to which it can be applied. If it can exist, I trust there are sufficient remains of sense and honour in the Irish nation to cut off the corrupted sources of these vile abominations."

Here, indeed, was "Satan lecturing against sin." In order properly to appreciate the brazen audacity of this insolent attack, it must be remembered that he who thus denounced the imputed iniquities of the patriotic party, was himself the *employé* of a Government who were openly and shamelessly practising every art of corruption in favour of their measure.

The work entitled "Public Characters of 1799-1800," thus speaks of Lord Clare's parliamentary tactics : "His firmness, his confidence in his own powers, and the bold tone in which he hurled defiance at his parliamentary opponents on every question connected with legal or constitutional knowledge, often appalled the minor members of opposition, and sometimes kept even their chiefs at bay. These qualities, however, did not always constitute a sure defence. The repulse, which on one memorable evening of debate he experienced on the part of the present Lord, then Mr. O'Neill of Shane's Castle, whose manly and honest mind caught fire at the haughty and dictatorial language with which the Attorney-General had dared to address him, is remembered by those who were then conversant in the politics of the day, and probably will not soon be forgotten."

Although Pitt had used Lord Clare in effecting the Union, yet, when the nefarious work was done, he heartily despised his Irish utensil. Clare fancied that attacks on his own country would receive the applause of the English House of Lords. In the "Life of Grattan" it is recorded that when Clare, in that assembly, dealt out his sweeping censures upon Ireland, "uttering very violent principles in a very violent and intemperate manner," Pitt, who had been listening for some time, at length turned to Wilberforce, who stood next him, and exclaimed : "Good God! did you ever, in all your life, hear so great a rascal as that?"

Clare, whose ambitious spirit was inflated with arrogance and success, soon tried the experiment of insulting the peers of England. He called the Whig lords Jacobins. The Duke of Bedford flung back the insult with the spirit that beseemed a British peer. "We would not," said he, "bear such language from our equals; far less will we endure it from the upstart pride of chance nobility."

The feeling of the whole House was with the Duke. Clare had not the poor consolation of sympathy or pity from any man, even of his own political party. His influence, once almost omnipotent, was now extinct. He returned, mortified and broken-hearted, to the country he had betrayed and ruined, cursing the part he had taken in promoting the Union. "There was a time," he said, with great bitterness, "when no appointment could be made without my sanction; now I am unable to make so much as a clerk in the Excise."

He tried to dissipate his chagrin by violent equestrian exercise. His death was hastened by a severe hurt he received while riding in the Phœnix Park. He died in January, 1802, expressing in his last hours deep though unavailing remorse for his criminal co-operation with Pitt against the Irish Constitution. His fall may be regarded as a signal instance of the retributive justice of Providence.

Of his lineage the following account is given in the publication already quoted: "He is removed but two degrees from a man in the humblest walk of society—a Catholic peasant—whose life was distinguished only by a gradual transition from extreme poverty to an honourable competency; and that, too, acquired by useful industry."

By his criminal political career he gained a peerage, which is now extinct. The so-called honours, for which he bartered the vital interests of his country, have passed away.

CHAPTER III.

PARLIAMENTARY CORRUPTION IN ENGLAND AND IRELAND.

How did they pass this Union?
By perjury and fraud.
By slaves who sold, for place or gold,
Their country and their God;
By all the savage acts that yet
Have followed England's track,
The pitch-cap and the bayonet,
The gibbet and the rack.
And thus was passed the Union
By Pitt and Castlereagh;
Could Satan send for such an end
More worthy souls than they?
Spirit of the Nation.

A SCOTCH essayist on Irish politics once expressed his curiosity to know by what magic William Pitt induced the minor members of the Irish peerage to consent to the Union. The great lords who had influence in the House of Commons were bought over on intelligible principles. The Earl of Shannon, for example, was paid £45,000 for his adhesion. Besides, the chiefs of the peerage could look forward to seats in the Imperial Parliament as Irish representative peers; whereas the smaller lords, in losing their Irish privilege of hereditary legislation, lost all that made their titles anything better than nicknames; whilst they had little or no chance of election to the central Legislature.

It certainly seems, at first sight, surprising that a considerable body of hereditary legislators should slavishly surrender the proudest privilege of the citizen, and receive for it no equivalent. Their act was an abandonment, apparently, of personal and national dignity. In 1785 Lord Lansdowne, in the British House of Lords, expressed his belief that an act of such degrading self-disfranchisement was impossible. An Union having been then casually mentioned, his lordship spoke of "the idea of an Union as a thing that was impracticable. High-minded and jealous," he said, "as were the people of Ireland, we must first learn whether they will consent to give up their distinct Empire, their Parliament, and all the honours which belonged to them." In point of fact the people of Ireland not only never did consent to the scandalous surrender, but opposed it to the utmost of their power. Nearly all the unbribed intellect of Ireland was against it. Our surprise at the share of the Irish House of Lords in enacting the Union is, however, diminished when we analyse the composition of the peers and examine their habits.

Let us first do all honour to the gallant band who, headed by the Duke of Leinster and the Earl of Charlemont, resisted the Union to the last. The Lords' Protest against the Union is a noble document, full of sagacity and patriotism. Alas! those who signed it were in a minority.

With respect to the rest of the peers, if we look into the Irish peerage list, we shall find that more than half of those existing in 1800 had received their creations from the then reigning monarch, George III. Of these men, thus personally bound to the Court, a considerable number were indebted for their elevation to the grossest political dishonesty. They cared nothing for their country, except for the purpose of trafficking upon it. Corruption had been carried to such an extent as to justify Grattan's indignant complaint that the Minister's familiar practice was to purchase the members of one House with the money obtained by selling seats in the other.

Again, a great portion of the Irish peers had nothing Irish about them but their titles. They had not a foot of property in the kingdom. They never entered it. They had no more compunction in voting for the extinction of the Irish Parliament than they would have had in voting away an Otaheitan Legislature. Take up a Dublin almanack for the year 1800, and run your eye over the peerage list; you will find many of the peers possessing also English titles and English residences. Exclusively of these, you will find that out of fifty-seven viscounts, there were no less than eighteen who had got no Irish residence at all. Run your eye over the barons, and you will find that out of sixty-five, there were in that year no less than thirty-four whose connexions, residences, and property were altogether English.

Again, some of the most bustling and prominent peers then residing in Ireland were either English lawyers, or the sons of Englishmen who had been thrust upon the Irish Bench, and thence into the Irish peerage. These men had not yet acquired Irish sentiments or feelings; they were still essentially foreigners; they rejoiced at an opportunity to strike a blow at Ireland.

Amongst those whom a descent of some half-dozen generations entitled to call themselves Irish, the greater number had so habitually looked on politics as a game to be played for the purpose of personal aggrandisement, that they had no conception of anything like political principle. There was a thorough moral recklessness about them which rendered them quite ready for any act of political desperation, provided it did not tend to enlarge the power of the people. Their personal habits necessarily fostered this recklessness. Their profusion and extravagance were great; and some of them—not a few—resorted to modes of raising the wind which showed that they mingled few scruples with their system of financial pneumatics. There was, withal, a strong dash of odd drollery in the brazen shamelessness of their expedients.

A curious specimen of this order of men was Lord M——y. His title was the result of some dexterous traffic in parliamentary votes. His manners were eminently fascinating, and his habits social. He had a favourite saying that a gentleman could never live upon his rents; a man who depended on his rents had money only upon two days in the year, the 25th of March and the 29th of September. He accordingly left no expedient untried to furnish himself with money every other day too.

It chanced that when Lord Kerry's house in St. Stephen's Green was for sale, a lady named Keating was desirous to purchase a pew in St. Anne's Church appertaining to that mansion. Mrs. Keating erroneously took it into her head that the pew belonged to Lord M——y; she accordingly visited his lordship to propose herself as a purchaser.

"My dear madam," said he, "I have not got any pew, that I know of, in St. Anne's Church."

"Oh, my lord, I assure you that you have; and if you have got no objection, I am desirous to purchase it."

Lord M——y started no farther difficulty. A large sum was accordingly fixed on, and in order to make her bargain as secure as possible, Mrs. Keating got the agreement of sale drawn out in the most stringent form by an attorney. She paid the money to Lord M——y; and on the following Sunday she marched up to the pew to take possession, rustling in the stateliness of brocades and silks. The beadle refused to let her into the pew.

"Sir," said the lady, "this pew is mine."

"Yours, madam?"

"Yes; I have bought it from Lord M——y."

"Madam, this is the Kerry pew; I do assure you Lord M——y never had a pew in this church."

Mrs. Keating saw at once she had been cheated, and on the following day she went to his lordship to try if she could get back her money.

"My lord, I have come to you to say that the pew in St. Anne's——"

"My dear madam, I'll sell you twenty more pews if you have any fancy for them."

"Oh, my lord, you are facetious. I have come to acquaint you it was all a mistake; you never had a pew in that church."

"Hah! so I think I told you at first."

"And I trust, my lord," pursued Mrs. Keating, "you will refund me the money I paid you for it."

"The money? Really, my dear madam, I am sorry to say that is quite impossible—the money's gone long ago."

"But—my lord—your lordship's character——"

"That's gone too!" said Lord M——y, laughing with good-humoured nonchalance.

I have already said that this nobleman's financial operations were systematically extended to every opportunity of gain that could possibly be grasped at. He was colonel of a militia regiment; and, contrary to all precedent, he regularly sold the commissions, and pocketed the money. The Lord Lieutenant resolved to call him to an account for his malpractices, and for that purpose invited him to dine at the Castle, where all the other colonels of militia regiments then in Dublin had also been invited to meet him. After dinner the Viceroy stated that he had heard with great pain an accusation—indeed, he could hardly believe it—but it had been positively said that the colonel of a militia regiment actually sold the commissions.

The company looked aghast at this atrocity, and the innocent colonels forthwith began to exculpate themselves. "I have never done so." "I have never sold any." "Nor I." The disclaimers were general. Lord M——y resolved to put a bold face on the matter.

"I always sell the commissions in my regiment," said he, with the air of a man who announced a practice rather meritorious. All present seemed astonished at this frank avowal.

"How can you defend such a practice?" asked the Lord Lieutenant.

"Very easily, my lord. Has not your Excellency always told us to assimilate our regiments as much as possible to the troops of the Line?"

"Yes, undoubtedly."

"Well, they sell the commissions in the Line, and I thought that the best point at which to begin the assimilation."

It is told of this nobleman, that when he was dying he was attended by a clergyman, who remonstrated with him on the scandalous exploits of his past life, and strongly urged him to repent. "Repent?" echoed the dying sinner; "I don't see what I have got to repent of; I don't remember that I ever denied myself anything."

We may well suppose that such a personage would have readily voted for the Union, or for anything else.

Mr. ——, a wealthy merchant, had aristocratic aspirings. Having amassed great wealth in trade, as well by lucky hits as by persevering industry, he resolved to add a peerage to his acquisitions. A bargain was made with the Irish Minister; the ambitious merchant was to be created a baron for the stipulated payment of £20,000. The patent was forthwith made out, and the new peer took his seat in due form. The Government never entertained a doubt that his lordship would faithfully pay them the price of his new honours; and in this happy confidence they gave him his coronet without first securing the money for it. Six months passed, during which the Castle took for granted that the new baron would fulfil his engagement at his earliest convenience. At length the secretary wrote a "private and confidential" epistle, to give his lordship's memory a gentle refresher.

The noble lord made short work of the matter. He wrote back, denying all recollection of the engagement referred to, expressing great indignation that anybody should presume to accuse him of being a party to the sale or purchase of a peerage; and threatening, should the claim be renewed, to impeach the Minister in Parliament for so grossly unconstitutional a proceeding. The Government were outwitted, and the ex-merchant got his coronet, as perhaps he had got other things also, without paying for it.

Many such scamps were to be found in the Irish House of Lords; and English lucubrators upon Irish affairs triumphantly point to their unprincipled conduct, and ask—as if the question were conclusive against Repeal—" Would you revive *such* a Parliament?" *

No, certainly. We seek not to revive corruption. We desire to restore the Irish Parliament, cleansed, purified, and placed beyond the reach of all corrupt influences. The unprincipled class, moreover, to which Lord M―――y and Lord ―――― belonged, cannot in any fairness be quoted against Irish claims or Irish rights. That class was manufactured by England in this country. It was prevented by English power and English artifice from becoming fully identified with Irish interests. When England, therefore, upbraids us with its moral rottenness, we retort that she was the instigator of its political crimes—that those crimes were disastrous to the great mass of the Irish people, who had no participation in them; and that the disgrace, consequently, rests not on

---

* Among the aristocratic eccentricities of the time was the Earl of Belvedere's *penchant* for people who had hideous noses. He is said to have given an annual entertainment called the Nosey Dinner, the guests being all remarkable for their large, red noses, or for some other sort of nasal deformity. His lordship's great delight was to invite two opposite proprietors of outlandish noses to take wine with each other, and to watch the converging inclination of their hideous profiles.

us, but on England herself, and on the individual criminals who yielded to her seductions in this country.

The corruption of the Irish Parliament is also often mentioned by our English censors as if English Parliaments had always been immaculate, and as if Ireland alone presented specimens of senatorial profligacy. English history, however, informs us that this species of iniquity has occasionally flourished in the Parliament of England. Lingard, for instance, says that when Charles II. received, in January, 1677, a portion of his annual pension from the King of France, the whole sum was immediately expended on the purchase of votes in the English House of Commons; the result of which traffic gave the Court, upon questions of finance, a majority of about thirty voices. But English senators did not restrict themselves to a market so limited as the English Court.

"It seemed," says Lingard, "as if the votes of the Members of Parliament were exposed for sale to all the Powers of Europe. Some received bribes from the Lord Treasurer on account of the King; some from the Dutch, Spanish, and Imperial ambassadors in favour of the confederates; some even from Louis at the very time when they loudly declaimed against Louis as the great enemy of their religion and liberties." In 1678 a test was proposed for the discovery of such Members of Parliament as had received bribes or any other consideration for their votes, either from the English or any other Government. "The popular leaders," says Lingard, "spoke warmly in its favour; but before the last division took place, about an hundred members slipped out of the House, and the motion was lost by a majority of fourteen." *

Lord Macaulay calls the management by corruption of the English Parliaments of that period, and of much more recent times, "one of the most important parts of the business of a Minister;" and, speaking of the long period between the reigns of Charles II. and George III., he says that it was "as notorious that there was a market for votes at the Treasury as that there was a market for cattle at Smithfield." †

Mr. Lecky, in his "History of England in the Eighteenth Century," ‡ quotes the following passage from Sir E. May's "Constitutional History," i. 317:

* Lingard's "History of England," *ad annos* 1676, 1678.
† Macaulay's "History of England," vol. iii. pp. 541, 546 (8vo ed.)
‡ Lecky's "England in the Eighteenth Century," vol. i. p. 436.

"Great sums of secret service money were usually expended in direct bribery; and places and pensions were multiplied to such an extent that it is on record that out of 550 members there were in the first Parliament of George I. no less than 271, and in the first Parliament of George II. no less than 257, holding offices, pensions, or sinecures."

Mr. Lecky, speaking of Sir Robert Walpole, says: " He (Walpole) governed by means of an assembly which was saturated with corruption, and he fully acquiesced in its conditions and resisted every attempt to improve it. He appears to have cordially accepted the maxim that Government must be carried on by corruption or by force, and he deliberately made the former the basis of his rule. . . . He employed the vast patronage of the Crown uniformly and steadily with the single view of sustaining his political position, and there can be no doubt that a large proportion of the immense expenditure of secret service money during his administration was devoted to the direct purchase of Members of Parliament. . . . If corruption did not begin with Walpole, it is equally certain that it did not end with him. His expenditure of secret service money, large as it was, never equalled in an equal space of time the expenditure of Bute."*

English politicians sometimes say that the Irish Parliament was so corrupt that it deserved extinction. To reason thus is to confound the turpitude of particular Parliaments with the existence of Parliament. It is to deprive the Irish people of their birthright because certain parliamentary majorities have been base and venal. Would the gentlemen who reason in this way apply the same logic to England? Would they argue that the English Parliament ought to be annihilated, and the English people deprived of self-government because English senators sold their votes to Dutch, French, Spanish, German, and native purchasers, and because the notoriety of the traffic equalled that of the public cattle-market?

If the Union struggle in the Irish Parliament developed on the one hand the political depravity which England had laboured so hard to produce, it also displayed on the other hand many brilliant examples of the most stainless and unpurchasable honesty. Every effort to debauch the Legislature had for a series of years been systematically made by

* Lecky's " England in the Eighteenth Century," vol. i. pp. 365, 367, 368.

An Honest Minority. 37

the Government; and yet in 1799 the first attempt to carry the Union was defeated by men who might have made for themselves whatever terms they pleased with the Minister. And in 1800, after every possible exertion to pack the Parliament had been resorted to, there still remained 115 members, a tried and trusty band, who, although in a minority, were yet miraculously numerous when we remember the enormous powers of corruption which the Government derived from the number of close boroughs, and from their other resources. Of the men who were returned by the people a majority stood firm to their trust. The traitors were chiefly found among those men whom private influence had introduced into the Legislature.

The Viceroy could not help entertaining respect for the anti-Unionists. On the 24th of May, 1799, he writes to General Ross : * "There is an opposition in Parliament to the measure of Union, formidable in character and talents."

The English Cabinet did not think that their Irish confederates were sufficiently active in pressing forward the Union. Lord Castlereagh, in a letter to John King, Esq., dated 7th of March, 1800, thus accounts for their imputed slowness : "It will be in the first place considered that we have a minority consisting of 120 members, well combined and united, that many of them are men of the first weight and talent in the House, that 37 of them are members for counties, that great endeavours have been used to inflame the kingdom, that petitions from 26 counties have been procured, that the city of Dublin is almost unanimous against it, and, with such an opposition so circumstanced and supported, it is evident much management must be used." †

When Lord Castlereagh boasted that the Union, by extinguishing a great number of pocket-boroughs, would operate as a measure of parliamentary reform, Charles Kendal Bushe immediately retorted that Lord Castlereagh's Union majority were to be found among the members for those very constituencies which his lordship proposed to abolish as a punishment for their impurity; and that it would be impossible for him to select one hundred members for the greater constituencies, amongst whom he would not find himself in a minority. "What, then," asked Bushe, "results from his own confession? This—that he is about to carry the Union against that part of the Parliament which

* "Cornwallis Correspondence," vol. iii. p. 101.   † *Ibid.*

he allows to be pure, and by the instrumentality of that part which he alleges to be corrupt. He does not merely state this as a matter of candour, but as a matter of boast. He glories in cutting off the rotten limb, and amputating the withered branch of Parliament, and yet, with that withered branch he beats down the Constitution."

Out of doors there was a nearly universal detestation of the Union, which would have been effectual in defeating it if it were not for the overpowering military force in the hands of the Government.

I have not sought to conceal the faults or vices of the Irish Parliament. It was an unreformed borough Parliament; and to the evils resulting from its construction must be added the mischief flowing from its sectarian bigotry during the long period between the restoration of King Charles II. and the relaxation of the penal laws. Yet, notwithstanding these very serious drawbacks, it is a fact of the highest importance that from the moment when, in 1782, this unreformed, bigoted Parliament acquired freedom from the usurped claims of England to legislate for Ireland, the prosperity of Ireland sprang forward at a bound, and its progress is attested by a host of unimpeachable witnesses, to whose evidence I shall advert in a subsequent chapter of this work. It is scarcely possible to conceive more effectual obstructions to the beneficial action of a free, resident Legislature than those which arise from the sectarian intolerance of its members, and from the prevalence of a close-borough system. Yet the Irish Parliament, despite those obstructions, conferred essential benefits on the country—benefits which greatly countervailed its evils. It kept the money of the country at home. It enacted several good measures. The individual interests of its members necessarily often ran in the same groove with the interests of the country; so that personal selfishness occasionally came in aid of patriotism. The very facts of residence and of discharging at home the high functions of Irish legislators produced in many of them sentiments of patriotic pride and of national honour. The general results appeared in the astonishing advance of trade, commerce, manufactures, and agriculture—an advance which forms a strong and melancholy contrast with the general decay that followed the Union, and the present condition of our flying population. By the Union, England obtained the dishonest control of the whole resources of Ireland; but she also obtained the lasting hatred of the people whose

Legislature she had first corrupted and then destroyed. The Union laid a sure foundation for Irish discontent and disaffection. It disposed the people to look anywhere for friendship rather than to the power that had robbed them of their birthright by an act that capped the climax of innumerable deeds of aggression. Great national crimes have seldom been forgiven by the injured parties. Oblivion of wrong is best promoted by ample and honourable restitution. Restitution is, in our case, absolutely indispensable to our national prosperity and dignity. "Keep knocking at the Union," were among the last words of Grattan to Lord Cloncurry. " Come it soon, or come it late," said O'Connell, "my deliberate conviction is that if the Union is not peacefully repealed, a sanguinary separation will be the ultimate result." This is pretty much what Saurin said on the 27th of February, 1800. " I consider," said he, " the present measure (of Union) as most dangerous .to that connection " (with Great Britain). "My opinion has been uniformly that it is a project to change an union and connection of safety and independence for an union of insecurity and dependence." Mr. (afterwards Earl Grey) said in the English House of Commons on the 7th of February, 1800: " Though you should be able to carry the measure, yet the people of Ireland would wait for an opportunity of recovering their rights, which, they will say, were taken from them by force."

I conclude this chapter with the following incident. On the night when the fatal measure passed the House of Commons, a large crowd, who had assembled in College Green, waited until Mr. Speaker Foster, the leader of the anti-Unionists, quitted the House. They took off their hats and followed him, sad, silent, and uncovered, to his residence in Molesworth Street. Ere he entered the house, he turned round, and sadly and solemnly bowed to the people, who then dispersed. No word was exchanged between the Speaker and the crowd. All felt the deadening pressure of a terrible national calamity. It was a sorrow too profound for utterance.

CHAPTER IV.

HOW IRISH DISCONTENT IS VIEWED BY SOME ENGLISH WRITERS.

"If it (the balancing check) keeps the three estates of Parliament together, all in their just proportion in each kingdom, why not depend on the same principle operating in the same way, and keeping the two Legislatures of both kingdoms in their just relations to each other, so as that their mixed powers, like those of the mixed Government, shall, by their separate exertions so checked, preserve the symmetry and union of the whole machine of the Empire, which a theoretic or unwise merging of the one into the other might so affect as to render incapable of working?"—RIGHT HON. JOHN FOSTER, 1799.

IT is in the highest degree desirable that England and Ireland should entertain mutual sentiments of friendship, and that both should willingly occupy their appropriate positions as constituent parts of a great Empire. It is in the highest degree desirable that all the inhabitants of Ireland should have reason to render to the throne of these kingdoms the homage of hearty and unqualified loyalty.

Ireland is dissatisfied with her position. While the Union, in its present shape, exists, Irish discontent will be ineradicable. It is an inquiry worthy of a statesman whether the position of Ireland is such as she ought to occupy; whether it is compatible with her rights, with her interests, and with her honour. And if it be compatible with none of these, it is worth inquiry whether a more satisfactory position could not be substituted for one which results in national suffering, in unnatural emigration, and in extensive disaffection.

The present condition of Ireland is a scandal to the civilised world, a curse to its inhabitants, and a disgrace to the Imperial Government. If experience can teach anything, the whole experience of the Union unquestionably teaches that Imperial legislation is incompetent to render Ireland prosperous and happy.

When Irish discontent is spoken of, English writers sometimes suppose that it is merely a traditionary sentiment still lingering in the national mind—the surviving result of injustice that has long since passed away. For instance, the *Times*, in an article on Fenianism in September, 1865, thus deals with the existing discontent: "The greater our former injustice to Ireland, the easier it is to account for existing discontent without assuming any present injustice. If there be any such present injustice, let it be pointed out. Unless it be the maintenance of the Irish Church, we know not where to look for it; and assuredly no English interest will be allowed to protect this institution if Ireland be united in demanding its abolition."

When the *Times* named the State Church as the only injustice subsisting in 1865, it forgot a greater and more grievous wrong—the Legislative Union. The State Church has since then been disestablished, and partially disendowed. It was doubtless a wrong of great magnitude, and created a severance of feeling between the two great sections of Irish people which has survived its disestablishment. I wish with all my heart that the words "Protestant" and "Catholic," as symbols of political party, could be obliterated from our vocabulary. The State Church was bad; but the Union is far worse.

The *Saturday Review* also says that injustice to Ireland is merely a matter of past history. It admits, indeed, that grievances existed at a former period. "But to our minds," it proceeds to say, "all that is passed now. We have turned over a new leaf. We have for some years tried to govern Ireland as a part of England, as justly, as patiently, as mildly as we could. The case for an aggrieved, a separate, an alien Ireland has passed away."

This self-complacent journal is unable to comprehend why discontent exists in Ireland. "We have," it seems to say, "done our best for your ungrateful nation. We have destroyed your Parliament, and yet you are not satisfied. We have thereby trebled the absentee drain, extinguishing numberless home sources of industrial profit, yet you are not satisfied. We extort from your poverty an enormous tribute —yet you are not satisfied. We make you pay a smart share of our own pre-Union debt-charge—yet you are not satisfied. We have drawn off to England the Irish surplus revenue, which the Act of Union promised should be appropriated to Irish purposes exclusively — yet you are not satisfied. We meet your demand for the redress of these grievances with chicanery and insolence; we call you sturdy beggars, and we mystify financial statements—yet you are not satisfied. We have got hold of your manufacture market —yet you are not satisfied. We have governed you in such a mode that your race seems in a fair way of being expelled from their native country, much to the delight of the leading organ of British opinion; yet you are not satisfied. O incorrigible nation of grumblers, how is it possible you can be discontented or ungrateful when we lavish such blessings on you? For, look you! this is governing Ireland as if she were part of England."

The free paraphrase I have given of the words of the *Saturday Review*, shows, not unfairly, the contrast between English opinion and Irish fact. The journalist innocently says, "We have for some years tried to govern Ireland as a part of England." The experiment has not brought prosperity to Ireland. Nor is it possible that it could. For Ireland is not a part of England. God has stamped upon her the indestructible features of national individuality. Self-Legislation is her vital need.

To govern her, therefore, as a part of England, is, in effect, to govern her for the benefit of England and not for her own benefit. We protest against that ruinous spoliation of her wealth, that insulting suppression of her individuality, which are termed "governing her as a part of England." We demand that she shall be governed as a distinct nation, with separate needs and separate rights, in accordance with the principles of the Irish Constitution of 1782, which, notwithstanding great obstructive influences, diffused unexampled prosperity through the nation during the period of its continuance.

In a part of the article of the *Saturday Review* to which I have referred, the writer, speaking of a projected Fenian invasion of Canada, says, "Fortunately the Canadians, by an overwhelming majority, are firmly attached to British rule." So they well may be. For the Canadians enjoy a free Parliament, and the uncontrolled regulation of their national interests. They are not robbed of their revenue for British uses. But Canadian attachment to Great Britain would sustain a rude shock if the Imperial Government attempted to rule Canada on the present Irish model; if it tried to govern Canada "as a part of England"—in other words, to destroy her Legislature, rifle her exchequer, and in every department of the State make English prejudice, English theory, or English sentiment supersede Canadian opinion. When in 1838 Lord Durham went to Canada to quell disaffection in the only statesmanlike way in which disaffection can be quelled—that is to say, by removing the grievances that caused it—he asked a question which we in Ireland may appropriately ask: What principle of the British Constitution holds good in a country where the people's money is taken from them without the people's consent? In Ireland our money is taken by the English Parliament without our consent; and the income-tax was imposed on us against the votes of a large majority of the Irish representatives.

Lord Durham's remedy for Canadian wrongs was precisely that which we claim for Irish wrongs. He advised that complete internal self-government should be given to the colonists; that the government of Canada should be put as much as possible into the hands of the colonists themselves. His advice was adopted; the Canadians got Home Rule; and the result shows a Transatlantic population transformed by that just and statesmanlike concession from a nation of insurgents into a nation of as loyal subjects to Her Majesty as can be found in any part of her dominions.

Among the most rational notions I have seen expressed by English journalists on Irish affairs is the following dictum of the *Pall Mall Gazette*, in an article on Fenianism in September, 1865: "The real prospect for Ireland is that of becoming in course of time a cis-Atlantic Lower Canada. It will no more amalgamate heartily with England than oil with water; but there is no reason why we should not be perfectly good friends, and very useful and convenient neighbours."

Not the least reason, if Ireland were treated as Canada is treated. Not the least reason, if Ireland had but the fair play of self-legislation, which is her indefeasible right. To call this dismemberment is to suppose that Foster, Grattan, Saurin, Ponsonby, and the other great opponents of the Union, were enemies of British connexion, instead of being, as they were, its firm friends.

The instinct of every Irishman—unless he is influenced by sectarian animosities and fears—will impel him not only to abhor the destruction of his country's Legislature, but to hate the destroyer also. There never was a greater blunder than to call the Union a bond of international affection. When I was a boy of ten years old, I was told by my seniors that we once had a Parliament in Ireland and that English influence extinguished it. I candidly acknowledge that my immediate impulse was to regard England with resentful abhorrence. Religious prejudices had nothing to do with the matter, for I was born of a Protestant family. I do not state this from the absurd notion that any importance attaches to myself or my sentiments. I make the avowal because it records and explains my individual participation in a sentiment that at this moment actuates millions at home, in

America, and in the Colonies, and which, by its general diffusion, assumes an aspect that is anything but contemptible.

Security of tenure for the tenant farmers, extinction of tithe rent-charge, which the Land Act of 1881 deprives the landlords of the means to pay—these, and other minor measures of relief would mitigate some of the external symptoms of the national malady. But nothing short of the restoration of the Irish Constitution—of the Government of the Irish people by the Queen, Lords, and Commons of Ireland—can reach the root of the disease.

"We may hope," said Grattan in 1780, "to dazzle with illuminations, and we may sicken with addresses, but the public imagination will never rest, nor will the public heart be well at ease—never! so long as the Parliament of England exercises or claims a legislation over this country."

And in his closing speech in 1800 against the Union, he predicts that although, for the present, the forces of military terror and corruption may overthrow the Irish Constitution, yet the country will at some future time throw off the incubus of foreign legislation and re-establish her rights.

"I do not give up the country : I see her in a swoon, but she is not dead; though in her tomb she lies helpless and motionless, still there is on her lips a spirit of life, and on her cheek a glow of beauty—

> "Thou art not conquered; beauty's ensign yet
> Is crimson in thy lips and in thy cheeks,
> And Death's pale flag is not advanced there.

"While a plank of the vessel sticks together, I will not leave her. Let the courtier present his flimsy sail, and carry the light bark of his faith with every new breath of wind; I will remain anchored here with fidelity to the fortunes of my country, faithful to her freedom, faithful to her fall."

CHAPTER V.

THE DIPLOMACY OF MARQUIS CORNWALLIS.

> As we are men and Irishmen,
> Scorn for his curst alliance ;
> As we are men and Irishmen,
> Unto his throat defiance.
>
> BANIM.

THE Union having been accomplished, the prevalent desire amongst the Irish people was, of course, to obtain its repeal.

For a few years no great effort was made for this purpose. The army of occupation, under the terror of which it had been forced upon Ireland, was to a great extent still continued in the country.

But the national desire for Repeal is coeval with the Union itself. It was not possible that a nation should sit quietly down in contented acquiescence in its own servitude. A sullen sentiment of enmity to England smouldered in the public mind. Men brooded angrily over the enormous crimes the English Government had committed against their country; and they felt (to use the language of Saurin, a lawyer of the highest ability) that "the exhibition of resistance to the measure became merely a question of prudence."

Ere I pass to later periods, let me pause for a few moments to notice a misrepresentation. It is frequently said that the Catholics supported the Union. The Catholics, as a body, are free from the imputed guilt. At a Catholic aggregate meeting held in Dublin in 1795, the Catholic leaders unanimously passed a resolution that they would collectively and individually resist even their own emancipation, "if proposed to be conceded on the ignominious terms of an Union with the sister kingdom." Imbued with this sentiment, O'Connell, in his maiden speech, delivered at a Catholic meeting held at the Royal Exchange, Dublin, to oppose the Union, on the 13th of January, 1800, declared that he would prefer the re-enactment of the whole penal code to the destruction of the Irish Parliament. On the 15th of January, the patriotic conduct of the Dublin Catholics was referred to in the House of Commons by Grattan, who said : "If she (Ireland) perish, they (the Catholics) will have done their utmost to save her. . . . They will have flung out their last setting glories and sunk with their country."

The Viceroy, Marquis Cornwallis, had made many attempts to gain Catholic support for the Union, and he had at one time flattered himself with hopes of success. But on the 12th of December, 1798, he wrote as follows to Major-General Ross :

" The opposition to the Union increases daily in and about Dublin; and I am afraid, from conversations which I have had with persons much connected with them, that I was too sanguine when I hoped for the good inclinations of the Catholics."

His failure to cajole the Catholic body is again mentioned in the following passage of a letter he addressed to the Duke of Portland, dated 2nd of January, 1799: "The Catholics, as a body, still adhere to their reserve on the measure of Union. The very temperate and liberal sentiments at first entertained or expressed by some of that body, were by no means adopted by the Catholics who met at Lord Fingal's, and professed to speak for the party at large."*

On the 12th of April, 1799, Mr. Secretary Cooke wrote to William Wickham, Esq., as follows: "The Catholics think it (the Union) will put an end to their ambitious hopes, however it may give them ease and equality." †

I find in an interesting compilation entitled "The Very Rev. Dr. Renehan's Collections on Irish Church History," the following incidental notice of Catholic hostility to the Union:

"1799, July 1.—Dr. Bray (Catholic Archbishop of Cashel), in reply to urgent appeals to procure discreetly Catholic signatures in favour of the Union in Tipperary and Waterford, says that Lord Castlereagh, at whose instance this application was made, should know that he, as a Catholic Bishop, had little influence. The Union might prove to be a useful measure; but bishops injure their own character and the cause of religion *by interfering against the wishes of the people*. It is plain that Dr. Bray intended this answer as a polite refusal. A few days after, he received a letter from the Archbishop of Tuam, expressing his fears lest some ecclesiastics should be seduced by the Government into approval of its measures, particularly the Union, from which he anticipated the worst evils." ‡

Despite martial law and Governmental interference to obstruct anti-Union petitions and to procure signatures in favour of the Union, we know that the signatures against it were 707,000, whilst those in its favour did not at any time exceed 5,000. Now, when we reflect that out of the 5,000,000 who then inhabited Ireland, 4,000,000 were Catholics, and also that the whole number of pro-Union petitioners, Protestants and all, was not greater than 5,000, is it not clear that the Catholic body stands exculpated from the ignominy of having supported the disfranchisement of Ireland? Lord Cornwallis, while trying to persuade the Bishop of Lichfield that, excepting Dublin, the general sense

* "Cornwallis Correspondence," vol. iii. p. 28. The meeting at Lord Fingal's was held 13th of December, 1798.
† *Ibid.*, p. 87.
‡ Renehan's "Collections," vol. i. p. 375.

of Ireland was favourable to the Union, inadvertently adds: "It is, however, easy for men of influence to obtain addresses and resolutions on either side." * If so, how did it happen, that notwithstanding the alleged popularity of the Union, the men of influence who favoured it could only stimulate 5,000 persons to sign petitions in its behalf; whilst the men of influence on the other side could muster an array of 707,000 petitioners? Lord Cornwallis discloses the truth. On the 31st of January, 1800, he writes to Major-General Ross: "The Roman Catholics, for whom I have not been able to obtain the slightest token of favour, are joining the standard of opposition."

To these proofs that the Catholics were not accomplices in the disfranchisement of Ireland I add the following extract from Daniel O'Connell's anti-Union speech, delivered on the 13th of January, 1800: "There was no man present," said O'Connell, " but was acquainted with the industry with which it was circulated that the Catholics were favourable to the Union. In vain did multitudes of that body, in different capacities, express their disapprobation of the measure; in vain did they concur with others of their fellow subjects in expressing their abhorrence of it—as freemen or freeholders, as electors of counties or inhabitants of cities— still the calumny was repeated; it was printed in journal after journal; it was published in pamphlet after pamphlet; it was circulated with activity in private companies; it was boldly and loudly proclaimed in public assemblies. . . . In vain did the Catholics individually resist the torrent. Their future efforts, as individuals, would be equally vain and fruitless; they must then oppose it collectively."

I have quoted the above testimonies in order to rescue the character of the Irish Catholics from a disgraceful accusation. That accusation, I presume, originated in the fact that the Government succeeded in cajoling a few Catholic prelates to sanction their measure, and that Lords Kenmare and Fingal were ready to surrender their country. I think the episcopal traitors did not exceed ten. Sir Jonah Barrington says:

* "Cornwallis Correspondence," vol. iii. p. 169. It is to be noted that in the accounts we possess of the public transactions of the period, the number of signatures to pro-Union petitions is sometimes set down at 5,000, and sometimes at 3,000; but as it is also stated that several of the petitions prayed, not for the enactment of the Union, but only that it might be discussed, I dare say the apparent discrepancy may be explained by assigning 2,000 of the signatures to the latter class of petitions.

"The Bishops Troy, Lanigan, and others, deluded by the Viceroy, sold their country, and basely betrayed their flocks by promoting the Union. But," Sir Jonah adds, "the great body of Catholics were true to their country." * This can be affirmed alike of the laity, the priesthood, and the majority of the Bishops.

The Protestants were not more favourable to the Union than their Catholic brethren. There were numberless resolutions of grand juries, Orange guilds, and Orange lodges, denouncing the project in the strongest language. Saurin declared that although the Union "might be made binding as a law, it could never become obligatory upon conscience; and that resistance to it would be in the abstract a duty." Numbers of the Protestant ascendency party were inaccessible to the bribes of the Minister. Their political integrity deserves honourable record, and enduring national gratitude. Sir Frederick Falkiner had four executions in his house at Abbotstown on the very day on which he rejected a large offer of money from Lord Castlereagh. There were numerous other instances of noble and disinterested patriotism amongst the leaders of Orangeism.

The Government had tried to delude both parties—the Catholics, by holding out hopes of their emancipation from the Imperial Parliament; the Protestants, by instilling into their minds a belief that the Union would render emancipation either impossible, or, if it should be granted, innocuous to Protestant ascendency. It must be observed that in the beginning of 1795 there was no active or extensive hostility entertained by the Irish Protestants to Catholic emancipation. But the machinations of the English Government had been so successful in reviving and inflaming the animosities of sects and parties (animosities rendered inveterate by the horrors of the rebellion), that in 1800 the liberal and generous feelings which had influenced the Protestants five years previously were to a large extent superseded by a stolid hatred of the Catholics, and a fierce resolve to resist their admission to any political privileges. George III. adopted the notion that under an Union emancipation would become impossible. In his published correspondence with Pitt, he tells that Minister that he had consented to the Union in the full belief that it would "shut the door" for ever against the Catholic claims. It required much dexterity on

* Barrington's " Rise and Fall of the Irish Nation," chap. xxvii.

the part of the Viceroy and his agents to infuse into the minds of the rival parties these opposite beliefs. Lord Cornwallis was, as we have seen, instructed by Pitt to assure the Catholics that the success of the Union was essential to the success of Emancipation. At the same time his subordinate ally, Mr. Secretary Cooke, while amusing the Catholics with some indistinct hope of "additional privileges" (which he did not specify), assured the Protestants in the same paragraph that under an Union "the Catholics could not force their claims with hostility against the whole power of Great Britain and Ireland."*

Of Mr. Pitt's ambiguous utterances Mr. Speaker Foster said: "Mr. Pitt's language is of such a nature that one would imagine he had the two religions on either side of him, and one was not to hear what he said to the other."†

Lord Cornwallis's task was to create among the Catholics a conviction that their claims would be much *strengthened* by incorporation with England. But what was the Viceroy's own conviction? Let him answer the question himself:

"The claims of the Catholics will certainly be much *weakened* by their incorporation into the mass of British subjects."‡

This he wrote to the Duke of Portland at the very time when he was labouring to convince the Catholics that the Imperial Parliament would emancipate them. So it did, twenty-nine years later; and so it would *not* have done at that, or probably at any other time, had not O'Connell's agitation created a belief in the Duke of Wellington's mind that the only alternatives were concession or civil war.

It is interesting to notice the doubts of success which Lord Cornwallis occasionally felt. In a pamphlet by a barrister named Weld, the author, speaking of the bribed supporters of the Union, says, "their penitential tears fall fast upon the wages of apostasy."

This reluctance to perform the execrable task for which they took payment is seen by Lord Cornwallis, who writes to the Bishop of Lichfield, on the 24th of January, 1800: "There can, I think, now be no great doubt of our Parliamentary success, although I believe that a great number

---

* Mr. Secretary Cooke's "Arguments for and against an Union Considered," p. 30.
† Mr. Foster's Speech, 11th April, 1799.
‡ Letter to the Duke of Portland, 24th December, 1798, "Cornwallis Correspondence," vol. iii. p. 22.

of our friends are not sincere well-wishers to the measure of Union." The Viceroy was right. Those men had not virtue to resist the wages of iniquity; yet their lingering *amor patriæ* would have been rejoiced if their country had escaped the blow of the executioner.

Again, the Viceroy writes to General Ross on the 4th of February, 1800: "God only knows how the business will terminate; but it is so hard to struggle against private interests, and the pride and prejudices of a nation, that I shall never feel confident of success till the Union is actually carried."*

This admission that he was fighting a hard battle against the pride and prejudices of a nation, contrasts rather curiously with his statements in other parts of his correspondence that the national sentiment was in his favour. On the 18th of April, writing to General Ross on the parliamentary supporters of the Union, His Excellency says: "I believe that half of our majority would be at least as much delighted as any of our opponents, if the measure were defeated."†

In fact they well knew that the measure struck a mortal blow at the best interests of their country, as well as at their own personal consequence. But the seduction of enormous bribes prevailed so far as to secure a majority for the Government in 1800. On the 27th of February in that year, Mr. Saurin described that majority as "consisting almost entirely of gentlemen holding offices or places at the pleasure of the Crown; of adventurers from the bar, of adventurers from the British army, of men who would have no scruple to subject the property of this kingdom, in which they have no share, to a foreign Parliament; to traffic the independence of Ireland for a personal independence for themselves."

In the English Parliament, Mr. (afterwards Earl) Grey thus described the Union majority in the Irish House of Commons: "There are 300 members in all. . . . One hundred and sixty-two voted in favour of the Union; of these 116 were placemen; some of them were English generals on the Staff, without a foot of ground in Ireland, and completely dependent on the Government."

The Union being carried against the will of nearly every inhabitant of Ireland, Protestant and Catholic, it appeared

* "Cornwallis Correspondence," vol. iii. pp. 169, 177.
† *Ibid.*, vol. iii. pp. 228, 252.

to the Government politic to conciliate the Protestants, as being the stronger party. Pitt indeed made a show of retiring from office, because the King's prejudices prevented him from carrying a Catholic Relief Bill. But he soon resumed office, having—as Lord Hawkesbury at a later period * publicly declared in the House of Lords—made a voluntary pledge that he never again would bring the Catholic question under the consideration of His Majesty. And in 1805 he positively refused to present a petition for Emancipation to the House of Commons, or even to lay it on the table of the House; he went so far as to say that if the petition should be presented by any other Ministerial member, he would feel it his duty to resist it. At the same time he politely informed the deputation who brought the petition, " that the confidence of so very respectable a body as the Catholics of Ireland was highly gratifying to him."

The confidence of the great body of Irish Catholics, Mr. Pitt had never possessed; and the few gentlemen (ten Bishops included) who styled themselves "Catholic leaders," and who were weak enough, or base enough, to consent to the Union in the hope of its being immediately followed by Catholic Emancipation, and in the hope, also, of episcopal pensions from the Government—those gentlemen deserved their disappointment. They deserved it for their folly in trusting the vague, indefinite intimations of Pitt and others that the English Parliament would immediately remove their political disabilities. They deserved it for their unprincipled readiness to sacrifice the legislative independence of their country for any consideration whatever.

No doubt there were multitudes who rejoiced in believing with King George III. that the Union had "shut the door" for ever against the claims of the Catholics. Those claims seemed for a while to be forgotten. The Government allowed the Irish Protestants to monopolise the local control of the country as the most effectual means of reconciling them to the Union. They had the Castle, the courts, the public offices, and the enormous revenues of the State Church. They had everything that remained after the suppression of the Legislature. Yet this monopoly did not avail to extinguish altogether the national sentiment that had grown up under the influence of home legislation.

Grattan, the illustrious founder of the Constitution of

* March 26th, 1807.

1782, retired on the enactment of the Union into private life, from which he did not emerge until 1805, when he was returned to the Imperial Parliament for the borough of Malton. On the first appearance of so distinguished an orator on the boards of St. Stephen's, there was necessarily great curiosity excited. There were in his style of speaking some marked peculiarities, and also in his voice some Hibernian inflections, which called forth an incipient titter of derision from certain of his English auditors. These symptoms, however, were checked by Pitt, who nodded his approval of the style and manner of the speaker.

What a type of Ireland's degradation! Her most honoured and venerable patriot exposed to the sneers of a foreign assembly, and indebted for exemption from insult to the patronising approbation of the bitter and triumphant enemy of his country! It was in the speech he then delivered that Grattan, in alluding to the fallen fortunes of Ireland, used the touching words, "I sat by her cradle; I follow her hearse."

In 1805 several of the guilds of Dublin met to prepare petitions for the repeal of the Union. The Stationers' Company met at their hall in Capel Street, and appointed a Committee of nine to draw up their petition. They were probably encouraged to commence the good work by Grattan's return to the English House of Commons. The Orange Corporation of Dublin followed the example of the guilds in 1810, and confided their petition for Repeal to Grattan and Sir Robert Shaw, father, I believe, of the gentleman who for many years was the Recorder of Dublin. Both these gentlemen promised to support the Repeal, and Grattan emphatically said : " Whenever the question shall come before Parliament, I shall prove myself an Irishman; and that Irishman whose first and last passion is his native country."

It is curious to hear modern Orangemen and Tories denouncing Repeal as being no better than treason, when we remember that Repeal was proposed in 1810 by the most ultra-Orange municipality in the kingdom. The example of Repeal agitation was then given by that body, whose anti-Catholic prejudices were so violent and inflexible, that it admitted only five Catholics to be freemen of the city of Dublin during the period of forty-eight years, from 1793, when the Catholics became legally admissible, to 1841, when the Orange Corporation was dissolved by the Municipal Reform Act. Mr. Butt, while still a Tory, once arraigned the Repealers as traitors in a speech at the Rotunda. He apparently forgot that his ancient friends and clients, the Orange Corporation, should necessarily be involved in this censure. The "treason" of Repeal was long enshrined in the Orange sanctuary in William Street, and many a true Orange knee was bent in that temple before the altar of the national divinity. Shall we ever see the Orangemen return to their ancient anti-Union principles? Shall we ever see them adopt the political faith which seeks not the ascendency of a class or sect, but the greatness, the prosperity, the dignity of the whole Irish nation?

I have mentioned that during the forty-eight years from 1793, when Catholics became legally eligible, to 1841, when the Corporate Reform Act disbanded the Orange Corporation, the Dublin corporators only admitted five Catholics as members of their body. Contrast their intolerance with the liberal conduct of the reformed Corporation of Dublin, in which there is an important majority of Catholics. Since 1841 to the year 1882, this reformed Corporation, in which Catholics predominate, has seventeen times elected a Protestant Lord Mayor; besides conferring on Protestants the situations of City Treasurer, City Engineer and Borough Surveyor, Assistant Engineer, Medical Officer of Health and City Analyst, Overseer of Waterworks, Superintendent of Fire Brigade, and Assistant-Superintendent. The names of these gentlemen will be found in the Appendix. The moral of the contrast is plain.

CHAPTER VI.

REPEAL ACTION—SECTARIAN OBSTRUCTION.

And will ye bear, my brother men,
To see your altars trampled down?
Shall Christ's great heart bleed out again
Beneath the scoffer's spear and frown?
Spirit of the Nation.

In 1810 public meetings were held in sustainment of the Repeal, and in order to encourage the Corporation. George III. became ill, prior to his madness, and the loyal corporators suspended their agitation lest they should embarrass the royal invalid. In 1813 the Repeal demand was renewed in Dublin, and the Repealers of all creeds held a meeting to promote their object. O'Connell, who had joined the movement in 1810, now again came forward, and exerted himself in conformity with the earliest declaration he ever had made of his political principles. In 1822 Mr. Lucius Concannon, a member of the House of Commons, gave notice of a motion for the Repeal of the Union. Mr. (afterwards Sir Robert) Peel inquired "if the honourable gentleman could seriously ask the House to violate that solemn compact?" Just as if a measure, which was literally forced upon Ireland at the point of the bayonet, could be rationally called a compact! From that period forward the Repeal was constantly mooted in private society. In 1824 Lord Cloncurry wrote a letter, which was read by O'Connell at the Catholic Association, recommending the Catholics to abandon for a time the struggle for Emancipation, and to coalesce with the Protestants in a struggle for Repeal. But this advice was premature; the Protestants of Ireland could not just then have been induced to combine with the Catholics for that or any other purpose. The demon of religious hatred was in the ascendant. Catholicity was familiarly designated "the beast" and "the accursed thing," by Protestant controvertists; and the more bigoted Protestant preachers inculcated envenomed hostility to the creed of the Catholics as a Christian duty paramount to all others. When sectarian hate 'is incessantly enforced it is speedily transferred from the creed of misbelievers to their persons. Those who recollect the exertions of the Biblical party in 1824, 1825, and 1826, have reason to rejoice that their pernicious activity has been to a considerable extent relaxed. The controversial excitement through the country was actually frightful. The Protestants were taught to look on the religion of the Catholics as a grand magazine of immorality, infidelity, and rebellion; while the Catholics, in their turn, regarded their enthusiastic assailants as the victims of a spiritual insanity derived from an infernal source, and as disastrous in its social results as it was bizarre in its exhibition. The kindly charities of friendship were annihilated; ancient intimacies were broken up; hatred was mitigated only by a sentiment of scornful compassion.*

* Lord Farnham was a leading patron of these Biblical exploits. One cannot help regarding with a feeling of melancholy interest the curious scenes to which the system of patronising proselytes from Popery gave rise. I knew more than one Protestant clergyman, remote from the headquarters of religious excitement, who had

Such were too frequently the mutual feelings of the two great sections of the Irish community—the one party having the immense preponderance in number, the other in wealth. Mr. Plunket, then Attorney-General, had declared that "the cauldron was already boiling over in Ireland ; and that it was not requisite that a polemic contest should be thrown into it."*

The advice was wasted. Many motives impelled the Biblical party to persevere. First of all, to do them every justice, there were some fanatics among their number who conscientiously believed that they were divinely commissioned to dispel the gross darkness of Popery. They were, as they conceived, authorised to walk forth, wielding "the sword of the Spirit, which is the Word of God." Then there were the political speculators, who looked on the furious theological

been asked by distressed wretches, "How much will I get from your reverence if I turn Protestant?" The universal conviction on the minds of the lower order of Catholics was that nobody "turned," as they called it, except for lucre, and that an enormous fund existed, under the control of the Protestant leaders, for buying up the religious belief of all Papists who were willing to conform. Weekly bulletins of the number of new converts from Popery were placarded on the walls, or suspended from the necks of persons who were hired to perambulate the public streets. Fourteen hundred and eighty-three converts were at one time announced as the fruit of Lord Farnham's exertions in Cavan; but when Archbishop Magee went down to confirm them their number had shrunk to forty-two. Lord Farnham was doubtless a sincere enthusiast; but his fanatical folly was excessive, and he was greatly imposed on. He kept open house for the crowds of proselytes, who were furnished with soup, potatoes, and in some instances with clothes. Pauper Protestants are said to have sometimes enjoyed his hospitality under the pretext of being "converts" from Popery ; and it is said that such Catholics as thought they could escape recognition among the multitude of strange faces, contrived to be "converted" three or four times over, in order to prolong the substantial advantage of being fed in a dear season at the noble lord's cost. When the supply of food, etc., was discontinued, they returned to their former Church. This Lord Farnham had been a determined opponent of the Union in 1800; and, not long before his death, he declared at a Conservative meeting that his hostility to Repeal arose from a religious, and not at all from a political motive. Alas! Lord Farnham was not the only man in whom sectarian fanaticism spoiled a good patriot.

* But although Mr. Plunket said this, he is also stated—I do not know with what accuracy—to have helped to set the cauldron boiling by advising Dr. Magee, the Protestant Archbishop of Dublin, to institute a controversial movement against the Catholic religion, which it was hoped would produce numerous conversions to Protestantism.

excitement as affording a useful diversion of men's minds from the grievances of tithes and legal disabilities to the abstract topics of purgatory, transubstantiation, and Saint Peter's supremacy. Again, it was hoped and expected by others that the ceaseless abuse launched at Popery would disincline Protestants to become emancipators, and possibly withdraw from the Catholics the political support of many who had already joined them.

It is probable that some of the Liberal members of Parliament, at that period, had but little sincerity in their emancipating zeal. The profession of Liberal politics effected two things for them—it obtained an agreeable popularity, and also what they considered the honour of seats in Parliament. Such persons voted for the Catholics year after year, entertaining, I verily believe, a full conviction that Emancipation would never be conceded. They thus enjoyed the cheap distinction of being senators on the easy terms of supporting a measure for which they cherished no affection, but of whose defeat they indulged in a comforting certainty. How ludicrously disappointed must such men have been when Peel and Wellington suddenly became champions of Emancipation in 1829!

Religious jealousy and sectarian distrust, like the poisonous exhalations of the upas tree, blighted and withered the natural, inborn sentiment of nationality in many a well-meaning man. When Lord Cloncurry, in the letter already alluded to, publicly advocated Repeal, a worthy Protestant gentleman said to me that it would be an excellent thing if we had a Parliament of our own in Ireland—"but then," he added, "the Papists are so numerous they would soon get the upper hand." I asked him what harm their emancipation would do him or any one? His reply was to the effect that they would rival the Protestants in everything; if a Papist was more eloquent or a better lawyer than a Protestant, he might get the start of the Protestant in Parliament, or he might be promoted to the Bench, while the Protestant of inferior talent lost the race. As matters stood, the Protestant could not be beaten in the race, for the Papist could not run; an advantage that should not be surrendered on any account.

I mention this trifling incident because it illustrates the sort of jealous feeling which operated, not only to enlist Protestants against the Catholic claims, but also to smother their national spirit as Irishmen. The mischievous efficacy of this jealous terror will be more apparent when I add that the gentleman in question had been connected with the United Irishmen in 1797. The impressions received from that connexion were effaced by the malign influence of sectarian partisanship. And yet there was no great bitterness, nor was there any personal hostility in his politics. He did not hate Catholics; he was not unkind to them in his landlord capacity; but he had taken up the notion that the doctrine of absolution authorised crime. He had accurately expressed the sentiment that actuated thousands—a sturdy resolve to sustain the monopoly the Protestants had got, not only to preserve a party advantage, but from a belief that the spiritual merits of Protestantism entitled its professors to that monopoly.

Meanwhile, O'Connell worked the Catholic question indefatigably. He was an inexhaustible declaimer, and astonishingly fertile in argument, in expedient, and in topics of excitement. There had been from the commencement of his career this novel feature in his agitation—there was nothing secret in it: no locked doors, no secret committees, no hidden springs, no machinery to which he would not at any moment have admitted the whole corps of Government inspectors. Former political leaders had conceived that secrecy was an indispensable element of success. But O'Connell early saw the perils of every scheme of which concealment formed a part. The very fact of supposing a junto secret would necessarily induce ill-regulated spirits to give utterance to illegal or treasonable sentiments. There was the presumed protection of silence. Then there instantly arose the danger of treachery; any rascal who was sufficiently base to betray his associates, any Reynolds or Newell, might instantly compromise the safety of the entire association by revealing the indiscretion, or the illegality, or the treason, of a single member. O'Connell's sagacity swept away all such danger. By resolving to hide nothing, his associates were sure to say and do nothing that required to be hidden.

O'Connell's immediate predecessor as a Catholic leader was John Keogh, a Dublin merchant. Keogh was far advanced in years at the time when O'Connell first became very celebrated; and it is believed that the old leader felt jealous of the popular talents as well as of the influence acquired by the younger one. It is certain that he sought to persuade O'Connell that the Catholics, instead of continuing their agitation, should relapse into silence and inertion, and try the effect of regarding the Government with a surly, awe-inspiring frown, indicative of hostility too deeply rooted to petition or negotiate. Keogh, in fact, proposed and carried a resolution to that effect at a public meeting at which his rival attended. O'Connell proposed and carried a counter resolution to that effect at the same meeting, which pledged the Catholics to unremitting activity.

Nothing could have gratified the Government more than the adoption by the Catholics of Keogh's advice. It would have released them from the annual parliamentary bore of the Catholic question. It would have retarded the success of that question incalculably. The policy of endeavouring to scare a hostile Government by a grim and silent scowl, was too melodramatic to avail on the political stage.

O'Connell, of course, persevered. In 1813 he was called "an agitator with ulterior views." He immediately accepted the designation, and declared that the ulterior object he had in view was the Repeal of the Union. When urged at a much later period to postpone the agitation of the Catholic claims to that of Repeal, he refused to comply, alleging as his reason that Emancipation, by removing one great subject of national difference, would facilitate the junction of all Irishmen to regain their national independence. O'Connell undoubtedly entertained at that time too favourable a notion of the patriotism of the Orange party. He did not anticipate the stubborn, inflexible, enduring Orange bigotry which has survived the emancipation of the Catholics, and thus outlived the chief pretext for its exercise. No doubt there were other pretexts too ; there were the corporations and the iniquitous Church Establishment; the former have been taken from the Orangemen ; but the so-called "disendowment" of the State Church has been so partially effected that it is in truth a re-endowment, not indeed of its original magnitude, but sufficiently large to make the Church a profitable institution to its officers, who are principally subsidised at the expense of the nation. So long as an anti-national institution is supported at the national expense, so long will the party that gains by its existence refuse to co-operate with the general mass of their countrymen.

John Keogh's belief in the inutility of political agitation is instructive. Lord Fingal was latterly impressed with that belief, and alleged it as his reason for declining to preside at a Catholic meeting in Dublin. How often have I—how often have all whose memory extends back to the latter years of the Catholic struggle—heard from all sides the exclamation, "Oh! they will never get Emancipation! The Government never will grant it! How are the Catholics to frighten the Government into concession? O'Connell is wasting his time; he has been haranguing for nearly thirty years, and has brought his dupes no nearer to it yet."

Thus do we hear the struggles of Ireland for domestic legislation denounced as a delusion, and in much the same language. That our claim should be derided by our enemies is natural. Among its friends—that is to say among the great bulk of the people of Ireland—there is too often an impatience of persevering agitation, a disposition to relinquish a pursuit that is not speedily successful. To all fickle patriots I would observe, firstly, that the object to be gained—namely, the restoration of the Irish Parliament in connection with the Crown of Great Britain—is our indefeasible right, and is vitally necessary to our national prosperity. It is a political pearl beyond price. Secondly, I would remind them that the pursuit of Catholic Emancipation occupied fifty-one years. The first relaxation of the penal laws occurred in 1778; the admission of Catholics to the Bench and to Parliament was not gained until 1829. Fifty-one years! Here is a lesson for impatient patriots. During that protracted period how many were the dreary intervals of hopeless depression! How often did ultimate success appear desperate! How many a heart was weary of the long, long struggle, which often seemed a vain and feeble protest against omnipotent hostility! Yet for fifty-one years the friends of the Catholic cause struggled on with varying fortunes, until at last success crowned their persevering efforts. And we must not forget that some of the worst enactments of the penal code had become law more than fourscore years before the earliest legal mitigation of that code's severity.

Hence we may learn a lesson of unfaltering perseverance in pursuit of Repeal. I do not underrate the difficulties of the task. England is now strong, and we are weak. Yet it is quite possible that political complications may arise which would render it worth England's while to purchase the fidelity of Ireland at the expense of that grand act of restitution. Repeal of the Union has ever had, has now, and ever will have, the great strength of incontrovertible justice and right. Let the people of Ireland be ever on the watch for a time when Imperial expediency may enforce from our rulers the concession of our righteous claim to self-legislation

Fenianism in America, despite its blunders and the glaring rascality of some of its leaders, is a portent too mighty to be despised. It is an exhibition to the world of the insatiable resentment of a people expelled by misgovernment, fiscal and political, from the land which "the Lord their God had given them" to inhabit. When, after 1798, the Marquis Cornwallis was congratulated because "the rebels were all crossing the Atlantic," His Excellency answered: "I would rather have three rebels to deal with in Ireland than one in America." Fenianism, as we have seen its exhibition in America, showed a great waste of power. The Fenians possess the raw material of great strength; but their strength is neutralised by mistakes in their programme, and by the turpitude of scheming leaders, who have filled their own pockets by trafficking on popular credulity.

The hatred entertained to England by the expatriated Irish, whom the Union has expelled from their native land by stripping it of the means of supporting them, has occasionally puzzled English commentators on Irish affairs. But the fact can be easily explained. England first corrupted the Irish Parliament, and then destroyed it. The destruction of home government was necessarily followed by national decay. Deprived by the competition of English capital of the resource of manufacturing industry, the great bulk of the people were thrown on the land as their sole means of subsistence. Mr. Mitchell Henry, member for the County Galway, stated in the English House of Commons on the 9th of February, 1880, that there were no more than 273 manufactories in Ireland, and that these included the flax-mills at Belfast. He added that the manufactories only gave employment to 80,000 persons in a population that then exceeded five millions. The people, almost exclusively dependent on the land for the means of existence, were in numberless instances persecuted by rapacious landlords, whose insatiable greed was often accompanied with fierce sectarian hatred of the tenants whom they fleeced. The landlords were generally Protestants. The tenants were generally Catholics. The whole ecclesiastical State revenues of Ireland had been wrenched by English power from the Catholics and given to the members of the English religion, whose ministers, naturally drawn towards the power that had given them the revenues, and as naturally hating the Catholic people who were wronged by that gigantic fraud,

Sectarian Insolence. 61

occasionally stimulated the religious zeal of their flocks by such utterances as the following :

"Again, sir," said the Reverend Francis Gervais at a meeting at Dungannon, held on Tuesday, 9th of December, 1828, " I consider the religion of Rome as under the curse of the Almighty, distinctly denounced against it, and that the time is at hand when the Divine judgment will fall on it, and everything connected with it—political institutions as well as others."

The report says these sentiments evoked " great applause."

In July, 1843, Doctor Robert Daly, Protestant Bishop of Cashel, delivered a charge to his clergy, principally against the Tractarians, in which his lordship thus expressed himself :

"It was said by a shrewd and pious man that Popery was the masterpiece of Satan, and that he never would bring into the world a second scheme of evil equal to it in cunning and mischief ; and the scheme now introduced (Puseyism) is not another—it is only a modification of the Popish views."

Isaac Butt, in his admirable " Plea for the Celtic Race," cites the following passage from a speech delivered at a great Protestant meeting in 1834 by the Reverend Marcus Beresford, afterwards Archbishop of Armagh :

" I trust that every good and faithful minister of his God would sooner have potatoes and salt, surrounded with Protestants, than to live like princes, surrounded with Papists."

It will be admitted that such utterances as these were not calculated to promote friendly feelings between the Protestant landlords and the Catholic peasantry. Enthusiastic clergymen vied with each other in assailing the popular creed.

The absence of manufactures necessarily caused a great subdivision of land. The interests of the landlords suffered from the overcrowding of their estates with human beings for whom there was no manufacturing outlet, and whose numbers exceeded the capacity of the land, as it was then cultivated, to support them. The system of clearing estates of their human inhabitants was vigorously acted on. The late Mr. Sharman Crawford showed, from parliamentary returns, that in the five years from 1838 to 1843 inclusive, ejectment proceedings had been taken against 356,985 persons; and he said he was prepared to show that the extermination of the people was going on in a rapidly increasing ratio. He called it "a dreadful and heartless persecution." The crowbar brigade has been actively employed from that day to this; and between its operations, and the general impoverishment of Ireland resulting from the want of home government, our population, which in 1841 was 8,196,597, has sunk in 1885 to 4,900,000. Lord Macaulay instances as a .proof of the destructive effects of war that the Prussian population was diminished ten per cent. by the wars of Frederick the Great. The Irish population has lost more than thirty per cent. under the Union since 1841 ; and if it be said that it increased between 1800 and 1841, we reply that it. multiplied in misery during that period. There were not then the modern facilities for emigration, and the Union starved our people in their own country. Now that magnificent steamers waft them cheaply and swiftly across the Atlantic, they emigrate, bearing in their hearts an ineradicable hatred of the power that has driven them into exile.

Can we conceive a condition of things more calculated to demoralise a nation, or to engender international animosity ? Mr. Godkin, editor of a New York journal, contributes to the *Nineteenth Century* for August, 1882, the following testimony of Irish feeling towards the English Government:

"I confess," he says, "I have until recently underestimated the strength and permanence of Irish hatred of England, which the English hatred of Irishmen has at last produced. . . . In America it is apparently cultivated by the Irish as a sort of religion, and is transmitted to the second generation, which knows Ireland only by hearsay. . . . The Irishman in this country and his son and grandson are tormented neither by landlord nor police, and never see an Englishman or the English flag, and yet they hate the English Government with a kind of frenzy."

This American writer ascribes Irish antipathy to England to the habitual hatred and contempt of Ireland which pervade English literature and conversation. That cause doubtless operates ; but a much more potent cause exists in the material injury and insult inflicted on Ireland by the Union. That measure permanently dislocated the social frame of Ireland, checked the growth of manufactures, intensified the mutual enmity of classes, overspread the land with pauperism by draining it of public revenue and private income, and became the prolific parent of crime by producing a hideous condition of social and political distortion and disease.

I respectfully suggest to the Irish in America and in the

Colonies, that in order to achieve legislative freedom for Ireland, they must renounce every principle that repels the great body of the Irish Repealers at home. They are sometimes accused of intending to substitute a republic for the Irish throne of Queen Victoria. It is our ardent desire that Her Majesty should govern Ireland through an Irish Ministry and an Irish Legislature, just as Francis Joseph now governs Hungary through a Hungarian Ministry and a Hungarian Legislature. The Fenians—I speak of the multitude of Irish-American emigrants, not of some ten or twelve dishonest leaders—must bear in mind that the Irish Repealers inherit the constitutional principles of 1782, by which the legislative independence of Ireland was combined with untainted loyalty to the sovereign of these realms. Any deviation from these principles must be fatal to an alliance between them and us; fatal to the strength which such an alliance, if wisely formed, would constitute.

Calculated as the Legislative Union is to alienate Irishmen from the English connexion, it is not unnatural that our exiles who have sought refuge in the American Republic from the wrongs inflicted by that measure, should sympathise in the Republican principles of the land of their adoption. But it does not therefore follow that they will not loyally and faithfully adhere to the Royal Constitution of Ireland when the Home Government Bill shall have removed the evil of foreign legislation, and re-established on a stable basis our exclusive right to legislate for our country. Their unanimous support of Mr. Gladstone's Bill sufficiently indicates their sentiments.

English writers have complained that they now have two Irelands to deal with, one on each side of the Atlantic. This is true; and in order that these two Irelands should effectively combine for the recovery of their rights, the Ireland now in exile must carefully shape her course in accordance with the principles and exigencies of the Ireland at home.*

It is needless to point out the political contingencies in which British statesmen may find it their true policy to give Ireland that contentment which can alone result from our possessing the sole control of our national concerns. War-clouds are blackening in various quarters of the horizon. It is vitally important to the integrity of the Empire, that in the

* There are also other Irelands growing up in Canada, Australia, and other British colonies.

event of foreign war, Ireland should be the fast and firm friend of England. There is but one way of making her so, and that is by the restoration of her stolen property, her power of self-legislation—in a word, by repealing the Union.

All this is of course unpalatable to the English lust of domination. But we in Ireland have our own experience of that domination. In an article on Fenianism in 1867, the *Times* asserted with sad truth that England "does but hold Ireland in the very hollow of her hand." Much more recently the *Economist*,* in an article on Secret Societies, repeated the same statement in these words: "It is the English people who hold Ireland."

True: we are strangled in the English gripe, and the results of this Imperial pressure are disclosed by the special correspondent of the *Times*, who writes from Cork to that journal on the 23rd of March, 1867. "In the country districts," says the *Times* correspondent, "the depopulation of Ireland is not brought to one's notice so forcibly as in the towns. The peasant's cabin, when its last occupant has gone across the blue water, is pulled down, and no trace is left that it ever existed. But town dwellings 'to let' and empty shops remain, sad witnesses of a population that has been and is not. To the Irishman this is a trite subject; the English traveller, accustomed at home to the rapid growth of numerous small towns in most of the counties he visits, is startled in this country by the almost uniform decay of towns, both small and great."

Yes; Ireland is held, as the *Times* says, in the very hollow of the hand of England; and the deadly consequence of that unnatural position appears in the evanishment of her people and in the decay recorded by the *Times* correspondent. It is well to bear in mind that when we were *not* held in the hollow of her hand—when, after 1782, we enjoyed for some years the priceless blessing of self-government—every element of national prosperity developed itself with a force which, contrasted with our present degraded and despoiled condition, demonstrates the absolute necessity of domestic legislation.

"It is the English people," says the *Economist*, "who hold Ireland."

This is the explanation of the ulcerated state of Ireland. The English people have no more right to hold Ireland than

* The *Economist*, quoted in the *Irish Times*, 1st of July, 1882.

the French or German people have to hold England. No condition can be more unnatural, more provocative of crime, more prolific of turbulence, more conducive to misery, than that of a nation gripped fast in the talons of another.

The extermination of great masses of the Irish people appears, from time to time, to have been a favourite object of English statesmanship. In the reign of Elizabeth, Lord Deputy Gray so conducted the Government that, as Leland informs us, the Queen was assured "that little was left in Ireland for Her Majesty to reign over but ashes and carcases."*

The Government raid on human life is thus described by Mr. Froude :†

" In 'the stately days of great Elizabeth,' the murder of women and children appears to have been the every-day occupation of the English police in Ireland; and accounts of atrocities, to the full as bad as that at Glencoe, were sent in on half a sheet of letter-paper, and were endorsed like any other documents with a brevity which shows that such things were too common to deserve criticism or attract attention."

In Mr. Prendergast's " Cromwellian Settlement," the author says: "Ireland now lay void as a wilderness. Five-sixths of her people had perished."‡

In the gracious reign of Queen Victoria more than three millions of the Irish race have been got rid of between 1846 and 1885. This is being held in the very hollow of the hand of England. The diminution still goes on; and so long as we enjoy that affectionate pressure, the same result may be expected. The *modus operandi* has indeed been changed from ancient times. In the days of Elizabeth and Cromwell there were sanguinary raids against the people, and troops were employed in destroying the green corn and carrying off the cattle in order to starve out the Irish race. The people perished because their means of support were destroyed or abstracted. And the people of our own time perish or emigrate precisely because their means of support are taken away from them—not, indeed, by the coarse, rude methods of a former age, but by the equally effectual methods devised by modern statesmanship. The Union, with its

* Leland, book iv. chap. 2.
† See his article in *Fraser's Magazine* for March, 1865, "How Ireland was Governed in the Sixteenth Century."
‡ Page 146.

consequent drain of Irish wealth in absentee taxes and absentee rental, and its destruction of the nascent manufacturing industries of Ireland by irresistible British competition, achieves the thinning out of our race which was formerly wrought by the sword. It deprives Ireland of the means of supporting the Irish; and it thus effectually replaces the murderous policy of Elizabeth and Cromwell. The work once performed by military violence is now accomplished by an economic process, and under legal, peaceful, and constitutional forms.

An Irishman who believes in the retributive justice of Providence may well be excused for doubting if such a system of iniquity is destined to be perpetual. *Quousque, Domine, quousque ?*

CHAPTER VII.

THE EMANCIPATION STRUGGLE.

"I think the character of the Irish Protestants not radically bad; on the contrary, they have a considerable share of good-nature. If they could be once got to think the Catholics were human creatures, and that they lost no job by thinking them such, I am convinced they would soon, very soon indeed, be led to show some regard for their country."—EDMUND BURKE.

DURING the struggle for Emancipation it must often have sorely galled the Catholic leaders to encounter the patronising condescension of Protestant nobodies, who took airs of protection and arrogated high consideration in virtue of being emancipators. Prompt payment in servility was expected for the assuasive courtesies which seemed to claim a measureless superiority over the Catholic *protégés* on whom they were bestowed. "We have now shaken off our chains," said Sheil after Emancipation ; "and one of the blessings of freedom is release from petty and contemptible political patronage. If a Protestant vouchsafed to be present at any of our meetings, it was, ' Hurrah for the Protestant gentleman ! Three cheers for the Protestant gentleman ! A chair for the Protestant gentleman !' And this subserviency, readily tendered by some, was perhaps the most provoking small nuisance of our grievances."

A species of humiliating advocacy consisted in alleging

that although the religion of the Papists was damnable, idolatrous, diabolical, degrading, and so forth, yet its wretched votaries might be safely admitted to political equality, inasmuch as the preponderating Protestant strength of the Empire would always avail to counteract any mischief that might be devised by the Papists. Nay, Emancipation might possibly be instrumental in converting the Papists to a purer faith; inasmuch as their legal disqualifications rendered perseverance in Popery a point of honour with its professors, whereas admission to equality of privilege would remove the suspicion which might otherwise attach to their motives in conforming to Protestantism.

Among the parliamentary advocates of Emancipation who took the occasion of supporting the Catholic claims to vituperate the Catholic religion was Mr. Perceval. He delivered a speech in which the ultra-virulent abuse of Catholicity was only to be equalled by the language of some orator at Exeter Hall, on a grand anti-Papal field-day; at the same time recommending the repeal of all disqualifying laws as conducive to the religious enlightenment of the Catholics. It scarcely needs be said that advocates of Mr. Perceval's class were among the politicians who would have clogged Emancipation with the royal veto on the appointment of Catholic Bishops. On this one point—that is, in supporting the veto—the illustrious Grattan went wrong. Mr. Daniel Owen Maddyn, in a work on Irish politics, upbraids O'Connell with having "laboured to make the venerable Grattan as unpopular as possible."

The accusation, when translated into the language of simple truth, merely means that Mr. O'Connell, with characteristic sagacity, opposed every scheme of accompanying Emancipation with measures calculated to secularise the Catholic Church in the slightest degree, or to bind up the priests in the trammels of the State. Grattan would have taken Emancipation, though encumbered with the veto; and although a Roman Catholic may condemn such a policy, yet he scarcely can blame Grattan for adopting it. Grattan was a Protestant, and, of course, could not fairly be expected to possess the watchful solicitude for the independence of Catholic spiritualities which should animate an intelligent Catholic, anxious as well for the religious interests of his Church as for the political freedom of his countrymen. In truth, the only point on which O'Connell differed from Grattan was the question of the veto.

But if Grattan needed any apology for the part he adopted, he could have found it in the fact that among the Catholics of note were some men who conceived that Emancipation should be purchased at the expense of handing over to the Government the appointment of the Catholic Bishops under the name of a veto. One of these Liberal Catholics was the late Chief Baron Wolfe, then a rising barrister on the Munster Circuit. He came into collision with O'Connell on this subject at a public meeting held in a church in Limerick, and made a powerful and effective speech from the front of the gallery in favour of the veto. O'Connell, in reply, told the story of the sheep who were thriving under the protection of their dogs, when an address, recommending them to get rid of their dogs, was presented by the wolves. He said that the leading *Wolfe* came forward to the front of the gallery, and persuaded the sheep to give up their dogs; that they obeyed him, and were instantly devoured; and he then expressed a hope that the Catholics of Ireland would be warned by so impressive an example against the insidious advice of any *Wolfe* who might try to seduce them to give up their proved and faithful guides and protectors. The hit was received with roars of applause, and the vetoists were routed.

Among the Protestant emancipators who combined patronage with insult, was the statesman immortalised in Disraeli's "Coningsby" under the pseudonym of Nicholas Rigby, a dexterous and lucky adventurer, of whose career a few brief incidents may not be uninteresting.

Rigby's father held a Government office near Dublin, and gave his son a college education. The young gentleman, whose critical taste was early on the outlook for subjects to dissect, published a metrical satire on the *corps dramatique* of the Theatre Royal, as it existed under the management of Mr. Frederick Jones. This production saw the light in 1804, and was entitled "Familiar Epistles to Frederick Jones, Esq." The authorship was not avowed until after the work had passed through two editions. The versification was easy and correct; the personal sketches flippant and piquant; the text, in short, was good of its kind, but the notes which encumbered every page were of helpless dulness, which quality was rendered the more striking by the perpetual and clumsy attempts of the author to be pointed and brilliant.

The dreary and ponderous pleasantry of Rigby's notes, irresistibly reminded the reader of the stupid German commemorated by Boswell, who, being charmed by the exuberant spirits of some humorist, endeavoured, when alone, to emulate his friend's vivacity by jumping over the tables and chairs, explaining the purpose of this saltatory exercise to an acquaintance who surprised him in the midst of his antics by saying, "*J'apprends d'être vif.*" Rigby's prosaic efforts to be *vif* were clumsy failures. But there was really a good deal of pungent sarcasm in his verses.* The amusing personalities of the "Familiar Epistles," rendered the book very popular in Dublin, and a good deal of interest was excited to discover the author. So long as the Epistles were anonymous, several of the small *literati* acquired a transient importance from imputations of the authorship—imputations which some of them encouraged. But at length the real poet came forth to claim his laurels; and Mr. "Nicholas Rigby" immediately began to lionise on the strength of his literary glories. Literary ladies asked him to their assemblies; dinner-giving dilettanti invited to their tables the young satirist who had revealed so just an appreciation of the scientific *gourmandise* of Frederick Jones. The "Familiar Epistles" soon rendered

E.g., the sketch of Richard Jones:

> But who is this, all boots and breeches,
> Cravat and cape, and spurs and switches,
> Grin and grimace, and shrugs and capers,
> And affectation, spleen, and vapours?
> Oh, Mr. Richard Jones, your humble!
> Prithee give o'er to mouth and mumble.
> Stand still, speak plain, and let us hear
> What was intended for the ear;
> For, faith! without the timely aid
> Of bills, no parts you've ever played.

Another sketch:

> Next Williams comes, the rude and rough,
> With face most whimsically gruff;
> Aping the careless sons of ocean,
> He scorns each fine and easy motion.
> Tight to his sides his elbows pins,
> And dabbles with his hands like fins.
> Would he display the greatest woe,
> He slaps his breast and points his toe.
> Is merriment to be expressed?
> He points his toe and slaps his breast.
> His turns are swings, his step a jump,
> His feelings fits, his touch a thump;
> And violent in all his parts,
> He speaks by gusts and moves by starts.

their author more familiar with champagne and turtle-soup than perhaps he had previously been.

One of the personages who bestowed their attentions on young Rigby was the late eccentric Baron Smith, father of Thomas Berry Cusack Smith, Attorney-General for Ireland at the time of the State trials of O'Connell and others, and subsequently Master of the Rolls. I have heard that the Baron warmly admired the sportive rhymes of Rigby; but however this may be, he bestowed some flattering attentions on their author, and affectionately invited him to his country-seat.

The Baron was proverbial for his oddity. Possessed of an acute and metaphysical mind, his great intellectual powers were often distorted by unaccountable caprice. One of his traits was the suddenness of his attachments and dislikes, the lightning rapidity with which he could adopt and discard an acquaintance. He would ask you to spend a month at his house with an air of affectionate cordiality. If you accepted the invitation, and seemed disposed to take your host at his word, you would speedily receive an unequivocal hint that the sooner you ended your visit the better.

He tried the experiment on Rigby. He asked him to stay for a month. Rigby accepted the Baron's hospitality, and was received with the blandest courtesy. For the first two days everything was *couleur de rose*. The Baron was enchanting; his guest was delighted with his condescension. Rigby was introduced to the company who filled the house as a young gentleman of extraordinary genius, and his host's most particular friend.

On the third day things were changed. The Baron scarcely deigned to glance in the direction of Rigby; or, if he did look towards the place where Rigby sat, it was with that wandering gaze that seems unconscious of the presence of its object. Rigby stood his ground unmoved. He, on his part, seemed unconscious of any alteration in the manner of the Baron. He rattled away, quite at his ease; lavished his stores of entertaining small talk on the company, who were charmed with the Baron's agreeable guest. At dinner the Baron did not speak to him; treated him with marked and supercilious coldness; and indicated by the mute eloquence of manner that Rigby had exhausted his welcome.

Next day Rigby took his usual place at the breakfast-table, conversed with delightful animation, and wore the appearance of a man so well satisfied with his quarters that, he had not the least notion of changing them. The Baron, finding that silence had no effect in dislodging his pertinacious guest, at last determined to speak out. Meeting him alone in the domain soon after breakfast, he thus addressed him : " I had hoped, Mr. Rigby, that you would have spared me the pain of telling you what I think that my manner sufficiently indicated—that your visit is no longer agreeable. Is it possible you cannot have discovered this ? "

" Of course I have discovered it," returned Rigby. "You do not suppose me such a fool as not to have perceived that you became capriciously rude—from what cause I am wholly unable to guess. But this I know, that you invited me to stay for a month, and for a month I *will* stay. Your station in the world is fixed, but mine is not. Before I quitted Dublin I boasted among all my acquaintance of the flattering invitation you gave me. ' I told them I was going to spend a month with you. If I returned at the end of a few days I should be their laughing-stock ; my social position would be seriously damaged, and my prospects would be more or less injured. No, no. You certainly cannot be serious, Baron, in the intention of converting your kindness into a source of mischief to me."

These words, spoken in a tone of civil but resolute impudence, tickled the Baron's fancy ; he saw that his guest was no every-day character, and, being an admirer of originality, he broke into a good-humoured fit of laughter, and permitted Rigby to remain until the month was expired.

The anecdote is very characteristic of the energetic perseverance which has marked through life the politician celebrated in Disraeli's novel as "The Right Honourable Nicholas Rigby."

Rigby's next adventure of importance was his return to Parliament. There was an election for the borough of Downpatrick.* The contest was expected to be very close. One of the candidates was detained by an accident, and his friends, in order to prevent his rival from getting ahead of him, set up Rigby—who happened to be in the town—as a stalking-horse. Rigby was proposed and seconded— harangued the electors against time—a poll was demanded, and *one* vote was given, which with the votes of the proposer and seconder, gave him *three* of the voices of the electors of the borough. Just at this stage of the proceedings the bonâ

---

* Query—should this be Athlone ?

fide candidate arrived. Rigby retired from the hustings, but made no formal resignation of his claims. Fierce raged the contest. There was on both sides a tremendous expenditure of bribery. The election ended in the triumph of the man who bribed the highest; and in due course of time his antagonist petitioned against his return. The sitting member was unseated for gross and corrupt bribery ; but the petitioner was not seated, for bribery to a great extent was clearly proved to have been committed by him also.

There had been, however, a third candidate, who had committed no bribery—a candidate who had got three votes. The committee accordingly reported that "Nicholas Rigby, Esquire," had been duly returned for the borough. This decision astonished the public, who had looked on Rigby's standing for the borough as a mere electioneering ruse, and who, in fact, had forgotten the circumstance in the interest excited by the more important candidates.

Here was a frolic of fortune. It is not every day that senatorial honours are flung at men's heads, and Rigby determined to make the most of his sudden and unlooked-for elevation. The gentleman as whose *locum tenens* he had been originally proposed to the electors wrote him a very friendly letter, requesting he would resign his seat, as the writer wished to offer himself again for the borough. But Rigby resolved to keep what he had got. What, resign his seat? How, in point of justice to his constituents, or consistently with his sacred duty to the country, could he surrender the important trust the electors had kindly confided to his hands? Forbid it honour! conscience! patriotism! Rigby's friend was compelled to submit to Rigby's virtuous determination.

Our hero, in the year 1808, published a pamphlet, entitled, " A Sketch of the State of Ireland, Past and Present," in which he bestowed a species of contemptuous advocacy on the Catholic claims. His arguments went to support Emancipation on the ground of its being too insignificant a boon to be worth refusing. He styled it " an almost empty privilege." He held the opinion that Emancipation would facilitate conversions to Protestantism.

"Trade," he wrote, " when free, finds its level. So will religion. The majority will no more persist—when it is not a point of honour to do so—in the worse faith than it would in the worse trade. Councils decide that the Confession of Augsburg is heresy, and Parliaments vote that Popery is superstition, and both impotently. No man will ever be converted when his religion is also his party. But expedient as Catholic Emancipation is, I think it *only* expedient, and concede it not without the following conditions."

He then enumerated four conditions, of which the most important were the payment of the priesthood by the State, the approval of the prelates by the Crown, and the disfranchisement of the forty-shilling freeholders. Curious timidity, that sought these protective conditions, in return for conceding "an almost empty privilege"!

It is creditable to our hero that in his "Sketch of the State of Ireland" he has anticipated the aphorism that acquired for the late Under-Secretary Drummond such extensive popularity. "A landlord," said Rigby, "is not a mere land merchant; he has duties to perform as well as rents to receive, and from his neglect of the former springs his difficulty in the latter, and the general misery and distraction of the country. The combinations of the peasantry against this short-sighted monopoly are natural and fatal."

Candidly and boldly expressed. This evidence, coming from such a quarter, is worth something. Rigby had previously given an accurate description of the rack-rent system. He, however, took care, *more suo*, to insult the objects of his advocacy: "The peasantry of Ireland are generally of the Roman Catholic religion, but utterly and disgracefully ignorant; few of them can read—fewer write." (Thanks to the Protestant Code that had made their education penal—but Rigby does not tell us so.) He goes on: "The Irish language, a barbarous jargon, is generally, and in some districts exclusively, spoken; and with it are retained customs and superstitions as barbarous. Popish legends and pagan traditions are confounded and revered." He elsewhere calls the people "utterly dark and blind."

I have mentioned Baron Smith. That wayward functionary was a member of the Irish Parliament, and supported the Union with a zeal which in due time was rewarded with elevation to the Bench. In 1799 he issued an ingenious pamphlet, entitled "An Address to the People of Ireland," recommendatory of the Union. He went largely into the question of the competence of Parliament to annihilate itself, which competence most of the anti-Unionists denied. He told the Catholics that he did not know whether an Union would better their chance of admission to the Senate, but suggested that at any rate it would not diminish it. On the question of commercial advantages he availed himself extensively of the *petitio principii*, assuming, as if it were an incontrovertible axiom, that the incorporation of the Legislatures would, *ipso facto*, incorporate the nations, extinguish their reciprocal jealousies, and identify their interests. How far he was sincere in the profession of these views it would now be useless to inquire. But as a sample of the readiness with which he accepted, or pretended to accept, empty professions for substantial securities, it is not uninteresting to record that he quotes the following passage from a speech of "that enlightened Minister," as he calls him, Mr. Pitt, to prove that Irish commercial and manufacturing interests would sustain no injury after an Union from English rivalry or jealousy:

"I will say," said Mr. Pitt, "that for a hundred years this country (England) has followed a very narrow policy with regard to Ireland. It manifested a very absurd jealousy concerning the growth, produce, and manufacture of several articles. I say that these jealousies will be buried by the plan (of Union) which is now to be brought before you." Having quoted the above words, Mr. Smith exclaims: "I can entertain no fears that the statesman who thinks thus liberally and speaks thus frankly, will, after an Union, make the influence of all Irish members submit to the mechanics of a single English town."

The English policy towards Ireland, described by Mr. Pitt as "very narrow," has more recently been described by Lord Dufferin in one of his letters to the *Times* in the following vigorous language: "From Queen Elizabeth's reign to the Union," says Lord Dufferin (he should have said from Queen Elizabeth's reign until 1779), "the various commercial confraternities of Great Britain never for a moment relaxed their relentless grip on the trades of Ireland. One by one, each of our nascent industries was either strangled in its birth, or handed over, gagged and bound, to the jealous custody of the rival interest in England, until at last every fountain of wealth was hermetically sealed."

But Mr. Pitt's frank and liberal acknowledgment that this policy was "narrow," and his generous promise that an Union would render such narrowness impossible, inspired the confiding breast of Mr. William Smith with implicit and unlimited trust in Great Britain. It is not thus, however, that men bestow their confidence in private life. Suppose, for example, that Brown says to Robinson: "My excellent friend, I acknowledge that I have always robbed and swindled you, I have counter-worked your honest industry, deprived you of a market, and done my utmost to starve your wife and beggar your children. All this, I confess, was very narrow policy. But, my beloved Robinson, let us henceforth join forces. Give me, O friend of my heart! the key of your strong box and the control of your estate; and you shall see with what noble and affectionate generosity I shall treat you for the future." If Brown, having plundered Robinson, thus addressed him, and if Robinson gave Brown the control of his estate and the key of his strong-box, we should certainly set down Robinson as a lunatic.

Pitt had admitted the past hostility, which, in truth, was undeniable. The leopard cannot easily change his spots. There was absolutely nothing in the Union to extinguish that hostility. On the contrary, there was everything to increase and perpetuate it. The Union invested our hereditary enemy with legislative power over Ireland. Irish commercial, manufacturing, and trading interests were then prosperous, because the Volunteers had won Free Trade for Ireland in 1779. Prior to that period, the British Parliament, deriving strength from the religious divisions of this country, had usurped the power of enacting prohibitory statutes and enforcing embargoes. British statesmen might calculate that after an Union the destruction of Irish industrial interests, which the prohibitory statutes and embargoes of a former period had achieved, could thenceforth be effected by the enormous hemorrhage of Irish income, whereby Ireland would be deprived at once of her domestic markets, and of the capital which is indispensably necessary to create or perpetuate manufacturing establishments."*

* The English jealousy of Irish prosperity sometimes peeps out in the shape of an apology for any suggestion that might seem calculated to promote Irish interests. The following appeared in the *Dublin Evening Mail* in September, 1861:—"The dread of a cotton famine has so demented the Lancastrians that one, writing in their behalf to the *Daily News*, advises a recourse to Irish linen as a temporary substitute. But the audacity of the proposal is so glaring that an apology is found necessary for counselling anything so desperate. '*Without wishing*' (says this friendly gentleman) '*in any way to promote Irish interests*, I venture to suggest, at this dull season, whether Irish linen might not in many cases be used instead of cotton?' If Irish linen could be grown near Glasgow or Preston, there might be no objection; but to encourage its manufacture on the West of St. George's Channel is only to be justified by the urgent pressure of necessity. Such inadvertent admissions betray the jealousy with which the efforts of this country to achieve a

Baron Smith did not like the agitators. He got into the habit of introducing political dissertations into his charges to grand juries. A speaker at some public dinner at Tullamore in 1833, had said that "Catholicity now held aloft her high and palmy head, unshaken by the stormy blasts of persecution." The Baron thought this bombast worth quoting and censuring in one of his charges. He used to come into court at two o'clock in the afternoon; and, when opening the commission, he carried a vast manuscript, the terror of grand jurors. This was his charge; and even although his auditors in the grand jury-box might concur in the political views which he announced, yet it is said that they were wont to cast many a weary glance at the ponderous composition, whilst the Baron perused page after page of a document which, to their impatience, appeared to be interminable.

It should be stated, to the Baron's honour, that as a judge he was humane, considerate, and painstaking. He went to the trouble of studying the Irish language in order to render himself independent of interpreters when witnesses were unable to speak English. Of his views on Catholic Emancipation I cannot speak with certainty. He tells us in his "Address to the People of Ireland" that he supported the Catholic claims in 1795; but it is clear that he considered that the preservation of the State Church Establishment and of Protestant ascendency should be carefully provided for in any measure of Catholic concession. I presume he held views on the Catholic question not dissimilar from those expressed by Rigby.

Advocacy which was blended with a lofty assumption of superiority, or with actual insult, could scarcely be acceptable to the Catholics. This sort of insolent patronage was symptomatic of the general Protestant feeling of contempt for Papists which I have already noticed.* In truth, this was to some extent the fault of the Catholics themselves. I have known a Catholic family of respectable station seize, with alacrity which seemed servile, the proffered acquaintance of Protestant neighbours who, at least in the article of wealth, were in no respect their superiors. Similar instances

---

commercial independence for herself are regarded by a great portion of the trading community in England."—*Dublin Evening Mail*, quoted in the *Cork Examiner*, 12th September, 1861.

* I once asked a baron (the son of an Union peer) whether any of his relatives were Catholics. "Oh, none," he replied, "except the bastards."

are consistent with my knowledge. A Protestant lady of fashion, angry with a female friend (also a Protestant) for introducing her to some ineligible acquaintance, exclaimed that she would avenge the affront by inviting the parish priest to meet the offending fair one at her house. This mode of punishing an affront, by inflicting the parish priest on the offender, was thoroughly expressive of the Protestant estimate of Catholic society.

Without disparaging the Catholic gentry, it must be owned that as a class they were inferior to the Protestants in all the refinements of polished life. Exceptions, no doubt, there were; but such was the general fact. The penal laws were the cause of this inferiority. It is uttering an obvious truism to say that the exclusive possession of power, official dignity, and political station, must necessarily have imparted to the habits and manners of the favoured class all the social ease which results from the consciousness of command. Their peculiar advantages placed within their reach every facility of refinement. Their monopoly of so many other valuable things gave them almost a monopoly of civilisation. It was a proverb, even so late as the first quarter of the present century, that you might know a Catholic in the street by his crouching appearance. The iron of the penal laws had entered into the souls of the people, and branded their manners with strong marks of their inferiority. The subservient spirit has long since passed away; but I am not quite sure that in other respects Catholic society has yet fully acquired the polish which, from the causes already stated, is to be found amongst the upper classes of Protestants.

On the other hand, there is no vulgarity so odious, so offensive, so pestilent, as that of the Orange squireen. It is the ingrained vulgarity of mind, of soul, of sentiment. It is the loathsome emanation of "malice, hatred, and all uncharitableness" in all its coarseness and deformity, unchecked and unconcealed by the conventional amenities of civilised life.

Decipit exemplar imitabile vitiis.

The squireen class could imitate the bigotry of their betters, but they could not imitate the graces of manner which sometimes invested the aristocratic bigot with something of a chivalrous and dignified air.

The Irish *noblesse* and leading gentry of the last century

lived magnificently. The edifices they erected, both in town and country, the scale of their household establishments, their equipages, were magnificent. In their manners there was *l'air grand;* their very rascality was of magnificent dimensions. There was no paltry peddling about them. You could hardly have found one of them capable of selling himself, like the Scotch Lord Banff, for the paltry trifle of eleven guineas. The *abandon,* the *laisser-aller* principle was carried amongst them to the greatest extent compatible with social politeness. Whatever was bad, bigoted, or unnational in the aristocracy was duly adopted and improved on by their industrious imitators, the small squires. Whatever tended to mitigate the evils of bigotry was beyond the imitation of the squireen class, because it was beyond their comprehension. How deeply are the Catholics of Ireland indebted to O'Connell for removing from them the galling indignities entailed by their political inferiority to such a thoroughly contemptible class!

An amusing volume might be written on the exploits of the Orange squires in Ireland.

Vulgarity of soul was of course often found among the possessors of thousands a year, as well as of hundreds. The squireen magistracy were a curious generation. While the smaller sort of justices occasionally rendered their judicial decisions auxiliary to the replenishing of their poultry-yards, those whose wealth gave them greater weight were in frequent communication with the Castle, recommending "strong measures" to keep down the people, such as the increase of the constabulary or military force, the proclaiming of the disturbed districts, the enforcement of the Insurrection Act, or the suspension of the Habeas Corpus. Complaints against obnoxious individuals were frequently made in these communications. The Government were earwigged by the "Loyalists," as the oppressors of the people thought fit to term themselves; and doubtless many a poor devil who never dreamed of plots or conspiracies, has been indicated to the executive as concerned in revolutionary projects.

One ludicrous instance of this species of volunteer espionage is deserving of record. The officious informant of the Government flew at higher game than ordinary. He was a magistrate, a grand juror, a man of family and fortune. The object of his attack was also a magistrate and grand juror, and of lineage and station at least equal to his own. They were both "good Loyalists." The former gentleman amused his leisure hours with a corps of cavalry yeomanry of which he was captain, and which he seemed to consider indispensable to the stability of British connexion.

These dignitaries quarrelled with each other. It was a private dispute—I do not know its nature; perhaps it concerned the comparative merits of their foxhounds. The Accusing Angel (whom I shall call Mr. A.) conceived that the most exquisite revenge he could take would be to procure the dismissal of his foe (Mr. B.) from the commission of the peace.

Mr. A. was in constant communication with the Government. He wrote frequent letters to the Viceroy or his secretary, expatiating on the demoniac disposition of the people, on the perpetual perils besetting the well-affected, and in especial on his own great merits. The literary qualities of his correspondence must have amused the official critics at Dublin Castle, for his orthography was unfettered by the usual rules, and he sometimes introduced a colloquial oath by way of giving additional emphasis to his statements. His despatches, with some such announcements as these, that " By ——! the country was in a truly aweful situation" —that "they ought to look sharpe to Mr. Murtogh O'Guggerty," etc., had been usually received with such respectful consideration by official persons that at last he began to consider himself all-powerful with the Irish Administration. His correspondence was private and confidential; so that he revelled in the double confidence of power and secrecy.

He accordingly wrote to apprise the Lord Lieutenant that Mr. B. was a political hypocrite, who, while wearing the outward marks and tokens of loyalty, was destitute of its inward and spiritual graces. One specific accusation, of which I was informed by Mr. B.'s son, was that persons of disloyal politics were hospitably entertained at his father's table. Mr. B. was represented as a dangerous character, who ought promptly to be struck off the list of magistrates. Mr. A. did not entertain a doubt that the return of the post would bring with it a supersedeas for his enemy from the Lord Chancellor; and he chuckled with anticipated ecstasy over B.'s mortification, and his ignorance of the quarter whence the arrow was aimed.

Although they had quarrelled, yet they had not quite discontinued their acquaintance. Mr. A., therefore, was not very much astonished when he saw Mr. B. one morning approaching his house on horseback. "Perhaps," thought he, "B. is coming to make up matters, if he can. I wonder has he heard of his dismissal yet?"

The visitor, seeing the man of the house on his hall-door steps, hastened forward, reached the mansion in a few moments, sprang from his saddle, and, horsewhip in one hand, presented with the other a written paper, saying:

"There, sir, is the copy of a document signed with your name, which I have received from Dublin Castle by this morning's post. It foully and falsely accuses me of being a disloyal subject, and demands my dismissal from the magistracy. I have come to ask whether you are the author of this rascally document?"

Mr. A. was so thunder-stricken at the suddenness, the total unexpectedness, of such an accusation, that he was quite at a loss what to answer. He stammered out an admission that he had written the letter.

"Then," said B., "walk into the house this instant, and write a contradiction of it, which I shall dictate."

Mr. A. could not choose but comply. B. immediately dictated a very full and unqualified contradiction, which A. duly wrote, and of which, the instant it was written, B. took possession. He then quitted the house with scant ceremony, and despatched to the Chancellor the exculpation he had extorted from his accuser. Of course he was not dismissed from the magistracy. Nor was his accuser dismissed; the Government probably attributing his escapade to an exuberance of loyal zeal.

Of the accusing justice the following anecdote was told me by a beneficed clergyman of the Established Church. His worship had an inveterate habit of profane swearing. At a meeting of magistrates, presided over by the Protestant rector of the parish, who was also a magistrate, he, as usual, gave emphasis to his opinion by a blasphemous oath. The rector, scandalised at the impiety, said: "I shall fine you tenpence, sir, for swearing in Court."

"Here it is, by ——!" said the other, handing up the tenpenny-piece (it was before the days of the shillings) and accompanying the coin with a repetition of the blasphemy.

"Another fine for that," said the rector. The justice tendered a second tenpenny with a similar profane accompaniment. And so on, the magistrate swearing, and the rector fining him, until he had emitted some eight or ten oaths, and got rid of a corresponding number of tenpennies.

His worship probably considered the affair an excellent joke.

This gentleman was the juror who, at the Cork assizes, presented to the Court, in the character of foreman, the verdict of "guilty," which he had spelled "gilty."

"That's badly spelled," said the counsel for the defence,[*] who was near the box, and seized the paper *in transitu*.

"How shall I mend it?" inquired the foreman, abashed and confused at this public censure.

"Put n, o, t, before it," returned the counsel, handing back the paper for the emendation, which the former immediately made, in bewildered unconsciousness of the important nature of the change.

"There—that will do," said the counsel, taking the amended document, and handing up "Not Gilty" to the Court. A fortunate interposition. The juror in question had a mania for hanging. He had, in his impetuous haste, handed in the issue paper without consulting his brethren of the jury-box. But if the prisoner in that instance escaped death, in how many instances were the miserable victims sacrificed? A verdict of guilty was easily obtained from jurors who belonged to a class that deemed accusation sufficient to establish criminality, and with whom the received policy was that of hanging the accused, "to make an example, and to preserve the quiet of the country."

CHAPTER VIII.

THE ZEAL OF A PACIFICATOR.

A man he was, to all the country dear.
GOLDSMITH.

THERE occurred in 1816 an incident strikingly illustrative of the Protestant ascendency policy of making examples to preserve the quiet of the country.

The gentleman who officiated as peace-preserver on the occasion to which I now allude, was the Rev. John Hamilton, Protestant Curate of Roscrea, in the King's County, and a magistrate. The reverend gentleman had been transplanted to Roscrea from the County Fermanagh. In politics he was an enthusiastic Orangeman; his per-

[*] Harry Deane Grady.

sonal disposition appears to have been romantic and adventurous.

Mr. Hamilton, on receiving his appointment to the magistracy, promised, as he afterwards boasted, to distinguish himself by his zeal in discharging the duties of his office. He speedily set about redeeming his promise. The Monaghan militia commanded by Colonel Kerr, were at that time quartered in Roscrea. They were all of red-hot Orange principles; and it was the familiar practice of the reverend gentleman to obtain from the commanding officer parties of the men, who scoured the country, firing shots, playing party tunes, and thus exhibiting their ardent loyalty in a sort of irregular ovation of perpetual recurrence. But these triumphant *feux-de-joie*, and the accompanying martial music, could not long furnish serious occupation to a spirit so adventurous as that of the Rev. John Hamilton.

There resided at Roscrea two highly respectable Catholic distillers, the Messrs. Daniel and Stephen Egan. There was also in that town a rival distiller named Birch, a wealthy Protestant, in whose family the reverend gentleman had officiated as tutor for some time after his appointment as curate.

It occurred to the Rev. Mr. Hamilton, J.P., to evince his magisterial zeal by implicating the Messrs. Egan in a criminal conspiracy to murder the Protestant gentry of the neighbourhood. He possibly also desired to serve the commercial interests of his patron, Mr. Birch, by getting the rival manufacturers of whisky hanged. He was bustling, active, and artful; and finding in many of his neighbours the ready credulity of prejudice, he soon succeeded in creating serious alarm in their minds. He procured the aid of a confederate named Dyer, who was groom or stableman in the employment of Mr. Birch (the reverend gentleman's patron); and Dyer, being duly drilled by Mr. Hamilton, swore informations, bearing that several persons engaged in the murderous conspiracy aforesaid, occasionally rendezvoused in a valley called the Cockpit, situated in the domain of the Hon. Francis Aldborough Prittie, M.P., for the purpose of concerting their organisation, and also of practising the manœuvres of military exercise.

Matters were not yet ripe enough to explode the plot against the Egan family. An assistant for Dyer was procured from Dublin, a dexterous practitioner in informations, named Halfpenny, alias Halpin. He was then in the police, an *attaché* of Major Sirr's office. He had, in 1798, displayed great activity as an informer. On this man's arrival at Roscrea, he was taken into the councils of the Rev. Mr. Hamilton.

That reverend gentleman, his wife, and Halpin, dressed up a straw figure in a suit of Mr. Hamilton's clothes. They placed this figure in a sitting attitude, at a table in a parlour on the ground floor of Mr. Hamilton's house; its back was turned towards the window; on the table before it was expanded a large Bible; a pair of candles stood upon the table. From without, the appearance of the pantomime was precisely that of the reverend pastor of the Roscrea Protestants, deeply immersed in the study of the Word of God. The scenic illusion in the parlour being thus prepared, the reverend gentleman furnished a pistol to Halpin, who, with Dyer, had received his instructions to fire through the window at the stuffed figure. A man named Quinlan was inveigled to join the shooting party. Dyer and Halpin, in obedience to Mr. Hamilton's injunctions, fired through the sash at that reverend gentleman's straw representative, the window shutters having been left open for that purpose. The figure was hit in the back with a bullet—the Bible was dislodged —two bullets struck the opposite wall.

Dire was the commotion that instantly prevailed through the town. The shout rang from mouth to mouth that the excellent pastor had been fired at whilst studying the Bible. He had escaped—hurrah !—by the special interposition of Providence. His preservation was, doubtless, miraculous; but who could say that the same overruling care would be vouchsafed to the other Protestant inhabitants, whose lives were equally menaced by the Popish conspiracy which had thus been mercifully baulked of its first intended victim ? The Protestants clearly must defend themselves.

The drums beat to arms. Parties of the Monaghan militia paraded the streets. In half-an-hour the Messrs. Egan, who were quietly sitting with some friends, were arrested by a piquet, and conveyed to the guard-house, where they were detained for a whole night on a charge of conspiring to murder the Rev. Mr. Hamilton. These events all took place on the night of the 28th December, 1815.

Next morning the two Egans were bailed out with great difficulty by the strenuous exertions of their friends. For some days a calm succeeded, interrupted only by the occasional nocturnal visits of Mr. Hamilton and the police to Mr. Egan's house, under pretext of searching for arms.

It was surmised—I pretend not to say with what truth—that the Government felt rather disinclined to follow up the prosecution in consequence of the excellent character always borne by the parties accused. But Lord Norbury and the Earl of Rosse so vehemently urged the prosecution, that the scruples, if any, of the Government were overruled. A fresh witness to sustain the accusation was procured in the person of one Hickey, brother-in-law of the first witness, Dyer.

Meanwhile, the rampant delight of the Orange inhabitants of Roscrea was evinced in the most noisy and extravagant manner. Colonel Kerr was an active partisan of the Rev. Mr. Hamilton. He permitted the tattoo to be beaten through the town every evening, the drums being followed by a large military escort, at whose head the reverend gentleman ostentatiously strutted, arrayed in an orange cloak, and wearing round his waist a belt studded with pistols. This melodramatic exhibition was enlivened by such tunes as "Boyne Water," and "Protestant Boys," played on the military fifes.

On the morning following the attack on the stuffed figure, the Hon. Mr. Prittie, son of Lord Dunally, visited the Rev. Mr. Hamilton to inquire the particulars, and asked him whether his (Mr. H.'s) son had not had a great escape?

"Yes, sir," replied Mr. Hamilton.

"*Where were you sitting,*" demanded Mr. Prittie, "*when the shot was fired at you?*"

"*There, sir,*" answered Mr. Hamilton, pointing to a table in the room. Mr. Hamilton thus sought to confirm Mr. Prittie in the belief which that gentleman had, in common with the public, then adopted—namely, that the shot had been actually fired at himself. This attempt at deception should be carefully borne in mind, because it neutralises the defence which the reverend gentleman set up for his conduct at a subsequent stage of the affair.

On the 11th of January, 1816, the Messrs. Egan were arrested under a warrant of the Rev. Mr. Hamilton's. They were placed in the custody of a party of soldiers and marched to the inn, where they found some eight or ten persons in custody on the charge of being also involved in the murderous conspiracy. The last-named parties were confined for the night in the guard-room.

At ten o'clock on the following forenoon all the prisoners set out for Clonmel, which is forty miles distant from Roscrea, escorted by a large body of military and police. The Egans travelled in a chaise which proceeded at a footpace; the other prisoners walked, handcuffed, after the carriage. The first day's journey was to Templemore. It was rendered extremely fatiguing by the slowness of the pace and the inclemency of the weather. The rain poured down in torrents, and the prisoners, on arriving at Templemore, were conducted to a miserable den without a fireplace, appropriately named the Black Hole, in which they would have spent the night but for the humane interposition of Sir John Carden, who obtained for them the accommodation of the inn.

Next day they proceeded to Cashel, where they were consigned to a small, dreary, damp apartment, without any sort of furniture. They applied for permission to occupy the inn, but met a refusal on the plea that the disturbed state of the country would render compliance dangerous. It was, however, resolved to forward them at once to Clonmel.

A curious incident occurred within a few miles of that town. Two of the escort appeared to quarrel with each other, and in the course of the dispute they fell from their horses. The steeds, released from their riders, ran away, and the whole escort, with the exception of a single policeman, made off in pursuit of them. The solitary guard approached the Egans and strenuously urged them to escape. "I will follow my comrades," said he, "in pursuit of the runaway horses, and you can then act as you please." But the prisoners, apprehensive of some trick, rejected the advice thus urgently offered, and quietly awaited the return of the party of police.

Arrived at Clonmel, they were met in jail by the Rev. Mr. Hamilton and Mr. Corker Wright,* a magistrate, who had sedulously interested himself in the prosecution. Mr. Wright on the following morning visited the prisoners,

* This Mr. Corker Wright's house, near Shinrone, was the scene of a bloody tragedy in 1815. A party had been got up to attack the house, it is supposed with his knowledge, and arranged by his steward, Hoey. At all events, the plan was fully known before it was acted upon; for a party of soldiers were in the house awaiting the assailants, in company with whom it is alleged that they marched for a part of the way. Arriving before the assailants, the soldiers were stationed on the stairhead. The aggressors entered without any opposition. One of them, lighting a candle, exposed the whole party to the soldiers, who immediately fired and killed them all. Not a man was left to disclose the agency by which the attack was concerted. The bodies were paraded on cars through the neighbouring villages on the following day, as trophies of the victory obtained by Mr. Corker Wright.

affecting great friendliness, and strongly advised them to confess all they knew of the "conspiracy," promising to exert his influence to procure their pardon. Of course an indignant disclaimer of all knowledge of any conspiracy was the only reply elicited by this treacherous suggestion. The Egans were then invited to see the various apartments of the jail. In one room they were shown the hangman busily preparing ropes for the next execution. But this sight failed to scare them into the false and foolish act of self-crimination.

In a few days the special commission was opened by Lord Norbury and Baron George. The Crown Prosecutor was Charles Kendal Bushe, then Solicitor-General, and afterwards Lord Chief Justice. The public augured very gloomily for the prisoners when it was known that Lord Norbury was to try the case. Norbury had a terrible reputation for severity. "We'll have great hanging next assizes—Lord Norbury's to come," was a phrase that familiarly heralded his lordship's approach to assize towns on the circuit.

Two witnesses came from Roscrea to bear testimony to the excellent character of the Egans. One of these was the Rev. Mr. L'Estrange, Protestant Rector of Roscrea. The other was a Protestant layman, Mr. William Smith, who informed the prisoners that shortly previous to the firing at the straw parson through the window, he had been present at a dinner-party given by Mr. Birch, of Roscrea, at the Rev. Mr. Hamilton's instance. It was there stated that the Egans were accused, on Dyer's sworn informations, of drilling men in the domain of the Hon. Mr. Prittie, for treasonable purposes; and Mr. Smith was then told that he should be apprised of the mode in which it was intended to proceed against them, provided that he took an oath to keep secret the particulars. Mr. Smith rejected this condition, stating his conviction that the Egans were incapable of the imputed criminal acts; and that, to his own personal knowledge, Dyer had sworn falsely, inasmuch as the Egans were in another place at the very time when they were sworn by that person to have been drilling men in Mr. Prittie's grounds.

Dyer was of course the principal witness. He gave his evidence with great self-possession and dexterity. He deposed to several meetings for military exercise in Mr. Prittie's domain. He was obliged to confess, on cross-examination, that he was in receipt of five shillings a week for suppressing his evidence against one Francis Cotton,* on a trial in which the said Cotton had been charged with the murder of a man named Quigley. The admission of his own infamy in compounding the felony of murder, necessarily deprived his evidence against the Egans of weight with the jury. Contradictions in his testimony were also elicited on cross-examination.

The Rev. John Hamilton was the next witness. The trick of the stuffed figure had transpired, and as he knew that a cross-examination on the subject awaited him, he resolved to put a bold face on the matter. Accordingly, in his direct evidence, he spoke of the effigy as a stratagem, employed for the purpose of ascertaining if Dyer's previous informations were true; but on his cross-examination he was constrained to admit that he had left the Government, as well as several of his brother magistrates, under the impression that the firing at the effigy was an actual firing at his person. The reader will remember that, when Mr. Prittie, on the morning following the attack on the straw figure, said to the Rev. Mr. Hamilton, in that gentleman's house, "Where were you sitting *when the shot was fired at you?*" Mr. Hamilton answered, "There, sir," pointing to a table in the room, and thus attempting to confirm, in Mr. Prittie's mind, the belief that he had been actually fired at.

When the reverend gentleman's testimony closed, the court-house rang with execrations, and the judges had some difficulty in restoring order.

Halpin, and Dyer's brother-in-law, Hickey, were next examined. Halpin gave his evidence with the composure and readiness of an expert informer. He inculpated Quinlan in the guilt of firing at Mr. Hamilton's effigy, under the belief that the effigy was the reverend gentleman himself. Hickey's evidence tended to exonerate Quinlan from having fired; but he swore that Mr. Stephen Egan had administered to him an oath to assist any one who should attempt to take Mr. Hamilton's life.

The infamous nature of the prosecution being manifest, the jury, without the least hesitation, unanimously acquitted the prisoners. Lord Norbury, deprived of an opportunity of hanging anybody, escaped from the Court under the

* This Cotton, and also Dyer, were subsequently in the employment of Mr. Birch, the distiller, at Roscrea.

pretext of sudden indisposition, leaving Baron George alone on the bench.

Dyer, with the concurrence of the learned Baron, was placed in the dock by the order of the Solicitor-General, and indicted for wilful and corrupt perjury. But the grand jury, thinking, perhaps, that he might be useful on some future occasion, committed the disgraceful act of ignoring the Bill.*

The liberated prisoners were warmly congratulated by their numerous friends. They had a narrow escape. Had the Rev. Mr. Hamilton's dexterity of execution been equal to the ingenuity of his invention, it would have fared hardly with them. He wanted only the opportunity to become a second Titus Oates. It was a romantic experiment, doubtless—that of the Orange divine who

> Stuffed a figure of himself—
> Delicious thought !—and had it shot at,
> To bring some Papists to the shelf,
> Who could not otherwise be got at.†

The Egans on their return were obliged to enter Roscrea by a back lane, in order to avoid the sanguinary ferocity of about one hundred of the Monaghan militia who had turned out, half intoxicated, ready for a desperate riot. There were also a large number of Orangemen, armed and prepared for mischief, who excited alarm by firing squibs through the town. Colonel Kerr was with some difficulty induced, by the strong remonstrance of a military gentleman, to draw the soldiers into the barracks. Mr. Hamilton published a pamphlet in his own vindication. He expatiated on his magisterial zeal—on the innocent nature of the exploit of getting men to fire at the effigy, which exploit, he loudly protested, was merely an ingenious device resorted to with the view of ascertaining whether designs against his life were really harboured by the persons whom Dyer had accused. He disclaimed having represented to the Government that the firing at the effigy was a firing at his own person; he alleged that he had made Major Sirr privy to the trick, and that he had requested the Major to convey that information to the Castle authorities. If he did so at all, it was somewhat of the latest.

* In 1844 Dyer was still living at Roscrea; he was then old, and seemed penitent for his former awful crimes. The witness Hickey was sent out of the country on the failure of Hamilton's plot by the parties who employed him, and is supposed to have gone to America.

† "Fudge Family in Paris."

The most amusing part of Mr. Hamilton's pamphlet is his solemn complaint that the Messrs. Egan showed no gratitude to Colonel Kerr. He was also dissatisfied with Peel, who was then Irish Secretary. "It is evident," says the ill-used clergyman, "that Mr. Peel's sole object was to vindicate the Lord Chancellor for not superseding me, and that he had no wish to defend me on my own account."

One would think that Mr. Peel, in all conscience, had quite enough to do to palliate the retention of such a person in the magistracy, without entering on a defence of his machinations against the Egan family.

My account of the transactions described in this chapter is derived from a manuscript narrative lent me by one of the Egan family, Alderman Egan of Dublin, and a pamphlet published by the Rev. Mr. Hamilton.

When we look back upon those dreary times; when we contemplate the social and political depression of the Catholics, and the supremacy of their enemies in all the departments of the State; when we think of the enormous influence possessed by a virulent faction; the vast array of selfish interest, deeply-rooted prejudice, and impenetrable ignorance, which had to be encountered and overcome; it is difficult to form an adequate estimate of the political merits of that leader whose voice inspired the timid and spiritless, whose sagacity restrained the intemperate and rash, and whose influence combined together the millions in that memorable organisation which wrung from reluctant bigotry the concession of the Catholic rights. O'Connell stated that a majority of the very House of Commons which in 1829 enacted Emancipation, had been returned in 1826 on pledges to resist that measure. As to the King, Lord Eldon has portrayed His Majesty's virtuous agonies at being compelled to give the royal assent to the Relief Bill. "What can I do?" exclaimed the disconsolate monarch. "What can I now fall back upon? I am miserable—wretched. My situation is dreadful—nobody about me to advise with. If I do give my assent I'll go to the baths abroad, and from thence to Hanover; I'll return no more to England; I'll make no Roman Catholic peers—I will not do what this Bill will enable me to do—I'll return no more. Let them get a Catholic King in Clarence—— The people will see that I did not wish this."

The Great Agitator triumphed, *pro hac vice*, over King, Lords, and Commons.

CHAPTER IX.

ANTI-TITHE AGITATION OF 1831-2.

He vowed before the captive's God to break the captive's chain,
To bind the broken heart, and set the captive free again.
ANON.

O'CONNELL's transition from the lawyer to the statesman was a change for which his long course of political agitation had prepared him. He intimately knew the people whom he was now to combine for the revival of the national Legislature, and whose scattered strength he was to consolidate. The Catholic Association was pronounced to be an *imperium in imperio* of vast magnitude and influence. And so it truly was. But the Repeal Association which O'Connell founded on the 15th of April, 1840, gradually swelled to larger dimensions than its predecessor. In 1843 it surpassed the Catholic Association in the number of its members, in the extent of its funds, in the steady enthusiasm of its friends, and in the exquisite perfection of detail with which its organisation reached every nook and corner of the country.

The sentiment of nationality had ever been a ruling idea in O'Connell's mind. It broke forth at first in his memorable declaration prior to the passing of the Union, that he would rather behold the re-enactment of the penal code than consent to the destruction of the Irish Parliament. With that declaration most of his subsequent acts have been consistent. That he who fleshed his maiden sword in opposition to the Union should devote his matured abilities to the repeal of that measure was naturally to be expected. He struck the right chord ; the sympathies of his countrymen responded. In September and October, 1830, he addressed four letters to the Irish public on the subject of Repeal. Those letters produced a deep and general sensation ; and if public adhesion to the cause was not then as universally declared as at a later period, the reason why men paused was the great magnitude of the measure, which led even those who most ardently desired it to fear that it was impracticable.

O'Connell's appeal to his countrymen was readily responded to. But it is a total mistake to suppose that such response originated solely in the leader's influence. It originated in the deeply-rooted conviction in men's minds that they were the worse for the suppression of their native

Legislature and would be the better for its restoration. What O'Connell openly uttered every man had felt before. The leader did no more than rehearse the popular sentiment.

By-and-by public meetings began to spring up in different quarters. The opposition to the tithe-impost at that time convulsed every parish in the land; and the two great questions of the Repeal of the Union and the Disendowment of the State Church were soon agitated together on nearly every rural platform.

The landlords in great numbers espoused the anti-tithe cause. Protestantism they affectionately loved, but the cheaper they could have it the better. Best of all if they could enjoy it gratis. I knew in 1823 a landlord of Conservative politics in collusion with his own Catholic tenant to defeat the exorbitant demands of the rector. The reverend gentleman claimed his tithe; but the landlord, by collusive distresses for rent, contrived for some time to outwit him. The landlord, disgusted at the grasping propensities of the rector, dropped his acquaintance, and the alienation continued for some years. It is said that the same landlord lay in ambush with a gun to shoot the parson's proctor, who presumed to enter his Protestant premises in order to make a valuation of the growing crops, and that the angry gentleman was only restrained from some deed of violence by the strong remonstrances of a friend on the consequences which the act must have entailed on the perpetrator. I knew all the parties. The anecdote was given me as a fact; but I think it must have originated in an angry threat which was interpreted too literally. Even thus modified, the story indicates a feeling of rage against the tithe system. In fact, a great proportion of the Protestant proprietary hated that system as intensely as the Catholics did; as intensely as it had been hated by their own Protestant predecessors, the members of the Irish House of Commons, who in 1735 passed the memorable Agistment Resolution that exempted all pasture-lands from the claims of the State clergy, and threw the burden of tithe exclusively on tillage.*

* This Resolution is generally described as having thrown the burden of tithes from the Protestant aristocracy on the Catholic tenantry. It indeed relieved the owner of pasture-land; but this relief imposed no additional burden on the owner of tillage. The man who tilled his land paid neither more nor less tithe after than before the passing of the Agistment Resolution. Moreover, tillage, in the early part of the eighteenth century, was so little practised in Ireland that the Legislature, not twenty years previously to the

"Down with the tithes," then, was the cry of many a Protestant landlord in 1831 and 1832. With some it was a purely selfish cry—a cry of men who simply preferred not paying money to paying it, and who dignified their conduct with the sounding phrases of "indignant resistance to an unjust and abominable impost," "sympathy in the sufferings of a Catholic people compelled to pay a Protestant priesthood," and similar expressions of generous and lofty principle. Unjust and abominable was the impost, doubtless ; and a flagrant spoliation of the Catholics, from whom the Church property had originally been torn, and on whom, consequently, the support of two Churches was thrown by the egregious malversation of the ecclesiastical State revenues ; but the animus of some of the anti-tithe landlords in 1832 was rather selfish than national. Many, however, were actuated by a purer motive.

There was another section of the Protestant landlords, more important in respect of their wealth and position, and including many of the nobility, who rallied round the parsons at their utmost need, paid their own tithes, compelled (where they could) their tenants to pay theirs, and entered into large subscriptions to enable the parsons to recover all arrears by legal process.

The anti-national Church Establishment, thus supported at home, and backed from without by the power of England, outlived a storm of well-earned popular vengeance that shook every stone and timber in the edifice. It was an institution totally indefensible on any ground of justice, honesty, or common sense. The remark is now trite that Ireland is the only country on the face of the earth, in which the whole ecclesiastical State revenues have been grasped by the pastors of a small fractional part of the population. Such a monstrous outrage on the great principles of equity, and on the great majority of any nation, may be elsewhere vainly sought, either in or out of Christendom. In truth, it was an outrage which no thoroughly free country would submit to for a single day. It has now been disestablished and partially disendowed ; but what is termed its disendowment has been so adroitly managed, that the tithes, under the name of tithe rent-charge,

extinction of tithe of agistment, had passed a law to compel every occupier of a hundred acres to keep at least five acres tilled. Grazing was general, and the Catholic tenant who grazed his land partook of the exemption secured to pasture by the Resolution of 1735.

still remain an oppressive burden on the landed property of Ireland.

The anti-Irish State Church has been so important a factor in Irish affairs, that a short retrospective view of its origin, of the objects of its authors, and of the results of its establishment, becomes necessary in a general sketch of the condition of Ireland.

Bacon recommended the "princelie policie" of fomenting the internal divisions of the Irish people as a means to facilitate their subjugation. It was "*Divide et impera.*" A more effective mode of carrying out this policy could scarcely be devised than the violent confiscation of the old Catholic ecclesiastical State revenues of the kingdom, and the transference of those revenues to an alien hierarchy, chiefly imported from England, and whose mission, accredited by the English Government, was to uproot, if they could, the ancient creed of the people whose Church property had been seized by the apostles of the new religion.

Whether that religion was right or wrong, I do not here discuss. I have only to do with its political results. The Irish were universally Catholics in the sixteenth century, as their ancestors had been from the days of Saint Patrick. Spenser, writing in 1596, says: "They be all papists by profession." The Rev. Maziere Brady has shown by the evidence of the highest Elizabethan functionaries,* that the instruments of the new apostolate were "fines, imprisonments, tortures, and death, unscrupulously employed by the ecclesiastical as well as the civil agents in that alleged reformation." Nor was their violence accompanied by the ascetic virtues which might have given an air of sincerity to the boisterous apostleship of the agents of the Reformation. Spenser deplores their immorality; he says:

"The clergy there (excepting the grave Fathers which are in high place about the State, and some few others which are lately planted in their new college) are generally bad, licentious, and most disordered."—*View of the State of Ireland.*

Sir William Drury (April 16th, 1577) mentions "the students of Ireland that are in Louvain, and come from thence." At that time our ecclesiastical students were under the necessity of seeking their education in foreign lands; and when they returned to keep the lamp of religion from extinc-

* Preface to "State Papers concerning the Irish Church in the Time of Queen Elizabeth," edited by the Rev. Maziere Brady.

tion in their own country, they did so at the risk of their lives. Spenser marvels at their zeal, and in a well-known passage contrasts it with the sloth of the Reformed ministers.

"It is," he says, "great wonder to see the odds which is between the zeal of Popish priests, and the ministers of the Gospel; for they spare not to come out of Spain, from Rome, and from Remes, by long toil and dangerous travelling hither, *where they know peril of death awaiteth them*, and no reward or riches is to be found, only to draw the people into the Church of Rome; whereas some of our idle ministers, having a way for credit and estimation thereby opened unto them, without pains, *and without peril*, will neither for the same, nor any love of God, nor zeal of Religion, nor for all the good they may do by winning souls to God, be drawn forth from their warm nests to look out into God's harvest, which is even ready for the sickle, and all the fields yellow long ago." *

The comparative ideas of religious toleration respectively held by the Irish Catholics and the Protestant Government in Spenser's time, are incidentally revealed in the above passage. The Catholic priests were in "peril of death" from Protestant intolerance, while the Protestant ministers could, had they so pleased, have assailed the old faith of the kingdom "without peril" from Catholic violence. It is, and always has been, a glorious trait in the character of our Catholic countrymen that their unshaken fidelity to their own religion is associated with the utmost tolerance of the religion of others.

Spenser says the Protestant preachers could "do small good" in converting the Irish, until the Irish "be restrained from sending their young men abroad to other universities beyond the sea, as Remes, Doway, Lovain, and the like."

A religion which emanated from England, and which was enforced in Ireland by "fines, imprisonments, tortures, and death," was naturally productive of two important consequences. It excited the abhorrence of the people to whom it was introduced by this species of sanguinary apostleship; and its position as a new and hostile element in Irish politics inevitably generated in its followers a strong anti-national sentiment, which is unfortunately inherited by too many of their successors at the present time.

In truth, no other results could have been reasonably expected. The new clergy, subsidised with the spoils

* Spenser's *View of the State of Ireland*, pp. 210, 211, 12mo edition, 1750.

wrenched from the old Church, could not, by the most tortuous exercise of sophistical ingenuity, have contrived to consider themselves anything else than intruders. When they looked around they saw a flock by whom their ministry was repudiated. Looking over to England they there beheld the power that sustained them in possession of the spoils of the Irish Catholic Church, in defiance of the natural resentment of the Irish Catholic population. Occupying such a position, it was inevitable that their affections should be given to England who supported their usurpation, and withdrawn from the Irish people to whom that usurpation was abhorrent. In November, 1626, the assembled Protestant hierarchy, having successfully ousted the Catholic Church from its ancient temporalities, issued the following declaration against tolerating the creed of the people they had robbed :

"The religion of the Papists is superstitious and idolatrous ; their faith and doctrine erroneous and heretical ; their Church, in respect of both, apostatical. To give them, therefore, a toleration, or to consent that they may freely exercise their religion, and profess their faith and doctrine, is a grievous sin ; and that in two respects : for, first, it is to make ourselves accessory not only to their superstitions, idolatries, and heresies, and, in a word, to all the abominations of Popery ; but also (which is a condition of the former) to the perdition of the seduced people which perish in the deluge of the Catholic apostasy."

In its nature the English Church thus established in Ireland was a potent engine of national discord. The practice which from the date of its origin had prevailed of largely importing English clergymen to occupy its benefices, excited the wrath of the Protestant settlers, who had got confiscated estates, and who deemed themselves entitled to monopolise Church patronage for the benefit of their families. Ecclesiastical incomes were in many cases rendered more attractive because they did not involve the necessity of residence. The incumbents were frequently non-resident. In many instances they had the excellent plea for non-residence afforded by the fact that their parishes contained no Protestants. They had no flocks requiring their ministry, and they knew that their prospects of preferment would be bettered by residence in Dublin.

Pluralities were numerous. In 1764 the County Clare contained seventy-six parishes, of which sixty-two were sinecures. The whole seventy-six parishes paid tithe to fourteen rectors, many of whom habitually lived in the metropolis. No doubt they never were missed by their Catholic parishioners. Without the slightest disparagement of the many excellent persons belonging to the Anglican religion, it cannot be denied that its existence as a State Church in Ireland was a grim burlesque on ecclesiastical establishments.

But the grim burlesque was so useful to the policy of *divide et impera* that in 1800 its preservation was specially provided for as an article of the Union; and the Union was defended on the express ground that it would render the grim burlesque impregnable. That nine or ten per cent. of the inhabitants of Ireland should style their Church the Irish Church was ludicrous. Mr. Under-Secretary Cooke accordingly argued that an Union would remove the anomaly by incorporating the people of this kingdom with their English neighbours, and thus converting the Irish Catholic majority into an Imperial Catholic minority. "With the Union," said he, "Ireland would be in *a natural situation;* for all the Protestants of the Empire being united, she would have the proportion of fourteen to three in favour of her [Church] Establishment, whereas at present there is a proportion of three to one against it."

This is a good sample of Unionist reasoning. The autonomy of Ireland was to be demolished, and her vital rights were to be trampled in the dust, in order to perpetuate the oppressive ascendency of the alien Church Establishment. And this monstrous subversion of all national and moral right was called putting Ireland in "a natural situation." The Catholics, however, could not see that the wicked suppression of the Irish Parliament rendered it a whit less dishonest to tax them for Protestant purposes.

The practice of bringing over Englishmen to enjoy the ecclesiastical revenues of Ireland had been to a great extent discontinued during the present century; and the State Church became a fruitful preserve for the junior members of the Irish landed aristocracy. Before the Composition Acts came into force the income divided among the ministers, great and small, of the Establishment, was probably a million per annum. After the enactment of the 1st and 2nd Victoria, chapter 109, which converted the tithe into a rent-charge, payable by the landlords to the rectors, and recoverable by them from the tenants, the gross income of the State Church has been calculated by the Rev. Maziere Brady at £700,000 per anunm.

Before I come to the period of Disestablishment, I wish to note some instances in which nobility of heart, and the instinct of honourable nationality, enabled Irish Protestants to escape from the demoralising influence of an establishment which was eminently calculated to make its followers bad Irishmen. Foremost among these stands Henry Grattan, a Protestant, whose belief was sincere and fervent, and who declared that his first and last passion was his native country. The fact was, that Home Legislation, except where English intrigue corrupted it, had the strongest tendency to generate national feeling among the Irish Protestants; and national feeling gravitated towards the inclusion of the Catholics in all constitutional privileges. Among the Protestant friends of Catholic Emancipation must be reckoned Plunket, Sir Lawrence Parsons, the Protestant Bishop of Derry,* Curran, Wolfe Tone, Valentine Lord Cloncurry, Lord Edward Fitzgerald, the Emmetts, Arthur O'Connor, Hamilton Rowan; the Belfast Volunteers, who, so far back as 1783, had instructed their deputies to the Dublin Convention to support the unqualified emancipation of the Catholics;† the numerous Protestants in the body of United Irishmen; the students of the Protestant University of Dublin, who, in their noble address to Grattan in April, 1795, expressed their hope "that the harmony and strength of Ireland will be founded on the solid basis of Catholic Emancipation;" and, I may add, on the authority of Earl Fitzwilliam, a majority of the Protestants of Ireland, many of whom asked for, and few in 1795 opposed, the repeal of all the then remaining Catholic disqualifications. Such was the state of good feeling, fraught with the promise of national prosperity and happiness, which was destroyed by the machinations of Pitt and his agents.

* Earl of Bristol in the English peerage.
† "Life of Wolfe Tone," p. 50 (M'Cormick's edition). Tone states (p. 77) that twelve Belfast citizens subscribed £250 each to establish a journal called the *Northern Star*, in which Catholic Emancipation was advocated.

CHAPTER X.

THE DISESTABLISHMENT CAMPAIGN.

"I well remember a phrase used by one not a foe to Church Establishments—I mean Mr. Burke: 'Don't talk of its being a Church! It is a wholesale robbery!'"—LORD BROUGHAM (1838), *on the Anti-Irish Church.*

I HAVE recorded the general outbreak against tithes in the years 1831 and 1832. The English Parliament gave the anti-Irish State Church a new lease of its life by transferring the liability of payment from the occupying tenant to his immediate landlord. The Act (1st and 2nd Victoria, chapter 109) to which I have already adverted, empowered the landlord to recover the tithe rent-charge from the tenant in the shape of additional rent. This was sometimes done. There were numerous instances in which it could not be done; instances where the landlord found it difficult enough to obtain his original rent. The law assumed that he could recover the whole of an equivalent to the rector's tithe, and enabled him to retain twenty-five per cent. of such rent-charge to compensate his trouble in becoming that reverend gentleman's tithe proctor. But it was frequently impossible to obtain more than the seventy-five per cent. from the tenant; so that in every such case the landlord got nothing for his trouble and liability.

In May, 1856, Mr. Miall, Member of Parliament for Rochdale, submitted to the House of Commons a resolution declaratory of the justice and expediency of impartially disendowing all churches in Ireland, and of applying their revenues to purposes of secular utility. He was in a minority of 93 in a House of 312. There were twenty-six pairs. The English Dissenters felt themselves aggrieved by being compelled to contribute to the support of the Established Church from which they or their ancestors had seceded. They therefore proclaimed the principle of voluntaryism; which principle had been preached from a thousand Irish platforms during the anti-tithe movement of 1831 and 1832. Our English allies also knew that in order to emancipate themselves from the incubus of State Churchism, they should first, by an active union with the Irish Catholics, effect the disestablishment, and, as they hoped, the disendowment of the anti-Irish State Church. Their efforts were responded to in Ireland by a meeting held at Clonakilty in the County Cork, on the 15th of August, 1856, at which resolutions were unanimously passed, expressing thorough approbation of the principles announced by Mr. Miall, gratitude for his advocacy, and promising to co-operate with his party in effecting the overthrow of the pernicious institution which he assailed.

The progressive steps of our agitation may be briefly summarised. The English voluntaries were active, intelligent, and indefatigable. Their alliance was indispensable to success. Yet, in seeking to promote that alliance, I encountered some difficulties. A Catholic Member of Parliament whose assistance I solicited, seemed averse to the proposed co-operation, not only because he deemed the theological principles of the English voluntaries violently anti-Catholic, but because whenever any measure affecting Catholic interests came before the House of Commons, their parliamentary representatives invariably "went into the wrong lobby." The objection thus started was by no means confined to the gentleman who made it. There was, however, a more practical and rational view of the question taken by an eminent Catholic dignitary, the Most Reverend Doctor Leahy, Archbishop of Cashel; he saw the great importance of accepting the assistance of the English voluntaries. I was honoured with much of his correspondence at the time when the English alliance was debated; and to his Grace's influence I consider the adoption of that alliance by the Irish Catholic hierarchy is chiefly attributable.

Shortly after the Clonakilty meeting I was visited by Mr. C. J. Foster, Chairman of the Parliamentary Committee of the Liberation Society. He was accredited by a letter from Mr. Miall, who introduced him as his *alter ego*. On both gentlemen I impressed the necessity of keeping attacks on Maynooth as much as possible in the background; not that the disendowment of Maynooth was to be relinquished, but that as heretofore every attack on that college had been made on purely sectarian grounds, it would be hard to separate an aggression on it, in ordinary Catholic apprehension, from an assault on the Catholic religion; even although the present assault was not at all sectarian, but merely directed against it as an endowed institution.

The agitation went on, slowly at first, but gradually acquiring momentum. Something more than eight years after the Clonakilty meeting, an association was formed in

December, 1864, for the threefold purpose of obtaining educational justice for the Catholics, a satisfactory settlement of the land question, and Disendowment of the anti-Irish Church. Our inaugural meeting was held in the Dublin Rotunda. Many Catholic prelates were present. To Archbishop (afterwards Cardinal) Cullen and myself was committed the Disendowment question. The Archbishop's resolution condemned the existing malversation of Church property in Ireland. My resolution affirmed the principle of voluntaryism, and disclaimed all desire on the part of the Catholics to acquire sectarian ascendency. Thenceforth the agitation proceeded with vigour. The English Liberationists were invaluable auxiliaries; held numerous meetings, disseminated pamphlets written with distinguished ability, while their able, accomplished, energetic secretary, Mr. Carvell Williams, essentially contributed by his personal exertions to prepare the public mind in England for the impending change. The question had now advanced so far that Sir John Gray, M.P. for Kilkenny, and proprietor of the *Freeman's Journal*, was induced to give it the support of his influential newspaper. He also issued a commission to inquire into the local details of the ecclesiastical anomaly in the different parts of the kingdom. Meanwhile petitions to Parliament for the abolition of State-Churchism were circulated for signature by the National Association, of which Alderman M'Swiney, Lord Mayor of Dublin in 1864, was one of the principal founders. These were extensively signed; and the signatures would have been greatly more numerous only for a strong popular distrust in the utility of asking the foreign Parliament for any measure of national justice.

In 1867, Sir John Gray introduced the question into the House of Commons in an able speech. His motion was supported by 183 votes against 195. His defeat by only twelve votes showed the great progress the anti-State Church cause had made, and encouraged the English voluntaries to redouble their efforts in behalf of Disestablishment. Early in 1868, Mr. Gladstone moved his celebrated Resolutions in the same direction. He was supported by 331 Ayes against 276 Noes. There were twelve pairs. Mr. Gladstone then introduced a Bill for suspending appointments to any Church benefices in Ireland which might become vacant prior to the final legislation of the following year. The Bill was easily carried in the House of Commons, but it was thrown out by the House of Lords on the 29th of June, 1868, by 192 votes to 97. A dissolution of Parliament soon followed. At the ensuing general election the Disestablishment of the State Church was made the principal test at every hustings. A large anti-State Church majority was returned to the House of Commons. The Bill was easily carried by Mr. Gladstone, and was then sent up to the Lords, by whom its provisions were so much mutilated that if it had passed as they returned it to the Commons, it would have increased, instead of diminishing, the ecclesiastical grievance.

A compromise between the conflicting parties followed the adverse action of the Lords. The Bill, as finally passed, dissolves the Union effected in 1800 between the anti-Irish State Church and the Church of England; dissolves the connection between the former and the State; protects the life-interests of its clergy; enables them to capitalise their incomes at a given rate of purchase, the Treasury advancing the money; appropriates the surplus of Irish ecclesiastical property to such secular uses as Parliament shall direct; and it provides for the total extinction of the tithes in fifty-two years from the date at which the landlords shall have gone through the form of what is termed "purchasing" them.

An impression extensively prevailed among the Irish landlords that the tithes, or tithe rent-charge, would expire in fifty-two years from the 1st of January, 1871, the day on which the Act came into operation. This was a mistake. Mr. Gladstone, with characteristic ingenuity, had introduced into the Act a clause which rendered the form of "purchase" a condition precedent of expiry; so that the payer of tithe rent-charge "purchasing" it now, or at any future period, is not credited in the purchase-money with one farthing of the hundreds, perhaps thousands, of pounds he shall have paid for tithe rent-charge since 1871. The fifty-two years are to be computed from the date of the purchase, not from the date of the Act. Thus an important obstacle has been placed in the way of extinction; as numerous landlords, unaware that the form of "purchase" was required by the Act, continued to pay the tithe rent-charge in the belief that the annual payment of the impost for fifty-two years would extinguish it at the end of that period.*

* The 32nd section of the Act requires "purchase." The Commissioners sell at twenty-two-and-a-half years' purchase, with the alternative of fifty-two annual payments as stated in the text.

CHAPTER XI.

STATE CHURCH ARGUMENTS EXAMINED.

"In parishes where there were no Protestants, or but the fewest, and which yielded their hundreds of pounds a year in tithes for dignitaries and incumbents, non-resident, and without duties, there were hundreds and thousands of Roman Catholics. That there was a tithe war is not to be wondered at; the only wonder is that any Protestant church was left standing, or any Protestant clergyman's life spared."—*The Irish Church*, by Herbert S. Skeats, an English Dissenter, p. 26.

IT is not uninteresting to record the pleas assigned by the friends of the ex-State Church for the preservation of that unprecedented injustice. Before entering on this retrospect, however, I wish to show the reader the view in which the injustice presented itself to a Dublin Quaker, Mr. James H. Webb, who seems to have been a rope-maker in St. Audeon's parish. The rector of the parish, the Rev. James Howie, had seized certain goods in Mr. Webb's warehouse in satisfaction of parochial dues; on which the aggrieved Quaker addressed the following matter-of-fact appeal, "To the inhabitants of St. Audeon's parish belonging to the sect called the Church of England:

"10, Corn Market, *Dec.* 7, 1848.

"DEAR FRIENDS;

"Well and truly may your pastor, James Howie, declare that 'he has done that which he ought not to have done;' for he has taken advantage of an Act of Parliament to take my property without giving me value. His collector called on me and made a demand of 18s. 6d. for certain prayers, sermons, &c., performed by James Howie; but as I had never employed him for such a purpose I declined paying the demand. On the 28th of November the collector, Joseph Conway, again called, in company with two bailiffs and two policemen, and on my again refusing his demand he carried away two pounds fifteen shillings' worth of my goods. I think it right that you should be aware that the person to whom you look for spiritual instruction makes out his livelihood by thus disobeying the simplest commands of Christ, and I ask you how you can be benefited by the teachings of such a man? It is as disgraceful to have other people's property taken for your religion as it would be to have it taken for your bread and butter. If you require such a person, you ought to make up a sum which would enable him to live honestly. It is well you should know that the same James Howie, by his collector, &c., took from me last June six pounds' worth of cords, for prayers, sermons, &c., valued by him at twenty-eight shillings.

"Yours truly,
"JAMES H. WEBB."

The terse, shrewd way in which the aggrieved Quaker puts his case may be taken to epitomise the national wrong, so far as its dishonesty was concerned. The pecuniary injustice, however, was the least of the evils engendered by the alien Church. It was a fertile source of irritation by which the social frame was grievously disjointed. It was impossible that the classes who were affected by the ecclesiastical outrage—those whom it benefited, and those whom it injured—could regard each other with the cordial friendliness essential to the national interests.

Let us here recapitulate the principal pretexts put forth in behalf of the anti-Irish Establishment.

I. It was urged by the transcendental pietists of the Protestant party, that the State, is bound to provide for the dissemination of true Christian knowledge among the community.

But those gentlemen had been in the habit of vociferating that "the Bible alone" is the sole arbiter of controversy. Yet here they made the State, and not the Bible, the arbiter of what is, and what is not, true Christian doctrine. It may be asked what authority the State, as such, possesses to define theological doctrines, and in virtue of such definition to tax the public of all creeds for their diffusion? The State in England has been Roman Catholic, has been Puritan, has been High Church Anglican, has been Latitudinarian. If the State have the right to hand over the national ecclesiastical endowments to the clergy who happen to accept its theological views, then it will follow that as often as the Government sees fit to change its religious belief, it may lawfully enforce a corresponding change in the destination of Church property.

II. The argument was sometimes put in this way: "The State is entitled to offer religious truth to the acceptance of the nation."

The nation, it was answered, has at least as good a right to deny, as the State has to affirm, that the commodity thus offered is religious truth. The State had been making that offer to the Irish people (at their bitter expense) for more than three centuries; and the people, strong in their own religious faith, persisted in believing that the article offered by the State was a counterfeit. Even if it were assumed that the Irish people erred in so believing, yet who, unless he were stone-blind from prejudice, could deny that a species of State-apostleship which the experience of three centuries had shown to be efficacious only in irritating, not converting, stood *ipso facto* self-condemned?

I desire in this work to keep clear of all doctrinal controversy. But without entering upon any, it may be observed that independently of all doctrinal grounds for rejecting the State Church, there is the significant fact that it is scantily believed in by large numbers of its own ministers. The Irish State clergy perpetually claimed identification with the State Church in England. The Union, they said, had incorporated the two Establishments. The Churches were "no longer twain, but one flesh." The Irish Protestant clergy imagined that they strengthened their position by hooking themselves on to the Anglican Establishment. But for several generations great numbers of the English State clergy had been clamouring against the hard necessity of subscribing their own doctrinal code. In 1772, and again in 1815, petitions from numerous Churchmen for exemption from what they called "the grievance" of subscription to the Thirty-nine Articles, were presented to Parliament. If the reverend petitioners really believed the Articles, they could not have termed their subscription a grievance. The Irish State clergy were apparently hard run for support when they sought strength in identification with a Church which was officered by a host of clerical unbelievers.

On the 15th of January, 1863, a meeting of 300 "evangelical" clergymen of the English Church was held at Bishop Wilson's Memorial Hall, Islington. At that meeting the Rev. Hugh Stowell thus delivered himself: "The astounding fact was now developed that numbers had avowed themselves believers in the Revelation of God, had actually taken upon themselves to teach that Revelation, and were yet all the while hollow of heart and unsettled in conviction." The reverend chairman of the meeting thus indicated the species of doctrine taught by these "numbers" of clerical dissidents: "The peculiarity of our present position is this, that the sceptical sentiments of the present day proceed, not from the school of Paine or Voltaire, but from those who are within the pale of our National Church—from men who, by their station and profession, are pledged to uphold themselves, and to teach to others, the doctrines of our holy religion." *

On the 9th of June, 1863, Mr. Buxton, M.P., brought a Bill into Parliament to abolish the necessity of subscription to the Thirty-nine Articles. He acted at the instance of ministers of the Anglican religion and candidates for ordination, who, as he described their pitiable case, felt their consciences tormented by the dire necessity of declaring their belief in doctrines in which they did not believe.†

Yet the Anglo-Irish Protestant clergy claimed to retain their grasp on the whole ecclesiastical State revenues of Catholic Ireland, on the pretext of diffusing among us a doctrinal code which their clerical brethren in England were trying to fling off as an intolerable burden on their consciences. To some extent the recalcitrant clergy were successful. By the Act, 28th and 29th Victoria, chap. cxxii., entitled, "An Act to amend the Law as to the Subscriptions and Declarations to be made and Oaths to be taken by the Clergy of the Established Church of England and Ireland," a less stringent form of Declaration of Assent is substituted for the previous forms of Declaration and Subscription. The short title of the Act is, "The Clerical Subscription Act," and it is dated 5th July, 1865. I cannot see that the dissident clergy have gained much by the change. Although the language in which profession of belief is henceforth to be made is undoubtedly to some extent relaxed, yet it still is, in express terms, a "Declaration of Assent"; which cannot, I think, be satisfactorily used by men whose real sentiment is Dissent. But whether the State clergy believed, or disbelieved, or doubted, or denied, the truth of their own religion, the Irish nation for more than three centuries have been taxed for the support of that religion; the Act [of Union professed to perpetuate its grasp on the national purse; and the 32nd section of Mr. Gladstone's Act of Disestablishment has dexterously thrown an obstacle in the way of the final extinction of the burden.

III. It was said in defence of the Establishment, "The

* London *Liberator*, 1st February, 1863.
† *Ibid.*, 1st July, 1863.

earliest Christians of Ireland were Protestants, whose belief was the same as that of the modern Anglo-Irish parsons. The parsons, therefore, are entitled, in virtue of their spiritual descent from the Irish Protestant Christians aforesaid, to enjoy the Church temporalities of Ireland."

To this plea we answered: firstly, that the statement was untrue; and secondly, that if it had been true, it could not establish any right to the national Church revenues on the part of the Protestant clergy of the present day.

The statement is untrue. For proofs of its untruth I refer the reader to a book by the Rev. Dr. Rock, entitled, "A Letter to Lord John Manners," sold by Dolman, of London. Dr. Rock's book overflows with irresistible demonstrations. A volume on the same subject by the Rev. Mr. Gaffney, sold by Duffy, Dublin, may also be consulted with advantage. A work by the Rev. Dr. Moran* is also worth the careful study of those who are interested in the history of the early Irish Church. Independently of the direct proofs contained in the works now referred to, there are historical statements made by the Rev. J. H. Todd, of Trinity College, in his "Life of St. Patrick," which seem wholly incompatible with the theory of early Irish Protestantism; and which are the more remarkable, inasmuch as Dr. Todd rejects the Roman origin of St. Patrick's mission.

Dr. Todd says: "The deadly hatred of England and of anything English, which has for so many centuries unfortunately rankled in the native Irish heart, was not at first created by any difference in religion." †

This is an important statement. The creed of the English invaders was admittedly Roman Catholic. Now, if the creed of the native Irish had not been also Roman Catholic, it is plain that religious dissensions between the two parties, exasperated by their national antipathies, must have widely prevailed through the kingdom. But while history is full of the struggles for political power between English and Irish, it is silent as to any theological warfare between them. The only rational solution of this silence consists in the fact that their creed was the same.

Accordingly, Dr. Todd candidly says: "There were two Churches in Ireland, separated from each other, *without any*

---

* "Essay on the Origin, Doctrines, and Discipline of the Early Irish Church," by the Rev. Dr. Moran, Vice-Rector of the Irish College, Rome. Dublin: Duffy, 1864.

† "Life of St. Patrick," Introduction, p. 242.

essential difference of discipline or doctrine, at a period long previous to the Reformation." *

Observe the important admission, " without any essential difference of discipline or doctrine." Now, one of these two Churches, or, more accurately speaking, these two hierarchies, is admitted on all hands to have been Roman Catholic. The other hierarchy, therefore, which did not differ essentially from Roman Catholic discipline or doctrine, cannot possibly have symbolised with the modern Protestant anti-Irish Church, which differs most essentially from both.

The doctrinal and disciplinary identity of the ancient Irish and Anglo-Irish hierarchies is further shown by Dr. Todd, who says: "At a subsequent period, when the Anglo-Irish Church had accepted the Reformation,† the 'mere Irish' clergy were found to have become practically extinct. *Their Episcopacy had merged into, or become identified with, the Episcopacy which was recognised by the law.*"—Ibid., p. 242.

This quiet identification into one body of the two

* " Life of St. Patrick," Introduction, p. 241.

† Which alleged acceptance is disproved by the Rev. Maziere Brady, D.D., and rejected as a monstrous historical error by so earnest a Protestant as Mr. Froude. Immediately following the passage last cited in the text, Dr. Todd, speaking of the post-Reformation period, says: " Missionary bishops and priests, therefore, ordained abroad, were sent into Ireland to support the interests of Rome; and from them is derived a *third* Church, in close communion with the See of Rome, which has now assumed the form and dimensions of a national established religion" (p. 242). What Dr. Todd here calls " a third Church " was precisely the same great mass of Irish and Anglo-Irish Catholics whom he admits to have been in communion with Rome up to the date of the Reformation. He seems, by the words, " a third church," to ignore the lay element of the Church, which constitutes the great body of its members, and which formed neither a third nor a second Church, but remained unchanged in its hereditary fidelity to Rome. It is true that the ferocity of the Reformed Government deprived the Catholic people of home education for their clergy, who were therefore compelled to pursue their ecclesiastical studies in foreign seminaries, whence they returned to preach the old faith in Ireland, where, according to Edmund Spenser, "peril of death" awaited them. But the people of Ireland were, and are, unable to understand how the tricks which the secular power played with religion in the sixteenth century could destroy their own inherited identity with the Church of their ancestors, even supposing that the alleged conversion of nearly all their bishops to Protestantism were historically true, instead of being, as it is, totally destitute of historical foundation.

Dr. Todd's work displays much research and possesses great interest, even for readers who do not acquiesce in all his views.

hierarchies shows that their religious belief was identical. This is evident when we consider the impossibility of such identification, or common merger into one hierarchy, of two Churches having different creeds. For instance, the identification of the present Anglican Church in Ireland with the Irish Roman Catholic Church is impossible. Fancy the Most Rev. Dr. Trench, the Protestant Archbishop of Dublin, celebrating mass in the Church of the Conception; or Cardinal Cullen preaching up the Thirty-nine Articles in St. Patrick's Cathedral! But Dr. Todd informs us that such an identification of the ancient Irish Church and the Anglo-Irish Roman Catholic Church had actually occurred before the Reformation; an identification which could not have occurred unless their religious belief had been previously identical.

But it may be suggested that the English invaders had, perhaps, infused their Roman Catholic notions into the minds of the Irish.

To such a supposition Dr. Todd supplies the answer when he tells us of "the deadly hatred of England and of everything English which for so many centuries unfortunately rankled in the Irish heart." That deadly hatred would have necessarily extended to any English religious opinions not previously held by the Irish themselves. The Irish were not likely to accept the apostleship of invaders whom they held in mortal abhorrence. The inference is inevitable; the Irish did not receive, and could not possibly have received, their undoubted Roman Catholic belief from England. Whence, then, did they derive that belief? There is but one answer —they derived it from the original founders of Irish Christianity. In fact, the difference between the early Irish and Anglo-Irish hierarchies was purely political or national, and not at all doctrinal.*

* Among the proofs of the connection of the early Irish Church with Rome is a rule, or canon, contained in the ancient Book of the Canons of Armagh, which enjoins that disputed matters, which could not be settled by the local ecclesiastical authorities, should be referred to the Roman See for final adjudication. Here is the canon as translated by the late Professor Eugene O'Curry: "Moreover, if any case should arise of extreme difficulty, and beyond the knowledge of all the nations of the Scots [*i.e.*, the Irish, who were then called *Scoti*], it is to be duly referred to the chair of the Archbishop of the Gaedhill—that is to say, of Patrick—and the jurisdiction of the Bishop (of Armagh). But if such a case as aforesaid, of a matter of issue, cannot be easily disposed of [by him] with his counsellors in that [investigation], *we have decreed that it be sent*

But in truth, the question whether the Church of Saint Patrick was Catholic or Protestant, was totally irrelevant to the claims of the anti-Irish State Church. Even if Saint Palladius and Saint Patrick had taught the Thirty-nine Articles, and converted the Irish of the fifth century to Anglican Protestantism, the modern Protestant hierarchy would not have been a whit the nearer establishing a righteous title to our national ecclesiastical revenues. For, in the first place, the legislator of our day has to deal, not with the fifth century, but with the nineteenth. Again, if the aboriginal Irish parsons of those early times were Protestants, they must have been an exquisitely good-for-nothing set of gentlemen, since it is clear that they suffered the whole nation to slip through their fingers into the hands of the Popish priests. On the modern "evangelical" hypothesis, those early pastors must have been given the Church-revenues as the salary for teaching Protestantism to the Irish people. But they did not keep their part of the bargain, for they suffered all their flocks to lapse into Catholicity. They did not give value for the money, and they consequently became disentitled to claim it.

How preposterous, then, to assert for the anti-Irish clergy of the present day, a right as derived from a long extinct generation of parsons, who, if they ever existed at all, manifestly forfeited all title to Ireland's Church property some thousand or twelve hundred years ago! Were such a plea valid, it would follow by parity of reasoning that if all the original holders of Irish Church property had been Mohammedans, then a hierarchy of Turkish muftis would, at the present day, have a rightful claim to our ecclesiastical State revenues.

IV. It was strenuously urged that as nearly all the Irish Roman Catholic Bishops at the period of the Reformation accepted Protestantism, they became entitled, in virtue of their corporate identity, to carry the Church property into the new creed of their adoption.

But, firstly, the story of their conversion is a figment. The Rev. Maziere Brady and the Rev. Dr. Moran have con-

---

to the apostolic seat—*that is to say, to the Chair of the Apostle Peter having the authority of the city of Rome.*

"These are the persons who decreed concerning this matter, viz., Auxilius, Patrick, Secundinus, and Benignus." See "O'Curry's Lectures on the Manuscript Materials of Ancient Irish History," pp. 373, 611. Dublin: Duffy, 1861.

clusively disproved it. Next, if the whole Catholic hierarchy of the Elizabethan period had adopted Protestantism, I do not see how their conversion could have justified them in carrying into the Protestant Church the Catholic ecclesiastical property of which they had been given the use on condition of their fidelity to the Catholic Church. On the contrary, it seems clear that by deserting Catholicity they would have forfeited their sole original right to enjoy the Catholic endowments. Suppose the whole English hierarchy were suddenly to become Anabaptists to-morrow, would they have a moral right, in virtue of their corporate identity, to carry the whole national Church property of England into the Anabaptist communion?

V. It was urged that the disendowment of the anti-Irish State Church would invalidate or shake the title to all other kinds of property. Sir Hugh (afterwards Earl) Cairns expresses the objection in the following words: "It was utterly impossible they could attempt to destroy any kind of property in the country without loosening the security of property of every kind. . . . They could not confiscate benefices without loosening the bonds that secured property of every kind in the kingdom."

I quote the following answer to the above objection from the report of a speech which I delivered at the National Association of Ireland on the day of its inauguration:

"Just as if the ecclesiastical endowments, which Grattan called the 'salary of prayer,' stood on the same basis with private property! The law creates the endowments. But the law only protects other kinds of property. The revenues instituted by the State as the salary or remuneration for the performance of certain specific public functions, are legitimately liable to interference on the part of the State that created them. But this gives no precedent for interference with property which the State did not create; property acquired from industry, inheritance, or gift. So much for the principle. Then, as to the fact. All this bugbear about loosening the security of secular property if the ecclesiastical revenues were meddled with—all these menaces were dinned in our ears when Parliament, about thirty years ago, struck twenty-five per cent. off the Irish tithe rent-charge. But what private property was loosened or lessened by extinguishing one-fourth of the parochial revenues of the Irish State clergy? Can Sir Hugh Cairns, can any man show that private property was shaken or diminished to the extent of one farthing by what the learned gentleman would doubtless call the confiscation of a fourth part of the Irish benefices?" *

VI. It was asked, "Would you make the tithe rent-charge a present to the landlords by a simple act of disendowment?"

When this question was asked, the landlords occupied a position very different from that in which the Land Act of 1881 has placed them. It was at that time fair to answer that the revenues of the State Church should be secularised, and applied to public uses of general benefit. Mr. Miall proposed that the tithe rent-charge should be sold to the landlords at ten years' purchase. It was also suggested that the poor-rate should be partially paid from the tithe rent-charge. The State Church property was a great national trust fund; and honesty imperatively demanded that it should be appropriated so as to benefit the whole Irish nation. Now, we said that although it was the trust estate of all, it was dishonestly monopolised by a small fractional part of the people. The Catholics had been robbed of it in the sixteenth century, and the robbery was perpetuated on hypocritical pretexts and defended by shallow and insulting sophistry. Restitution, we said, could be made in either of two ways—by reinvesting the Catholic Church with the ecclesiastical revenues; or by appropriating those revenues to secular objects for the benefit of the whole people. The former mode was heartily deprecated (and for excellent reasons) by nearly all the Irish Catholics. The latter mode, as matters then stood, commended itself as being an effectual and satisfactory mode of restitution.

I say, as matters then stood; for matters stand quite otherwise now with the Irish landlords. This we shall see when the next plea in behalf of the State Church comes to be examined.

VII. It was said, by way of showing that the Catholics had no right to complain, that the incidence of tithe, or tithe rent-charge, fell upon the landlords, who were chiefly Protestants, and not upon the tenants, who were chiefly Catholics.

This was in most cases a delusion. The English Parlia-

---

* Page 14 of my speech, which was printed as a pamphlet by the English Liberation Society, from whom it can be had at 2, Serjeants' Inn, Fleet Street, London. Nobody can pretend that the recent agitation against excessive rents had any connection with the disestablishment of the State Church. It arose from various other causes, of which one was the existence of the rack-renting system.

ment took care to leave the burthen of tithe rent-charge on the tenants, by enabling the landlords to exact the amount from them in the shape of additional rent. Only the impost, when paid by the tenants, was to be called "rent," and not "tithe;" and was recoverable as rent by the landlords. Compositions for tithe had frequently been made by the tenants with the Protestant rectors. It was not unusual, while the system of "middle-men" prevailed, that two, three, sometimes even four lessees and sub-lessees were interposed between the head landlord and the actual occupier of the land. To enable the landlords, when saddled with tithe rent-charge, to extract it from their subordinate lessees and sub-lessees, the Act 1st and 2nd Victoria, chap. cix., provided a process of recovery which is thus described in the marginal summary of the 10th section of the Act:

"If any person who would have been liable to tithe-composition hold mediately or immediately under the person liable to such rent-charge, *the amount of such rent-charge may be recovered as rent from the next tenant and so downwards to the person primarily liable.*"

Thus the occupying tenants were reached by the parsons, not indeed directly as of yore, but by the device of transforming the landlords into tithe-proctors. The tenants paid the impost to the rectors through the receivership of the landlords, instead of paying it as formerly through the receivership of the old tithe-proctors. To be sure the name was changed; but "a rose by any other name would smell as sweet;" and the tithe, whether styled rent, or rent-charge, or modus, or whatever else you please, had as foul a stench in the nostrils of justice as in the days of Captain Rock and the tithe-riots.

Many landlords added the tithe rent-charge to the previously reserved rent. In all such cases the burden fell upon their tenants, in full accordance with the spirit of the Act to which I have referred. But there also were many cases in which the landlords found it extremely difficult, occasionally even impossible, to obtain the tithe rent-charge from their tenants; and of course in such cases the burden unquestionably fell upon themselves. It was, and is, paid in such cases from their rents, unassisted by the additional rent which Parliament empowered them to extract from their tenantry.

An erroneous impression prevailed in some quarters that the Rent-charge Act conferred a boon upon the landlords, because, in rendering them responsible to the rectors for the tithe, it professed to allow them to retain twenty-five per cent. for collecting and handing to the clergy the remaining seventy-five per cent. Judging from my own experience, from my knowledge of the country, and from my communications with other landlords, I feel certain that very few landlords, if any, pocketed a farthing of the twenty-five per cent. The tithe rent-charge was paid out of a gross rental which was greatly diminished by the repeal of the corn laws, while the septennial valuation of the impost was measured by comparison with the standard of high prices that preceded that repeal.

So stood matters up to 1881. But the Land Act of that year has essentially changed the position of the landlords, and largely increased the grievance of the impost. The Land Courts, constituted by the Act, have, on the average of Ireland, reduced the rents of landlords by from twenty to twenty-five per cent. This reduction of the rental cuts away the source from which the Rent-charge Act empowered the landlords to obtain the tithe rent-charge for which they were responsible to the rectors, and since Disestablishment, to the Commissioners of Church Temporalities.

Let us suppose the case of a landlord whose original rental was £1,000 per annum, and the tithe rent-charge on whose estate was £100 per annum. The Rent-charge Act enabled him to recover £1,100 per annum from his tenants; at the same time requiring him to hand the tithe rent-charge to the rector from the additional £100 per annum. But now comes the Land Act of 1881. The landlord is brought into court. A judicial rent is fixed. The Court takes twenty or twenty-five per cent., often more, from the rent; thus sweeping off much more than the portion of the landlord's income which had been previously appropriated to the payment of tithe rent-charge. The tithe rent-charge is extorted, while the means of paying it is taken away by the law. A plainer case of injustice than this one can hardly conceive. If the English Parliament were actuated by a spirit of fair play, that body would advance from the Treasury a sufficient sum to buy off the anti-Irish clergy. They advanced twenty millions of money to buy off the slave-owners, an excellent precedent to follow in the present case. In point of justice England ought to pay the cost of purchasing out her clergy in Ireland, inasmuch as it was England that forced Protestantism on the Irish people. England committed the wrong by which Ireland for three centuries had been fleeced and otherwise afflicted; and England, having now discovered that the imposition of the Anglican Church on Ireland *was* a wrong, should emphasize her penitence by paying the pecuniary penalty. This, however, has not been done. The negro slaves were not required to repay the £20,000,000 advanced from the Imperial treasury for their emancipation. The Irish landowners *are* required to recoup that treasury for the cash advanced for Disestablishment.

VIII. Some Protestant clergymen pleaded that the State Church revenues of Ireland were little enough for the support of their order; and on this ground they deprecated reduction or alienation. For ministering to a small fractional part of the Irish people they were not ashamed to claim the whole ecclesiastical State property of the country. It was, they said, little enough. It was, as I have remarked, about £700,000 a year.* If this were little enough for the Church purposes of a fraction, let us ask to what annual sum should the payment of the Irish clergy of all denominations, rated on the same scale, amount? If the State Church clergy, with flocks not more than eleven or twelve per cent. of the whole, required £700,000, then the collective Irish clergy of all denominations would have needed something about six millions sterling per annum. It was lucky for Ireland that her Catholic priests and her Presbyterian ministers had less inflated notions than the State Church clergy entertained respecting the pecuniary value of their ministrations.

I have now noticed a few of the current sophisms which were employed to defend the infliction of a Protestant State Church on Catholic Ireland. As an institution of the State, it was a marvellous system of incorporated fraud and insolence. It robbed the people and it insulted their religion. When its advocates, clerical and lay, had exhausted their eloquence in sounding its praises, we had only to look it in the face—to look at its shameless monopoly of a nation's Church property for the benefit of a small and wealthy minority—in order to condemn it as an abominable outrage

* The Rev. Maziere Brady, in a letter to the *Times*, March, 1867, having enumerated various items of Church revenues and Church property omitted from an annual income of £420,000, which Lord Dufferin appeared to think was the whole, says: "If those sums were added to the £420,000 a year of which Lord Dufferin spoke, the total would, perhaps, exceed £700,000; but in the absence of any reliable return, it is impossible to calculate with certainty the present revenues of the Establishment."

on every principle of justice and of honest policy. Englishmen were often asked to make our case their own; to tell us what they would think of a Roman Catholic Church Establishment quartered by law on every parish of Protestant England; of fiery Roman Catholic polemics extorting payment from English Protestant flocks for ferocious vituperation of Protestantism ? *

Why, it may be asked, was the anti-Irish State Church so long upheld by English statesmen? Why did they persist for three centuries in inflicting on us a wrong to which the English nation would not submit for an hour?

The true answer, I doubt not, is to be found in the traditional Irish statecraft of English parties—in the belief that Ireland could not be governed without a plentiful application of exasperating injustice. To keep Ireland down, it was deemed necessary to perpetuate the distractions and miseries of her people. The policy was not new. "Some of her (Elizabeth's) counsellors," says Leland, "appear to have conceived an odious jealousy which reconciled them to the distractions and miseries of Ireland. 'Should we exert ourselves,' said they, 'in reducing this country to order and civility, it must soon acquire power, consequence, and riches. The inhabitants will thus be alienated from England; they will cast themselves into the arms of some foreign power, or perhaps erect themselves into an independent and separate State. Let us therefore connive at their disorders; for a weak and disordered people never can attempt to detach themselves from the crown of England.'"—LELAND's *History of Ireland*, book IV., chap. 3.

In the species of statecraft here described by the historian, we discern the policy that inspired the establishment of an anti-national State Church of Ireland. "Let us connive at their disorders." It would tax human wit to connive at our disorders more effectually than by forcing on the country a corporate incubus of which social hatred and heart-burning were the necessary consequences; which generated an angry sense of wrong on the one side, and a sentiment of arrogant superiority on the other. With such a social gangrene among

---

* It would be most unjust to inculpate all the Protestant clergy of Ireland as firebrand polemics. Great numbers of them were incapable of the insulting malpractices referred to in the text, and were personally very estimable; but there were also many whose controversial zeal rendered them intolerable nuisances. All alike were in a false position.

us, it cannot be a matter of surprise that a thousand acrid humours diffused their poison through the nation's veins, and kept the body politic in a chronic condition of disease.

This was the true purpose and mission of the anti-Irish State Church.

Before I close this chapter I shall say a few words on the proposals which previously to Disestablishment had been from time to time suggested, to purchase the clergy by pensions, or glebes, or some other sort of State endowment.

Statesmen regard the endowment of any Church by the State in the light of a bribe to the clergy. Thus, Lord Castlereagh speculated on purchasing the support of the Presbyterian clergy for the Union by an augmentation of the *Regium Donum*. On the 23rd of November, 1798, he wrote as follows to William Wickham, Esq.:

"Of late they (the Presbyterians) are rather tired of the treason in which they had very deeply embarked; perhaps they may be inclined to compromise with the Union; *some additional provision for the clergy, connecting the Church more closely with the Crown, would probably disarm the opposition, if not secure the support, of that body.*" *

In the recently published "Correspondence of Earl Grey," † we find the following passage in a letter addressed by Sir Herbert Taylor to that nobleman: "Your lordship is aware that I was private secretary to King George III., when the correspondence took place with the Administration of which you were a member, on the Catholic question, and I was of course privy to all that passed (His Majesty being blind), and had opportunities of learning his sentiments not consigned to paper. I am almost confident that he more than once said that he should not object to a proposition for giving a stipend to the Roman Catholic clergy, and that he observed that no better expedient could be found for reducing the influence of the Pope in Ireland, and transferring their dependence to the Government from which they would derive their means of support. I have heard the late Duke of York express the same opinion; and the King assures me that the late Mr. Perceval had frequently stated it to him as an arrangement he should be glad to effect."

It is needless to observe that the Catholic clergy give no

---

* "Cornwallis Correspondence," vol. ii. p. 247.

† "The Correspondence of Earl Grey with King William IV. and with Sir Herbert Taylor." Edited by Henry, Earl Grey. London: John Murray, 1867.

allegiance to the Pope inconsistent with their temporal allegiance to their sovereign. What demands our attention is this—that the project of giving them a pension was considered in the light of a bribe by its authors—a bribe which was to buy them off from certain principles which it was presumed that they held. And in the light of a bribe would any possible scheme of endowing the Catholic clergy of Ireland by an English and Protestant State be inevitably regarded—not only by the Government, but, what is more important, by the people of Ireland. If the clergy of the people became the paid officers of the English Government, they would utterly and finally forfeit the confidence of their flocks. We shudder to contemplate the scenes of anarchy and irreligion which would follow from such a loosing of the bands that now unite the people and their pastors. Let us hope that in the wisdom, the honesty, and the Christian fidelity of the priesthood, a sufficient security exists against such a terrible result.

In Cardinal Cullen's Pastoral at the beginning of Lent, 1866, he said, with reference to the pensioning project, "*Timeo Danaos et dona ferentes.*" Now, in whatever shape the *dona* may be offered, whether in glebes, in pensions, or in any other mode whatsoever, it is certain that the offer would be meant as a bribe to purchase off the priesthood from the national interests of their country. Both English Whigs and English Tories—combined in hostility to Mr. Gladstone's Home Government measure—are resolved on preserving the Legislative Union as long as they can. That is to say, they will do their best to perpetuate the legislative disfranchisement of Ireland ; to prolong a system that deprives her of the sole control of her own national interests, and that gives to Great Britain about nine parts in eleven of the formal control of those interests, and in real fact, the whole of it; to prolong a system that results in the wholesale spoliation of the wealth which God has bestowed upon our island, and in the consequent depopulation that afflicts almost to madness every man who has a heart to feel for the wrongs of his expatriated brethren, and a conscience to abhor the diabolical wickedness of plundering a country of its riches and driving out the inhabitants.

All this the Union does, and the people of Ireland know it. How could they retain their confidence in a priesthood capable of accepting any species of endowment from a Government resolved to perpetuate that Union ?

The scheme of dividing the national ecclesiastical endowments between the Protestant and Catholic Churches was started by a gentleman whose personal character, position, and abilities entitled him to our respect. I publicly stated my objections to this scheme. The attempt would have been extremely impolitic, for it would have turned against us our only reliable allies, the English voluntaries. Desirous, as a matter of principle, to obtain the disendowment of the State Church in England, from which they or their progenitors had gone forth, and irritated by being made to contribute to its support, they knew that the ultimate success of their attack on it would be much facilitated by the overthrow of the State Church in Ireland. Hence, in working for us they worked for themselves. To attempt an endowment for Irish Catholicity would have deservedly forfeited their support. Moreover, such an attempt would have entailed upon our cause the weakness of division. For the mass of Irish Catholics would not have deserted the voluntary banner under which they had previously rallied, in order to fraternise with the claimants for Catholic endowment. Our agitation would have been encumbered with miserable by-battles between the friends of total Disendowment and the gentlemen (few, though indefatigable) who demanded the division of the spoil between the Churches. Thus, we should have furnished to the Whigs a plausible pretext for leaving the giant evil undisturbed. They would have been only too glad of an opportunity of telling us that until we were agreed among ourselves as to the proper remedy, they would deem it inexpedient to interfere with existing arrangements.

We proclaimed that the Irish Catholic Church in Ireland had thriven and flourished for more than three centuries on the voluntary system; that it had struck its roots deep into the hearts of the Irish people, not only unsustained by, but in defiance of, the powers of this world. We said that among the human motives which act in harmony with the principle of Divine faith, supporting that principle and in turn receiving strength from it, a leading motive was the deep, enduring, passionate love of country that burns in the hearts of our people. We warned the claimants for Catholic endowments from the alien State against the terrible experiment of separating our devotion to the Catholic Church from our Irish nationality. " Let no fantastic theorist," we said, " seek to reduce us to the awful alternative of abandoning our accustomed ecclesiastical obedience; or of rendering that obedience to a hierarchy who would have forfeited our confidence by accepting endowments from a Power that, whether nationally or religiously, cannot possibly have any common sympathy with Catholic Ireland."

There was not, however, much real chance that the advocates of a State endowment for the Irish Catholic Church would succeed in their movement, which was chiefly supported by one bishop, a lay gentleman of much poetic talent, and a handful of West-British Whigs. Against their scheme was the vast and powerful array of British voluntaries; the British anti-Papal multitude, who would have resented the endowment of "Popery" as treason to Protestantism; and, finally, the great body of Irish Catholics, clerical as well as lay, who felt that the union between the clergy and their flock would be rudely shaken by placing the former under pecuniary obligations to the alien Government. During the prevalence of the Fenian conspiracy, an intelligent priest in the south of Ireland, conversing with me on the efforts the Catholic clergy had made to check Fenianism, said: "The people were just hanging on to us— we could hardly hold them in; but if they had been able to point to an endowment in our hands we could not have held them in at all."

Of the general principle of State endowment of religion I shall here say nothing. But of its particular application by the Protestant Government of another country to our national Church, I will say this: Every Church which is endowed by the State must to some extent rely upon temporal support; but "the vital power of religion is generally found to exist in an inverse ratio to its reliance on temporal support." *

This is at any rate true of Catholicity in Ireland. And may God defend us, and defend our remotest posterity from the fatal pecuniary alliance between our national Church and an alien, uncongenial Government!

* Rev. H. B. Liddon.

CHAPTER XII.

PROGRESS OF THE ANTI-TITHE MOVEMENT.

Then who's the wretch that basely spurns
The ties of country, kindred, friends;
That barters every nobler aim
For sordid views—for private ends?
One slave alone on earth you'll find
Through Nature's universal span,
So lost to virtue, dead to shame:
The Anti-Irish Irishman.
Spirit of the Nation.

I HAVE said that "Repeal" and "No Tithes" were associated on the platforms. The journals in the State Church interest, and the speakers and writers, lay and clerical, by whom that interest was defended, generally represented Repeal as a purely Popish scheme, designed to overthrow Protestantism, and fraught with peril to the properties and persons of Protestants. The true merits and facts of the question were carefully suppressed; the most baseless falsehoods were boldly affirmed and reiterated; the fanatical engine was incessantly worked; and a profound impression was made on the credulity, the ignorance, and the religious prejudices of a large class of Protestants.

So far as concerns the miserable wrangling of adverse religionists, let it pass for what it is worth. A ferocious polemical divine imagines that he has discharged a telling shot when he has let off some fanatical impertinence about "idolatry," or "wafer-gods," or "the priest-ridden people." Well, he has been impertinent; what matter? None, surely —unless we get too much of his impertinence. I bear no enmity to any man for calling me a limb of Antichrist, and telling me I must go to the devil as a follower of the Pope. Certainly such language is not civil, and I am convinced it is not true. But there is little wisdom in quarrelling with men for mere incivility, or for a mistaken view of my chances of salvation. It is impossible to conceive anything more intrinsically unimportant than the anti-Catholic speculations and incivilities of our polemical assailants. "Antichrist" shouted at a Catholic by some delirious enthusiast should no more excite his wrath than "d——n your blood" from a drunken trooper. But the case is altered when abuse of our faith becomes the watchword of a powerful party. When it becomes the rallying cry of men who avail themselves of the spirit it excites to assail our pockets or abridge our liberties, we are called on to resent it; to resist the party who use their fanaticism as an engine wherewith to work out our oppression.

It was preposterous to talk of the anti-Irish Church Establishment as a religious institution. Of the personal piety or of the doctrinal convictions of its numerous estimable members, I say nothing disrespectful. I speak of it solely as a State Institution. During the period of its Establishment it was in Catholic eyes a political instrument designed and calculated to create and intensify class animosities. I fear that a good deal of the bitterness which it engendered has survived its Disestablishment.*

Its advocates defended it on the plea of its being what they termed "a Missionary Church." It was supposed to have a mission from the State to convert the Catholics. From a Protestant standpoint it cannot seem, in this sense, valuable; for it has not converted the Catholics of Ireland to the Protestant religion. They were but as three to one during part of the last century; now they are seven to one as compared with the Protestants of the Episcopal Church—poor evidence of its missionary efficacy.

Had it diffused through the land the Christian fruits of peace, goodwill, and mutual tolerance? There for three centuries it stood—hating and hated, plundering and execrated; in past times prolific of tears, outrage, and wailings; in our own day prolific of bitter politico-sectarian animosity between classes who ought to have one common interest as Irishmen. The people regarded it as a monument of English power and Irish degradation.

* In a paper entitled "Ritualism in its Missionary Aspect," by an Anglican clergyman—the Rev. Dr. Littledale—that reverend gentleman says of the State Church in Ireland: "Though called by some of its panegyrists a Missionary Church, how completely it has broken down in dealing with the Roman Catholic population need not be insisted on. It is enough to say that even if the reports of the proselytising societies were as true as they are unscrupulously mendacious, the results would be a very poor return for three centuries of monopoly."—*The Church and the World: Essays on Questions of the Day.* By various writers. First Series. Edited by the Rev. Orby Shipley, M.A. Second Edition. London: Longmans.

Archdeacon Stopford, in order to demonstrate the vast success of the State Church in converting the Irish from Catholicity, published in 1853 in his work called "Income and Requirements of the Irish Church," a table professing to give the number of State Protestants

These were the qualities that constituted its real value in the estimation of our Whig and Tory rulers. The Whigs, when out of office, had often made political capital by denouncing it as an intolerable grievance. The Whigs, when in office, were accustomed to look with complacent philosophy at the intolerable grievance, and would to this day have continued equally sympathetic and equally inactive, if the English Liberation Society had not forced the question on the notice of the nation and of its rulers by such a vigorous and persistent agitation that the Government were at last compelled to abate the great scandal by complete Disestablishment, and by a partial and inadequate Disendowment.

Looking back on the anti-Irish Church, on its English origin and its historical sympathies, it would be impossible to conceive a more useful auxiliary to English Whigs and Tories in the misgovernment and robbery of Ireland. It held out rich rewards to an important class to sustain in every possible mode the (so-called) interests of Imperial England as opposed to those of their native country. The injury of being thus rendered subservient to the powerful rivalry of another land became the more galling, when, as in the case of Ireland, the depressed nation was compelled to be the paymaster of those officers who enforced and perpetuated its own servitude. A man who supposed he could smooth his path to station and salary by crying, "Up with England! Down with Ireland!" found the inducement to anti-national politics much augmented, when to the motive of self-interest was added the stimulant of sectarian partizanship.

That such a wealthy exclusive institution as the State

in forty-eight selected parishes in 1834 and 1851 respectively, by which he made it appear that the Protestant inhabitants were greatly increased by conversions, and amounted in 1851 to no less than 12,372 persons. Mr. Herbert Skeats, in his excellent pamphlet styled "The Irish Church; a Historical and Statistical Review," follows the Archdeacon through each of his forty-eight parishes, and finds, by comparing the Archdeacon's figures with the figures of the (then) last census, that if there were really 12,372 Protestants in those parishes in 1851, there must have been "the most alarming declension, in ten years, of the number of converts, or of members of the Established Church, that has probably taken place in any part of Ireland or in any other country." And well might Mr. Skeats say so, for the census of 1861 only gave a total of 6,939 State Protestants in the parishes in question. The other alternative suggested by Mr. Skeats is probably the true one—namely, that the Archdeacon's statement was inaccurate.

Church should have kept a considerable portion of the Protestant body from merging into the great national mass, is not greatly to be wondered at. Religious bigotry, combined with pecuniary profit, has availed to perpetuate the original hostility to Ireland of the Elizabethan, Cromwellian, and Williamite adventurers in the breasts of their descendants of the present day. This long-cherished hatred of a domestic faction to their countrymen has no parallel in any other country. You will find all Frenchmen, of whatever party in the State, zealous for the glory of France; all Germans ardent for the honour of Germany; Spaniards for Spain, and so on. It is in Ireland only that you will hear from the lips of her unnatural children the frequent expressions, "this odious land!" "this detestable people!" "England will drag her triumphant cannon over your prostrate carcases if you dare to resist;"* with innumerable similar ebullitions of venomous hatred of the unoffending people among whom their lot is cast, and whose only crime is that they agitate for the common liberties of their revilers and themselves. I recollect reading some years since in a Limerick paper a letter written by an English gentleman named Potter, who had spent some time in Ireland, and who had expressed his surprise that all the Irish Protestants he met seemed to him to have been trained to hate their native country. A trivial circumstance will illustrate the satanic activity with which, under the pretext of religion, hatred of the Irish Catholic peasantry is instilled into the Protestant mind. I chanced to converse with a young lady who had been carefully brought up under parsonic influences. She abused our poor country-folk as a set of ferocious and immoral savages. Of course she had derived that impression from her intercourse with teachers and companions. I tried to undeceive her, and stated one or two reasons to show she was mistaken.

"Ah!" said she, "I wish you had been the other night at the lecture we heard from the Rev. Mr. ——! He said the country people were a dreadful set, and told us how, when going among them, his life had been more than once in danger from the ferocity of fellows who were hounded at him by the priests. I can tell you he was well cheered."

I have no doubt he was well cheered. On my fair friend's table was a "religious" work, in which it was

* I found this anti-national brag in the report of a speech delivered by Mr. Emerson Tennent.

affirmed that the Irish Catholics considered it a greater sin " to eat meat on Friday, than to murder a Protestant for a consideration." These details may seem trivial. But such prejudices are not trivial in their consequences when kneaded into the minds of possibly well-meaning people, the current of whose affections has been thereby turned from the land that supplies them with their means of living, and from the people whom they ought to love.

What, I ask, is the inexhaustible fountain of this pestilential hatred of Ireland by Irishmen? What feeds the stream of ceaseless calumny, insult, and political enmity? Prior to the Disestablishment of the English Church in Ireland, the obvious answer to this query was—the anti-Irish State Church, acting through the interests it affected. Since Disestablishment we must ascribe the anti-national feeling partly to the bigotry bequeathed by that pernicious institution to its disestablished successor, but also in some measure to the violent onslaught on the whole body of Irish landlords got up by Mr. Parnell, which fatally widened the traditionary chasm between them and the people—a chasm which we, of the Repeal Association and the Home Rule League, had laboured hard to close.

Despite the lapse of ages, despite even the connexions formed by marriage with many of the native families, the hostile spirit of the invader is as fresh, as vivid, in the modern descendants of the ruthless soldiery of Essex or St. Leger, of the sanguinary fanatics of the Commonwealth, or of the military settlers of the Williamite era, as it was some centuries ago in the breasts of their forefathers. They have never become blended with the people. I have heard language redolent of the most contemptuous and envenomed hostility to the national population of Ireland proceeding from tongues whose rich Hibernian brogue contrasted ludicrously with the anti-Hibernian sentiments they uttered. Even the ignorant Orange tradesman still fancies himself a sort of Englishman in virtue of his English creed, and the long habit, not yet extinguished by emancipation, of regarding its profession as a badge of social superiority.

To any dispassionate observer at a distance, not aware of the source of the unnatural hostility of Ireland's domestic enemies to their country, how strange, how unaccountable must that hostility appear! How strange that no national yearnings should be excited in their minds by the hallowed associations of home, the ties of kindred, the casting of their lot in the old land of their birth; that the blending of their forefathers' dust for many a generation with Irish earth, should yet leave the living descendant as alien in feeling—nay, as hostile, as if no such associations existed to bind his heart to his fatherland! Strange that the mystic voices of the breeze that stirs the sycamores over his ancestors' graves should not whisper to his spirit to love Ireland—to strive for her liberties! Strange that he should have no pride of country; that not only is he destitute of the ordinary sentiment of patriotism indigenous to every other land on earth, but that from *his* tongue should emanate the bitterest insults to Ireland and her sons—from *his* brain should proceed the wickedest devices to enthral his own countrymen! I once heard a jovial Irish squire of Cromwellian descent, whose estate lay in as peaceable a district as any in the world, exclaim that if it were not for the personal supervision his property required from him, he would quit "this abominable country and go to live in England." An orator named Harte proclaimed at a meeting of the Dublin Conservative Society some years ago, that "it was perfectly notorious to every man who heard him, that to be a Protestant in Ireland was sufficient to render life insecure." These instances are not isolated. The party who display this astounding hatred of their country are indefatigable in their calumnies. The inspiring source of that hatred is clearly discernible in the pseudo-religious character of their attacks. Take two instances which accidentally met my eye some years ago; they are both typical. The first of these is an extract from the *Cork Constitution* newspaper of July 27th, 1844. It is headed:

"DOINGS IN DINGLE.

"On Sunday last, the Rev. Mr. Brasbie read his public recantation from the errors of Popery in Dingle Church. The fact of a priest abjuring Popery caused great excitement; and the magistrates, having got full notice that the mob were determined to execute lynch law on the priest on his road to the church, took full precautions to preserve the peace. Before service commenced, the townspeople were astonished to see the Hon. Captain Plunket, of H.M. steamer *Stromboli*, march into the town from Ventry with a force of about one hundred men, including the marine artillery and marines, with drums and colours. This fine body of men, armed to the teeth, having joined the seamen and marines of H.M. brigantine *Lynx*, under command of Captain Nott, presented such an imposing appearance that, we need not say, everything passed off very quietly. The coastguard from the surrounding stations were marched to church, fully armed, and conveyed the reverend gentleman to the house of the Rev. Mr. Gayer, where he at present remains. Mr. Gillman, our active sub-inspector, had all his police ready to turn out at a moment's notice. Dingle for the last twenty years never presented such a force."

Lord Aberdeen, about that period, apologised in Parliament for the non-transmission of a marine force to Morocco, as Her Majesty's war vessels were on duty on the coast of Ireland. His lordship ought to have explained the tremendous nature of the duty which deprived the Mediterranean of the presence of the British flag. He should have announced that the *Stromboli* and the *Lynx* were required to assist the "missionary Church" (as the *Evening Mail* delighted to term the Establishment) in the acquisition of the Rev. Mr. Brasbie to her fold.

The whole paragraph is redolent of Irish State Churchism. The transition from Popish error to Protestant truth is performed by the beat of drums and the flourish of military colours. The triumph of having caught a priest who will renounce holy water and purgatory is combined with the congenial triumph of saying to the mob, "My lads, we have 100 marines all armed to the teeth, who will make smithereens of any man who dares to wag a finger." The orthodox parade of "such a force as Dingle had not seen for twenty years," is requisite to give due *éclat* to the Rev. Mr. Brasbie's exchange of Pope Gregory XVI. for Pope Victoria as the head of his Church; and, moreover, to protect the sacred person of the convert from the truculence of the "mob," who in all probability did not care three straws for the exploits of the reverend gentleman.

The other instance is the allegation by the Rev. Mr. Nangle, of Achill, that eleven Achillonians had attempted to induce one Francis M'Hugh to enter into a conspiracy to burn Mr. Nangle's House. That reverend gentleman also printed in the *Achill Herald* (of which he was the editor) a statement that the Catholics of the island had conspired to break into his dwelling, and strangle the inhabitants. His charge of meditated murder and arson elicited from Mr. S. C. Hall, the well-known writer, an indignant letter to the *Times*, from which the following paragraph is an extract:

"The intention of the conspirators (writes the Rev. E. Nangle in his own newspaper, the *Achill Herald*—fruitful source of incalculable mischief!) was to have come down in considerable force at night, to have entered by one of the senior missionary's (*i.e.* Mr. Nangle's) houses, to have strangled him and the other heads of the mission in their beds, and, after robbing them, to burn their dwellings.

"Rely on it, sir, there is not a shadow of foundation for this 'horrible plot.' For the sake of mercy and justice, lend your powerful aid to prevent so foul a slander from obtaining credit in this country.

"Without meaning to insinuate that this cock-and-bull story of conspiracy to murder wholesale has been got up for the occasion, I may at least say that it occurs at a lucky moment for the colony, inasmuch as within the next month the Rev. E. Nangle will make his customary round of visits to several English towns, and deliver his annual oration at Exeter Hall; the result of which, once a year, is a freightage of English gold to his small colony at Achill. I append my name, which you will either print or withhold at your pleasure.

"S. C. HALL."
"Jan. 8th, 1884."

Mr. Hall is not only a Protestant, but a Conservative. I mention his religious and political opinions, not that his personal truth and honour are in the slightest degree thereby affected, but because there are readers who will more readily accept the testimony of a gentleman who holds his views than if it were the evidence of a Catholic nationalist. In fact it is extremely difficult to suppose that Mr. Nangle believed in the truth of his serious accusations. They were, of course, interspersed with affecting expressions of pious regret at the dense spiritual blindness of the people. Mr. Nangle prosecuted the alleged culprits. The charge of attempting to involve M'Hugh in a conspiracy to burn the house was sworn to at the Mayo assizes of July, 1844, by that person himself, who appeared to be a convert, probably of Mr. Nangle's manufacture. His sworn testimony was rejected by Judge Jackson as totally incredible.*

* Mr. Hall's appreciation of the moral merits of the onslaught on the faith of the Achill Catholics, sustained by English contri-

The work of pious slander is incessant. In July, 1863, a circular address was issued from "The Metropolitan House, Bachelor's Walk, Dublin," to the Protestant employers of Ireland. It is headed with the words, "Assassination—Self-Preservation," and seems to have been chiefly meant to work upon the nervous fears of ladies, inasmuch as it commences, "Dear Madam." I copy the first and last paragraphs of this most characteristic document:

"The assassinations that are taking, and have taken place, almost daily, in our unhappy, but alas! too notorious country, prove beyond a shadow of doubt that it is neither safe nor prudent for landlords to employ Roman Catholics as domestic or farm-servants, or to locate them on their lands as small farmers or stewards. To illustrate this statement by numerous examples would be to waste your time, and trifle with the most serious evil of the age in which we live."

The address goes on to urge, as the best means of preservation from Popish assassins, the employment of "Protestants only who are in favour of British connexion." Roman Catholics, indeed, may be employed; but only "in stations unaccompanied by risk and personal danger." They are to be shown a holy and edifying example, and to be taught to live "in the constant practice of godliness, industry, and every Christian virtue."

Having thus exhorted the Protestant employers to keep their dangerous neighbours at a prudent distance, the address concludes as follows: "This method of self-preservation would, we are convinced, be found a golden rule—a royal road to domestic safety, security, and protection, for Protestants individually and collectively. It would check the assassination and decimation of our gentry; and it would

butions of money, may be learned from the following passage of his "Tour through Ireland," p. 400. "It was impossible," says Mr. Hall, "not to appreciate the magnanimity of the poor, miserable, utterly destitute, and absolutely starving inhabitants of Achill, who were at the time of our visit enduring privations at which humanity shudders—and to know that by walking a couple of miles and *professing* to change their religion they would be instantly supplied with food, clothes, and lodging. Yet these hungry thousands—for it would scarcely be an exaggeration to say that nine-tenths of the population of the island were, in the month of July last, entirely without food—preferred patiently to endure their sufferings rather than submit to what they considered a degradation. Such fortitude we do believe to be without parallel in the history of any 'ignorant and unenlightened' people since the creation of the world."

reflect its blessings on those who are not of our communion. It would elevate our class, edify the Church, receive the approval of the Most High, and attract the attention of the civilised and uncivilised inhabitants of Great Britain, of Europe, and of the World.

"Your very humble servant in Christ Jesus,
"THE SECRETARY,
"Employment and Aid Society for Protestants.
"July, 1863."

This address was intended for private circulation; but a copy of it accidentally reached the hands of Mr. A. M. Sullivan, the able and patriotic editor of the *Nation*, in which journal that gentleman published it on the 15th of August, 1863.

One mode of keeping up the sectarian excitement was by displaying anti-Catholic placards in the streets. This was for a long period constantly and offensively done. An English gentleman, one of the most illustrious of the Oxford converts, wrote to me from Dublin that if the Catholics were to retaliate with anti-Protestant placards, a state of things would be produced which would probably compel the Government to put a stop to that species of warfare. There were controversial handbills profusely scattered over the country—thrown upon the highways, flung into the fields, and pasted upon walls. The piers of my entrance-gate were thus decorated. Whether any of the handbills displayed talent, I am unable to say. The attempts at argument in those which I saw were the veriest sweepings of controversial rubbish. But they attacked "Popery," helped to exasperate Catholics, and gave an appearance of activity in return for the large sums of money with which the managers of the affair were subsidised by credulous English fanatics.

Let me here observe, that, great as has been the evil resulting from religious bigotry, yet the presence of two rival creeds within the land has not been totally without its good. I have heretofore spoken of the Protestant Church with reference exclusively to its temporal Establishment.

I now speak of it as a religious system, and, as such, it has derived some moral advantage from the presence of antagonist Catholicity. The advantage has been mutual. Two rival Churches will watch and purify each other. Not that this is any justification of religious differences; not that

K

such differences are necessary to preserve religion pure; but simply that where they happen to exist, God can educe good from the evil of disunion.

Contrast the morals of the Protestants of the present day with those of their fathers in the heyday of the penal laws, when Catholics were too insignificant to be their rivals—when Protestantism had everything its own way. Then were the golden days of duelling, of drunkenness, of profligate clubs in the metropolis—the Cherokee, the Hellfire, the Pinkers and Sweaters, whose orgies are still preserved in the local traditions of Dublin. Then were the days of gallant, jovial, hard-drinking parsons—men who were paid by the State for talking every Sunday about religion, and who, accordingly, pronounced some cold and formal sentences to small congregations, who, on their part, conceived that they performed a meritorious duty in listening with grave faces to the solemn homilies. Catholicity, however, uprose in renovated strength, shook off its penal bandages, and assumed the attitude of spiritual rivalry. The State Church was alarmed. If the Protestant clergy and their flocks became more bigoted, they certainly became more virtuous. The majority of the parsons of our day are moral and pious. Apart from the drawbacks of anti-Irish prejudice and anti-Catholic slander (in which latter not one-twentieth part of them actively participate) they are in general personally virtuous and exemplary.

Would to God that Irishmen of all creeds could recognise and rejoice in each other's good qualities; that they could turn the rivalship of antagonist creeds to its legitimate account—the promotion of religion and morality; discard all unchristian acerbity, and unite with cordial, mutual trustfulness in the national cause!

CHAPTER XIII.

THE REPEAL CAMPAIGN OF 1832.

'Tis only to gather
Our strength and be ready,
The son with the father,
The wild with the steady.
In front of the danger,
To tramp all together;
Defying the stranger
In hall or in heather. J. DE JEAN.

THE continued existence of the Union for thirty years had a powerful effect in benumbing nationality among those whose religious teachers had inspired them with a suspicion of their countrymen. They had become accustomed to be legislated for by England, and use had rendered them insensible to the degradation which had aroused in 1800 the Irish spirit of the very Orangemen. The Union had debased and degraded many of the generation who had grown up since its enactment. They sneered at the Repealers as visionaries, and—prejudging the whole matter in dispute—they flippantly asserted that there was nothing Ireland could gain from native legislation that she could not also obtain from the Imperial Parliament.

The Reform agitation of 1831 necessarily excited the English mind to a pitch of intensity. The Irish were busy with their own agitation; and when Reform had been carried, and some enlargement of the constituencies temporarily effected, the Repealers mustered their strength to send members to St. Stephen's who should represent their principles.

Many Irish agitators, with the prospect of Parliamentary distinction, were speedily in the field. Ere the senatorial vision had crossed their aspiring thoughts, some three or four had acquired more than ordinary notoriety by their agitation. Of these, one of the most conspicuous was Feargus O'Connor. Feargus was fourth son of Roger O'Connor, who, in 1798, resided at Connorville, near Dunmanway, in the County of Cork. Roger O'Connor was involved in the rebellion of which his brother Arthur was one of the principal leaders. Arthur wished, at the later period of his agitation, to make Ireland a republic on the French model of 1792. He was a thoroughly honest politician. Of his disinterestedness there is conclusive proof in the fact that he deliberately forfeited the splendid inheritance of his maternal uncle, Lord Longueville, who was childless, and who would have made him his heir on condition of his adopting his lordship's politics. Roger's views were monarchical; I believe he intended to exercise the sovereign authority himself.

Roger employed his military skill in fortifying Connorville to sustain an attack from the King's troops. He planned a trap for them also, of which I had a detailed description from a gentleman who was personally cognisant of the device.

There were two fronts to Connorville House. From the front that faced the public road the hall-door steps were removed, and the windows of the basement storey on that side of the house were strongly built up No hostile entry could have been effected upon that front. The other front opened on a large courtyard, nearly surrounded with high buildings. From the eastern side of this courtyard ran a broad, straight avenue, some hundreds of yards in length, between two very lofty walls, overgrown with ivy of extraordinary luxuriance. At the extremity of this avenue, farthest from the house, was a high and massive iron gate. The whole length of the avenue was commanded by cannon, which were placed in a shed in the courtyard, and managed by French artillerymen. The massive gate at the eastern end of the avenue was left constantly open, to invite the entrance of his Majesty's troops in the event of a hostile descent upon Connorville. There were men always stationed *perdu* in the huge ivy bushes at the top of the piers, to lock the gate the instant the military forces should have passed through. The soldiers would thus be caught in a complete trap; hemmed in by the lofty walls that flanked the avenue, their retreat cut off by the iron gate behind them, and their position fully raked in front by the cannon in the courtyard.* The scheme seemed feasible enough, but it never was realised. The soldiers came to Connorville; they entered the avenue and courtyard; but whether the artillerymen had deserted their post, or whether Roger had not completed his intended preparations, certain it is that the redcoats scoured the premises without molestation, and Roger surveyed them from the friendly shade of a hollytree in which he was ensconced, on a rocky eminence that overlooked the courtyard from the north. He escaped on that occasion; his capture did not occur for some months after. His subsequent imprisonment at Fort George in Scotland is well known. I possess, in his manuscript, a poetical "Invocation to Sleep," which he composed during his incarceration. It is manifestly an unfinished production; a few lines may serve as a sample of its merits:

> Far from my native land, far from my wife
> And all my little babes, on Moray Firth

---

* This account of Roger O'Connor's preparations was given me by my father. A lady, who professed to recollect Connorville at that period, had, I am told, asserted that the preparations were not actually made. It is, therefore, proper to say that my father may possibly have described to me a plan which Roger only devised, but did not bring to the point of preparation; but my impression of the communication I received is such as I have given it in the text.

> Incag'd and barr'd with double bolts I drag
> My weary days and lengthened nights of pain.
> On Sleep, that dull and partial god, I call
> In vain! Unheard or slighted are my plaints.
> The constant tramp of feet, and watchful cry
> Of "Who comes there?" the sentry's hollow cough
> Contracted from the midnight cold and damp,
> Assail my ear, still conscious of the sound;
> The bell's loud voice, which speaks Old Time's decay,
> Is so familiar grown, I still conceit
> That I can tell his numbers by his note.
> O! for a cup of Lethe's pool to steep
> My weary senses in forgetfulness.

When Roger was released from Fort George, he was permitted to reside in England, but not for some time to return to Ireland. When at last this restriction was withdrawn, he returned to Ireland, and purchased the magnificent mansion and domain of Dangan Castle, in the County Meath, the family seat of the Wellesleys. Dangan was long supposed to have been the birthplace of the Duke of Wellington; but the minute researches of Sir Bernard Burke have conclusively established that his Grace was born in Mornington House, No. 24, Upper Merrion Street, Dublin, which mansion is at present occupied by the Commissioners of Church Temporalities and the Commissioners of the Land Court. The purchase money of Dangan was to remain for some time in Roger O'Connor's hands, bearing interest.

The following brief notice of Dangan occurs in Arthur Young's "Tour in Ireland," under date 28th of June, 1776: "Went in the evening to Lord Mornington's at Dangan, who is making many improvements which he showed me. His plantations are extensive, and he has formed a large water having five or six islands much varied; and promontories of high land shoot so far into it as to form almost distant lakes; the effect pleasing. There are above 100 acres under water, and his lordship has planned a considerable addition to it."

The extensive plantations had grown up into lofty woods before Roger became their proprietor. His declared object in becoming the occupant of Dangan was, that he might possess a house fit for the reception of Bonaparte, as he professed a firm faith in the advent of the Emperor to Ireland. Wellington, however, was less hospitable, and effectually prevented the visit of Napoleon to his hereditary residence.

Feargus was born at Connorville in 1796. He resided a good deal with his father at Dangan until that mansion was consumed by a fire said to have been accidental. He had, however, been sent to two or three schools, at which he distinguished himself by a number of irregular pranks. At a school in Portarlington he fell desperately in love with the schoolmaster's fascinating daughter, and received a severe paternal admonition on the impropriety of sullying the glory of his illustrious lineage by such a *mésalliance*. He ran off from his family to England, and amused himself haymaking one summer in Wiltshire. His father was eccentric and imaginative. Feargus early acquired a taste for an adventurous life, and politics naturally had a place in his ruminations. In 1822 he resided, with other members of his family, at Fortrobert, a spacious house—now a roofless ruin—on a hill adjoining the domain of Connorville. There he lived a jolly life, enjoying the society afforded by the neighbourhood, to which his entertaining conversation rendered him a welcome acquisition; playing whist, riding to foxhounds, outrivalling all his competitors in desperate horsemanship; and giving occasional indications of the spirit within him by attacks on prominent local abuses. He published a pamphlet fiercely denouncing the oppressors of the peasantry—parsons, tithe-proctors, grinding middlemen, jobbing grand-jurors—with especial censure of all magistrates trafficking in justice.

As yet Feargus had not tried his rhetorical powers in public. But the exciting political transactions of 1831 and 1832 necessarily called forth so active and ardent a spirit. He first appeared at a Whig meeting held in Cork in December, 1831, for the purpose of forwarding Reform of Parliament. Messrs. Jephson, of Mallow ; Nicholas Philpot Leader, then member for Kilkenny; Delacour, a banker ; Stawell, of Kilbrittain ; Baldwin, of Cork ; with some youthful scions of the Shannon and Kingston families, and several other Whig notables of the county, were mustered in the old Court-house on the Grand Parade at an early hour. They all rehearsed the usual commonplaces of Reform ; talked in a tone of aristocratic condescension of the claims of the democracy ; announced that in order to establish a right to full citizenship it was not requisite that men should exhibit rent-rolls and pedigrees ; with a great many equally respectable political truisms. Up to four o'clock the most amusing speaker was Leader, the member for Kilkenny. He was a stout, thick-set man, with a wild, ferocious eye ; he shouted and bellowed, gesticulated like a harlequin, slapped his thighs, spun nearly round on tiptoe, emphasised remarkable hits by bobbing down his head within a couple of feet of the floor, roared, stamped, ranted, blustered, and perforce of a thundering expenditure of personal energy, elicited vociferous applause.

Late in the day Feargus came forward to the front of one of the galleries; distanced all the Whigs and Reformers by exclaiming that Repeal alone could save Ireland from ruin; and certainly so far as concerned the external matters of voice, action, and delivery, he made beyond comparison the best speech of the day.

Feargus now set himself to work in earnest to attain political leadership. He had not yet contemplated an attack on the representation of the county, for he had not yet seen to what extent the Reform Bill would popularise the constituency; but he dearly loved the greeting cheers of the multitude; he revelled in the consciousness of possessing unusual volubility; and he had a strong conviction that his popular talents would soon exalt him into a position of political command.

In the summer of 1832 the anti-tithe agitation extended all over the County of Cork. Feargus was ubiquitous; Macroom, Dunmanway, Enniskean, and several other places, were visited in rapid succession. "Fargus," as the country folk familiarly called him, soon ingratiated himself into every one's favour; and by the frankness and ease of his address, and his great colloquial powers, disarmed the suspicious enmity of many in the middle ranks who had previously anathematised both himself and his cause.

He soon received the distinction of two or three public entertainments. At Macroom he got a dinner from about three hundred farmers and shopkeepers, at which he, for the first time, publicly announced himself a candidate for the representation. He declared, in accents of affecting pathos, that his advocacy of the people's rights had deprived him of the affections of his nearest relatives.

"Since I last," said he, "met my friends of Macroom, there has been no smile on my cheek, no comfort in my breast. My nearest relations have turned from me; it is true they recognise me privately, but in public they have wounded my feelings. I leave them to that awful moment when the sacred Monitor shall arouse them to reflection—when he shall tap here" (pointing to his breast), "and cry, Awake! be judged."

It behoved the people on whose behalf the sufferings in question were incurred, to apply the salve to the patriotic victim. It especially behoved the tradesmen of Macroom to indemnify him for his sorrows, inasmuch as he claimed the honour of membership with their fraternity in virtue of his having taken part in a meeting held in the large square in that town in the month of June previously.

The electors in the popular interest had been urged by the Catholic clergy to register their votes, and the shrewd ones began with confidence to augur a very large Liberal majority at the next general election. At the Macroom dinner, as we learn from the Cork *Southern Reporter* of that date, " the subject of the representation was freely discussed. Mr. O'Connor announced his intention of becoming a candidate for the County of Cork at the approaching election. He was received with great enthusiasm, and all present confirmed his pretensions by the highest eulogy of his claims and character. A general pledge was made by the company of their support and influence. At the suggestion of the chairman, a resolution was entered into for the formation of an Independent Club to organise the representative franchise in the county, the better to secure the return of Mr. O'Connor in conjunction with any other popular candidate who should present himself. The conditions laid down for the future candidates were a full support of the Repeal of the Union, total abolition of tithes, vote by ballot, and universal suffrage."

It was late at night when Feargus rose to announce his resolution to become a candidate for the county. The candles had nearly burned down to their sockets, and threw a dim and doubtful gleam upon the large apartment. A very prosy, windy speaker had occupied a great deal of time in delivering a speech which I cannot better describe than by saying that in matter and structure it resembled an interminable leading article in a tenth-rate country newspaper. Listeners got tired—Feargus was especially impatient; yet the orator not only prosed on, but seemed to regard his newly-found capacity for public speaking as a subject of particular congratulation. "This," he exclaimed, " is the first time that I ever made a speech, and I never thought I could have talked so long without stopping—it appears to me that I'm inspired ;" and he continued to give the audience the benefit of his inspiration, either until he had exhausted the afflatus, or until the chairman checked him on the plea that the hour was now far advanced. The crowd had drawn close to the small daïs, or platform, on which were assembled the chairman, the guest, and two or three other country gentlemen. There was great exultation at the prospect of seeing the popular favourite returned to Parliament. When Feargus announced that he would stand for the county, a rapturous "hurrah!" testified the general delight. The candidate resumed his seat, much pleased with the sympathy of his friends, when a movement was discerned among the throng, as of some stalwart fellow elbowing his way to the front. Feargus rose, and recognised the person who was forcing himself forward; he was a broad-shouldered, red-haired, athletic Protestant farmer, named Whiting, who bore a strong personal resemblance to the burly candidate himself.

"Make room for Mr. Whiting," said Feargus in his blandest accents. Room was immediately made for his passage. "How are you, my worthy friend?" continued Feargus, courteously shaking hands with Whiting. "Would you wish to get on the platform? We've plenty of room for you."

Whiting accepted the invitation and was given a chair, on which he seated himself. He gazed for some moments at Feargus in mute ecstasy, and then broke forth: "O, Fargus, Fargus! is it not the murdher of the world to see you looking after the representation of a county in their English Parliament, instead of enjoying (as by right you ought) the royal crown of Ireland upon that honest red head, as was worn by your ancesthors in the ancient times of ould!"

Feargus, however, limited his ambition to a seat for the county, despite this stimulating burst of post-prandial enthusiasm. He smiled assuasively in return for Mr. Whiting's complimentary allusion to his ancestral honours. The scene was amusing, and its effect was heightened by the personal resemblance of the sturdy yeoman and the patriotic orator, who exchanged the most affectionate glances with each other.

Feargus lashed all jobbers, particularly jobbing magistrates who made a profitable trade of their justice-ship; "they ate justice, drank justice, lay upon justice, rode justice, wore justice—ay, threadbare!"

He complimented the tradesmen of Macroom by whom he was surrounded: "Tradesmen we are all, in fact, from the monarch who fills the throne, and whose trade is that of cabinet-making, to the humble chimney-sweeper who loudly proclaims his calling from the house-tops. I am a tradesman of Macroom. I was bound apprentice in the great square on the 10th of June last" (alluding to the anti-tithe meeting held on that day); "and on my show-board shall be Peace, Industry, Union, and Freedom."

At the Enniskean anti-tithe meeting Feargus gallantly defied the Duke of Wellington. "I did hear that a military force was to have attended. If I saw that force under the command of the great Captain of the age, I would tell him he was in his dotage, and that the power of knowledge was greater than the power of cannon."

He defended himself from calumnious imputations: "Here I stand in the midst of thousands and tens of thousands to whom I have been known from my birth, and I fearlessly ask them if the breath of slander has ever dared to assail my character?" ("No, no!" and cheers.) "Have I ever oppressed the meanest individual among you?" ("No, no! hurrah!") "Have I not ever been your adviser and director?" ("Yes, yes! hurroo!")

He announced the religious object of his agitation at a dinner given him in Enniskean: "My object is to purify the religion I profess by lopping off its rotten and redundant temporalities"; and he fiercely inquired "whether the religion of the Almighty was to be set in blood?" alluding to the fatal tithe affrays.

At a dinner given in Cork to the late Bishop England, Feargus concluded a vehement speech in these words: "No! though our sea-bound dungeon were encompassed by the wooden walls of Old England—though the 300,000 promised Cossacks marched through the land with all the emblems of death, the rack, the scaffold, and the axe, yet I would suffer martyrdom ere I would throw up my hat and cry 'All hail' to him* who dragged my country's Liberator through the streets of the metropolis to answer a charge made crime by proclamation. No! though stretched upon the rack I would smile terror out of countenance, and die as I have lived—a pure lover of liberty!"

The critic in his closet who laughs at this fantastic bombast, will scarcely believe that when volubly thrown off, *rotundo ore*, and recommended by graceful and emphatic action, and an air of intense earnestness, it not only could

---

* The Marquis of Anglesea.

pass for "fine speaking," but produce to some extent, upon a sympathetic audience, the effect of genuine eloquence. It seems to have found an admirer in the reporter for the *Cork Mercantile Chronicle*, whose comment ran thus: "This splendid effusion of masculine eloquence created a most extraordinary sensation, coming, as it did, like a thunderclap on all. The talented speaker was long and loudly cheered on resuming his seat; and we will augur that it will be long before he is forgotten by the people of this city."

Feargus had now established his fame through the county as "a fine speaker." In the city of Cork he was generally called "the Rattler." Those who have not heard him in public in his best days, and who have only judged of his abilities by his printed effusions, have frequently done great injustice to his powers. He was remarkably ready and self-possessed. He was capable of producing extraordinary popular effect. He had very great declamatory talent. He had also great defects. As a stimulating orator in a popular assembly he was unexcelled. It is true he dealt largely in bombast, broken metaphor, and inflated language; but while you listened, those blemishes were lost in the infectious vehemence of his spirited manner; you were charmed with the melodious voice, the musical cadences, the astonishing volubility, the imposing self-confidence of the man, and the gallant air of bold defiance with which he assailed all oppression and tyranny. The difference between his spoken and printed harangues was surprisingly great.

He mingled the exciting qualities I have enumerated with a very small amount of argumentative power. He blended the facility of at first acquiring popular influence with a sad incapacity to retain it. He displayed an exhaustless fund of vituperative vigour in lashing all the parties disliked by the people; but he was sometimes betrayed, by want of reflection, into receiving and announcing as truths the most incredible exaggerations. For instance, he proclaimed to a numerous meeting in Bandon that certain portions of the parish of Timoleague paid tithe at the rate of £90 per acre; and that the fact of that extravagant tithe-charge had been confirmed upon oath before two magistrates.

During the agitating summer and autumn of 1832, scenes of a highly exciting and picturesque character were constantly exhibited. The meetings for Repeal and No

Tithes were usually held on Sundays after mass. It was impossible to see without interest the rustic worshippers wending along the glen and down the hill-side, sauntering through "the lone vale of green bracken" beneath the brilliant morning sunshine; crowding to the Catholic church at the call of the bell; stragglers from the outskirts of the parish endeavouring to recover lost time by short cuts and increased speed, as they sprang with agility over the ditches. Then there was the muster of the hardy peasants in the churchyard; the more thoughtless occupying the interval before mass in inquiring the news of the day; the more devout kneeling apart before the altar rails, or under the rude pictures called the Stations of the Cross; or in some shaded spot without the sacred edifice, where, unmolested, they might recite a litany or a rosary beneath the shadow of an old hawthorn. Then came the last quick toll of the bell, announcing that divine service was just going to commence; then the hurried gathering into the church of a crowd that often overflowed its precincts; the Mass; the homely discourse in Irish; and after the "Ite, missa est," an announcement of the meeting of the day.

The meeting frequently comprised the inhabitants of many parishes. The dark multitudes streamed from the hills to one common centre—many on horseback, but the greater number on foot. There was a proud thrill in every man's breast; all felt the ennobling consciousness that a nation was peacefully mustering and banding together to assert and recover their rights. The Irish peasantry are not mere clodpoles. Many of them are imaginative and intellectual. They love their native land, and they are proud of it. They are susceptible of every external influence that can heighten the sentiment of patriotism; and as the multitudes traversed the grand scenery of the parishes on the sea-coast, doubtless many a foot was arrested on the heights which commanded a view of the bold mountain peaks, the magnificent expanse of ocean, the steep cliffs, and the rich green glens often winding from the shore among the hills; and many a heart felt to its centre that the freedom of such a glorious land was worth any struggle men could make—any peril men could encounter.

The meeting usually mustered in full strength at the appointed place about three o'clock in the afternoon. The chairman was often a Protestant, whose hatred of tithes was not less intense than that felt by the Catholic concourse around him. I only knew of one Protestant gentleman who was said to occupy his post with reluctance. He was a landlord of some hundreds a year. He was deemed a prize by his anti-tithist neighbours, who made many attempts to secure him for their chairman, which he always coquettishly evaded, until it was delicately hinted that in the event of his persisting in refusal, the requisitionists would develop to the Board of Customs certain smuggling transactions in which he had been engaged. The hint was sufficient. Mr. —— consented to preside, and he delivered a philippic against the Church temporalities, of which the pungent bitterness amply redeemed his previous apathy.

Feargus was quite in his element at all these public meetings. The first of them which he attended was, I think, a very large gathering held near Dunmanway on the 29th of June, 1832, at which my brother, Thomas Wilson Daunt, presided. Feargus delivered himself with a voluble energy which called down tumultuous cheers, and found so much favour with some of his hearers that they declared he was "finer than O'Connell." He hated the Union with cordial bitterness; he hated the tithes with equal intensity; and he had stories of ecclesiastical mismanagement at his fingers' ends much better authenticated than the legend of the £90 per acre. He spoke of the parish in which his own residence, Fortrobert, was situated; told how the rector, Mr. Hamilton, had never set his foot within the parish for thirty-five years; exposed the vestry that had enlarged the clerk's salary because the clerk went to live at a distance from the parish, and required additional payment to remunerate him for the additional road to be travelled on Sundays to his church; and finally the orator denounced the jolly sexton who kept a house of ill-fame near the church gate.

Mr. Hamilton, the rector, resided in a remote part of the kingdom, and never visited the parish. I know nothing of his personal character or of his professional accomplishments, and am therefore unable to say whether his small Protestant flock were losers by his absence. Non-residence has often been stigmatised as a grievance. Certainly it withdraws the expenditure of the incumbent's income from the parish. But there have been, and perhaps still are, cases in which the incumbent, when inflamed with anti-Catholic bigotry, is so great a public nuisance, that his absence would be a blessing; and it would, in such cases, be often worth the

Catholics' while to subscribe some increase to his revenue on condition of his living elsewhere.

The people were enchanted with Feargus's scathing exposures of clerical, magisterial, and legislative iniquity; and "Fargus" was unanimously pronounced to be "a devil of a fellow." His manners were excessively conciliating; in private they were courteous and refined; in public they were hearty, rattling, and impulsive. He had frolicsome touches of mimicry, nickname, and claptrap; he now and then let off a telling pun. His courteous demeanour alternated with a certain indescribable swagger, which, however, was not in the least degree offensive, and merely indicated the excellent opinion which he entertained of himself, without disparagement to any one else. He was a capital *raconteur*. His talents as a mimic were considerable. His was not that mere parrot mimicry that imitates sounds only; he was a mimic of sentiment and feeling; he could take up the whole train of thought as well as the voice, and present you with an exquisitely ludicrous resemblance of mental as well as vocal characteristics. He also excelled in repartee. He had strong satirical powers, a formidable readiness in retort, and could pounce with merciless sarcasm on the weak or ludicrous points of an antagonist; so that, whenever any incivility was attempted at his expense, he retaliated with a pungency that made his opponent repent the rash assault. But Feargus, when not attacked, was remarkable for suavity and excellent temper.

He was fond of puns, and sometimes made them tell. At a meeting which he attended, after having been for some time absent from the country, it chanced that there stood at his right hand a patriotic paper-maker named Kidney. Feargus assured his audience that his absence from home had not altered his politics. "Here I am," cried he, "unchanged —the same pure lover of liberty you have ever known me, with the same honest heart, and the same stout *Kidney* too!" patting his worthy and stalwart neighbour on the shoulder amidst shouts of laughter.

Feargus's strongest point was his great physical energy. He was indefatigable in his agitation. In all the quarters of the compass, wherever a popular muster of sufficient magnitude was announced, there was usually to be seen the popular agitator with the brawny muscular figure, the big round shoulders, the red curly tresses overhanging the collar of his coat, the cajoling smirk, the insinuating manners, and the fluent tongue. His taste in eloquence was not rigorous; his language might, to borrow a Homeric phrase, be termed "poluphloisboios." He was fond of sounding and redundant sentences. He often declared, for example, that the people were "wrecked by disunion, torn by discord, revolutionised by faction." This description of talk rolled off his tongue in continuous torrents.

He considered it politic to assume towards the Catholic clergy an air of profound and affectionate reverence. He boasted that he had a larger number of clerical acquaintances than any other layman in Ireland. He talked of convening an assembly of the Catholic clergy of the County Cork, at which he was to preside. Feargus's *concio ad clerum* would have been a curious deliverance.

The Whig and Tory squirearchy laughed to derision his prospects of success. They sneered at the rustic meetings, the public dinners got up among the village shopkeepers and farmers. "He had a genteel day of it!" writes one of them, who was scandalised at the overwhelming preponderance of the frieze coats at a public entertainment given to Feargus. Meanwhile Feargus persevered with continually increasing activity. Some of the advertisements of his movements were headed with the appropriate words in huge types, "Up and doing!"

Whatever were the merits or defects of his public speaking, his manner and delivery were those of a gentleman. A clever writer remarks that in the earlier period of his agitation he addressed the people more in the style of a chieftain encouraging his gallant clansmen than of a commonplace agitator talking down to the level of an unenlightened auditory. The people appreciated his aristocratic demeanour, for the Irish democracy—(and this is a trait in the national character well worth the attention of politicians)—are eminently aristocratic in their prepossessions. They love ancient lineage; they can quickly discern, and they ardently relish the demeanour that should mark the far-descended gentleman. Those who in O'Connell's time, and still later in the time of Isaac Butt, feared that the Repeal of the Union would result in democratic anarchy, evinced by that fear their ignorance of the feelings, dispositions, and prejudices which then characterised the Irish nation. Writing of them many years ago, I said that there was not in the Empire a people more desirous to give practical efficacy to the theory of the British Constitution; to carry into practice the theoretic equipoise of Crown, Lords, and Commons. Loving the liberty of Ireland as their dearest earthly birthright, they rejoiced when they were led in pursuit of it by men of high station and old lineage. Loyal to the Crown (but not to the Legislative Union), they honoured the coronet—those Irish worshippers of freedom. They merely desired to convert the aristocracy from oppressors into protectors.

But the aristocracy were hard to convert. At that time the State Church existed, offering a bribe of £700,000 per annum to the scions of the Protestant nobility and gentry to support the Legislative Union. There were large parochial incomes; great prizes in the wheel; bishoprics, archbishoprics, deaneries. The preservation of the State Church was especially provided for in the Act that destroyed the Irish Parliament. Then there was the spectre of Catholic ascendency; a spectre as unreal as Pepper's Ghost; yet held forth from pulpits and platforms to scare the Irish Protestants from nationality. There was also the elaborate ignorance of the facts of Irish history—ignorance in which the Irish Protestants were generally trained, by narratives that represented England as being always in the right, and Ireland always in the wrong.

Their attitude to their own country was hostile, and few of their number supported O'Connell in his noble efforts to recover the priceless possession of Home Legislation.

CHAPTER XIV.

ELECTIONEERING AGITATION IN 1832.

My inmost heart is in your cause. I pray
God speed your quarrel. Yet my hands are bound;
There is a golden fetter that restrains
The energies that should of right be yours.

ANON.

REPEAL was now a topic of universal interest. The Rev. Charles Boyton, a Fellow of Trinity College, made several speeches at the Dublin Conservative Society, strongly impregnated with Irish nationality. In one of those speeches he ably dissected and exposed the fallacies which even then Mr. Spring Rice had begun to put forth, about the incalculable benefits produced to Ireland by the Union. Mr. Rice had been triumphant in the English House of Commons—that is to say, he had the votes, the majorities, the cheers, which in general await in that assembly the exploits of an Irishman who does the dirty work of England. It was easy to prove to the perfect satisfaction of an English audience that the subjugation of Ireland to England was an overflowing source of prosperity to the former country. His miles of figures, his tables of statistics, his carefully-contrived arithmetical legerdemain, made an imposing show in an assembly whose members cared nothing for the merits of the case, and cared everything for their own grasp on Irish resources.

But Mr. Rice's statistical jugglery did not prove so convincing to the Irish people. He did not find it so easy to persuade them that their starving population were comfortably fed; that their unemployed half-naked tradesmen were warmly clothed; that the manufactories crumbling into ruins in many parts of the country were hives of happy thriving industry; that the 14,000 silk-weavers just then stalking unemployed through Dublin were models of prosperity and comfort; that the crowded metropolitan mendicity demonstrated the brisk state of trade; that the insolvency of one-fourth of the number of houses in Dublin indicated the increasing opulence of the metropolis; that the Dublin people were greatly enriched by the removal to London of all the public Boards; and that the drain of four millions of absentee rents out of Ireland, and the further drain of Irish public revenue, were a source of remunerative employment and national wealth to the Irish people.

All these brilliant paradoxes might easily be received as gospel-truths by a body of Englishmen interested only in keeping down Ireland, and wringing all the profit they could out of her poverty; but the suffering people themselves felt the poignant addition of insult to injury when they saw the great cause of their sorrows held forth to the world as the fountain of blessings to their country.

Boyton, despite his Conservatism, felt as an aggrieved Irishman would naturally feel, and in a speech which displayed full knowledge of the subject, he refuted with contemptuous sarcasm the fallacies of Mr. Rice. Boyton's mind and body were alike of athletic powers and proportions. He had the reputation of being an able pugilist, and, no doubt, in his reasoning there was many a knock-down blow. The man was in spirit, feeling, and conviction an Irish Nationalist, but he was bound up in the golden fetters of the State Church; his national vigour was therefore necessarily paralysed.

A gentleman on terms of intimacy with the leading members of the Repeal movement made (I believe at the instance of Mr. O'Connell) private overtures to Boyton for a junction between his party and the Repealers. Boyton's reply was in substance, and nearly in terms, as follows: "I would gladly acquiesce in your proposal if I thought there was the slightest probability of its being effectual. But, were I publicly to unite myself with the Repealers, I should only separate myself from my own party; I could not possibly carry them along with me. Sir, they hate you —their enmity is bitter, and cannot be mitigated. I trust I need not say that I do not participate in it; but I know that any overture of mine to unite them with the O'Connellites would be perfectly fruitless, from the personal hatred they bear to your leader, and their bigoted horror of the great body of his followers."

The negotiation, of course, fell to the ground; but Boyton now and then made excellent speeches savouring strongly of Repeal. One of his best was on the celebrated interview which took place in Cork between the Viceroy* and Dr. Baldwin, a highly respected advocate of national self-government. The Doctor beat the Viceroy hollow in the controversy; and the Viceroy threatened to blockade the Irish ports with four English gun-brigs, and to effect a total suspension of intercourse between England and Ireland.

"A total suspension of intercourse!" exclaimed the Rev. Charles Boyton; "and, supposing the intercourse was suspended, which of the parties would be the worse for it? England, whose exports are articles which derive their value from the great manufacturing skill exerted on materials of small intrinsic worth, or Ireland, whose exports chiefly consist of articles of food—the staff of human life? If the gallant Viceroy could suspend the intercourse between the countries and prevent our exporting Irish beef, butter, and corn to England, why, I really think that in so awful an extremity we could manage to eat those commodities ourselves. Whereas, it would task the powers of even John Bull to masticate and digest a Sheffield whittle, a Worcester tea-cup, or a Kidderminster carpet."

Meanwhile, Feargus undertook to enlighten the Viceroy upon Irish affairs in "A Letter from Feargus O'Connor, Esq., Barrister-at-Law, to His Excellency the Marquis of Anglesea."

---

* The Marquis of Anglesea.

Feargus had been threatened with a prosecution for his political misdeeds; and in the indictment were included James Ludlow Stawell, of Kilbrittain,* Francis Bernard M'Carthy, of Laurel Hill, with some others who had made themselves conspicuous by agitation. The principal subject of Feargus's Letter to Lord Anglesea was Feargus himself. He apprised the Viceroy that he (Feargus) was a barrister—a member of one of the most respectable families in the kingdom; that he possessed an unencumbered property beyond his wants; that when Lord Anglesea had been mobbed some time previously in Dublin, he (Feargus) followed him into Parliament Street and raised his arm in His Excellency's defence.

He also boasted of an exploit he had performed in 1822; the incident exemplifies the necessity of caution in accepting the assertions of habitual accusers of the Irish people.

"The parsons," said Feargus, "were then with the people, proclaiming that tithes had nothing to do with the disturbance, and that the cause was to be found in exorbitant rents. I convened a meeting of the neighbouring parishes in the Roman Catholic Chapel of Enniskean, at which nine or ten Protestant clergymen attended; they were principally rectors. They all spoke of the perfect tranquillity their respective parishes enjoyed, and unanimously signed the resolutions which strongly expressed that tranquillity, under the belief that they would not go farther. I, however, had a duty to perform. I published them in two of our provincial journals; and what will be your lordship's astonishment when I tell you that this publication was deemed by the clergy who attended the meeting a crime for which my head would scarcely have atoned! Because the declarations made by some of those reverend gentlemen

---

* I cannot cursorily mention James Ludlow Stawell without a passing tribute to his memory. He was a sincere Protestant; he was also a warm-hearted and enlightened Irishman. Descended from an ancient house, and possessed of an ample estate, he felt that he owed an account of his stewardship to the Providence who had bestowed on him the gifts of high birth and large fortune. He honestly and zealously laboured to render those advantages auxiliary to the freedom of his countrymen. He threw himself into their struggle; they revered and loved him. His useful and honourable career was cut short by sudden death. A feverish cold, of which the inflammatory symptoms were increased by the patient's anxiety about the prosecution, terminated fatally on the third or fourth day. He was deeply regretted by all parties. "Requiescat in pace."

at the meeting were diametrically opposite to those made by the same persons with respect to the state of their parishes but a day or two previously."

Feargus demanded from Lord Anglesea the publication of the informations on which he and his confederates had been charged as conspirators and dangerous persons.

The prosecution was abandoned by the Government. Stawell died after a few days' illness; and as his death was generally believed to have been accelerated by the harassing annoyance of the threatened proceedings, it is not improbable that the Government regarded it as a sufficient expiation of the political sins of the whole batch of offenders. But the fact of having been indicted was an additional feather in Feargus's cap. His having incurred the peril of martyrdom increased his popularity.

The summer and autumn passed away. The registries had been well worked, and in the month of December the general election took place. The second popular candidate for the County Cork was Mr. Garrett Standish Barry, of Lemlara, a Catholic gentleman of private worth, but not adapted for public business. He was brought in for the county under Feargus's wing, being, in truth, indebted for his success to the stirring agitation got up by his active and adventurous colleague.

The electors from the rural districts now poured into the city. Parties of the frieze coats, each detachment headed by the parish priest, came in for four successive days, the voters from the more remote parts of the county having generally travelled all night. I accompanied one of the nocturnal parties from the district around Dunmanway.

The night was cold, and the pace was slow. I occupied a seat in a gig belonging to the parish priest, who had called at my house after midnight. Our slow progress was rendered still slower by delays at various points, where accessions of voters from other districts were expected to swell our cavalcade from bohereens and by-roads. My reverend companion seemed insensible to the discomforts of a journey performed at a snail's pace under the darkness of a chill winter's night. His mind was engrossed by the coming struggle, and elated by the prospect of a triumph. On the first day of the election the rival candidates met upon the hustings. Lord Bernard (son of the Earl of Bandon) and the Hon. Robert Boyle (son of the Earl of Shannon) appeared on the Conservative side. The Hon. Robert King (afterwards

Earl of Kingston) was a candidate in the Whig interest. Lord Bernard read a short speech from a paper which lay in the bottom of his hat, all about keeping up the tithes and the Union. Feargus made the audience laugh by remarking that if the noble lord had not spoken from his head, he had at any rate spoken from his hat. I do not recollect that Mr. Boyle made a speech. He had published an address to the electors in which he promised nothing—a promise which there was no doubt of his ability to redeem. Mr. King said that if returned he would vote for the discussion of Repeal. Garrett Standish Barry said that if the reformed Parliament in its first session should not give (what he called) justice to Ireland, he would vote for Repeal. He professed unqualified hostility to the tithes. Feargus made an eloquent declamatory speech for full, unqualified, unconditional, immediate Repeal.

The election terminated on the fifth day in the return of Feargus and Mr. Barry. The announcement of the victory was answered by a hurricane of cheering in the Court-house, which was echoed by the multitude without. Out of the eight seats for the city, the county, and its boroughs, the Tories only obtained one, namely, Bandon, for which the Hon. William Bernard was returned. The Tories were infuriate at the success of their opponents. Speaking of Feargus's triumph, the well-known Hedges-Eyre of Macroom swore deep oaths as he paced the Conservative club-room, that the county was lost, disgraced, destroyed for ever.

Whatever may have been Feargus's subsequent career, we must do justice to his really gallant achievement of wresting the County Cork from the families who had monopolised the representation prior to 1832. The task required indefatigable energy, a thorough contempt of all difficulties, a facility of rousing the despondent and nearly torpid population with fiery harangues, an undaunted audacity, and a superlative self-confidence. All these qualities Feargus enjoyed in perfection, and without them he never could have displaced the former parliamentary families. The people were fascinated, too, by the marked and respectful deference with which the Protestant agitator invariably treated the Catholic priesthood, to whom he never omitted an occasion of paying a well-turned compliment. He bragged loudly and constantly of his own aboriginal extraction; adverted frequently to the losses his family had sustained in the people's cause ; and succeeded in producing a general conviction that the bold, dashing, voluble, swaggering champion of the people's rights was the *beau idéal* of a popular member of Parliament. Feargus's services were on that occasion very great. The truth is that no other man in Corkshire possessed the combination of qualities requisite to open the county at that period.

It is usual with the Tory, and often also with the Whig landlords, to accuse the Catholic clergy of unduly influencing the tenant-farmers in their exercise of the franchise. The charge is retorted. Of the multitude of tenants expelled from their holdings it is commonly believed that a large number have been punished by eviction for voting at elections against the will of their landlords, and that, previous to the enactment of the ballot, the tenure of many who still occupied their farms depended on their obedience to the landlord's political commands. The accusers of the priests assumed that if the tenant were uninfluenced by any party, and wholly left to his own free choice, he would by preference give his vote to the landlord's candidate. Those persons forget that the natural sympathies of the priest and of the Catholic tenant-farmer are the same, and consequently that when the priest exhorts the elector to support the advocate of tenant-right, or of Repeal, he only exhorts that elector to act upon his own principles, and to do that which his real inclinations would lead him to do. By investing the humble elector with a vote the Constitution plainly supposes him to have a political opinion. But those who assume that the landlord should be the master of that vote, suppose, on the contrary, that the humble elector has got no political opinion; or else that if he has one, he should sacrifice it to the dictation of another man. If this were the real spirit of the Constitution it would have saved, before the introduction of the ballot, much trouble and much misery if the landlord, instead of driving his tenants to the hustings under terror of his wrath, had been empowered by law to tender, in his own person, as many votes as he had tenants on the roll of electors. Such a personage might have presented himself at the hustings, saying : "I give you twenty votes, or forty" (as the case might be), " for Mr. So-and-so." The tenants could have remained at home while their landlord did the voting for them ; and they would have escaped the cruel alternative of being compelled to vote for some sturdy supporter of national wrongs, or of being exposed to the vengeance of, possibly, a spiteful and malignant tyrant.

It would be grievously unjust to the landlords of Ireland

to deny that there are amongst them many excellent men, who have always respected the electoral liberty of their tenants. But landlords of the opposite stamp were unhappily plentiful. The system of the ballot has sheltered the tenants in most cases from the dangers to which they were exposed under the system of open voting. The protection, however, is incomplete. Some landlords, knowing, or strongly suspecting, that their tenants would vote for a candidate distasteful to the ruling caste, have prohibited them from voting at all, under the ancient penalty of landlord displeasure.

Looking back at the former system, it is interesting to recall the contrast between the English and Irish constituencies, as described a good many years ago in the House of Commons by the late Earl of Derby. He said that in England the rural tenants followed the command of their landlords with implicit submission; that they inquired for my lord's man, or the squire's man, and voted as their masters directed. In the towns venality was the dominant influence. In Ireland, however, notwithstanding the terrible and frequent exercise of landlord power, it was not so easy to drive electors like swine to the market. There was, and is, a much greater spirit of constitutional independence among the Irish electors than among their English brethren. They have more frequently voted, in proportion to their numbers, in accordance with their political preferences. Year after year they had seen before their eyes the bitter penalty of being politically honest; they had seen the old homesteads of their neighbours levelled to the earth and the miserable inmates turned adrift; they had seen that the crime of which this was the punishment, was the honest discharge of a trust committed to them by the Constitution, and yet great numbers of them persevered.

There is in this gallant defiance of local tyranny something grand and high-souled. It stamps the brave peasants with the ineffaceable character of political integrity. They were willing martyrs for their country's freedom. Men who could thus perseveringly and readily incur the bitterest persecution for the sake of principle, stand infinitely higher in the moral and intellectual scale, and are infinitely more capable of the duties of self-government than a people who surrender the Constitutional trust of the franchise at the dictation of another's will, or for the sordid and dishonest consideration of pelf. Of course there have been in Ireland, as elsewhere, many instances of corrupt voting, some of which are recorded in this volume. But the Irish electors, taken as a whole, have displayed true nobleness of character, and at no time more conspicuously than in the general election of 1826, when the forty-shilling freeholders defied the utmost wrath of anti-Catholic landlords and agents, and gave their support to the candidates who were pledged to sustain O'Connell in his struggle for Catholic Emancipation. For this honest and spirited discharge of their electoral duty they were disfranchised by Sir Robert Peel. At the present time the prevalence of electoral corruption in England has compelled the Government to introduce a Bill (46th and 47th Victoria) "for the better prevention of corrupt and illegal practices at Parliamentary elections." Instances of scandalous traffic in the franchise were elicited by commissions appointed in 1880 to inquire into the extent of the evil. Commenting on these revelations, the London *Spectator* said : " It is not too much to say that they (the Commissioners) have revealed the existence of constituencies in which the mass of the electors were mere hirelings, and the man who gives an honest vote is a noteworthy person. Even when this extreme has not been reached, and the open transfer of votes for money is still avoided, the evidence shows that the more indirect forms of bribery are practised upon a truly heroic scale." *

"There is no sign whatever," says the *Times*, "that Sandwich and Gloucester and Canterbury are shocked in any way at the exposure of their own demerits. Men come forward with a smile and a smirk to tell the Commissioners that they have taken bribes from both parties, or that they have put their votes up for sale and have given them to the highest bidders, or have promised them and had the money for them, and have not given them. Their belief seems to be that the common laws of morality are suspended while an election is going on, and that proceedings for which in ordinary times a man would be sent to prison are quite honest at election times. It is in vain that the Commissioners attempt to set up another standard. It is much if they can succeed in putting a damper on each joke as it arises. The next barefaced disclosure of fraud or corruption is taken for as good a joke as ever, and is as certainly and as heartily laughed over."†

---

* Cited in the *Nation*, 23rd October, 1880.   † *Ibid.*

In its issue of the 23rd of October, 1880, the *Nation* quotes some items of the evidence :

"At Macclesfield 'voting is frankly treated as a matter of business.' Prices ranged from 3s. 6d. to 15s. a vote. Out of £2,000 distributed by a prominent manager on one side, only £100 is admitted to have been legally spent, while another manager, on the other side, took each voter who came to him into a dark pantry and there made the best bargain he could. 'Out of every six voters, certainly four, and probably five, voted as they were paid.'"

I have referred to the late Lord Derby's assertion that in England the rural electors generally followed their landlords to the hustings. Apart from bribery, and with reference solely to the landlord influence over electors in England, it must, however, be admitted that the English voters have not the same reason for opposing their landlords that the Irish voters too often have. Whatever be the political party of the English candidate, the elector may be certain at the present day that he is zealous for the honour and power of England. Whig, Tory, or Radical, he will equally desire to uphold the glory of the British Lion.

But in Ireland the Nationalist elector has been frequently called on to vote for a candidate zealous only for the servitude and subjugation of his country ; eager to revile and disparage her creed and her people ; flippant to announce (as Lord Wicklow did in the days of O'Connell's agitation) that there is not in Ireland the material for self-legislation. He is called on to vote for some person whose political convictions originate in the false, degrading, calumnious, self-stultifying principle that the land of Swift, and Grattan, and Malone, and Flood, and Hussey Burgh, and Burke, and Sheridan, and Bushe, and Foster, and Plunket, and O'Connell, and many other men whose names shed lustre upon human intellect, is inhabited by a race incapable of making laws to govern themselves. The soul of the Irish peasant instinctively spurns the impudent libel on his country. There cannot be a cordial community of feeling between the peasantry and the landlord class until the owners of the soil learn to regard their native land with sentiments of just respect ; until they learn to rejoice in Ireland's honour, to take pride in Ireland's fame, and to feel every insult to their country as an indignity inflicted on themselves.

CHAPTER XV.

NATIONAL COUNCIL CONVENED BY O'CONNELL IN 1833.

Each voice should resound through our island;
"You're my neighbour; but, BULL, this is *my* land;
Nature's favourite spot,
And I'd rather be shot
Than surrender the rights of our Island."
LYSAGHT'S *Anti-Union Song.*

O'CONNELL suggested, in December, 1832, to the members who were pledged to the Repeal of the Union, the expediency of meeting in Dublin to discuss various matters connected with Irish legislation. Between thirty and forty of them assembled in January, 1833, under the denomination of the National Council. The first meeting took place at Home's Hotel, in College Green, directly facing the principal front of our old House of Commons. The proximity was suggestive of some mournful recollections, associated, however, with some high resolves and hopes. The forms of a legislative assembly were strictly observed by the National Council. The first day was chiefly occupied in the examination of Michael Staunton, the able proprietor and editor of the *Dublin Register*, on the grievous fiscal wrongs which the Union enabled England to inflict upon this kingdom. On the subsequent days the members met in the Great Room of the Corn Exchange, Burgh Quay; there were a strangers' gallery and a bar, admission to which was charged the parliamentary price of two-and-sixpence. O'Connell's object in bringing together this embryo Parliament, was partly to present to the people of Ireland the spectacle of their own legislators deliberating on Irish affairs in the capital of their native land; to habituate the members to home service; and thereby to excite both the representatives and the represented to continuous energy in the great national enterprise.

"The cork," said the *Dublin Evening Post*, "was flying out of Feargus's high-bottled eloquence;" and at the National Council, as also upon some other public occasions in the capital, Feargus well sustained the reputation he had acquired in the South, of a ready, rattling speaker.

In Parliament he was not so successful. True, he talked away in the House with his customary fluency; but he failed to impress the public with any strong faith in his senatorial wisdom. He amused the Legislature with local anecdotes, sometimes extremely well told. He amused them also with occasional bursts of exaggerated energy; as, for example, when in the debate on the Coercion Bill, some foolish English member had blustered about opposing the Repeal *vi et armis*, Feargus resolved to outbluster him, which he did somewhat after the following fashion:

"The honourable gentleman," said the member for Cork County, "had declared that rather than consent to the Repeal of the Union he would submit to be pistoled and bayoneted. But he (Mr. Feargus O'Connor) would reply, that rather than submit to the oppression of Ireland, he would readily encounter swords, bayonets, guns, pistols, blunderbusses, muskets, and firearms of all sorts."

But to do Feargus justice, he often uttered very good Liberal principles, and he gave occasional expression to bold and spirited sentiments of liberty. He was deficient in logic. His speeches were what the French expressively term *inconséquent*.

In 1833 he made an effort to force forward the discussion of Repeal prematurely in the House of Commons. O'Connell was desirous to keep back the question until the organisation of the Irish Repealers should have become more effective and general. There had been undoubtedly a great deal of popular noise and excitement; but O'Connell did not deem that the people had been yet sufficiently organised to enable them to give to their representatives that steady and sustained support out of doors which was absolutely necessary to the success of the question in Parliament. O'Connell, in this cautious policy, could appeal to the authority of the venerable Henry Grattan, who, when in 1810 announcing to the people of Dublin his readiness to advocate Repeal, at the same time explicitly stated that it would be neither prudent nor possible to bring Repeal into the House of Commons until the question should be backed by the whole Irish nation. Feargus, however, overlooked all such considerations, and announced to the Repealers that if O'Connell should decline to lead them, he would himself become their leader.

Notwithstanding this intrepid announcement, he was fortunately induced to withdraw the notice he had given upon the subject, which, in truth, he was very ill qualified to discuss. He could declaim, indeed, about slavery and liberty, and give vehement utterance to popular feelings and sentiments; he could accumulate instances of local suffering; and denounce usurpation in sentences of thundering sound;

but he knew nothing about the details of the financial swindle involved in the Union, nor could he reason with accuracy on its defects in a Constitutional point of view. He, however, had succeeded in exciting the popular impatience for a parliamentary discussion; so that O'Connell found it requisite to bring forward the question in the following session.* Feargus made a very long speech about Repeal in the debate. The sentiments of course were good, but the logic was *nil*, and the orator did not touch the marrow of the subject.

Parliament being dissolved in December, 1834, Feargus was again returned for the County of Cork. In his address to the electors he declared his intention of excluding for the future the *new* families—namely, the Shannons, Kingstons, and Bandons—from the representation; and on the hustings he told Lord Bernard that the best blood in his lordship's veins was derived from "a Kerry strain," a connexion with the O'Connor family.

Feargus's majority was on this occasion large, but not so overwhelming as it had been at the previous election. The landlord persecution had already begun to work upon the county franchise. A petition against his return was briskly undertaken. He was unseated in June, 1835, and Mr. Longfield, of Longueville, near Mallow, slipped into the representation.

Feargus had evidently conceived the idea of supplanting O'Connell in the leadership [of the Irish people; and in furtherance of this project he now published a pamphlet containing numerous allegations of political dishonesty against the Liberator. The pamphlet sold well among the Conservative party, but it necessarily alienated the Repealers of Ireland from its author.

Before long he formed a connection with a political society in London, of which the Rev. Doctor Wade, a Protestant clergyman, was a member. The principles of this society were those subsequently known as the five points of the Charter, and its members assumed the designation of Chartists. He soon established in Leeds the *Northern Star*, a weekly newspaper, which was designed to propagate the principles of the society. He had talked the Chartist public into a belief that the new journal would work wonders; and showers of five-pound notes rained down on the projector to

---

* O'Connell's motion was made 22nd April, 1834.

enable him to establish it.* Before long it acquired an enormous circulation. I have heard of 60,000 copies of a single publication being sold by the agent at Manchester; and it is said that—railway conveyance being then far from general—the Post Office authorities were in some cases obliged to hire carts or waggons for its transmission, as it occasionally overflowed the restricted accommodation of the mail coaches. It is long since defunct. While it lasted, many of the traits of the proprietor were amusingly chronicled in its columns.

One curious mode of extending his influence was by having the infant children of his followers christened by his name. A string of such baptisms was for a long time to be found in the columns of each successive *Star*, as for example: " On Monday, the 8th instant, the wife of Ichabod Jenkins, nailer, was delivered of a fine thriving boy, who was christened Feargus O'Connor Ichabod ;" and so on for the best part of a column. Girls were also christened after Feargus. A whole population of Feargus O'Connors, male and female, seemed rapidly springing up; and the lists of these baptisms were usually headed with the words : " More Young Patriots."

There was also a religious institution got up under the name of "The Chartist Christian Church ;" and I presume that the Mr. Cooper who combines, in the following extract, the celebration of O'Connor's humility with the baptism of one of the young patriots was a minister of that society.

" We learn from the *Leicester Mercury* that Mr. Thomas Cooper, the leader of the O'Connorites in that borough, preached a sermon in the Amphitheatre on Sunday week, from Daniel ii. 34, 35. In the course of his address he said : ' The disciples of truth, and all great men, were humble, and did not like to have others depreciated for the purpose of exalting themselves ;' and as instances he noticed Sir Isaac Newton, Haydn, Mozart, and Feargus O'Connor. After the sermon he announced that the tragedy of *Douglas* wonld be performed on the following Tuesday, and that *Hamlet* was in preparation. He then baptized a child, 'Feargus O'Connor Cooper Beedham.' " †

Ordinary agitators had for a long time adopted the system of banners at their public processions. The original genius of Chartism for once discarded such ensigns as stale, flat,

* So I was told by a person who, at that time, was employed in the office.
† *Dublin Evening Post*, 3rd January, 1843.

and commonplace; and in lieu thereof startled the crowd at a meeting in Burnley with an infinitely grander conception: "The attention of the multitude was arrested by the ascent of a large balloon, with the words 'FEARGUS O'CONNOR' inscribed in large characters."

Banners, however, were admitted into other localities. On a banner at one of O'Connor's processions were inscribed the following stanzas:

> Lo! he comes! he comes!
> Garlands for every shrine;
> Sound trumpets—strike the drums!
> Strew roses—pour the wine!
>
> Swell, swell the Dorian flute,
> Triumphal to the sky;
> Let the millions' shout salute,
> For THE PATRIOT passes by.

Feargus now seemed to sweep through the world in the midst of a continuous triumph. Garlands, libations, Io Pæans. It was like the majestic advance of one of Homer's demigods. But Feargus was not exalted by these celestial honours above the old terrestrial mode of dealing with political questions *par voie du fait*; and accordingly, when confined at a subsequent period in York Castle for certain alleged misdemeanours, he published an "Appeal to the Working Men of Yorkshire" to obstruct by violence the proceedings of a meeting at which O'Connell was expected to be present at Leeds. The appeal was exceedingly vehement, and much of it was eloquently written. He inquired whether, if he were at large, would O'Connell dare to come to Leeds to meet him? And to this query he responded, "No! a million times no!" He then urged the great debt which he said the Yorkshire Chartists owed to himself, and declared that all would be cancelled—nay, infinitely overpaid—if they gave "O'Connor his day, and Dan his welcome." The conclusion of this eloquent incitement to a row is eminently characteristic:

"I live and reign," says Feargus, "in the hearts of millions who pant for an opportunity to prove their love, and who will embrace that which is now presented, to convince me of their approbation of my honest endeavours to serve the cause of universal freedom.

"I am, my friends and brothers, the Tyrant's Captive, the Oppressor's Dread! the Poor Man's Friend, and the people's Accepted Present, "FEARGUS O'CONNOR."

The people did not respond to any great extent to the belligerent call of their Accepted Present. It was supposed, or promised, that 100,000 Chartists would assemble to oppose O'Connell; but the contemporary journals state that from two to three thousand at the utmost assembled upon Holbeck Moor.

Feargus, during the earlier part of his imprisonment in York Castle, was treated with atrocious severity. He published in the newspapers statements of the barbarous indignities inflicted upon him. In a letter to the *Times* he expressed a fear lest the prison discipline should abridge his existence; and desired that, in the event of his death, his body should be opened by three surgeons whom he named; one residing at York, another at Hammersmith, and the third in London. Before he had ended his epistle, however, he evidently thought that it would be better to live for future political squalls than to die in jail for a post-mortem examination. "Adieu, world," he exclaims, "for seventeen months : but, by heaven! I'll make a storm in you yet."

In jail he performed some eccentric exploits. On the first Sunday after his arrival he was conducted to the chapel of the prison, where he astonished the congregation and scandalised the parson by bellowing the responses of the service in stentorian tones. He was not again required to attend the chapel during his imprisonment.

He early acquired supremacy among the apostles of Chartism. Joining the Chartists as a volunteer, he speedily worked himself into the supreme command, although he had competitors of by no means contemptible ability. A Chartist gentleman once said to me, "He began with us as a disciple, but he soon distanced all of us."

In the *Evening Star*, a sort of adjunct to the *Northern Star*, and, like it, edited for a time by Feargus, an amusing writer published a series of sketches of the Chartist leaders, commencing with a portrait of the Chartist Chief. The writer, describing an interview with Feargus and a Scotch Chartist leader named MacDouall, acquaints us that the latter gentleman claimed a diabolical pedigree. "'Son of the Devil,' said the gallant little doctor, 'is the meaning of my surname.' 'And I am a lineal descendant from Roderick O'Connor, the last King of All Ireland!' said Feargus, kindled into a momentary pride of ancestry by this flash of the untameable spirit in the brave Scot. 'There were five Kings of Ireland, all O'Connors, at the same time, but I am lineally descended from the Ardrigh, or High King. You see in me a specimen of what my countrymen of the true Milesian descent would all have been, had it not been for the dwarfing effects of bad living and ill-treatment.'"

It would seem that in thus offering himself as a specimen of the splendid proportions to which his countrymen might, if unpersecuted, have arrived, Feargus produced on the narrator an impression that he was, in truth, a being of mysterious and undefinable greatness.

"From that period," continues the writer, "I have never seen O'Connor without regarding myself as in the presence of a true representative of the ancient Celtic chieftains— beings who depicture themselves to us out of the mist of time as characterised by simple and unaffected majesty of form and deportment, without the adornments of civilisation —the frippery of jewels, crowns, and sceptres." The writer ends by remarking that "the reality of O'Connor's greatness, as a devotee of principle," overawed his enemies.

All this was doubtless very complimentary—not more so, however, than Feargus himself could be on an appropriate occasion. In Dublin lived a Mr. Patrick O'Higgins, who got up a nibbling opposition to O'Connell, and devoted a room at the back of his house to the reception of a few discontented deserters from O'Connellism. Mr. O'Higgins professed himself an ally of Feargus, and promised to propagate Chartism in Dublin. Feargus acknowledged his merits in the *Star*, and ended an eloquent eulogium by exclaiming: "Rome had her Brutus—Ireland has her O'Higgins."

When Joseph Sturge, the Quaker, was candidate for Nottingham on the principles of moral-force Chartism, Feargus gave him active assistance in the preliminary agitation. An affray took place in the market square of Nottingham, in which Feargus displayed strength and valour befitting the descendant of the Ardrigh Roderick; for although beset by numbers on every side, he knocked all down right and left. Next day twenty-one men swore that Feargus had severally knocked each of them down in the riot. The *Univers* translated the English accounts of the transaction into French, heading the narrative, "Mœurs Electorales Anglaises."

At one of the meetings for the Nottingham election Feargus exclaimed, "Hurrah for Sturge and Nottingham! or for the Devil, if he supports the Charter." I should like to have seen the quiet Quaker-face of honest Joseph Sturge on being thus hypothetically coupled with the Prince of Darkness by his reckless ally. Perhaps the hurrah for the Devil was intended as a compliment to Doctor MacDouall, who asserted the diabolical derivation of his patronymic. When Charles Gavan Duffy heard that "Son of the Devil" was alleged by the Doctor to be the meaning of his name, he drily remarked, "It is a pedigree we see no reason to question."

The report of O'Connor's meetings and speeches in the *Star* are full of traits illustrating that wild energy which formed so marked a feature in his character. We are told how he sat down after a two hours' speech so exhausted that the perspiration oozed through his dress; how he said he would work the flesh off his bones or have the Charter; how he cheered his followers by declaring that he was "as strong as ten bulls;" how he described Lane End as the place "where the lads beat the cavalry and made them retreat," adding, "in this town all the people are born marksmen. I learn that a lad of fourteen or fifteen could kill a crow flying with a stone." He was resolved to lose nothing by unnecessary modesty. In one of his addresses to his followers he thus stated his achievements and his consequent responsibilities: "I have made the mind of England, and it is my duty now to guide it."

He was ambitious of the reputation of possessing classical and scientific knowledge, as appears by the following extract from the *Manchester Guardian:* "Mr. O'Connor next referred to the charge of the *Times*, that he did not know how to spell; and challenged any editor of that paper to be examined with him by any Fellow from one of the colleges in Greek, Latin, Hebrew, Geometry, Algebra, Arithmetic, etc., and if he (Mr. O'Connor) did not beat him, he would consent to be banished from the country for life."

In 1847 he was returned to Parliament for Nottingham, defeating Sir John Hobhouse by a majority of over six hundred. In 1848 an enormous Chartist demonstration, in which Feargus was of course the principal hero, took place in London. Serious disturbances were apprehended, and among the special constables then sworn in, it is said that Louis Napoleon, afterwards Emperor of the French, was enrolled.

Feargus had instituted a land scheme which elicited a vast number of five-pound subscriptions from members of the Chartist body who believed that the payment of that sum would entitle them to profitable settlements on four-acre allotments. The scheme broke down, and with it broke down its author's intellect. His insanity displayed itself in a number of strange freaks in the House of Commons and its immediate precincts. He was confined, by order of the House, in one of its apartments for some days. During that period the newspapers gave constant accounts of his condition and his actions. From one of those accounts I take the following: "He still indulges in rapid, rambling aberrations; reciting to his attendants snatches of what he states to be his own poetical compositions—uttering now and then an *éloge* on the late Sir Robert Peel, abruptly broken off to descant on the disasters of an old woman and her pig in the bogs of Ballinhassig—of a stud of some twenty long-tailed black horses his brother kept in Ireland—all whimsically interwoven with such canticles as are heard at the Coal-Hole, or by the recital of a litany interlarded with tears on the failure of the unfortunate land-scheme."

The exhibition was at once grotesque and melancholy. We discern among the shattered fragments of his once strong intellect, faint traces of the facetious humour which in his better days had rendered him an entertaining companion. He was removed to the asylum kept by Dr. Tuke, at Chiswick, and thence, in 1855, to lodgings at Notting Hill Terrace, where he died on the 31st of August in that year, in the sixtieth year of his age. The Chartists of London gave him a grand public funeral. He was buried at Kensal Green Cemetery. His admirers at Nottingham have erected a statue to his memory.

O'Connell preserved the Irish Repealers from the alliance with the Chartists which Feargus wanted to effect. O'Connell had no confidence in the leaders, and he condemned the unfair and intolerant policy repeatedly practised by their party, of violently obstructing all meetings held for any other political object than the attainment of the Charter.

CHAPTER XVI.

IRISH POLICY OF THE FIRST REFORMED PARLIAMENT.

Justice hath done her unrelenting part,
If she indeed *be* Justice, who drives on,
Bloody and blind, the chariot-wheels of death.

SOUTHEY.

WE have been constantly told to expect vast benefits for Ireland from the English Legislature, consequent on the extension of the Parliamentary franchise. We have been told, in like manner, to expect great benefits for Ireland from the Reform Bills of 1831. Our experience of that period does not encourage us to entertain sanguine hopes of any good from that source. The proceedings of the first reformed Parliament furnished a conclusive answer to those Irish Whig-Liberals who opposed Repeal on the plea that Reform in the English Legislature would supersede the necessity for domestic legislation for Ireland.

The Irish agitation in 1831-2 was not opposed by the Whig Government so long as it could be considered auxiliary to the English agitation for Reform. But as soon as the triumph of Reform was certain, and the Irish agitators were no longer required to subserve English purposes, prosecutions were threatened. Lord Anglesea proclaimed down meetings; and the Sailor-King was instructed by his Ministers in 1833 to express from the throne his "surprise" and "indignation" at the efforts of the Irish to obtain a restoration of their national Legislature, of which they had been deprived by a system of Machiavelian fraud and diabolic crime.

O'Connell denounced the King's speech as "a brutal and bloody speech—a declaration of war against Ireland." The address, echoing the speech, was of course carried by an enormous majority. The Coercion Bill, for restricting the people of Ireland from meeting to petition Parliament, was shortly afterwards introduced. There was a very full muster of Irish and English members on the night of its introduction. Expectation was strongly excited; it had been announced that disclosures of an appalling nature would be made to justify its enactment. Lord Althorp (afterwards Earl Spencer) opened the case for the Government. His delivery was heavy, hesitating, and unimpressive. He laboured under a disadvantage which, in an impartial assembly, would have been fatal—namely, that of requiring implicit belief in a tale of Irish outrages and horrors, in which the names of the informers were to a great extent suppressed. The House was called on to ground coercive legislation upon unauthenticated charges; and the pretext for withholding the authentication was, that to publish the names of the informers would expose them to personal outrage from their lawless neighbours.

The House was perfectly ready to ground coercive legislation for Ireland upon anonymous information. It was not nice as to pretexts. It was boldly alleged that prædial outrage was the result of political agitation, and that in order to put down the former the latter should be suppressed. Any other origin of prædial outrages than political agitation appeared to be ignored by the friends of coercion.

Lord Althorp's speech was a failure. O'Connell left the House immediately on its conclusion and remained for some time in the lobby, offering triumphant congratulations to all the anti-coercion members whom he met, on the wretched exhibition of his lordship. "Did you ever hear anything more miserable? Why, the Government have literally got no case at all. Bad as the House is, it will be impossible to get them to pass the Bill on such statements. Hurrah!" Thus did the Great Dan cheer the members of the Tail and his friends in general, expressing in the most sanguine terms his conviction that the Government must be defeated.

By-and-by Mr. Stanley (afterwards Lord Derby) rose. He enjoyed one great advantage — he had an audience strongly predisposed in his favour. But in other respects he laboured under difficulties. He had, in fact, to repair Lord Althorp's failure. He had to restate a series of allegations which had fallen, feeble and dull, from the incompetent lips of the blundering leader. And well did he perform his task. Before he had spoken for five minutes the attention of friend and foe alike was riveted in admiration of the orator's abilities. Clear, rapid, and animated, he scathed the Liberals with the fire of his sarcasm, and combated their arguments with his showy and plausible parliamentary logic. The natural graces of his unconstrained and easy action, the vivid glances of his eagle eye, the air of bold and well-sustained defiance which no one could better assume, greatly enhanced the effect of his eloquence. He had gathered up some of the unconsidered sayings of his Irish antagonists, and paraded them before the House with wicked ingenuity as indicative of seditious intentions. He closed with a ferocious invective against O'Connell personally, and sat down amidst thunders of Whig and Tory plaudits.

Well did he merit the cheers of his party. The rickety and misshapen bantling of Lord Althorp was moulded by the plastic powers of Mr. Stanley into showy proportions and apparent strength.

The Bill was obstinately contested. Mr. O'Connell led the opposition, and displayed all the qualities of a great parliamentary debater. An Irish Conservative exclaimed to me with astonishment as the House adjourned one night: "How stoutly Dan battles it out among these English!"

O'Connell had, in the course of the evening, thus concluded a fiery invective against the Whigs: " You have brains of lead, and hearts of stone, and fangs of iron!" He displayed inimitable tact and dexterity in defence, promptitude and vigour in assault, and knocked about Whigs and Tories with an easy exercise of strength which astonished the members who had not previously witnessed such a brilliant display of his abilities.

Despite the opposition of the friends of Ireland, the Bill finally passed, and the Constitutional privileges that yet remained to the Irish people were temporarily invaded— ostensibly to check prædial disturbance, but in reality to thwart the agitation for Repeal. Mr. Stanley had boasted that he would make his Government feared before it should be loved. He did not make it either feared or loved; he only succeeded in making it hated.

The crime thus committed against Ireland was aggravated by the fact that it emanated from the English Reformers in the full flush and heyday of their triumph. The first use the friends of English liberty made of their great victory was to crush the Constitutional freedom of their Irish fellow-subjects. What a pregnant lesson to Irishmen! What a practical commentary on the doctrine of Imperial identification! Lord Campbell, "who," says Sir Charles Gavan Duffy, "associated with Englishmen of every rank in succession during his slow ascent from the position of a writer of paragraphs for the daily papers to be Lord Chancellor of England," accounts for his party promoting the Coercion Bill without incurring unpopularity among the people of England in the following manner:

" They were probably tranquillised by recollecting how essentially Ireland is hated by the English nation, and what a lenient view is taken of any measure which tends to degrade the mass of the Irish population."*

Lord Campbell thus attests the contemporaneous existence of that inveterate anti-Irish sentiment among his countrymen, of which we in Ireland have had seven centuries' experience. Mr. Gladstone, in one of his speeches, expressed a desire to attach us to Great Britain " by the silken bonds of love." His past financial operations did not encourage Irish confidence in his friendship. He had greatly over-estimated our taxable capacity—he had mercilessly increased our taxation

* "Life of Lord Campbell," vol. ii. p. 27; cited by Sir C. G. Duffy in " Four Years of Irish History," p. 51.

fifty-two per cent., and given a stimulant to the exodus by draining the country of the means that ought to circulate at home for the sustentation of our people. In fiscal affairs he has shown himself our unscrupulous foe; but he has given expression to the sentiment that Ireland, in all matters purely local, should be ruled in accordance with the feelings and principles of the Irish people.

He now seems to be sincerely desirous to atone for all past errors by restoring to the Irish nation their ancient possession of a resident Parliament. If he can succeed in this noble and statesmanlike policy, and if his measure of Home Rule shall contain a just arrangement of the fiscal difficulty, he will have proved himself a real benefactor to Ireland, entitled to enduring national gratitude.

It may be observed that on the 18th of March, 1846, Sir James Graham made the following remarkable statement: "I think," said Sir James, "it is our bounden duty, in legislating for Ireland, not to legislate with regard to English feelings, English prejudices, and still less with reference to English law, which has long obtained the sanction of usage in this country. But we are bound to consult Irish feelings, Irish habits, Irish laws, as they have existed for centuries, though they may be at variance with the provisions found in the English statute book."*

Sir James spoke these words under the pressure of O'Connell's agitation. Mr. Gladstone now attempts to give practical effect to the principle they announced.

CHAPTER XVII.

RESULTS OF THE COERCION ACT OF 1833.

They came in the morning, scoffing and scorning,
Saying: "Were you harassed—were you sore abused?"
O Orange haters! ye beat the traitors
That betrayed our Saviour to the wicked Jews."
Rockite Song.

WHEN the Coercion Act was passed by the first Reformed Parliament, the Repealers were angry, but not depressed. If agitation was suspended for a season, its objects and purposes survived with undiminished vitality and vigour in the affections of the people. Affairs, however, wore a very dreary

* Report in *Morning Chronicle*, 19th March, 1846.

aspect. There was a cessation of the cheering, spirit-stirring activity which had enlivened the previous year, whilst the Catholic tenantry were, in many instances, mercilessly scourged for their anti-tithe and anti-union offences. Ejectments were served on non-voters as well as on voters by some of the more bigoted landlords of the Tory-evangelic school. I have two cleared districts at this moment before me—that is, districts from which the Catholic tenantry were swept out to make room for a docile Protestant colony. The town lands, respectively named Castletown and Shanavagh, are situated in the County of Cork, and in 1837 were part of the estate of a Union-Earl of high Tory politics and warm evangelic zeal. That noble lord is since dead; his political and evangelic mantle descended on his son, who is since also deceased, and who, whatever were his politics, was reputed, I doubt not deservedly, to possess an amiable disposition and a character of unimpeachable morality.

It is right to premise that in the instance now mentioned the landlord appeared to have acted from religious enthusiasm, not from political resentment; for the ejected occupiers had not registered their votes. But expulsion is the same, whether proceeding from fanatical ardour or political vengeance. I have selected the townlands in question, because, from their proximity to my residence, I had access to the best information respecting them.

It may not be amiss to devote a few sentences to the past and present memoranda of these districts—the rather as the tale, with a few slight changes, is that of many a spot in Ireland Instruction sometimes lurks in the simple annals of the poor.

Kinneigh, the parish in which Castletown is situated, is a wild, upland tract, rising into abrupt and rocky eminences abounding in furze and coarse herbage. The hills are savage without grandeur; there is nothing picturesque in their outline, and none of them ascend to any considerable elevation. There has, some years since, been erected a handsome Protestant church, which replaces the former barn-like edifice, and in its immediate vicinity stands one of the inexplicable round towers, seventy feet high. This tower is the only thing in the parish worth looking at. A stern old monument it is of days so long gone by that man's memory retains no trace of their annals.

Having mentioned the church, I may as well waste a few words in commemoration of an ancient parson, now deceased, by whom the church-goers of Kinneigh were for a long time illuminated. This gentleman, the Reverend Gilbert Laird, dropped into the parish, no one could tell whence, about the beginning of this century, or perhaps a few years previously. All that the Protestant parishioners knew about the matter was, that a queer-looking little brown bunch of a man, whose appearance suggested the idea of an enlarged species of hedgehog, suddenly ascended the pulpit one day and delivered a discourse containing nothing about which anybody who heard it could predicate any quality in particular. The slight curiosity which was excited by the first appearance of the new parson died away when it was found that all inquiry as to his origin, birthplace, former associates, or habits, was fruitless. On all those matters he preserved to the end of his days an impenetrable silence. He bore with him due credentials from the absentee rector, so that his title to the curacy was undoubted and unquestionable; and that, he conceived, was all that his flock were entitled to know. He continued to officiate and to preach. I believe the only effusion of his pulpit eloquence which survives in the parochial memory was an exhortation to the practice of industry, preached from the sixth chapter of Proverbs: "Go to the ant, thou sluggard; consider her ways, and learn wisdom;" and illustrated by a reference to the nursery fable of the "Idle Grasshopper and the Industrious Ant," with appropriate amplifications from the preacher himself. Feargus O'Connor, who was one of the Rev. Gilbert Laird's congregation, excelled in his mimicry of this sermon, and often delivered it with great comic power for the amusement of his friends. No two human faces could be more dissimilar in form and feature than those of the clergyman and his imitator; but this dissimilarity seemed to vanish, so exquisite was Feargus's presentment of the voice, the manner, and the expression of countenance proper to the reverend original.

Mr. Laird became a sort of favourite with one or two squires who played backgammon and lived loose, rollicking lives. He rattled the dice with more sociability than he had displayed in any other occupation, and although personally free from vice, he was not the man to annoy his patrons with many troublesome moral remonstrances. By-and-by the queer little man acquired a sort of small popularity, probably because his absurdities furnished matter for mirth. Whimsical stories were told of him; people were amused with his odd habits, such as getting his bed thrashed with short flails every morning by the housemaids, and his sleeping with a bolster at the bed-foot in order to accommodate himself in the event of his choosing to reverse the relative positions of his head and feet during the night. His penurious style of living also supplied matter for irreverent jests. He existed on the smallest possible modicum of his salary as curate; and the residue he regularly invested in the purchase of a life-annuity. The whole income arising from these investments he invested again; so that if the insurance offices had given him ten thousand per cent., they would have still been gainers by their singular annuitant. Thus he went on—investing and reinvesting; and he flattered himself with the hope of enjoying the income thus created by the time it should reach £500 per annum.

He continued unmarried until about the age of eighty-seven. He then united himself with a lady who was some fifty years his junior. The union was not happy, for he bitterly reproached the bride with her deception in concealing the malformation of her left foot, which deformity he had not discovered until after the matrimonial knot was irrevocably fastened. He did not long survive the discovery, and he now reposes in one of the graveyards of the city of Cork. The old gentleman, although far from being a model clergyman, yet possessed the negative merit of doing no mischief.

Such was the pastor to whose care the souls of the Protestants of Kinneigh were for many years committed. While the spiritual interests of his small flock flourished under his tutelage, the temporal concerns of the Catholics were not in a very prosperous condition. It is indeed true that they enjoyed one important advantage —the rector was an absentee, who for many years never visited the parish. He had another benefice in a distant county where he always resided. The Kinneigh farmers were therefore relieved from the vexatious presence of a reverend spy, with his eye perpetually on the outlook for every agricultural production from which tithe could be extorted; and as the resident curate, Mr. Laird, was a quiet, harmless man, with a fixed salary, he had no interest in prompting his absent principal to harass the farmers by increasing his exactions. They were, however, harassed enough. They held the land from a middleman, named Gillman, who was the immediate tenant of the Earl of Bandon. Some of them eked out their rents from the proceeds of illicit distillation; and the necessary consequence of such a system was the demoralisation of the parish to a considerable extent. The falsehood and chicane indispensable to those who carry on a contraband trade are not the worst results of their illegal occupation. Men who live in defiance of the law become desperate, and blood has been shed in that unhappy district in defence of the pottheen stills. Undoubtedly the whole blame of these evils should not be cast upon the people. Those squires and squireens who encourage their traffic by becoming their customers, are to a great extent culpable.*

Let it not, however, be supposed that Castletown was an unmitigated pandemonium of pottheen desperadoes. There were many of the inhabitants who had nothing to do with the stills, and who were of very fair average characters.

The middleman from whom the people held their farms died, and their leases all expired with him. His term was for his own life; the town-land at his death reverted to the Earl of Bandon. Here was a glorious opportunity to plant a Protestant colony. The noble Earl rejoiced with exceeding great joy at the facilities now presented of serving an eject-ment on Idolatry and Wafer-worship, and inducting a colony of true believers into the evacuated district. The number of persons to be expelled, young and old, good, bad, and indifferent, was 247. The expulsion of such a multi-tude excited public interest. The Earl of Mulgrave, then Lord-Lieutenant of Ireland, adverted to the circumstance in the House of Lords, and elicited the following reply from the noble proprietor:

"The Earl of Bandon felt, as the noble Earl had alluded to him in so pointed a manner, it was necessary that he should trouble their lordships with a very few words. The noble Earl had brought a charge against him founded on a newspaper report. He (the Earl of Bandon) was not in the habit of attending to newspaper reports, and he never con-descended to answer them. He thought he had some reason to complain of the noble Earl for advancing so grave a charge against him, founded upon no more authentic infor-

* An instance in point occurred not long since. A landlord at the quarter sessions of a southern town preferred a number of accusa-tions against a tenant he was anxious to evict. Among the evil deeds imputed to the latter, he was charged by his landlord with keeping an illicit still. The accused turned round to his censor, and, amidst the laughter of the Court, exclaimed: "By virtue of your oath, didn't your honour often find a gallon of pottheen at your honour's hall door?" His honour was unable to deny the fact.

mation than that contained in a newspaper. He would not trouble their lordships by entering into a detail of his arrangements with respect to his own estate (hear, hear). He would only say that those whom he was accused, at that inclement season, of having turned adrift in the world, were, all of them, in their respective houses (laughter and cheers). Having made that statement he must repeat that he felt himself rather ill-used by having been called to defend himself from a charge founded on no better authority than that of a newspaper."*

Lord Bandon's virtuous indignation imposed on Lord Mulgrave, who immediately withdrew the accusation. The natural inference from Lord Bandon's words was, that the tenants were not to be molested. It is true that he did not directly assert that they should not be disturbed, but his complaint of ill-usage at being accused of disturbing or expelling them, was calculated to convey that impression to his audience. The real fact was that the tenants had all received notice to quit, but the notices had not then yet taken effect. The time of ejectment soon arrived. The aboriginal occupants were turned out, and new tribes of Hosfords, Applebys, Swantons, Dawleys, and Burchells were introduced. Three of the former tenants were permitted to retain a portion of their holdings; of these a man named Hurley sought favour with the noble proprietor by promising to abjure Popery. The man accordingly went to the Protestant Church, pursuant to his undertaking; but conceiving that a domestic calamity—the idiotcy of his son —was a mark of the Divine vengeance at his change of religion, he threatened (according to the information I was given at the time) to return to his former creed. Whether he did so I know not.

The whole machinery of proselytism was put in motion at Castletown and Shanavagh. Reverend personages exhorted; readers and teachers besieged the Catholics on highways and by-ways; schools were erected, to which some of the not yet extirpated Papists gave their trembling and reluctant attendance. The noble Earl's family occasionally visited these schools to watch the expansion of the nascent Gospel seed, and to accelerate the process of its ripening by the warmth and light of their countenances. They were, I doubt not, sincere enthusiasts; and when we consider the

* Parliamentary Report in Cork *Southern Reporter* of 2nd December, 1837.

vast influence their station and fortune, if properly used, might invest them with, it was deplorable to witness the direction their zeal had taken; to contrast what they have been with what they might have been; to see them in the front rank of the anti-national interest, instead of being the honoured, cherished leaders of their countrymen to national independence. I cannot help remarking that there was a time when Francis Bernard, afterwards first Earl of Bandon, was associated with the people of Ireland in demanding the restoration of the Irish Constitution. On the 25th of March, 1782, at a meeting held in Bandon, he occupied the chair. There were three resolutions passed, of which the last affirmed:

"That no power on earth can make laws to bind Ireland, except the King, Lords, and Commons thereof.

(Signed)   "G. STAWELL, Col., Bandon Cavalry.
           "F. BERNARD, Col., Bandon Infantry."

Grattan had fired the mind of the nation, and the sacred flame ignited many persons who themselves, or whose descendants, have degenerated into anti-nationalists.

At Shanavagh, the politico-religious movement produced its natural results. A man named Hurley (a suspicious patronymic, it would seem, in these districts) attended the school with great assiduity, and after a due course of instruction, professed his willingness to attend the Protestant church. He accordingly became a church-going Protestant, and his new *confrères* thought that a valuable fish had been hooked. One day a tenant of mine met this convert on the road, and asked him wherefore he had quitted his earlier faith to adopt Protestantism.

"Musha, God help us!" responded the convert, "I have got a small family to support, and I thought by turning I could maybe get a lase of the ould ground from Lord Bandon."

"But you'd lose your poor sowl," remonstrated the other.

"Och, maybe not—maybe not. I expect God won't take me so short entirely but that I may quit them all and go back to mass once more afore I die."

The convert also told my informant, that, by way of an additional safeguard, he did not give attention to the preaching or prayers of the Protestant service, but rehearsed his own prayers mentally, while the parson performed the service.

Some time subsequently to the above conversation (which

I took down from the lips of one of the parties), Mr. Hurley's duplex policy was curiously exhibited. He fell ill, and being afraid of death, despatched a messenger to bring the parish priest to administer the last rites of the Catholic Church. "But, hark ye!" added the politic invalid, "tell his Reverence not to come up till after dark, for fear any of the Protestants should see him and tell the minister."

Mr. Hurley had considered his alternative—death, then Popery and Father O'Sullivan; but if he should recover, then Protestantism and another attempt to conciliate his landlord's patronage. Father O'Sullivan (then priest of the parish) informed me that he refused to attend him, stating that his pertinacious duplicity at that awful period totally disqualified him from the profitable reception of the rites of the Church.* He recovered, and continued to attend the Protestant place of worship; but although he was permitted to remain in his farm, I am not aware that he obtained a lease of it. About the period referred to he sent an infant

* A reviewer, commenting on this narrative, said that it cut two ways, and that the priest must have left Hurley in a state of great ignorance. But Hurley was not ignorant that his conduct was criminal. He was plainly acting against conscience, and the priest had nothing to do with his conduct except to condemn it.

In 1845 public attention became excited by the case, tried at the Tralee Assizes, of the Rev. Charles Gayer, one of the leaders of a proselytising establishment at Dingle, County Kerry, *versus* Patrick Robert Byrne, proprietor of the *Kerry Examiner* newspaper. The defendant was convicted of what, in the rigid acceptation of the law, was deemed libel; but the organised system of rank bribery to proselytise the Catholics, which the evidence disclosed, must, I think, have received a salutary check from the publicity thus entailed upon it. TIMOTHY LYNCH, a witness and *ci-devant* convert, deposed that he got from Mr. Gayer the sum of £12 10s. and two half-crowns as the price of his adhesion. EDWARD HUSSEY, another witness, also deposed to having received money from Gayer in consideration of his becoming a Protestant. JOHN POWER, a fish-jolter, deposed to having received from Gayer "about £5 or £6 pound" for a similar consideration." THOMAS HOGAN deposed to having got from Gayer 17s. in two different sums, and two pecks of potatoes, and a house rent-free from another proselytiser named Moriarty, in consideration of which benefits he became a Protestant. JAMES KEARNEY, another convert, deposed that the considerations for which he conformed were plentiful employment and good wages from Gayer, and a house and garden rent-free; "he never paid a farthing rent; taxes and all are paid for him; has a garden behind the house the same way, and every one else has the same; none of them pay any rent." MAURICE POWER, a second fish-jolter, deposed to having bargained with Gayer to become a Protestant for the price of a horse to carry his fish. These statements were uncontradicted by Gayer, who was in court child to the priest to be christened; the child was smuggled in a covered basket to escape the observation of the Protestants.

It is but justice to say that the Protestant clergy then, and since, in the parish, have been men of irreproachable morals. They, in common with their brethren all over the kingdom, were startled at the march of nationality; they trembled for the stability, if not of their Zion, at least of its temporalities. Hence their itching and uneasy zeal to make an inroad on the enemy's territories. I suppose Mr. Hurley's conversion has been chronicled in some exulting report of the progress of "the Gospel."

Well, Castletown was now peopled with a Protestant tenantry. Shanavagh also was pretty well dotted with the new settlers. A sort of miniature millennium was to be exhibited amidst the Kinneigh furze-brakes for the edification of the surrounding community. The noble landlord doubtless regarded his work with sentiments of self-applause. But—it is pleasant to be able to say it—the proselytising zeal of past

during the trial; and some of them (such as that of the houses being rent-free for converts) were of such a nature as, from the public notoriety of the facts, rendered denial in Kerry impossible.

It is difficult to resist a smile at the ludicrous character of the proselytising system, thus exhibited on the uncontradicted oaths of competent witnesses; but the horrible results of that system, the spiritual recklessness which it necessarily engenders, suggest solemn and mournful reflections. The total insensibility to real religious conviction of what nature soever, the organised hypocrisy resulting from the traffic of the people with the "Dingle Mission," appears in the following incident. A batch of Gayer's proselytes, finding their adhesion to the State Church less profitable than they had expected, turned off *en masse* to the Rev. Mr. M'Manus, Presbyterian minister at Miltown, and inquired what terms he would give them for becoming Presbyterians.

In Molière's *Bourgeois Gentilhomme*, Coviel denies that Monsieur Jourdain's father was a linendraper. He had, indeed, from disinterested benevolence, accommodated the public with linens; and the public, from their grateful sense of his kindness, had gracefully and delicately presented him with certain monies. On both sides it was an elevated interchange of practical philanthropy—there was nothing of traffic in the transaction. Precisely thus did Messieurs Gayer and Company deny that they ever bribed "converts." True, some pauper Papists, from the force of sudden and simultaneous conviction, came rushing headlong into Protestantism—true, also, the Protestant agents gave money, and free houses, and employment to the converts; but there was nothing of a *quid pro quo* in the transaction. On the one side it was conscientious adoption of religious truth; on the other it was the most exalted benevolence and "mercy to the household of faith."

years has died out at Shanavagh. The displacement of Catholics was not carried to the same extent as at Castletown. Among the tenants now residing on the land are Catholics, not at present molested by their landlord, who, it is needless to say, cannot be considered responsible for transactions that occurred before he succeeded to the property.

The people in numerous parts of the kingdom feel the paramount necessity of efficient protection from the irritating persecution of which I have given a specimen. The best protection would be found in the principle of nationality. Were that principle well developed in Ireland, it would speedily absorb all wretched sectarian contentions. It would extinguish the pernicious desire to exalt any one sect or Church at the expense of any other. The doings I have briefly recorded are exploits of what is called the English interest in Ireland. The people can never be prosperous or happy until the magnates of the land cherish the Irish interest —which, if they did but know it, is their own true interest— as paramount to every other.

Every unprejudiced person will concede that the interests of real religion cannot be advanced by the system of evangelical bullyism. That much of the crime and insubordination of Ireland has arisen from the extermination— whether pious or profane—of the inhabitants, will be readily admitted, when it is remembered that in the five years from 1838 to 1842 inclusive, ejectment proceedings were taken against no less than 356,985 persons, as appears by the parliamentary papers to which the public attention was called in June, 1843, by the late Mr. Sharman Crawford, who then affirmed that the clearing process went on at an increasing ratio. And from that day to this, among the incidents most familiar to those who watch Irish events with anxious interest, are the evictions of the Irish tenantry, often under circumstances which show that the work of expulsion is prompted by political vengeance or sectarian bigotry.

It seems a curious and perverse fatality that the possession of the elective franchise, and also the want of it, have alike been fraught with bitter evils to the Irish peasantry. The exercise of the franchise in opposition to the landlord's will has drawn down extermination upon tens of thousands. That the want of the franchise in former days also caused the expulsion of the people from the soil, appears from a statement of John Keogh's in the published correspondence of Edmund Burke.

"It is a known fact," says Keogh in 1792, the year before the concession of the forty-shilling franchise, "that the Roman Catholics have been, and are every day turned out of very beneficial farms, deprived of the maintenance of themselves and their families, have lost their honest occupations, and the exercise (the most beneficial to the State) of their industry and capital, because they could not vote at an election, and to make room for those who could. *A fortiori* they have in multitudes of instances failed to obtain leases, nor can they ever obtain them on equal terms." *

It was natural that a peasantry thus trained to regard the franchise as conducive to their livelihood, should, on first acquiring it, have used it for several years with greater subserviency to landlord dictation than they have done in more recent times. When political corruption was at its greatest height, the landlords occasionally disposed of their electioneering interests to the candidates who bid the highest. The tenants saw that their votes were a subject of traffic by their landlords. An instance of impartial rascality is recorded of Mr. B—— F——. He sold the votes of all his tenants to two rival candidates, and pocketed the money of both. As he did not indicate to his tenantry the particular candidate for whose success he was desirous, one of the tenants, on behalf of the rest, asked his honour for which of the candidates they should vote?

"Faith, boys," answered Mr. F——, "you may take your choice. I have knocked the highest penny I could out of your votes already, so it would be unhandsome of me to hinder you from selling yourselves now to whoever will bid the best."

The tenants thanked his honour for his liberal permission, and proceeded as fast as they could to take his advice.

It is said that at a hotly contested election in the olden time, Denis D—— and his opponent ran so close to each other that the numbers were equal—a blacksmith only remaining unpolled. The blacksmith's horse was for sale. Denis bid twenty guineas; his rival bid thirty; so they went on bidding alternately, each bid being an advance of ten guineas, till at last Denis stopped, the horse being knocked down for two hundred guineas to his antagonist, who triumphantly cried to the blacksmith, "Come off and be polled." "Ay," whispered Denis to the blacksmith,

---

* Burke's "Correspondence," vol. iv. p. 67.

"but remember who put up the horse to auction for you." The whisper was effectual—the artisan voted for Denis.

The expedients used to manufacture voters for an emergency were sometimes very curious. The well-known MacCoghlan, of the King's County, when hard pressed for a batch of electors to turn the scale in an approaching contest, granted freeholds to the requisite number of voters; the terms of the leases being for the life of one Jack Murphy. The voters were put in possession—the election came on— and MacCoghlan's friend, with the aid of the newly-made freeholders, carried the day. MacCoghlan, however, had not the least notion of allowing the new corps of voters to occupy his ground, now that their services were no longer necessary. He accordingly ended all their leases by shooting Jack Murphy, the common life in all. Be not horrified, good reader : Jack Murphy was an old spavined horse.

CHAPTER XVIII.

THE REPEAL DEBATE OF 1834.

> Ireland rests 'mid the rush of progression,
>   Like a frozen ship in a frozen sea;
> And the changeless stillness of life's stagnation
>   Is worse than the wildest waves could be,
>   Rending the rocks eternally.
>
> Trumpet-tongued to a people sleeping,
>   Who will speak with magic command,
> Bidding them rise—these dead men keeping
>   Watch by the dead in a silent land?
>
> SPERANZA.

O'CONNELL was at last obliged by the pressure of some members of the Tail, as well as by the remonstrances of the Repeal newspapers, to bring the question of Repeal before the foreign House of Commons on the 22nd April, 1834.

For some days previously Mr. Spring Rice, who was selected as the special champion of the Union, was observed to frisk about the purlieus of St. Stephen's with the smirking self-complacency of anticipated triumph. He knew that he should have an overwhelming majority against O'Connell's motion; he knew that whatever assertions he might make, however delusive, however contrary to truth, would be received with enthusiastic plaudits by that alien Parliament; and he had availed himself of his peculiar facilities of reference to official documents to prepare lengthy tabular statements illustrative of what he termed the giant-stride prosperity of Ireland under the Union. With these he expected to demolish O'Connell's allegations of Irish decay.

The 22nd arrived; the House was crowded with members, the gallery with strangers.

O'Connell's opening speech rehearsed the outrageous crimes committed by England against Ireland from the earliest date of their connexion. Having, by this historical retrospect, demonstrated the systematic enmity of England to this country, the speaker thence passed to the measure of the Union, dilated on the means by which it was carried, exhibited the falling off in national prosperity which had been its consequence, and concluded by moving for a select committee to inquire and report upon the means by which the destruction of the Irish Parliament was effected; of the effects of that measure upon Ireland, and upon the labourers in husbandry, and operatives in manufactures in England, and on the probable consequences of continuing the legislative Union between both countries.

O'Connell's able and comprehensive speech occupied five hours.

On the next day (the 23rd), Mr. Rice delivered his reply. He deprecated Mr. O'Connell's references to the English atrocities of former times, as being in their nature irritating, and irrelevant to the question before the House.

He alleged the danger of two independent Parliaments in one Empire, and inferred the likelihood of separation under such a system from the differences on the Regency Question in 1789. I shall not recapitulate his arguments here, as the subject will be examined in the Appendix to this work.

He alleged that the Irish Volunteers had tried to intimidate the Irish Parliament subsequently to 1782. Well had it been for Ireland if their interference had been potential. What the Volunteers sought was to procure a reform of the Irish House of Commons; of which measure the principle has been since recognised, and incorporated with the British Constitution by the English Legislature.

He alleged that the Irish Parliament had been notorious for bribery and corruption. Not more so, certainly, than the English Parliament. Lord Macaulay says that there was a time when the only way in which the Minister could manage the English Parliament was by corruption.* That the Irish Legislature was in this respect culpable only proves that it needed the reform which the Volunteers sought; not that it ought to be extinguished. To urge the corruption of the unreformed Irish Parliament as a reason for putting an end to it, is extremely like saying that as death puts an end to disease, the best mode of treating a sick man is to kill him outright. Mr. Rice was amusingly impartial in his criticism. He censured the Irish Parliament on the score of its corruption; he also censured the Volunteers for trying to put an end to that corruption.

He next quoted Grattan to show that the Irish Parliament had not realised his expectations. But he took care not to quote Grattan's declaration that the Irish Parliament, with all its faults, had done more good for Ireland in fourteen years than the English Parliament had done for England in a century.

He denied that the rebellion of 1798 had been fomented in order to carry the Union.

He alleged the parental care of Ireland evinced by the Imperial Parliament; stating that no less than 175 Commissions on Irish affairs had been appointed by the House since the Union. He, however, forgot to state that the immense majority of those Commissions had ended abortively; and that the Committee of 1825, for which he claimed the merit of carrying Emancipation, was in fact the product of O'Connell's Irish agitation.

He claimed merit for England in admitting Irish corn and butter duty-free; as if it were a boon to Ireland to increase the supply of food to English customers and to cheapen its price for them. England has, since then, done the same for all the world; compelled by the exigencies of the English stomach to import as much food as she can get, and on the cheapest possible terms.

He inferred the giant-stride prosperity of Ireland from her largely increased exports of corn and cattle, omitting to notice that the producers of the corn and cattle were disabled by poverty from consuming the food of their own raising; and that much of the price received for the exports was again exported to England in the shape of absentee rents and absentee taxes.†

* "History of England."
† In truth, a table of exports and imports may afford no true test of a nation's prosperity. Let me borrow the following illustration

Mr. Rice stated some Acts of beneficial tendency which the United Parliament had passed for Ireland. But in claiming credit for the Union on this score he omitted to show that a reformed Irish Legislature would not have passed every one of the good laws in question, and many more into the bargain.

He produced multitudinous tables to demonstrate the improved condition and increased comforts of the Irish people generally after the Union. Cruel mockery! At the time when he spoke there was the evidence of the Railway Commissioners showing that 2,385,000 of the Irish people—being more than one-fourth of our then population—were destitute paupers for thirty weeks in every year.

He stated many grants made by the Imperial Parliament to Ireland from 1800 to 1834. But he did *not* state that the greater part of those grants had been made prior to 1821, in virtue of a stipulation at the time of the Union for their continuance for twenty-one years; nor did he state that the Imperial Parliament commenced the work of reduction as soon as the stipulated period had expired. And he did not state that the aggregate of the absentee rents and absentee taxes extorted from Ireland largely exceeded the whole of his boasted grants.

He stated that the consolidation of the Exchequers of England and Ireland in 1817 had been precipitated by the bankruptcy of Ireland. But he did not tell the House that Ireland had been made bankrupt by the fraudulent financial terms of the Union, which had forced her to contract for an expenditure she was totally unable to meet. The reader will

from my able friend, Mr. Staunton (1814) : "Fifty years ago we manufactured our own cloth; at present we get cloth from England. Fifty years ago £100 worth of corn sent from Tipperary to Dublin was consumed in Dublin, and was paid for with £100 worth of cloth made in Dublin. Here was a transaction which occasioned no exports or imports. Contrast this transaction with the present condition of affairs. The £100 worth of corn goes from Tipperary —not to Dublin, but to England ; it is paid for with £100 worth of cloth made in England. An item is furnished to Spring Rice's table of exports and imports, and he cries out, 'Hurrah! I have got a triumphant proof of Irish prosperity.' But how stands the fact? In the former transaction, which exhibited no imports or exports, the Irish corn fed the Irishman, and paid for Irish manufactures. In the latter transaction, which exhibits both an import and an export, the Irish corn feeds the Englishman, and is paid for in English manufactures, while the Irish operative perishes for want of employment."

find in the Appendix a paper in which the nature of the fiscal grievance is examined.

Mr. Rice quoted the amount of tonnage of the vessels clearing out from Irish ports, in proof of augmented commercial wealth; relying on his hearers' ignorance of the fact that tonnage is frequently a delusive index.*

He repeated the old fallacy that Irish agitation kept English capital out of the country. Just as if English capitalists were not constantly investing their money in countries where real danger and real obstacles are encountered —in foreign lands, where a single hostile shot between the countries would destroy the security for repayment. "England," says Captain Marryat, "has now fifty-five millions sterling invested in American securities, which is a large sum; and the majority consider that a war will spunge out this debt."†

At a later period Lord George Bentinck gave the House of Commons a list of English investments in foreign speculations, both civil and military. He was urging an advance of money for Irish railways, and contrasting the reluctance of Parliament to give a farthing for that purpose with the lavish profusion displayed by Government as well as by private

---

* To illustrate this position I subjoin the following table of Dublin tonnage, which I obtained in 1842 from a well-informed source. It is close enough to accuracy to serve the purpose of the argument:

In 1832 there were about 130 vessels cleared outwards to foreign ports from Dublin. Of these 130 vessels,

        43 were in ballast (timber ships), and
        52 carried passengers. Thus,

95 out of 130 represented no profitable commerce.

Again, in 1833 there were about 180 vessels cleared out to foreign ports. Of these,

        90 were in ballast, and
        30 with passengers. Thus,

120 out of 180 represented no profitable commerce.

Again, in 1834 there were 150 vessels cleared out to foreign ports. Of these,

        64 were in ballast, and
        49 with passengers. Thus,

113 vessels out of 150 betokened no profitable commerce.

Before a table of tonnage, therefore, can be accepted as a test of commercial prosperity, it is necessary to ascertain the nature of the traffic which that tonnage represents. Of course a profitable export trade involves large tonnage; but on the other hand, large tonnage may exist without a profitable export trade.

† Captain Marryat's "Diary in America," vol. ii. p. 118. London, 1839.

speculators in squandering English wealth on the objects he enumerated. "Send it abroad," said his lordship, "as you did some £70,000,000 for three years to foreign countries, to support their wars and to subsidise foreign nations. Send it abroad, as you did £10,000,000 or £12,000,000 in 1825 ; and invest £7,000,000 sterling in Peruvian mines, Mexican gold, and Mexican silver, as you did in 1825. . . . Sink your capital in no less than twenty-three foreign mining companies. . . . You also sent £13,000,000 to Portugal, and you sunk £22,000,000 in Spanish Actives, Spanish Passives, and Spanish Deferred. To America in 1836 you sent millions. You got rid of £100,000,000 in this way." *

The English capitalist can scatter his investments broadcast all over the globe except in Ireland. Dangers of climate, dangers of war, perils of earth, air, or ocean deter him not. It seems there is only one scarecrow on the face of the earth that has terrors for his adventurous soul ; and that scarecrow is Irish agitation. Mr. Spring Rice affirmed in 1834, with as much parliamentary gravity as if he expected a single human being to believe him, that the capitalists who were undeterred by the vast variety of real and substantial dangers that beset their undertakings in the most remote corners of the globe, were frightened out of Ireland by Irish agitation—that is to say, by the clack of our platform eloquence. Our subsequent experience teaches us a different lesson. There was, for a good many years after the famine, a cessation of what is called Irish agitation. We were nearly as quiet as the graves into which myriads of our countrymen had been precipitated by English misgovernment. Did English capital stream into the country, to reward our quiescence, and to verify the prophecies of Mr. Spring Rice? On the contrary, Mr. Gladstone seized the moment of our helpless prostration to add fifty-two per cent. to our previous taxes; which friendly achievement constitutes, I presume, his claim to the enthusiastic confidence so warmly expressed by some of his Irish admirers.

To talk about English capital coming to Ireland is an impudent mockery. We should not want a shilling of English capital if England did not rob us of Irish capital. We are plundered of our own by a ceaseless process of abstraction, and then it is said to us, "Do but keep quiet, and suffer English capital to stream into your island."

* Speech of Lord George Bentinck in the House of Commons, 4th February, 1847.

Whatever other reasons may exist to prevent the investment of English capital amongst us, it is certain that the Union, by giving the English manufacturing capitalist the command of the Irish manufacture market, deprives him of at least one motive to expend his capital in establishing manufactures here. He has already got our market. What more does he require? From his mill or his factory in Yorkshire or Lancashire he can pour any amount of his fabrics into Irish circulation. Why, then, should he incur the needless risk and expense of establishing a factory in Tipperary or Roscommon?

Mr. Rice's oration occupied six hours and a half. At its close he was unable to find the amendment to which his long speech was a prelude. Some mirth was excited by his perplexity. The amendment was found on the following day, read by the Speaker, and seconded by Mr. Emerson Tennent in a speech which, pursuant to his invariable habit, he had carefully written out and got by heart. The only part of it worth extracting is the following ludicrous specimen of flippant nonsense:

"Ireland was, we were told, annihilated and extinguished by the Union, inasmuch as it then ceased to be a distinct kingdom. But on the same principle, Scotland must likewise have been annihilated when she, in 1707, ceased to be a distinct kingdom on being incorporated with England; and by a parity of reasoning, if the mere fact of incorporation, by destroying distinctness, involves extinction, England herself must have been extinguished when she became incorporated with the other two." (Loud cheers.) "So that, according to the doctrine of the Repealers, the whole Empire must at this moment be ideal, and exist, like the universe of Berkeley, only in the imagination of its inhabitants." (Renewed cheering.)

What an index to the discerning sagacity of the House is afforded by the plaudits elicited by Mr. Tennent! Here, now, are the facts:

Ireland lost two-thirds of her representation by the Union; England preserved her representation whole and intact.

Ireland lost the power of legislating for herself; England retained, unimpaired, the full power of self-legislation, and acquired, in addition, the power of legislating for Ireland.

Ireland lost the advantage of a resident Legislature and its consequent expenditure; England lost nothing, and acquired the residence not only of the Irish delegates, but of the largely augmented crop of Irish absentees whom the transfer of power to the London Legislature attracted thither.

And yet a parrot-statesman is cheered by the collective wisdom when he glibly rehearses the absurd proposition that if the Union politically annihilated Ireland, which had lost much and gained nothing, it necessarily also annihilated England, which had gained much and lost nothing.

Richard Sheil made a brilliant speech in the debate. He had for some time after 1830 coquetted with Repeal. The Great Agitator had made many public appeals to him to join the movement; but vainly, until the general election of 1832 necessitated a decisive declaration on the subject. Sheil then declared himself a determined and unqualified Repealer. His accession was hailed with delight by O'Connell, who triumphantly exclaimed : "Richard's himself again." The important recruit proved a powerful ally in the parliamentary debate. Of his speech I shall quote one or two passages :

"At the time of the Union Ireland was charged with the contribution of two-seventeenths.* Was that fair? Sir John Newport and Lord Plunket both asserted that it was most unfair; but the fact was far better than the authority of either of them, for it turned out that Ireland was unable to pay it. It was necessary to make up her deficiency by a loan. Where was that loan borrowed? In England; and the revenue of Ireland was devoted to paying the interest on that loan to British capitalists."

Sheil produced great effect by his allusion to the case of Belgium :

"Now turn to Belgium. Does not the example bear us out? Hear an extract from the Declaration of Belgian Independence. After stating that the Union was obtained by fraud, the document goes on and states that 'an enormous debt and expenditure—the only dowry that Holland brought us at the time of our deplorable Union ; taxes, overwhelming by their amount; laws, always voted by the Dutch *for* Holland only, and always *against* Belgium, represented so unequally in the States-General ; the seat of all important establishments fixed in Holland; the most offensive partialities in the

* Not two-seventeenths of the *whole* Imperial revenue, but two-seventeenths of that part of it which remained after the debt-charge of each country had been first provided for by separate taxes upon each.

distribution of civil and military employments—in a word, Belgium treated as a conquered province, as a colony; everything rendered a revolution inevitable.'" (Loud cheers from the Repealers.) "You fear," continued Mr. Sheil, "separation may be the result of Repeal. What may not be the result of maintaining the Union? Let a few years go by; Catholic and Protestant will become reconciled (their divisions cannot last for ever); the popular power will augment; the feelings of the people will be extended to their representatives—the absentee drain will continue—the Church system will still be maintained—the national mind will become one mass of heated and fiery emotion—the same disregard for the feelings and interests of Ireland will be displayed; and then (may God forfend that the event should befall!) if there be an outbreak of popular commotion here; if the prediction of the Conservatives should be fulfilled, and if your alliance with France, which is as unstable as its dynasty, should give way—then you may have cause to lament, but lament when it will be too late, that you did not give back her Parliament to Ireland."

Sir Robert Peel followed Sheil in a speech of great ability and eloquence, but which partook of the fallacious character necessarily attaching to all that was urged in defence of the Union. He treated the legislative Union as a measure whose necessity was an instinct of the British mind. "There are," he said, "truths which lie too deep for argument; truths to the establishment of which the evidence of the senses or the feelings of the heart have contributed more than the slow process of reasoning; which are graven in deeper characters than any that reasoning can either impress or efface."

This is undeniably true; and to this class of truths belongs the necessity to Ireland of self-legislation. Reason will enforce that necessity, but the slow process of reasoning is anticipated by the instinctive consciousness that an Irish Legislature, bound to Ireland by the very fact of residence, and the interests of whose members must generally run in the same groove with the interests of their country, is infinitely better qualified to promote Irish prosperity than a Parliament of strangers who inherit the traditionary British feelings towards Ireland of jealousy, hostility, or apathy, and whose idea of Union consists chiefly in taxing Ireland for British uses. All this is intuitively felt by our nation. Sir Robert's above-quoted words are indeed true, but they apply in a sense quite opposite to that which he intended. He went on to say :

"The conviction in favour of *the Union* springs from every source from which conviction in the human mind can arise. Consult your senses, consult your feelings, consult reason, history, and experience—they all concur in enforcing the same truth."

All true, provided that for "the Union" we substitute the words "self-government for Ireland."

He quoted Canning's smart saying, "Repeal the Union! Restore the Heptarchy!" but he omitted to state that the Repeal of the Union and the restoration of the Heptarchy had been instanced by Canning as absurdities analogous to a reform in Parliament. What Canning had said was, "Reform the Parliament! Repeal the Union! Restore the Heptarchy!"* Canning, in a debate in the British House of Commons on the Union in 1799, termed Catholic Emancipation "a wild and impracticable measure." These random expressions of statesmen are worth little or nothing. The supposition that the man who would give Ireland a Parliament is bound by his own principles to give separate Governments to Essex and Kent, was unworthy the intellect of Canning.

Sir Robert next urged that Repeal would be a dismemberment of the Empire.

He said that absenteeism was caused, not by the Union, but by "the cursed system of agitation."

He tried to terrify the Irish Protestants by predicting that they would have real dangers to encounter should Repeal be achieved. Since Sir Robert spoke, the Irish Protestants have had to endure a large share of the general poverty entailed by the Union, as the vast reduction of their numbers, the records of the Encumbered Estates Court, and other records also bear witness.

He manfully avowed the spirit of British usurpation by declaring that "he, for one, would never consent that to an Irish Parliament should be left the determination of the proportion of the amount that country should contribute in future to defray the general expenses of the State, and contribute to the diminution of the general public debt."

Considering that Ireland, by a system of barefaced fraud, had been swindled into an enormously disproportioned lia-

* So O'Connell told me. I have not seen the report of Canning's speech containing the passage cited. The speech next referred to I found in an old volume of the Debates of 1799.

bility to that same public debt, Sir Robert's cool avowal of the robber principle, "We will put our hands into your pocket whether you like it or not," was a miracle of impudence. It was just the thing to tell effectually with an English audience.

He denied, in defiance of O'Connell's proofs, that Pitt and Castlereagh had fomented the rebellion of 1798; alleging that those statesmen could not have afforded a rebellion at a time of foreign war, and when a mutiny broke out at the Nore. They could, however, afford to pour 137,000 troops into Ireland; and the forces thus left at their disposal well enabled them to afford a rebellion.

He defended the application to Ireland of the ruinous and infamous principle of *Divide et Impera;* alleging that this principle had protected the two parties from each other; and that he regarded it as the mediator by which, in all domestic quarrels, the fury of both sides had been allayed.

He quizzed Mr. Feargus O'Connor about the Irish King Roderick, quoting some ancient account of a barbarous ceremonial at the coronation of the kings of Ireland. Much laughter was excited by this sally.

He then wound up by a very eloquent allusion to the tremendous conflict which agitated Europe from 1803 to 1814, calling the attention of the House to the fact that among the bravest military leaders were the Irish Generals, Ponsonby and Packenham; that the British Army had been commanded by the Irish Wellington, "who, standing with his back to the sea on the rock of Lisbon, saw all Europe in dismay and her liberties jeopardised, but who never ceased from his glorious labours till he saw the whole Continent emancipated."

What the Union had to do with the valour of Ponsonby and Packenham, or with the glories of Wellington, it were difficult to tell. I presume that even if the Irish Parliament had continued to exist, England would have readily availed herself of Irish valour and Irish military genius.

"During that period," said Sir Robert (namely, from 1803 to 1814), "the reins of Government were placed in the hands of a Castlereagh and a Pitt,* and a Grattan was seen to join with a Fox in the deliberations of the Legislature of the country." It is political blasphemy to class the illustrious Grattan in the same category with the execrable patricide Castlereagh.

* Pitt died in 1806.

The conclusion of Sir Robert's speech was eloquent: "With the return of a separate Parliament, after the Catholic disabilities had been removed, what might not be expected from the triumphant rancour of religious hatred? It would amount to a complete disbanding of society. Who could set bounds, who could regulate the force of those antagonist powers? Who could so adjust the centrifugal force, if he might so term it, which ought to keep Ireland within her proper orbit in the system of the empire, as to prevent her flying away into the chaos of lawless agitation, or a boundless sea of revolution? (Continued cheers.) To set such boundaries was beyond any power that man could possibly employ. To effect such a state of things required the might of that omniscient and omnipotent Power which in the material world had separated the light from the darkness (loud cheers), and prescribed the eternal laws by which the magnificent harmony of the planetary system was arranged and sustained."

Sir Robert sat down in the midst of a perfect tempest of applause, of which the enthusiasm was not diminished by the shameless libel on the Irish Catholics which he deemed it expedient to pronounce. "Triumphant rancour of religious hatred." The Protestant Parnell, in his "Historical Apology for the Irish Catholics," does their character justice in this respect: "The Irish Roman Catholics bigots!" he exclaims; "the Irish Roman Catholics are the only sect that ever resumed power without exercising vengeance." And another Protestant historian, William Cooke Taylor, LL.D., speaking of the Catholics of Ireland, says: "It is but justice to this maligned body to add, that on the three occasions of their obtaining the upper hand, they never injured a single person in life or limb for professing a religion different from their own."*

In truth, one of the most prominent traits in the Irish Catholic character is the absence of religious bigotry. This trait is displayed in the fairness with which Catholic majorities in Corporations elect Protestant Mayors in due rotation. It is manifested in the fact that priests and people prefer Protestant candidates of popular principles to Catholic candidates of unpopular politics. The contests between the Protestant Spaight and the Catholic Ball, between the Protestant White and the Catholic Waldron, between the

---

* Taylor's "History of the Civil Wars of Ireland," vol. i. p. 169.

Presbyterian John Martin and the Catholic Preston, are instances in point. Our people are steadfastly faithful to the Catholic religion. But their politics are influenced, not by theological predilections, but by their desire for the success of some legitimate political object. It was stated in the debate of 1834, by Mr. Lambert of Wexford (an anti-Repealer), that the Catholic Bishop of Waterford was pelted with mud in the streets of that city because he was not a Repealer. No man of right feeling will approve such an outrage; but the fact shows that even among the lowest and most violent of the populace religious partisanship was absorbed in national prepossession. The Repealer was, with them, a character more sacred than the non-repealing prelate. The mitre was unable to protect its venerable wearer from the indignation of those who deemed their nationality outraged by his non-adhesion to their cause. "Triumphant rancour of religious hatred." Sir Robert, in this outrage upon truth, calculated that his words would influence that class of persons whom a blind, unreasoning hatred of Catholics and Catholicity diverts from the real interests of their country and of themselves. He calculated accurately.

After some further skirmishing among the smaller fry, the debate was closed by Mr. O'Connell in a speech remarkable for its vigour and vivacity. I extract from it the following passages:

"I have insisted on the incompetence of the Irish Parliament to create a new Legislature, and I am convinced I was right in that part of my argument. There was nothing to authorise the Parliament of Ireland to dispose of the Irish nation, any more than there was anything to authorise the British Parliament to dispose of the British nation to any other on the face of the globe. As to the fomenting of the rebellion in order to bring about the Union—upon that point I have been perfectly triumphant. 'But why,' said the right hon. baronet, 'should Mr. Pitt and Lord Castlereagh excite a rebellion in Ireland at a time when there was a mutiny at the Nore?' That mutiny had broken out suddenly and unexpectedly. What, therefore, had its existence to do with the fomentation of the rebellion? The English Ministry did not foresee the mutiny, though they might have conjectured the outbreak of the rebellion.* Could the Union ever have been carried but for the rebellion? What answer

---

* They might have more than conjectured it, seeing that it was designedly provoked by their intolerable tyranny.

could be given to the Report of the Secret Committee of the Irish House of Commons, from which it appeared that a person holding the rank of colonel of the United Irishmen, had given to the Government monthly reports of their secret meetings from March,* 1797? It was clear from this that the Government were cognisant of the plot, and had it in their power to put it down. But the right hon. gentleman said there were traitorous materials in Ireland. Undoubtedly there were; otherwise there could not have been a rebellion; but those materials were not of a formidable nature. They existed to a certain extent in Leinster and Ulster, and produced two skirmishes, in one of which Lord O'Neill was killed; but the only really formidable occurrence took place in Wexford. These matters were encouraged—not repressed; and the Union was brought about by fomenting the rebellion till it exploded."

Mr. O'Connell continued in a strain of great animation to reply to the arguments of several of his opponents seriatim.

The motion for the Repeal Committee was negatived by an enormous majority, the numbers being 525 against 40, including the tellers.

Mr. Stanley took no part in the debate. He was probably muzzled by Sir Robert Peel, who, with characteristic policy and caution, contrived that the debate should sustain as little interruption as possible from the indecent shoutings and ferocious yells with which the Irish Members had been assailed during the discussion of the Coercion Bills in the previous year. Mr. Stanley's silence was remarkable. His feelings against the Repeal were very strong; he had in 1833 declared he would "resist it to the death." That he did not now avail himself of the opportunity of renewing that declaration, is probably to be ascribed to the management of his more cautious leader, who naturally doubted his discretion.

The ministerial and English journals generally were loud in their glorifications. Spring Rice's speech they pronounced to be an unanswerable manual. No Repealer could in future dare to raise his voice against the demonstrations, clear as light, of the infinite benefits the Union had conferred upon Ireland. The question, they said, was finally set at rest; and they added much more to the same purpose.

Meanwhile, the result of the debate upon the Irish people

---

* This should have been April.

was precisely what any man who knew the country and its inhabitants must have expected. They saw in the division a fresh proof of English hostility to their rights and of English indifference to their grievances. Mr. Rice's tabular dexterities—his "giant-stride prosperity" on paper, seemed a heartless and insolent mockery to a people of whom every fourth individual was a destitute pauper. The alacrity and fervour with which the House applauded the most hollow fallacies, afforded, to the minds of the Irish nation, fresh evidence of its total ignorance of their condition and its consequent incapacity to legislate for their advantage. Our people felt that the Constitution of Ireland was the indisputable property of the nation, and not of its Parliament, which, consequently, had no authority to sell it in 1800. Their resolve to struggle for the Repeal, to seize whatever opportunities God might send for its achievement, was thenceforth more firmly fixed than ever.

Both Houses had addressed the King, who replied in an echo of their joint address. The address and the reply contained a promise to uphold the Union; but at the same time a pledge "to remove all just causes of complaint, and to sanction all well-considered measures of improvement." The Irish people were not so foolish as to place the least faith in this pledge of King, Lords, and Commons; but they acquiesced in O'Connell's policy of testing their truth by the celebrated six years' experiment, at the end of which, as the pledges were demonstratively proved to have been mere delusions, the Repeal Association was established, and the agitation directed once more into its natural and legitimate channel. O'Connell was wrong, in my opinion, to have suspended for six years the national demand. It is scarcely conceivable that he believed the joint pledge of King, Lords, and Commons, "to remove all just causes of complaint." Moreover, the most important cause of just complaint was the refusal to restore the Irish Parliament; our greatest grievance was the Union; and this the King, Lords, and Commons declared they would uphold.

I shall pass over the six years of Whig ascendency, and the fruitless struggles for that chimera, Equality with England under the Union.*

There was, to do the Whigs justice, a fair administration of the law; and their legal appointments were excellent.

* In the *Anti-Union*—a most interesting periodical, commenced on the 27th December, 1798, and which reckoned Saurin among its

CHAPTER XIX.

O'CONNELL'S FINAL EFFORT FOR REPEAL.

Resolve! resolve! and to be men aspire;
Let godlike Reason from her sovereign throne
Speak the commanding word, "I will," and it is done.
                                                THOMSON.

THE time was now come when O'Connell deemed it right to abandon for ever all attempts to obtain "justice for Ireland" from the English Parliament. He accordingly embarked in his final effort to procure a Repeal of the Union. On the 15th of April, 1840, he founded the Repeal Association. Its first meeting was held in the Great Room of the Corn Exchange, Burgh Quay, which is capable of accommodating about five hundred persons. The room was not one-fifth part filled; there was a discouraging display of empty benches—a commencement that might well have disheartened a leader less sanguine than O'Connell. He remembered the commencement of the Catholic Association, the seven men who congregated in Coyne's back parlour, in Capel Street, and the magnificent result of that small beginning; and he confidently looked forward to a yet more brilliant termination of his new enterprise.

Still the meeting had a very discouraging appearance to those who had not the sagacious forecast of the leader. It seemed as if the word Repeal had lost its potent magic. But the fact was far otherwise. The thinness of the attendance arose from no apathy as to the national cause. It arose from a strong fear on the part of the Repeal public that the new experiment was not made *bonâ fide*. Repeal had been temporarily abandoned before. Such might be again its fate. Men dreaded lest O'Connell merely meant to rattle it about the ears of the Government *in terrorem*, as a means of compelling them to make minor concessions to Ireland.

contributors—I find, at p. 63, the following : "It has been asserted that the powers of Irish representatives will be enlarged, and the rights of Irish electors improved, by Irish representatives having two shares in eleven in the direction of affairs relative to their own country only, instead of having the sole disposal of them in themselves alone."—The other nine shares being in the hands of a jealous rival! Such is the Union.

"As soon," said O'Connell, "as they begin to find out that I am perfectly in earnest, they will come flocking into the Association."

The chair was taken by Mr. John O'Neill, of Fitzwilliam Square, a Protestant merchant of great wealth and sterling patriotism. He had been in early youth a member of the Volunteer army of 1782. "I was then," he said to me, "too young to be of much use to Ireland, and now I am too old." But, young or old, his country had always commanded his best services. That good old Protestant patriot is long since dead. He descended to the tomb full of years, and deeply honoured by his fellow-countrymen.

For more than half-an-hour the few who had congregated at the Corn Exchange anxiously awaited the opening address of the Liberator; but he still lingered, apparently unwilling to commence, in the hope of a more numerous attendance. But no reinforcement came. There were manifestations of impatience among those who had assembled. O'Connell at length rose, and with the air of one deeply impressed with the high and solemn responsibility which he incurred, spoke as follows :

"My fellow-countrymen, I rise with a deep sense of the awful importance of the step I am about to propose to the Irish people, and a full knowledge of the difficulties by which we are surrounded, and the obstacles we have to contend with. I trust that my heart is pure, and my judgment on the present occasion unclouded; and I declare, in the presence of that God who is to judge me for an eternity of weal or woe, that I have no object in view but the good of my native land, and that I feel in the deepest sense the responsibility I am about to incur. We are about to enter on a struggle that will terminate only in having the most ample justice done to Ireland by placing her on an equality with the sister country,* or by the establishment of our legislative independence. The struggle commences now—it will end only then. We commence under auspices that may afford little prospect of ultimate success to some; but those

* I never could understand what is meant by "equality" between Ireland and England under an Union. Said C. J. Fox, on the 7th of May, 1800, at a meeting of the Whig Club : "It was idle to talk to Ireland of the word union, since there could be no such thing as a real Union on an equal footing between two countries so disproportionate and unequal. Could the Irish believe that in this connection they were to have an equal voice in legis'ating for England as the English had in legislating for Ireland ?"

O

who know the character of the brave, moral, religious, and patient Irish people, cannot be of that opinion. We will, no doubt, be laughed at and derided on all sides, and sneered at by friends who believe everything is impracticable, and opposed by those malignant enemies who will be delighted to find any opportunity of manifesting their hostility. But no matter; we were derided and laughed at before by persons of this description when we set about the accomplishment of that great moral revolution which won religious freedom for ourselves and others."

He then referred to the small origin of the Catholic Association, its progress and triumph; exposed the delusive nature of the Union, and repeated his proofs of the anti-Irish spirit in which laws were made for Ireland by the Imperial Legislature. He promised perseverance.

"We have assembled to take part in proceedings that will yet be memorable in the history of our country. Yes, this fifteenth of April will be yet memorable in the annals of Ireland. It shall be referred to as the day on which the flag of Repeal was unfurled; and I shall fearlessly, legally, and constitutionally keep it unfurled until the day of success shall have arrived, or the grave shall close over me, and on my tomb shall be inscribed 'He died a Repealer.' . . . We must be up, I say, and stirring. We can do no good by quiescence; it may do us evil, but it can do us no service. We must take counsel from the French proverb, which says: 'Help yourselves, and God will help you.' We must not forget the story of the fellow, who, when the wheel of his cart stuck in the mud, prayed to Jupiter to help him. 'You lazy rascal,' said his godship, 'put your shoulder to the wheel, and get along out of that.' I tell you there is nothing else for us but to help ourselves; and help ourselves, with the aid of God, we shall."

Having quoted the well-known denunciations of the Union, pronounced in 1799 and 1800 by Charles Kendal Bushe (the Chief Justice), and William Conyngham Plunket (the Chancellor), he continued: "These are

Thoughts that breathe, and words that burn.

I have them here. They shall be spread through the land in the course of next week for the perusal of the youth of Ireland; not one of whom, I trust, will be found, whose eye will not glisten with fire, whose young heart will not burn with indignation at the spoliation resorted to by our enemies.

There was a bargain, forsooth! Why, is not the Chief Justice* still living? and is he not a witness for me? Is not the Lord Chancellor of Ireland,† with all his Asdrubals or Hannibals, living also to bear his testimony? What care I whether he has changed his opinion or no? He was honest then, because he had no sons to quarter on the State. Let him change now if he wish. In his day of virtue he felt and spoke those sentiments which I have read for you. Let him now change them in the day of his power and authority."

In the opening passage of O'Connell's speech, he had mentioned "justice to Ireland" as an alternative. But how visionary he deemed the prospect of obtaining that "justice" is evident from the following passage: "If we get that justice we desire, then our Repeal Association is at an end; but I know we will not get that justice, and that there is nothing left for us but to pursue vigorously the course we have commenced this day.... Why should we for a moment deceive ourselves? This justice will not be done to Ireland, and we will at once set ourselves right by declaring that there is a Repeal Association, and that unless the moral miracle be performed of having justice done to us by England, we will never cease until we have a Parliament established in College Green.‡

"Not one single benefit has the Union conferred upon Ireland, but, on the contrary, it has brought in its train poverty, degradation, and sorrow. When once the public

* Charles Kendal Bushe.
† William Conyngham Plunket.
‡ As this passage appeared to contain an admission, even although a hypothetical one, that justice from England could supersede the necessity of Repeal, O'Connell guarded himself from such an objection in a subsequent speech, delivered on the 1st of May, 1840. He explained his meaning in still retaining the semblance of an alternative thus: "I have declared for the Repeal, and from this declaration nothing shall ever take me. It has been said that even in the formation of this society I held out the alternative of justice. Let them do us justice; let them increase our representatives to 150 in number; let them remove the Church grievance; let them increase the franchise—let them do all this, and though they will not have convinced me that Repeal is unnecessary, they will deprive me of the forces by which I hope to succeed..... But who supposes they ever will be brought to do us justice? Not even a dreamer who dreamed soundly in his sleep; no one short of an idiot could be brought to believe it..... I hold out the alternative, to be sure; but it is to the English Members of Parliament. The alternative is not for me—it is for them."

mind is aroused, and the evils which we have suffered pointed out to the people, the Union cannot continue. It is not the writing of a single letter, nor the delivery of a single speech, that can effect the Repeal; it is the concentration of public opinion, directed as a galvanic battery, that will have that effect. That opinion will then become powerful as the lightnings of heaven, destroying everything that may impede its course."

He concluded by moving the adoption of a set of rules; the seconder of the motion being Mr. John Redmond, a patriotic citizen.

So ended the first day's meeting. The Whig Liberals did their best to throw contempt and ridicule on the proceedings. The paucity of the attendance was pointed out with scorn. Those gentlemen said to their acquaintances as they met in the streets, " Dan will never work this question —he is not in earnest—the people don't care about it "— (this was a very favourite allegation)—" he will not be able to get over the priests to help him." The word "Repealer" was pronounced with a derisive curl of the lip by the "genteel" Liberals, who religiously abhorred all treason against Whiggery. More sagacious men, however, knew that the question was workable. They remembered the popular enthusiasm of 1832, and they did not believe that enthusiasm to be a mere fever-fit.

O'Connell was accused, as a matter of course, of embarking in what he knew and intended to be a delusive agitation. To create an impression that the leader was insincere, was a dexterous mode of damaging the cause. O'Connell, however, had the most intense conviction that success was possible, provided that the parties who were interested in its attainment would apply their whole strength to the task. Those parties were the people of Ireland. He had great faith in the manifest truth and common sense of his statements and arguments. When dictating Reports and Addresses to Mr. Ray, the able and energetic Secretary of the Association, he would say: "Well, Ray, I am acquitting my conscience; I am giving the people of Ireland an opportunity to have their Parliament restored, and if they do not aid me the fault is their own."

He held that the Act of Union—which Saurin had pronounced to be destitute of any other sanction than coercive force—did not need a formal Act of the Imperial Parliament for its repeal; and he published in May, 1840, a masterly argument to show that Her Majesty possesses the constitutional right of convoking the Irish Parliament in Dublin, notwithstanding the iniquitous suppression of that body by the monster-crime of 1800.* And he believed that it was not impossible to create a condition of public affairs in which Her Majesty's advisers might deem such exercise of her constitutional prerogative expedient.

O'Connell lost no time in placing before the public, in the fullest detail, his plan for the reconstruction of the Irish Parliament. He was resolved to avoid the reproach of a vague, indefinite agitation; an agitation for the Repeal of the Union, unaccompanied with a clear, minute statement of the system he proposed to establish. Accordingly he issued, on the 4th of May, 1840, an elaborate scheme for the construction of the restored Irish Parliament; which, like its suppressed predecessor, he proposed should contain 300 members. Of these, 127 were to represent cities and towns, and 173 were to represent counties. The local electoral forces he computed on the basis of the population returns of 1831.

"It may be alleged" (so runs his Report †) " that in proposing to give to the agricultural districts 173 members, and to the towns, or mercantile interests, but 127, an undue proportion is thus struck between the one and the other. But we think there is no weight in such an objection. There is no antagonism of interest between the mercantile and agricultural classes in Ireland; and we consider that in point of fact the greatest interest our commercial men can have, is in the increase of the number of landed proprietors whose duty or whose ambition would lead them to continue to reside in their respective counties; thus employing the income derived from lands in Ireland, in the consumption of the articles in which our mercantile men principally deal.

"It may be objected that it is premature to bring before the public the plan for the reconstruction of the Irish Parliament, before we have made more progress towards that combination of public opinion from which alone we can hope for success. But we deem it most fair and reasonable, at the earliest possible stage of that agitation, which can terminate only in the Repeal, to submit to the good sense and calm consideration of the people of Ireland, the best mode of reconstituting their House of Commons. At present, our plan can be discussed coolly and dispassionately; and its defects,

---

* The reader will find O'Connell's argument, which he supports by historical references, in the Appendix.

† First Series of Repeal Reports, printed by Browne, Dublin, 1840, p. 51.

if any, can be pointed out without creating heat or animosity. Not so, if the period of Repeal were actually at hand. Then local interests would create or magnify objections, and accusations of personal or particular motives might be made, which cannot now be even dreamt of. We have, therefore, deemed it the wisest course to procure the discussion and adoption of a settled plan of reconstruction of the Irish House of Commons, at a period when it can be discussed and adopted without the smallest intermixture of passion, prejudice, or private interest." *

Thus careful was O'Connell to explain, with the utmost minuteness of detail, what he meant by the Repeal of the Union. It will be observed that in the distribution of seats he proposed to give a predominating influence to the landed interest. If the Irish landlords had been wise enough to throw their strength into his movement, Repeal could have been easily carried; and the landlords would have deservedly possessed, as patriots, that commanding power in their native country, which they have deservedly forfeited as the servile and degraded supporters of the alien rule that strips their country of its wealth, banishes its people, and largely helps to beggar themselves. But the landlords were in most cases bewildered by a bigoted fear of their Catholic fellow-countrymen, and withheld their assistance from O'Connell's effort to restore legislative independence and consequent prosperity to the nation in which Catholics were a majority.

For a good while after the establishment of the Repeal Association, the English press was wholly, or nearly, silent on the subject. By-and-by the English journalists condescended to laugh at the Repealers. After their wit was exhausted at our expense, they began to be abusive. The Repealers were denounced as political criminals of the worst description, and floods of coarse vituperation were poured upon them from the copious reservoirs of the *Times* newspaper. O'Connell returned the compliments of the *Times* in these verses :

> Vile press without a parallel,
> Organ meet for fiends of hell,
> Lies thy trade; thy master-sense,
> Bribed and brutal insolence;
> From Puddledock to either sea,
> Toryism stinks of thee.

---

* First Series of Repeal Reports, printed by Browne, Dublin, 1840, p. 52.

To account for the virulence of these lines I should remind the reader that the *Times* had termed the Irish nation "a filthy and felonious multitude," and the Catholic clergy a tribe of "surpliced ruffians."

CHAPTER XX.

GRADUAL PROGRESS OF THE REPEAL ASSOCIATION.

> Such men as these,
> Give grace to holy mysteries,
> And make the pure oblation rise,
> A God-accepted sacrifice.
>
> ANON.

THE Repeal Association gradually expanded. Every week brought fresh recruits. Of these, some few were the ancient relics of a former age—old men who in early youth had stood in the ranks of the Volunteer army, and who now, ere they sank into the grave, were glad to enrol themselves once more in the service of their country. I have already named my old Protestant friend, John O'Neill. Another of our patriarchal adjuncts was Robert M'Clelland, a northern Presbyterian, who, although past eighty, was a regular attendant at the weekly meetings at the Corn Exchange as long as his health permitted him. It would be unjust and ungrateful to omit this mention of those venerable Protestant patriots, whose aid was ever heartily rendered to every movement having for its object the enlargement of the liberties of Ireland. "Requiescant in pace."

Repeal progressed. The Catholic clergy sent in their adhesions pretty numerously. On one occasion a bishop* and eighty-three of his clergy were enrolled together. There were three great provincial meetings for Leinster, Connaught, and Munster. At the Leinster meeting, which was held near Kilkenny, in October, 1840, a quarter of a million of persons were computed to be present. John O'Connell occupied the chair. It was a grave autumnal day; there was a quiet beauty in the fertile, undulating landscape, with the city in the middle distance, the proud towers of the Ormonds rising high above the mass of city buildings, and the hills of Mount Leinster and Blackstairs in the far horizon.

* Right Rev. Dr. Foran, Bishop of Waterford.

The muster was a noble display, and was distinguished, like all other meetings for Repeal, by that rigid observance of decorum, preservation of peace, and perfect sobriety, which no great popular gatherings of similar extent in any other nation could exhibit.

Father Mathew's movement was essentially useful to Repeal. By withdrawing the people from the odious and stultifying vice of inebriety, it raised them in the intellectual scale. Freed from the degrading influences of intoxication, they were the better able to think and to reason. A reasoning, thinking people are not destined to slavery. The arguments in favour of Repeal come so home to the common-sense of Irishmen, that it needs only to rescue the people from habits of intemperance to convert the impulsive and unreasoning shout for liberty into a calculating, sagacious, and well-sustained struggle for legislative independence. The enemies of Ireland, both domestic and English, saw this; and accordingly the temperance movement was made the object of ferocious vituperation. It is amusing to look back at some few of the exploits of the anti-temperance party. Religious fanaticism was of course pressed into the service of drunkenness. A parson named Whitty refused to grant Father Mathew the use of the Rock of Cashel to accommodate his postulants, alleging that "temperance was of the devil." * Another clergyman, named Edgar, residing in the diocese of Derry, declared, in a letter to Mr. Buckingham, the ex-Member for Sheffield, that "teetotalism was highly insulting to the majesty of God;"† at the same time expressing his fear that Mr. Buckingham was affected with the disease in its worst form. The Rev. Mr. Sewell, of Oxford, wrote an article in the *Quarterly Review*, entitled "Romanism in Ireland;" asserting therein that superstition was the chief agency of the temperance movement, and murder its ultimate object.

Passing from the high priests of inebriety to its profaner organs, the *Protestant Magazine* for June, 1841, complacently quoted from the congenial *Times* the following awful passage : " We cannot but suspect that this temperance movement is, substantially, a sort of Trojan horse, within whose ribs there lurks an overwhelming phalanx, which some of these nights will sally on the sleeping sentinels of Ireland and make it an easy prey."

* *Morning Chronicle*, 27th April, 1841.   † *Ibid.*

The Ulster Orangemen were at all events resolved that they should not be caught napping. At Loughgall, a number of Orange farmers entered into a resolution that they would not employ any labourers who had taken the temperance pledge. In other places there were anti-temperance riots, especially at Newtownhamilton and Lurgan. The Orangemen apparently were not satisfied with the privilege of getting drunk, unless they could deprive their neighbours of the privilege of pledging themselves to sobriety. The Cootehill Orangemen published a manifesto, redolent of the choicest inspirations of the Orange divinity, exhorting the Protestants to oppose the entrance of Father Mathew into their district, where he proposed to administer the pledge. The document, having first adverted to the priest's threatened advent, proceeded thus: "Insulted Protestants! will, ye, can ye bear it any longer? Has the spirit of your fathers, of immortal William, died within you? .... Arouse! be steady and courageous. Let not the *religion* * of your fathers be trampled on by idolaters. Let the spirit of William, that whispers to you at this moment, animate your hearts and souls, and let not the anti-Christian apostle depart from Cootehill in boasted triumph.

> Arise, I say, arise, my boys, and raise your standard high,
> The man that will not join you now, treat as an enemy;
> Fear not O'Connell—Mathew—Devil! but let your motto be,
> To put your trust in God, my boys, and keep your powder dry.
> Remember Gideon's chosen few,
> The arm that guarded them guards you.

This delirious *mélange* of politics, bigotry, and truculence, demonstrates the fatal success with which the Whittys and Edgars had instilled into their followers a virulent hostility to national amelioration. The Divine assistance is invoked by the Cootehill devotees to preserve their drunken license. The arm that guarded Gideon's chosen few is expected to guard the Orange Bacchanals from the fatal invasion of temperance. At a later period, however, the spirit of the North became improved. Leading men of all political shades looked with favour upon temperance; and as virtues are gregarious, the same result which attended the success of Father Mathew's movement in the South also marked its progress in the North. As morality and sobriety advanced, nationality kept pace with them. Let the mere

---

* Query, the whisky bottle?

enthusiast, whether Orangeman or Repealer, forswear his drunken orgies; the latter will become a more zealous and useful, because a more enlightened and intelligent supporter of national liberty; the former will be led to inquire whether that which is manifestly good for Ireland can be bad for himself. The result of this inquiry will make him a Repealer.

The agitation for Repeal went on, sometimes in places which conjured up interesting historical associations. A Repeal meeting was held at Carrick-on-Suir, which was followed by a public dinner, presided over by a Protestant gentleman, Mr. Power. The dinner took place in an apartment at the top of the principal inn. I was told that many persons had wished to obtain a room in the Castle of Carrick-on-Suir for the festivity; but a fear lest Lord Ormond, the proprietor of the Castle, might visit with his vengeance the gentleman who rented the old building as tenant at will, induced the managers of the dinner to select the less commodious apartment in the hotel.

I chanced that day to be at Carrick, and I walked to see the old Castle. It is beautifully situated in a secluded lawn overhanging the Suir, at the distance of a few hundred yards from the eastern end of the town. I could not ascertain the date of the older, or castellated portion of the edifice; the more modern part was erected by Thomas Butler, Earl of Ormond, in 1565, which date is displayed on the wall of the hall, on which, also, there is a rude fresco, representing Queen Elizabeth, with the initials E.R. On the opposite wall there is another fresco, representing the founder, who is said by the tradition of the Castle to have found favour as a lover with that princess. The tradition found its way into France, and the family of Lord Galmoye is stated, in a French genealogical work, to descend from Her Majesty and her Irish admirer. In Burke's " Peerage and Baronetage for 1830," the following very curious notice of the Galmoye family is extracted from the " Dictionnaire de la Noblesse," published at Paris in 1771, second edition, tome iii.:

" Le comte Thomas de Butler, dit le noir, quelques années après être allé en Angleterre, envoya en Irlande un jeune enfant portant son nom, et déjà créé Lord Vicomte de Galmoye. Il est certain (dit le Mémoire envoyé sur lequel nous avons dressé cette généalogie) que le comte le reconnaissoit pour son fils, et la tradition veut que la reine Elizabeth fût sa mère; c'est de cet enfant que descendoit milord de Galmoye, mort à Paris en 1740, lieut.-général des armées du roi, créé comte de Newcastle en France par le roi Jacques II., dont il était premier gentilhomme de la chambre," etc. A tradition of the same import prevails in the Irish branch of the family.

The curious old mansion founded by "Black Tom Butler" is still habitable.* Its front presents a long row of gables in the fashion of Elizabethan manor-houses, with a large oriel window over the porch. Its large, deserted chambers are just such as spectral personages might readily honour with their visits. I accordingly asked if the house was haunted, and was told by the person who showed it, that in the days of the Ormonds a ghost had been constantly there—a utilitarian ghost, apparently; for he used to officiate as volunteer shoe-black, and to discharge other duties of domestic labour.

The largest apartments are in the upper storey. There is a noble drawing-room about sixty feet long, which contains two decorated chimneys. Whatever be the worth of the Galmoye tradition, old "Tom Butler," as the guide familiarly called him, was anxious to record his devotion to Elizabeth; and this he has done by the frequent repetition of Her Majesty's initials and arms in the quaint stucco ornaments of the ceiling. There is another spacious room on the same floor, with an oriel overlooking the river.

I was inclined to regret that Mr. O'Connell was not entertained in this old stronghold of the Butlers. The old

* 1842. I have not seen it since. Thomas Butler, the founder of the Elizabethan part of Carrick-on-Suir Castle, was the tenth Earl of Ormond, and died there in his eighty-eighth year in 1614. He was great-uncle to James, the celebrated Duke of Ormond, who often mentioned his recollection of his aged relative as "a blind old man, having a long beard, and wearing his George about his neck whether he sat up in his chair or lay down in his bed." In 1632 James made a journey from London to Carrick, which, even according to modern ideas, seems a rapid one. On a Saturday morning in September he left London, and rode post to Acton, within eight miles of Bristol. At 8 next morning he sailed from Bristol to Waterford in a vessel called *The Ninth Whelp*, and at 9 a.m. on Monday they ran up to Waterford, whence his lordship immediately took horse for Carrick, which is distant from Waterford only sixteen miles.

Henry Hyde, second Earl of Clarendon, in a letter to Lord Rochester, dated in 1686, says of this old seat: "Carrick, an ancient seat belonging to the Duke of Ormond, is, I think, one of the prettiest places I ever saw in my life."—*Clarendon's Letters*, London, 1828.

walls speak eloquently to the imagination. There would have been a romantic interest in beholding the great advocate of Irish legislative independence working out his mighty task in the deserted residence of one of the most powerful of Norman-Irish families; enforcing the right of Ireland to self-government in the ancient halls of Elizabeth's favourite, who performed his share of the duty of riveting the English chain upon his country; in those halls which at a later period were the habitation of James, Duke of Ormond, who exercised such potent influence, partly for good, but more for evil, on the destinies of Ireland.

I lingered until twilight in the Castle. The echo of the closing doors sounded weirdly and solemn through the dusky chambers; it came upon the ear like the voice of ages past. The guide bore in his hand the ponderous old keys, which, to judge from their great size and rude workmanship, might have been coeval with the edifice itself. When I reached the lawn, I turned to look once more at the venerable pile reposing in its solitude and silence, and then retraced my steps to the town.

At the Repeal dinner, O'Connell said: "I am often asked, how can I expect to obtain Repeal from the Imperial Parliament when I have not been able to obtain minor benefits? I answer this question by reminding the querists that upon the minor advantages I sought I have not been supported by the whole Irish people; whereas the Repeal agitation accumulates around me their entire strength. Minor objects were not of sufficient importance to enlist their full energies. The eagle does not catch flies. The eagle spirit of Ireland soars above these individual advantages and perches on the lofty pedestal of national independence." He proceeded to predict the certain attainment of Repeal so soon as universal Ireland should be actively aroused in its behalf; and he then, in a strain of fervid eloquence, described the long perspective of Irish prosperity which he expected to result from that measure.

Carrick had its own sad experience of decay since the Union, there having been prior to that measure a thriving woollen trade in the town and its immediate vicinity, giving bread to about 5,000 persons; whereas now* there is but partial employment for about one hundred persons there. Go where they would, the Repeal agitators had the dismal

* 1844.

and terrible advantage of being able to point to the surrounding crowds instances of decay with which their local experience was familiar—practical fulfilments of John Foster's memorable words: "Where the Parliament is, there will the manufacturer be also." In Limerick there had been before the Union over a thousand woollen weavers; the number had shrunk to less than seventy. In Bandon—Protestant Bandon—there had been before the Union a flourishing manufacture of camlets, cords, and stuffs. That trade had all but vanished; the only branch of the woollen manufacture remaining there when our Repeal missions were organised, being that of frieze for the peasantry. And similar decay had widely overspread the land on all sides.*

The Viceroy, Lord Ebrington, now made an effort to arrest the progress of Repeal by announcing that no member of the Repeal Association should be appointed to any office in the gift of the Government. This declaration necessarily scared all the place-hunters from joining the movement, and thus preserved it from the adhesion of a good deal of rascality. Lord Ebrington's threat was undignified, but not unnatural. He probably thought that as the Union was originally carried by bribery, Repeal could best be averted by bribing men through their hopes of office to refrain from junction with the agitators.

CHAPTER XXI.

PROPAGATION OF REPEAL BY MISSIONS.

> Arouse thee, youth! it is no idle call;
> Our rights are leaguered—haste to man the wall;
> Haste where the old green banner waves on high,
> Signal of honoured death, or victory.

AMONG the public men who played fast and loose on the question of Repeal, was Mr. Sharman Crawford. That gentleman had ably and persistently advocated the cause of the Irish tenant-farmer, and had, by his advocacy, acquired wide and merited popularity. He denounced the crimes committed against the people by exterminating landlords,

* For copious and authentic details of the general decay see Mr. Secretary Ray's admirable "Report on the Disastrous Effects of the Union on the Woollen, Silk, and Cotton Manufactures."

and contended for the system of small farms, which he said could be worked with a profit to the tenant by the application of increased skill in cultivation, while the landlord would possess full security for his rent in the value enjoyed by the tenant.

O'Connell expected that Crawford would assist the Repeal agitation—an expectation which was not unreasonable, for Crawford, in 1833, had published a pamphlet entitled, "The Expediency and Necessity of a Local Legislative Body in Ireland supported by a Reference to Facts and Principles." In page 27 of that pamphlet, its author says : " Sad experience now proves to Ireland, as on former occasions, that England's freedom is Ireland's slavery ; that England's prosperity only dooms Ireland to a more depressed state of misery and political degradation. She finds the same abuses retained—the same disregard of her complaints ; and what renders the case still more hopeless is the general apathy and indifference of the British nation, and the worse than indifference of the Scotch, towards matters connected with Irish policy." At page 53, speaking of the reformed Parliament of England, Mr. Crawford asks : " Have not the proceedings of that Parliament forced a conviction on many of the most attached friends of British connexion, that the union of the nations can only be upheld by the separation of the Parliaments ? "

These extracts afford a fair sample of the general spirit of Mr. Crawford's pamphlet. But on the revival, by O'Connell, of the agitation for Repeal, Mr. Crawford ranged himself among the anti-Repealers. In October, 1841, he published " Observations addressed to the Repealers of Ireland," in which he declared that he would not be "a party to a delusive agitation." He recommended, instead of the pursuit of Repeal, that the Irish should unite with "the aggrieved and unrepresented classes in England and Scotland," in demanding a new distribution and equalisation of electoral districts all over the United Kingdom. He denied that it was possible for Ireland to possess an independent Parliament in connection with the British Crown. And he censured the patriots of 1782 for establishing "a nominally independent" Irish Parliament, instead of seeking a federative connexion with England on the American principle.

Mr. Crawford's attacks on the Repealers had a wide circulation. The task of reply was entrusted to me. My answers went the round of the Repeal press in Ireland, and were published as a pamphlet both in Dublin and Belfast. As long as O'Connell lived, Mr. Crawford retained his attitude of hostility; but after the death of O'Connell he publicly joined the Protestant Repeal Association which had been instituted at Belfast, recanted his imperialism, and declared his assent to the principles of 1782. But I must not anticipate.

Hitherto the agitation, although occupying the minds of the people, and engaging much of their support, had not been efficiently organised. To supply this defect, and at the same time to inculcate the principle of nationality in the various rural districts, it was now deemed advisable to send missionaries through the land. The persons selected by the Committee of the Association to discharge this arduous duty were Mr. John O'Connell, third son of the Liberator, who was appointed Repeal Director for Connaught; Mr. Ray, the Secretary of the Association; and myself. I was appointed Repeal Director for Leinster.

On the 12th of September, 1842, we left Dublin for our several routes. Mr. Ray proceeded to Limerick, Munster having been assigned as the district of his labours. As John O'Connell's route and mine for the first and second days lay in the same direction, we travelled together in the canal-boat to Mullingar. At that town we waited on the Right Rev. Dr. Cautwell, the bishop of the diocese, who promised his cordial co-operation to the cause in which we were engaged. Next day we proceeded to Ballymahon, where the Bishop of Ardagh had invited a large party of his clergy to meet us. There was much grave and earnest discussion on the subject of the movement. The prelate pledged himself that all the influence he possessed should be placed at the disposal of the Repeal Association. The Bishop of Meath had given a similar pledge, and nobly were their promises redeemed.

Without the active co-operation of the priesthood, the Repeal cause could never have acquired the commanding position it soon began to occupy. It is not uninteresting to trace the gradation of its progress in the rural districts. Three men, animated with the most ardent desire to promote national freedom, travelled from town to town, from parish to parish. They solicited and obtained the hearty and powerful support of the priests. They assembled their countrymen in the market-place, in the church, on the bleak hill-side; they told in plain and energetic language the story of England's crime and Ireland's degradation; they enumerated the grinding wrongs, the oppressions, and the robberies inflicted on the ill-starred land, which in losing the power of self-government had lost the power of self-defence; they asked their countrymen whether this national dishonour should continue; whether the Irish people should not stretch forth their hands to seize and fashion into strength the rich elements of power and prosperity that everywhere lay scattered around? They made it a personal question to each individual. They charged it home upon the conscience of each whether he would be a guilty partaker, by his criminal apathy, in the wrongs inflicted by England on his country? They asked,

"Could the wrong'd realm no arms supply,
But the abject tear and the slavish sigh?"

They stirred into energetic life the slumbering spirit of old nationhood; they wakened the political sleeper from his trance. "Repeal" began to be a gathering shout in many a district that had long dozed on in torpid inactivity. The connexions of the central institute in Dublin were extended through the land. The pulsations of the heart began to be felt at the extremities; and the question soon exhibited in the various rural districts a vitality and vigour which astonished the whole tribe of anti-Irish gentlemen with wooden heads and stony hearts—men whose diseased and stunted intellects were perfectly incapable of regarding any great public question except through the medium of the narrowest, the paltriest prejudice.

It was in the rural dwellings of the clergy that the question was now efficiently worked. In the priest's humble home a power was being organised which was destined, as we fondly hoped, to make tyranny reel in high places. And how simple the process! how easy the details! Look at that anxious, thoughtful group, gathered round the pastor's table. The shutters are closed, the candles lighted, the faggot blazes brightly on the hearth; "the autumn breeze's bugle sound" is heard from without; it has swept from the hills, and its wild voice awakens in the heart a mystic thrill for freedom. The priest tells his guest the effective strength of the district, availing himself, in the detail, of the local information possessed by the parishioners, or the neighbouring clergy who have assembled at his house. It is then ascertained who will work, who will undertake the duty of Repeal Warden, who will collect the Repeal rent, and who will assume the charge of particular plough lands if in the country, or wards if in a town. The obstacles are also canvassed; the hostility of Lord So-and-So, or of Captain ——, his agent, who swears he will eject every tenant who gives sixpence to any of O'Connell's devices. Or perhaps there is the anti-Irish Catholic landlord—a greater scourge than the Orange proprietor—who, since shuffling off his penal coil in 1829, has affected the courtier and fine gentleman, and conceives that he establishes his claim to aristocratic distinction by mimicking the tyranny of those by whom his creed is denounced as satanic; the supple slave of Tory squires; the petty tyrant of his village, who redeems the vulgarity of going to mass by the severity with which he grinds the unfortunate tenantry who go there along with him. To elude the spiteful vigilance of this most execrable class is a problem which engages the attention of our coterie. The problem is easily solved. What needs Squire A. or Lord B. know about the tenants' contributions? A discreet warden, who can be silent when occasion requires, is appointed to receive their subscriptions; so that matter is settled. Then speculations arise respecting the possible adhesion of men whose countenance would be advantageous; they are alleged to have uttered very national sentiments on certain occasions; could they now be got to realise their patriotic declarations?

Having arranged all these practical matters, and set the agitation in a working train, the missionary next inquires respecting the past and present state of trade, and the social condition of the people in the district. The information thus elicited is painful. It reveals the national decay and the popular destitution. Nearly all over Leinster the linen trade—once the great staple—is now only a memory. The inquirer is told that in the immediate vicinity of Clara in the King's County, capital amounting at least to £150,000 had been invested in that trade, which is now extinct in that locality. The old men who have joined the priest's party tell the visitor that prior to the Union they remember from forty to fifty head of cattle killed at Christmas by the villagers and farmers, who could then afford to eat beef; whereas now, instead of forty or fifty, not half-a-dozen Christmas cows are consumed by the impoverished people. At Mullingar he hears there had been a flourishing linen trade before the Union, and that it is now gone. At Athlone that trade gave bread to from 4,000 to 5,000 persons prior to the Union. There is now no linen trade at Athlone, but there is

P

a large poor-house there. The country round Banagher, Ferbane, Ballycumber, and Cloghan, had once been covered over with the linen manufacture. The visitor is told that it has shared the same fate as at Athlone and Mullingar—extinction.

The numerous deserted mansions, formerly the seats of splendid hospitality, but now decaying from the neglect of their absentee owners, also form a painful item in the missionary's information. On one point a great unanimity prevails—namely, that all these evils, and nearly all other grievances affecting the country, have their source either remotely or immediately in the denial to Ireland of the power of making her own laws, and in the anti-national, anti-Irish spirit which the Union and sectarian bigotry have infused into the aristocracy. There is among the Irish peasantry a natural respect for old descent, an attachment to families whose progenitors for some generations have been lords of the soil. This is a sort of feudal instinct, but it is needless to say that it is uprooted in cases where the lord of the soil is the fierce and reckless enemy of the popular religion, or where he is a heartless, greedy extorter of rack rents, or where he is violently opposed to the national rights of his country. But under a right order of things—an order, that is to say, in which the aristocracy should exhibit a spirit of religious fair play and of Irish nationality—the Celtic sentiment of just and manly reverence for superiors truly entitled to respect, would be found an element of great practical utility in binding the social frame of Ireland together. This source of strength is suppressed by the present unnatural system.

Such are the topics that occupy the group in the priest's humble parlour.

At the Repeal meeting next day, the thousands who assemble round the missionary drink in his words with an eagerness that evinces the depth and fervour with which they are ready to fling themselves into the Constitutional strife. They exhibit intellectual quickness in their just and accurate perception of the points brought before them by the speakers. Their appreciation of the arguments addressed to them is clear and instantaneous. They evince this mental power by the judicious mode in which they cheer, or otherwise testify the impression made upon their minds. A striking and honourable feature in the national character is also developed at those gatherings—namely, the profound reverence the Irish people entertain for religion. If the name of the Deity be pronounced every hat is raised. If the Divine blessing be invoked on Ireland—if the speaker expresses his reliance on Providence for the ultimate success of the movement, and the consequent greatness and happiness of the land, there follows a deep murmur of reverential acquiescence from the multitude; there is an earnestness of voice, gesture, and countenance which demonstrates how intense is the reliance of the Irish people on the overruling care of their God.

There cannot be a more interesting occupation than that of the Repeal missionary. He penetrates into retired rural districts; he mingles with the people; he learns from personal inquiry and actual observation to know their condition more truly than if he had trusted for information to the monstrous fallacies of Spring Rice and Montgomery Martin.* He finds that condition grievously deteriorated since the time when Arthur Young wrote his "Tour in Ireland." In enlarging his acquaintance with his countrymen he augments his indignant horror at their wrongs and his zealous devotion to their service.

The Catholic churches and the abodes of the priests often afford interesting mementoes of the penal days. In the more remote parishes the house of the pastor is sometimes a thatched cabin adjoining the chapel, which is also thatched; both nestling in the nook of a hill, or in some retired situation which seems to evidence that concealment from observation was an object with the founder. In the chapel is the old, rough, unpainted woodwork; there are the deal benches, rails, and altar, clumsy in their construction and brown from age; the rude, whitewashed walls, the decaying windows, the simple roof that has sheltered the worshippers for four generations from the inclemency of the weather. On the altar is the tiny sacring-bell, which has tinkled perhaps for a century to announce the "Canon," the "Elevation," and the "Agnus Dei." Relics are these of the dark times of Catholic depression—relics which, notwithstanding their humble appearance in modern estimation, were doubtless in their day the source of modest pride and triumph to the priests and the flocks who had been accustomed to celebrate their worship in the glen or on the plain, beneath

* Mr. Staunton, formerly proprietor of the *Dublin Register*, wrote a trenchant castigation of this impudent quack, in a pamphlet published at the expense of the Repeal Association.

the chill blasts of winter or the scorching sun of summer. To them a roof, however rude, under which to adore their Creator, was indeed a luxurious novelty. Then the priest's cabin—containing four miserable closets, two bed-rooms, a parlour, and a kitchen.

In wet weather the Repealers sometimes got the use of the chapels for their meetings. The rude old walls which had witnessed the timid orisons of a persecuted flock in penal days now echoed to the proud and joyous voice of reviving nationality.

These remnants of a former period contrast strongly with the spacious and substantial churches raised in later years by the voluntary subscriptions of the people. The Catholic clergy in the wealthier parishes now reside in excellent and comfortable houses. The traveller is forcibly impressed by the contrast between the past and the present. He sees in its obvious moral a powerful evidence of the fidelity with which the Irish people adhered under persecution to the creed which they deemed the best, and of the pious zeal with which, when disenthralled from penal shackles, they have reared temples to the worship of the Most High God. He sees in it also an evidence of the efficacy of the Voluntary System in support of religious institutions. Small individual contributions from a numerous population can, without severe pressure upon any one, produce great results.

The missionaries forwarded to the Association weekly reports of their progress. Mr. Ray especially turned his attention to the condition of the peasantry; and from one of his reports I extract the following passages descriptive of the wretchedness endured by the poorer inhabitants of Charleville, County Cork:

"At the meeting on Sunday," says Mr. Ray, "the Rev. Mr. Meagher mentioned a most revolting case of destitution connected with this subject, occasioned by the head of a family being thrown out of employment. He was a check-weaver of sober, industrious habits, but reduced to such a state that, after having parted with every article to support nature, his wife actually perished for want; her helpless babes were lying beside their dead mother unconscious of their loss —the unfortunate man himself in agonised bewilderment. In this condition the Rev. Mr. Meagher found them on Christmas Day. Innumerable appalling cases here and elsewhere might be added of the effects of that fatal Act which robbed Ireland of her industrial occupations, and her people of their spirit and nationality.

"Immediately adjoining Mr. Dudley's in the town there is a row of wretched cabins; these were formerly the happy residences of busy inmates. They are erected on a plot of ground held originally by lease for lives under the Earl of Cork, an absentee nobleman. I understand the lessee, some years ago, consigned the occupying tenants to his lordship, the rents being applotted on their respective holdings. One of the cabins is held by a widow named Dalton; that and the adjoining one were erected by her late husband—the rent £2 a year. The roof was blown off the latter cabin at the great storm last January, and so it remains. The other is so dilapidated that the rain pours all through. Next to this is one held by Widow Meehan, at 7s. 10d. per year, almost roofless and perfectly untenantable; her son-in-law died, leaving his wife and an infant, now two years old, an incumbrance upon the poor widow. They are supported chiefly by charity. She told me that she had to pawn her bed-clothes last year to pay the rent, and was never since able to release them, and that she wished she had them now to pawn again, for the present year's rent is due.

"A man named Clifden held another of these cabins and a small plot at £1 15s. a year. He is a labourer at sixpence a day when he can get work. The surviving life in the original lease was supposed to have died a couple of years since, and possession was taken of the entire range under ejectment process. The day this occurred Clifden had the roof partly stripped, and was in the act of repairing it with new thatch. They had, of course, to quit, and this roof was also blown off by the wind. It was presently discovered that the life in the lease was in being (as the respected lady is still), 'and the tenants were allowed to continue; but this man with a wife and a number of young children had to hire a miserable cabin at the end of the town, and he is liable to the two rents. The very next hut is still worse; the roof of this was also blown down by the great storm; it is held by John Molony, labourer, at 15s. a year; it is exactly twelve feet square; the clay walls about six feet high. The poor man made a sort of covering from the old sticks and thatch of the fallen roof, but from its flatness totally incapable of resisting the wet. I found his wife and five of his children huddled together in a corner of this hut, scarcely covered with a few loathsome rags; the youngest was in her arms, the two next had only dirty, coarse, tattered bibs, the others little better; the two elder boys were out helping their father to dig, etc. This was on

Tuesday last; the two preceding nights had been most wet and inclement, and this unhappy family could get no rest, as there was not a dry spot they could lie on. I observed the remains of an old deal bedstead in a corner, with as much broken straw and rags as would make a bed for a dog; the floor under it, and indeed through the entire in a complete bog with wet. I asked, was *that* where they slept? The woman said, 'Aye, is it.' ' Have the entire family no other sleeping-place ?' said I. ' None other.' I could ask no farther questions. They were standing round two or three sods of half-burned turf, trying to dry their rags; it was so, in fact, with the rest. I did not see in all those places together as much as would equal one good fire. This poor woman told me that up to two months ago the elder children used to attend school, but were now too naked to go there. . . . 1 have given a sample of what is prevalent everywhere about the towns and in the rural districts. ' They starve themselves,' said an intelligent man to me, ' to feed the pigs for the rents.' It is impossible to witness these things without deep sensation."

Mr. Ray also furnished a report on the fallen condition of Bandon; but instead of quoting from it, I shall give the following memorandum, which was kindly communicated to me by William Connor Sullivan, Esq., a gentleman who exhibits the practical patriotism of employing sixty persons in a factory he has established in Bandon in connection with his tanning trade, and who, if he could depend on sufficient support, would make an effort to re-establish the cotton mill at Overton near that town. Here is his memorandum: " In 1825 the population of Bandon was 14,000, according to Lewis—of these, 7,000 persons were supported by the manufacture of linen, woollen, ticken, and corduroys, or cotton. In 1861, according to the census, the population had fallen to 6,100. The Overton Mills, which gave employment to 2,000 persons, have been long since abandoned, the trade gone, and the buildings dilapidated."

When some instances of Irish poverty, suffering, and decay were once mentioned in the English House of Lords, the late Duke of Wellington observed that it would not mend the matter to set up a Parliament in Ireland, because there was also deep misery in England, which country did actually enjoy the residence of the Legislature. "There is a Parliament in England; there is also misery there; therefore seek not the Repeal of the Union."

There will be a mixture of poverty in every human society till the end of time. "The poor you have always with you."* But the Duke's argument implies that the numbers of the poor and the intensity of their privations are not diminished by the presence of the wealthy, and are not increased by withdrawing from among them the great source of expenditure. It is also to be noticed that when his Grace used that argument, a good deal of the misery existing in England was directly traceable to the Irish poverty caused by the Union. The poorer Irish, having no manufactures to employ their surplus hands at home, emigrated in shoals to England, where they lowered the wages of labour in the English market, and frequently dragged down the English operative to the level of their own wretchedness. Had his Grace remembered this, he would perhaps have doubted the soundness of his anti-Repeal inference from the distress existing in certain English districts.

Every political quack will supply his own nostrum. The social diseases of Ireland are admitted on all hands. You can scarcely find any man of any party who does not laugh to scorn Spring Rice's "giant-stride prosperity." It was available to call forth a parliamentary cheer, and for a parliamentary pretext for opposing Repeal; but it was the very hyperbole of audacious falsehood; it was too monstrous to endure in the real conviction of any human being. The social diseases, I repeat, are admitted on all hands. The condition of Ireland is professedly anomalous. There is the startling incongruity of an anti-Irish aristocracy enlisted against the just rights of the masses of the people. There is a vast ecclesiastical income still exacted from landlords, from whose rentals an amount in general exceeding the tithe-tax has been taken by the Land Act of 1881. There is a proprietary hating the land whence their wealth, their rank, and their social status are exclusively derived. There is a soil proverbial for its fertility, yet inhabited by the yearly diminishing remnants of a people whose poverty is declared by travellers to exceed all they ever had witnessed of human destitution elsewhere. There is productive power, which, if developed, and its fruits retained at home, could support in comfort a larger population than ever inhabited the island, yet which either lies waste, or else is diverted from its natural and legitimate purpose—the support of the Irish people—to

---

* Matt. xxvi. 11.

swell the wealth and greatness of the neighbouring nation that has struck its fangs into our vitals.

There is the spectacle of a people, who, plucked bare by the Union-drains of many years, and crushed to the dust by famine, were just at that juncture made the subject of new and enormous taxation to liquidate the liabilities of wealthy England.

That all this leaven should not powerfully work for disaffection, no rational man could expect. We have various nostrums recommended by a multitude of political physicians. But it is not the absentee legislator, nor the cold, utilitarian political economist, nor the clever political speculator who can string together flippant paragraphs, nor the Cockney tourist who posts through Ireland to construct a marketable book from the salient traits which appear on the surface of society—it is not one of these who can prescribe, or even comprehend, an adequate remedy. They have not the requisite knowledge of the people; and if they had, they have not the hearty sympathies which are requisite to render that knowledge available. Cold, self-sufficient dogmatisers too many of them are, viewing all that they see (and how little is that all!) through the medium of preconceived political theories, nine-tenths of which are inapplicable to the condition of the country.

He whose intercourse with the people has been extensive and prolonged; who has mingled with his fellow-countrymen on terms of the most unreserved mutual confidence; who has seen the struggles of the oppressed against the tyranny that would grind them into powder; who has witnessed the anxious heavings of the nation's breast; who knows the intense sincerity and unalterable determination with which his compatriots are actuated; who witnesses the persevering efforts of the anti-Irish class to prevent the disenthralment of the people from their bondage; he who has seen the pernicious antagonism of the two great sections of the Irish nation, is compelled to trace the origin of Irish evils to English influence operating through an alien Legislature and anti-national prejudice, and to recognise in the Repeal of the Union the only possible cure for the social disease—the only possible guarantee against relapse.

It is manifest that the bitter hatreds engendered by exclusive political institutions could not, in the present day, survive the restoration of the Irish Legislature. The class who are now infected with a vicious hatred of their country would then become nationalised in spite of themselves. They could not help it. The preponderating pressure of the national sentiment, having a Legislature for its organ, would overcome their resistance. Their prejudices would be swept away in the national torrent. They would, despite some contortions and grimaces, be made auxiliary to the national prosperity and greatness. They would at last be amalgamated with the great mass of Irishmen.

Nothing short of the Repeal of the Union can fulfil the requirements of Ireland. Imagine every minor boon conceded that the most liberal Whig-Radical could proffer; imagine tithes abolished, the franchises enlarged, the representation extended, the magistracy popularised, tenant-right conceded; yet, so long as Ireland possessed no Parliament, we should still have England's robber-hand in our pockets, abstracting our money for her own uses under the pretext of Imperial identification; we should still be impoverished by the drain of an absentee rental, computed to have often reached four millions sterling a year; our people would still be driven as if with flaming swords out of their own country by the colossal plunder of the means that should circulate at home for their support; we should still be subjected to a system devised to substitute cattle and sheep for the human inhabitants of Ireland; we should still remain degraded by the absence of that privilege without which man is a despised slave—the uncontrolled management of our own country for ourselves. Thus, if England were to give us everything else, yet, so long as she withheld from us our Parliament, we should be deprived of that which would be far more valuable than all the rest put together.

The instinct of nationality cannot be rooted out of the Irish mind; if its eradication were practicable, it would have long since been effected. What, let us ask, is that instinct? What are its lessons? Here are the words of an authority who will at any rate be respected by many who are not well-wishers to Ireland:

"It is by virtue of a providential design that the human species is found distributed in groups distinct by race and language, and established in certain definite territories, where each has contracted a certain unity of tendencies and of institutions, so that it does not trouble the habitation of another and suffers no interference with its own. God has shown what value man should attach to his nationality when, wishing to punish the Hebrew people, rebellious against warnings and chastisements, He inflicted foreign domination on them as the most terrible punishment of all .... The Christian idea does not admit that the social power should issue in the oppression of one individual by another. Conquest cannot legalise the domination of one nation over another, for force is powerless to constitute right."

Whether the doctrines here enunciated were correctly applicable to the purpose for which they were employed by the author, I do not pronounce. But it is certain that as applied to Ireland they find a cordial echo in the minds of millions of our countrymen at home and in exile. The words I have quoted are taken from a letter addressed by Baron Ricasoli to the Pope, in August, 1861.

Nationality is the principle which teaches us to take care of the interests of our own country, and to protect ourselves against the aggression of our neighbours. It is not a merely sentimental or romantic idea. It is eminently practical. It teaches us for instance, in Ireland, that the physical and mental gifts bestowed by the Creator on our country and on its inhabitants—the fertility of the island—the wealth which it produces—the intelligence of its people—their industrial capacities, were clearly designed by the Divine Giver for the use and benefit of the Irish nation; and that the system is wicked and execrable which deprives that nation of the bounties of Providence; which expels them by the million from the despoiled land, and which grasps for the benefit of England the gifts bestowed by God upon the people whom a multiform, subtle tyranny has hunted into exile. The principle of nationality is the principle of self-protection against such monstrous wrong. It is in the spirit of a friend to the British Empire, not an enemy, that I quote from a very able New York letter in the *Dundee Advertiser* the following description of the progress of the Irish in America: "They are building up a mighty nation, and raising up an enemy for their hereditary foe, that will assuredly strangle her at some future day."

England, in the day of her strength, may deride such predictions. Her scorn, however, is not wise. Despite the follies and blunders of Fenianism, and the crimes of some of its leaders, its animating principle will survive and acquire fresh strength with every shipload of emigrants landed from Ireland on the American coast. It is not reasonable to suppose that the Fenians will always be destitute of leaders

How to make Ireland "*loyal, proud, and happy.*" 219

of ability. A cause that enlists all the Irish in the United States must sooner or later furnish champions endowed with a formidable capacity for command. I leave to statesmen to consider the perils probably resulting from the fixed resentment that inspires the large and growing community of exiled Irish. There is an effectual mode of extinguishing that hatred. Let England deal with Ireland as Austria dealt with Hungary. Let her undo the hideous crime of 1800. Let our revered Sovereign open in Dublin the first session of the restored Irish Legislature, leaving thenceforth her faithful Irish subjects to possess their own country and develop for themselves its resources in accordance with the claims of justice and with the evident purposes of Providence —let our Queen do this, and Ireland, resuming the prosperous career which commenced in 1782, and which the Union interrupted, will become the right arm of the Empire —loyal, proud, and happy; contributing to the general prosperity in time of peace, and to the general defence in time of war. Let our Queen do this, and Irish disloyalty, deprived of its pabulum, will at once become a thing of the past.

Mr. Gladstone is doing his utmost to produce that result. Every rational patriot on either side of the Channel should give him every possible support in his noble enterprise.

CHAPTER XXII.

THE YOUNG IRELANDERS COME PROMINENTLY FORWARD.

True, my friend, as if an angel said it.
Would that an angel's pealing voice were thine,
Until thy words were rooted and imbedded
Deep in every Irish heart as mine,
Battling for our isle's regeneration.
Still we know the future holds no chance,
Hope, or prospect for this Irish nation,
Save in trampling down intolerance—
Trampling down the bigot's broils, that pandered
Through the past to England's foulest deeds;
Writing broadly on our souls and standard
This unchanging motto: DEEDS, NOT CREEDS.

A NOTABLE event in the year 1842 was the establishment of the *Nation* newspaper.

The proprietor and editor, Mr. (now Sir) Charles Gavan

Duffy, had previously exhibited the self-reliance of conscious talent in setting up the *Belfast Vindicator*, despite the discouraging predictions of various friends well acquainted with the North, who assured him that the failure of a Repeal journal in Saxonised Ulster was a matter of certainty. Duffy, nothing daunted, persevered in his experiment and speedily reached a circulation of 1,300; establishing a firm footing in the heart of the enemy's quarters. The ability with which the *Vindicator* was conducted soon acquired for its editor a high reputation as a journalist. Mr. Duffy felt before long that his talents required a wider scope for their exercise than could be afforded by the conduct of a provincial journal, however respectable. He resolved to start the *Nation*. In this new undertaking he encountered discouragement similar to that which had waited on his Northern experiment. Intelligent, observant men, who wished him well, treated his hopes of success as chimerical, asserting, with much colour of probability that the whole ground was preoccupied by the two respectable weekly metropolitan journals which were already the exponents and propagandists of Repeal doctrines.

The *Weekly Freeman's Journal* had been edited in succession by several warm and able advocates of Irish independence. The *Weekly Register*, conducted by its proprietor, Michael Staunton, had acquired great value from the extensive and accurate financial and statistical knowledge profusely scattered through its leading articles. Mr. Staunton has been truly called the father of a distinct school—and a most useful one—of Irish politics. He devoted his abilities to the elucidation of the knotty question of international finance—a question the most easily obscured by the ingenuity of official chicane.

The *Nation* appeared contemporaneously with the Repeal missions. Its projectors little heeded the vaticinations of timid prophets. In the words of their prospectus, "they were prepared, if they did not find a way open, to try if they could make one." And a way they *did* make, and that speedily. They were encouraged to their task by the conviction that since the success of O'Connell's great struggle for civil and religious liberty, a new mind had grown up in Ireland; a mind filled with new thoughts, new aspirations—panting to achieve new victories.

The style of the *Nation* was eminently fervid and earnest; it told home upon the hearts of the people. It spoke forth the singleness of purpose and the energy whereby its editor was characterised. One of its attractive features was its poetry. There were many poetical contributors, of whom the principal were Mr. Duffy and Mr. Thomas Osborne Davis, a Protestant barrister. Their minds were stored with the annals of their country—the feuds, the wrongs, the struggles of elder ages—the gallant exhibitions of an often foiled, but never vanquished, spirit of liberty. The thoughts inspired by those annals—now flowing in a dark and vengeful current—now rushing along in impetuous tumult—now softening into deep and solemn pathos—now concentrated in stern defiance—now soaring aloft upon the buoyant wings of lightsome hope—were thrown into verses glowing with a passionate fervour, that awakened into life every slumbering pulse of Irish patriotism.

Here is " Young Ireland's" poetical compliment to O'Connell:

I.

I saw him at the hour of prayer when morning's earliest dawn
Was breaking o'er the mountain-tops—o'er grassy dell and lawn;
When the parting shades of night had fled—when moon and stars
    were gone;
Before a high and gorgeous shrine the Chieftain kneel'd alone.
His hands were clasp'd upon his breast, his eye was rais'd above,
I heard those full and solemn tones in words of faith and love;
He pray'd that those who wrong'd him might for ever be forgiven;
Oh! who would say such prayers as these are not receiv'd in
    Heaven?

II.

I saw him next amid the best and noblest of our isle,
There was the same majestic form, the same heart-kindling smile.
But grief was on that princely brow—for others still he mourn'd;
He gaz'd upon poor fetter'd slaves, and his heart within him burn'd:
And he vow'd before the captive's God to break the captive's chain,
To bind the broken heart, and set the captive free again.
And fit was he our Chief to be in triumph or in need,
Who never wrong'd his deadliest foe in thought, or word, or deed.

III.

I saw him when the light of eve had faded from the west,
Beside the hearth that old man sat, by infant forms caress'd;
One hand was gently laid upon his grandchild's clustering hair,
The other, rais'd to heaven, invok'd a blessing and a prayer.
And woman's lips were heard to breathe a high and glorious strain—
Those songs of old that haunt us still, and ever will remain
Within the heart like treasur'd gems, that bring from mem'ry's cell
Thoughts of our youthful days, and friends that we have lov'd so well.

IV.

I saw that eagle glance again—the brow was mark'd with care,
Though rich and regal were the robes* the nation's Chief doth wear;
And many an eye now quail'd with shame and many a cheek now glow'd,
As he paid them back with words of love for every curse bestow'd.
I thought of his unceasing care, his never-ending zeal,
I heard the watchword burst from all—the gathering cry—REPEAL!
And as his eyes were rais'd to heaven, from whence his mission came,
He stood among the thousands there a monarch save in name.

I select the following poems, not so much as specimens of poetical excellence, as from the plain exposition they afford of the policy, principles, and objects of their authors. The first is entitled:

A LAY SERMON.
BY CHARLES GAVAN DUFFY.

I.

BROTHER, do you love your brother?
  Brother, are you all you seem?
Do you live for more than living?
  Has your life a law, and scheme?
Are you prompt to bear its duties
  As a brave man may beseem?

II.

Brother, shun the mist exhaling,
  From the fen of pride and doubt;
Neither seek the house of bondage,
  Walling straightened souls about;
Bats! who from their narrow spy-hole
  Cannot see a world without.

III.

Anchor in no stagnant shallow;
  Trust the wide and wondrous sea
Where the tides are fresh for ever
  And the mighty currents free;
There, perchance, O young Columbus,
  Your new world of Truth may be.

IV.

Favour will not make deserving—
  (Can the sunshine brighten clay?)
Slowly must it grow and blossom,
  Fed by labour and delay;
And the fairest bud to promise
  Bears the taint of quick decay.

---

* The municipal robes of Lord Mayor.

V.

You must strive for better guerdons;
　Strive to *be* the thing you'd seem;
Be the thing that God hath made you,
　Channel for no borrowed stream;
He hath lent you mind and conscience;
　See you travel in their beam.

VI.

See you scale life's misty highlands
　By the light of living truth;
And with bosom braced for labour,
　Breast them in your manly youth;
So, when age and care have found you,
　Shall your downward path be smooth.

VII.

Fear not on that rugged highway
　Life may want its lawful zest;
Sunny glens are in the mountain
　Where the weary feet may rest,
Cooled in streams that gush for ever
　From a loving mother's breast.

VIII.

"Simple heart and simple pleasures,"
　So they write life's golden rule;
Honour won by supple baseness,
　State that crowns a cankered fool
Gleam as gleam the gold and purple
　On a hot and rancid pool.

IX.

Wear no show of wit or science
　But the gems you've won and weighed
Thefts, like ivy on a ruin,
　Make the rifts they seem to shade.
Are you not a thief and beggar
　In the rarest spoils arrayed?

X.

Shadows deck a sunny landscape,
　Making brighter all the bright;
So, my brother, care and danger
　On a loving nature light,
Bringing all its latent beauties
　Out upon the common sight.

XI.

Love the things that God created,
　Make your brother's need your care;
Scorn and hate repel God's blessings,
　But where love is, *they* are there,
As the moonbeams light the waters,
　Leaving rock and sandbank bare.

XII.

Thus, my brother, grow and flourish,
    Fearing none, and loving all;
For the true man needs no patron,
    He shall climb, and never crawl;
Two things fashion their own channel—
    The strong man and the waterfall.

The next is a song of triumph, by Thomas Davis, at the union of all Irishmen. Davis was sanguine in his expectation that the plain common sense that prompted the recovery of self-legislation for Ireland would overcome the obstinate bigotry of the Orange party; whose interests as Irishmen were equally involved with ours in a measure that would rescue Ireland from the grasp of a hostile power, and restore to her the control of her own resources. He accordingly took for granted the fusion which he ardently laboured to promote.

I.

Ireland! rejoice, and England! deplore;
    Faction and feud are passing away.
'Twas a low voice, but 'tis a loud roar;
    Orange and green will carry the day.
        Orange! Orange!
        Green and Orange!
Pitted together in many a fray;
        Lions in fight,
        And linked in their might,
Orange and Green will carry the day.
        Orange! Orange!
        Green and Orange!
Wave them together o'er mountain and bay;
        Orange and Green,
        Our King and our Queen,
Orange and Green will carry the day.

II.

Rusty the swords our fathers unsheathed,
    William and James are turned to clay;
Long did we till the wrath they bequeathed,
    Red was the crop, and bitter the pay.
        Freedom fled us,
        Knaves misled us,
Under the feet of the foemen we lay;
        Riches and strength,
        We'll win them at length,
For Orange and Green will carry the day.
        Landlords fool'd us,
        England ruled us,
Hounding our passions to make us their prey;
        But in their spite,
        The Irish "Unite,"
And Orange and Green will carry the day.

III.

Fruitful our soil where honest men starve,
  Empty the mart and shipless the bay.
Out of our wants the Oligarchs carve;
  Foreigners fatten on our decay.
       Disunited,
       Therefore blighted,
Ruined and rent by the Englishman's sway;
       Party and creed
       For once have agreed,
Orange and Green will carry the day.
       Boyne's old water,
       Red with slaughter,
Now is as pure as an infant at play;
       So in our souls
       Its history rolls,
And Orange and Green will carry the day.

IV.

English deceit can rule us no more,
  Bigots and knaves are scattered like spray;
Deep was the oath the Orangemen swore,
  "Orange and green must carry the day."
       Orange! Orange!
       Bless the Orange!
Tories and Whigs grew pale with dismay
       When from the North
       Burst the cry forth,
"Orange and Green must carry the day."
       No surrender,
       No Pretender,
Never to falter and never betray;
       With an Amen
       We swear it again,
Orange and Green shall carry the day.

Such were the strains that aroused the spirit of Young Ireland, and of Old Ireland also. Their moral was self-reliance, internal union, and the extinction of sectarian animosities. In that moral I thoroughly concurred. We had in the Repeal Association many Protestant members, of whose conscientious attachment to their own religious belief I never entertained a doubt. Those men had a noble, generous, well-deserved trust in their Catholic countrymen. Enemies themselves to the political ascendency of Protestantism, they felt no fears of Catholic ascendency in the event of Repeal. Their principle, and ours, was the thorough political equality of all. For myself, I must be permitted to say this: I am a Catholic, deeply convinced of the truth of the Catholic faith, and claiming for Catholics the fullest equality of citizenship with Protestants. Yet, while recognising the infinite importance of the Catholic faith in a spiritual point of view, I feel that, in a temporal aspect, Home Government is so much more important than Catholic privilege, that if I were reduced to the alternative I should greatly prefer to have Ireland governed by an exclusively Protestant Irish Parliament than by an exclusively Catholic English or Imperial Legislature.

On a balance of advantages and disadvantages the scale would immensely preponderate in favour of self-legislation, even although clogged with the drawback of Catholic disability. Should any theological enthusiast find fault with this opinion, I would remind him that the Catholic aggregate meeting, held in Dublin in 1795, unanimously declared that they would resist even their own emancipation if offered as the price of an Union. And O'Connell said something not dissimilar when he announced on the 13th of January, 1800, that he would prefer "the penal code in all its pristine horrors to the Union, as the lesser and more sufferable evil."

Young Ireland was ardent and eager. Her fiery vehemence was a useful ingredient in our great Constitutional warfare, so long as it was tempered with the judgment and experience of her elder friend and namesake. Old Ireland had been the victor in one prolonged and hard-fought contest—a triumph due to her wisdom, her virtue, and her perseverance. The sagacity of the one, restraining but not extinguishing the impetuous ardour of the other, produced a combination of qualities which would have been resistless in their union, if the demons of jealousy and division, followed by the crushing evils of the famine, had not dashed the councils and paralysed the strength of men whose movement, so long as they acted in concert with each other, had so fair a prospect of success.

Davis's jubilant hopes of an Orange accession to the national cause were premature. It is not easy to extirpate the inveterate anti-national venom that festers in the Orange heart. The existence in Ireland of the Orange institution presents a strange and melancholy spectacle to every intelligent lover of his country. It seems at first as unaccountable as it is unnatural, that a body of men should detest the great mass of their countrymen, and glory in the degradation of their country. Elsewhere, we do not see the bitter animosities of a distant century kept alive by noisy and insolent annual celebrations. These displays, they allege, are intended to assert their "principles;" which principles are manifested by outbursts of hatred, malice, and all uncharitableness. Their outbursts are associated with vociferous boasts of their devotion to "a free, open Bible," and loud professions of religious fervour. This pretext of religion suggests the clerical source of their anti-social virulence. Davis not improbably founded his hope of an Orange contingent to the National ranks on the fact that in 1800 many of the Orange lodges had passed spirited anti-Union resolutions,* and he may have deemed it possible that the anti-Union feeling of that period might survive in the Orangemen of 1842. On the other hand, there was the fact that the Orange institution was founded in 1795 as an anti-Catholic organisation; that the sectarian bigotry of its members was constantly inflamed by furious anti-Catholic sermons from State Church pulpits, and equally furious harangues from Orange platforms; there was also the important fact that the State clergy, who must have felt their position insecure as monopolists of the whole ecclesiastical State property of a Catholic country, felt interested in stimulating the ferocious zeal of the Orange adherents of the State Church by fiery appeals to their anti-Catholic prejudices; and finally, that the Orangemen, thus influenced, were unlikely to unite in a national movement which appeared to them to be a Catholic movement, because Catholics formed the large majority of the nation.

I know not what proportion of the Presbyterian community belonged to the Orange institution. Presbyterians

* The following Resolutions, passed by Orange lodges in 1800, are identical in spirit with many others:

"LODGE 391, WATTLE BRIDGE, CO. FERMANAGH, 1st of March, 1800.

"That, strongly attached to the Constitution of 1782—a settlement ratified in the most unequivocal manner, so far as the faith of nations is binding—we should feel ourselves criminal were we to remain silent while an attempt is made to extinguish it. That, impressed with every loyal sentiment towards our gracious Sovereign, we trust that the measure of a legislative Union, which is contrary to the sense of all Orangemen and the nation at large, will be relinquished.

"JOHN MOORE, Master."

"LODGE No. 883, AT NEWTOWNBARRY, 16th February, 1800.

"That Orangemen ought to come forward as Orangemen and Irishmen and declare their sentiments against a legislative Union, which now, or at any other time, would be of the most fatal and pernicious consequences to the real liberty of Ireland.
"EDMUND BEATTY, Master.
"WILLOUGHBY BUSTARD, Dep.
"ALEX. M'CLAUGHRY, Sec."

had been extensively involved in the insurrectionary movements that preceded the Union. Lord Castlereagh contemplated "an increased provision for their clergy" as a good mode of buying them for the Court. The *Regium Donum* was accordingly swelled up to a large amount; and the patriotic ardour which had characterised the Presbyterians disappeared.

The *Nation* first appeared on the 15th of October, 1842. John O'Connell had, I think, returned to town, but Mr. Ray and I were still pursuing our missionary avocations. The result of the missions on the Repeal Rent was remarkable. The week before we set forth to the provinces the rent was £45 14s. 8d. The week after our return it reached £235.

CHAPTER XXIII.

REPEAL DEBATED IN THE DUBLIN CORPORATION.

ACRES.—By my valour, then, Sir Lucius, forty yards is a good distance. . . . I tell you, Sir Lucius, the farther off he is, the cooler I shall take my aim.

SIR LUCIUS.—Faith, then, I suppose you would aim at him best if he were out of sight?

ACRES.—No, Sir Lucius; but I should think forty, or eight-and-thirty yards. Do, my dear Sir Lucius, let me bring him down at a long shot.

The Rivals.

O'CONNELL's next step was to bring the Repeal Question into the Dublin Corporation. Early in February, 1843, he gave notice that on Tuesday, the 21st of the month, he would move a resolution affirmatory of the right of Ireland to a resident Parliament, and the necessity of repealing the Union.

Shortly prior to the 21st, he suddenly announced the postponement of his motion for a week. The Tory members of the Corporation complained of being unfairly treated. Alderman Butt declared that he had remained in town at much personal inconvenience in order to oppose the motion, and strongly remonstrated against the postponement. O'Connell, however, was inexorable, whereupon there was a sort of triumphant growl among the opposite party, who said that he only manœuvred to get Butt out of town, from a well-grounded fear of discussing the merits of Repeal with so able an adversary.

The postponement was useful. Had the discussion taken

place on the day originally fixed, it would have passed off as a matter of course, without exciting half the interest it afterwards created. But, by putting it off, an additional fillip was given to the public mind. The anti-Repealers alleged that O'Connell was shrinking from Butt; the Repealers indignantly denied the accusation. People upon both sides were thus set talking about the matter, and the public curiosity was wound up to a pitch of intensity when the day for the discussion arrived. O'Connell had planned this, in order to give additional *éclat* to the discomfiture he intended for the anti-Repealers.

And a signal triumph he achieved. The Unionists had long been in the habit of saying, "O'Connell and his party have always kept out of the way of discussing this question—if we had them face to face we could expose their delusions." They had now got an opportunity of realising their boast.

The Assembly House in William Street was crowded to the utmost. A vast concourse of people thronged the street without, unable to obtain admittance, yet rooted to the spot by the interest which the question awakened in all breasts. Twice or thrice in the course of the day I passed through the crowd, and the people invariably asked me how Repeal was getting on, and who was speaking now, with as eager an anxiety as if the success of the Repeal in the Dublin Corporation would secure its final and immediate triumph.

O'Connell's opening speech occupied four hours and ten minutes. He had arranged the whole subject under nine distinct propositions. These were:

I. The capability and capacity of the Irish nation for an independent Legislature.

II. The perfect right of Ireland to have a domestic Parliament.

III. That that right was fully established by the transactions of 1782.

IV. That the most beneficial effects to Ireland resulted from her parliamentary independence.

V. The utter incompetence of the Irish Parliament to annihilate the Irish Constitution by the Union.

VI. That the Union was no contract or bargain; that it was carried by the grossest corruption and bribery, added to force, fraud, and terror.

VII. That the Union produced the most disastrous results to Ireland.

VIII. That the Union can be abolished by peaceable and constitutional means without the violation of the law, and without the destruction of property or life.

IX. That the most salutary results, and none other, must arise from a Repeal of the Union.

"These," said O'Connell, "are the nine propositions which I came here to-day to demonstrate. I say to demonstrate, not as relying on any intellectual powers of my own, or any force of talent, but from the truth and plainness of the propositions themselves."

His speech was luminous and masterly. Notwithstanding its length, the physical vigour of the orator continued unimpaired to the end. The *Nation's* description is so accurate and discriminating that I cannot do better than quote it:

"O'Connell," says that journal, "may have made more eloquent speeches—speeches more calculated to heat the blood and stir the passions—but he never excelled this one as an elaborate and masterly statement of a great case. The arrangement he adopted was remarkably skilful and judicious. He threw down, as it were, a single proof, and heaped others in succession on the top of it, till they grew up to a gigantic pyramid which all the world might recognise. The effect of this process on the audience was magical. The truth seemed to dawn upon them like the rising sun growing plainer and plainer by degrees, till at length, as he drew near his peroration, it admitted of neither question nor dispute, and men seemed to say to each other with exulting looks, 'This is unanswerable.'"

Such was the oration Mr. Butt was obliged to reply to. It is not the least disparagement of his great abilities to say that his reply was a failure. There was a case made out for the Repeal which could not be rebutted. In the total absence of legitimate argument he was compelled to resort to small dexterities, such as challenging, *not* the doctrine that the Irish Parliament was incompetent to effect its own destruction, but the alleged consequences of that doctrine, which Mr. Butt asserted would invalidate all the Acts of the Imperial Parliament. Mr. Butt also prophesied that as forty years had elapsed since the Union, we might look forward to some future good results from that measure; a prediction which he tried to sustain by alleging that after the lapse of forty years the Scottish Union had begun to bear fruits of benefit to Scotland. Mr. Butt, a few years later, saw reason to change his opinions. In his admirable "Plea for the

Celtic Race," he admits "the decay that unquestionably followed the Union;" and instead of retaining the confidence which, in 1843, he reposed in the justice of the British Parliament, he writes as follows in a letter on the County Cork election, dated 10th of February, 1867 : " I have lost all faith in what is called parliamentary action. Just measures for Ireland will not be passed by the British Parliament, unless under the pressure of external danger, or the influence of some great and powerful organisation combining the Irish people."

In other words, we have nothing to expect from British justice. Any rights obtained from the British Parliament must be forced out of that assembly by fear or by expediency. So said O'Connell in 1843. So said Butt in 1867.

To return to his speech in reply to O'Connell. He defended the Anti-Irish Church Establishment on the ground that it was the duty of every State to consecrate itself to God; just as if the mode of consecrating Ireland to God was to invest the pastors of the eighth or ninth part of the population with a legal power to fleece the whole people! He strongly urged repose for Ireland; just as if a wronged and suffering nation ever gained anything by silent acquiescence in her injuries!

Mr. Butt was a man of great intellectual power and of generous impulses. It would indeed have been impossible that, possessing his high qualities of head and heart, and with the experience of the intervening quarter of a century, he should have retained the opinions expressed in his anti-Repeal speech in the Dublin Corporation.

While he spoke, O'Connell repeatedly exclaimed, "I never made so unanswered a speech! Why, he doesn't even try to make a case!" The solution was, that in the midst of an Irish assembly there was no case to be made. Mr. Butt once or twice tried Spring Rice's expedient of alleging our giant-stride prosperity; but although that line of argument might call down vociferous cheers in the foreign House of Commons, it could not elicit one solitary cheer from the Conservative party in the Irish Corporation; for to all in that assembly the adverse facts were too well and too painfully known.

The *Warder* newspaper, of Evangelico-Orange politics, an able organ of the anti-Repeal party, and to which Mr. Butt had been often a literary contributor, in its number for the 5th of October, 1844, gave the following emphatic contradiction of Spring Rice's prosperity case :

"Squalid half-starvation is the desperate lot of the Irish peasant—destitution which no exertion of his own can relieve; there is no labour too hard for him—he shrinks from no toil or hardship—but employment there is none for him; privation and misery which could not be borne for two days by Englishmen without the riot of insurrection, are here endured from weary month to month with a stoical patience."

So spoke the Tory *Warder*. It may be easily supposed that the allegation of Irish prosperity did not meet an encouraging reception from men who, though holding various politics, were yet perfectly cognisant of the dreary facts thus announced on high Protestant authority. I may parenthetically remark that in the face of such severe and widely spread privation, the Whig Parliament of 1833 might have discovered some other cause of predial outrages than political agitation.

The Corporation debate was adjourned till the following day, when it was resumed with much ability by other gentlemen. Mr. Staunton's speech was an admirable financial statement. The debate was a second time adjourned.

On the third day the public anxiety continued unabated. The vicinity of the Assembly House was again densely crowded. Several speakers preceded O'Connell, who rose to reply at two o'clock. Near him sat his two staunch friends, John O'Neill, the Protestant, and Robert M'Clellan, the Presbyterian. The countenances of both those old patriots expressed their triumph at O'Connell's anticipated victory.

No report, no description, could possibly do justice to that magnificent reply. O'Connell took up in succession all the objections of all his opponents, and dashed them to pieces, one by one. The whole phalanx of Unionists looked like pigmies in the grasp of a giant. The dexterities of Butt shrank and withered into nothing when touched by O'Connell. The consciousness of a great moral triumph seemed to animate his voice, his glance, his gestures. Never had I heard him so eloquent; never had I witnessed so noble a display of his transcendent powers.

The House divided on the question; forty-one members to fifteen affirming the principle of Repeal by a majority of twenty-six. The decisive blow thus struck in the metropolitan Corporation was promptly followed up in all the reformed Corporations in the kingdom. Nothing could be more manifest than the superiority in argument of the corporate Repealers of Dublin. The *Evening Mail*, which had long puffed and blustered on the side of the Unionists, clearly saw that no rational case could be made against Repeal; and it therefore, with becoming prudence, gravely advised the enemies of Irish legislative independence in the Cork Town Council, not to argue the question at all, but simply to record their political servility by silent votes.

The impulse given to Repeal throughout the kingdom appeared in a rapid augmentation of the rent. The national question was now enthroned, moreover, in the different municipalities; and the temper and ability with which it was discussed in those assemblies demonstrated the powerful hold it had taken on the thinking and intelligent mercantile classes of the kingdom.

But the enemy did not relax his activity. The most daring mis-statements of facts, the most reckless falsifications of the purposes of the Repealers, were profusely circulated by a large portion of the anti-Repeal press; and with an amount of success proportioned to the ignorance, bigotry, stolidity, or prejudice of each reader. We, whose earnest aim and labour were to raise Ireland from her prostrate condition; to retain for Irishmen the blessings which God has bestowed on their country; to retain for the country the expenditure of its own wealth, and thereby to rescue the Irish peasant from the squalid half-starvation which the Tory *Warder* pronounced to be his desperate lot; to obliterate sectarian distinctions and to place all Irishmen upon a common level of fair play and equal privilege; we, whose efforts sought the welfare and honour of all, were maligned as dark and dangerous conspirators against the rights of property, against the lives of Protestants, against order and civilisation, against British connection.

Among the modes adopted to produce false impressions of the question of Repeal, was the circulation of a pamphlet by Mr. Montgomery Martin, entitled "Ireland Before and After the Union with Great Britain." The object of this pamphlet was, of course, to show that Ireland had prospered largely by the destruction of her power of self-legislation. Mr. Martin's production was hailed with a burst of acclamation by the anti-Repeal press. The *Times* led off by saying: "Mr. Montgomery Martin has published a valuable recital." The *Morning Herald* said: "The publication at such a juncture of this so demonstrative a work is invaluable; it will convict the Impostor. To the Government proceedings it will give great assistance. It ought to be circulated throughout every town, village, and hamlet in Ireland." And so on, in strains more or less laudatory, through numerous anti-Repeal organs in all the three kingdoms. Mr. Martin had, some time previously, tried to set up a Repeal newspaper in London under the patronage of Mr. O'Connell. He was advised by Mr. O'Connell not to attempt it, inasmuch as the only readers of the paper would be the Irish in England, whose support would not render the experiment remunerative. Mr. Martin, however, persevered; set up the paper, and called it the *Repealer*. O'Connell's prediction was fulfilled—it did not pay ; and Mr. Martin, after publishing a few numbers, desisted from the profitless attempt, and resolved to adopt the opposite side of the question as more probably lucrative. His pen, equally ready to advocate either the Repeal of the Union or the continuance of that measure, was now employed to prove, not only that Ireland had made vast advances since 1800, but that she had been in a state of progressive decay during the existence of her free Constitution. To demonstrate the alleged decay, Mr. Martin exhibited fifteen items of exports, in which, during a carefully selected portion of that period, a decrease had occurred. But he took care to omit nineteen other articles of export (including the staple commodity, linen), in which, during the very same years, there had been a large increase. On the whole thirty-four items, the nineteen and the fifteen taken collectively, there was a large increase. The audacious fraud was exposed by my old friend, Michael Staunton, in a learned and able reply which was published as a pamphlet by the Repeal Association, and widely circulated. I mention the circumstance to show the base methods that were taken to deceive the public mind on a question of vital importance to Ireland.

CHAPTER XXIV.

THE MONSTER MEETINGS OF 1843.

Oh, come, then, Erin, come away ;
Oh, haste, my love, no longer stay.
Oh, haste, thy cruel sister leave;
Her words are false, her smiles deceive.
" UNION," she cries, with vip'rous breath;
UNION with *her*—is Erin's death.
Beauties of the Press.

THE coming summer and autumn were rendered remarkable by the great gatherings called monster meetings. The utility of those meetings lay in the evidence they afforded that the voice of the nation was for Repeal. Whig and Tory alike had incessantly asserted that the people cared nothing for Repeal. The people in 1843 turned out in their multitudinous strength to give the lie to that laboriously reiterated calumny. The whole population were astir. Invitations to attend public meetings in distant quarters poured in upon those who had been chiefly conspicuous in the agitation. The attendance on the weekly meetings of the Association overflowed the capacity of the apartment in which we had been accustomed to assemble. O'Connell resolved on erecting a hall of larger compass; and on Thursday, the 30th of March, 1843, he laid the foundation stone of the new edifice, on which he bestowed the name of Conciliation Hall.

Meanwhile, meeting followed meeting in the country. O'Connell displayed astonishing mental and physical elasticity and vigour. He was then sixty-eight years old; and he flattered himself that when accumulating years should have deprived him of the strength required for his public exertions, he could still, from his closet, regulate the agitation, and guide the men who might occupy, under his instructions, a species of deputy leadership. During all this year the Young Ireland party, whose organ was the *Nation* newspaper, seemed to work in harmony with the old Agitator; but in their writings, and especially in their poetry, there rang the clash of arms—there were significant allusions to the sword which O'Connell did not like. He could not control his impetuous allies; but he took comfort by observing that fiery thoughts, which, if expressed in prose, might be legally unsafe, could be clothed in a poetic dress consistently with legal security. He had, with wondrous skill, kept the public mind of a whole generation at a pitch of the highest political excitement, yet restrained it from unconstitutional or illegal action. He feared that the Young Ireland party would stimulate his followers to compromise at once their own safety and the interests of Repeal by deviations from the old, safe course they had hitherto pursued. But as yet the public saw nothing except mutual confidence and harmony of action between Old and Young Ireland.

The greatest of the monster meetings was held on the Hill of Tara in the County Meath, on the 15th of August, 1843. In O'Connell's speech occurs the following passage: "We are at Tara of the kings. We are on the spot where the monarchs of Ireland were elected, and where the chieftains of Ireland bound themselves by the sacred pledge of honour and the tie of religion to stand by their native land against the Danes, or any other stranger. This is emphatically the spot from which emanated the social power—the legal authority—the right to dominion over the farthest extremities of the island, and the power of concentrating the force of the entire nation for the purpose of national defence. I here protest in the face of my Creator—in the face of Ireland and of God—I protest against the continuance of the unfounded and unjust Union. My proposition to Ireland is that the Union is not binding upon us; it is not binding, I mean, upon conscience—it is void in principle—it is void as matter of right—and it is void in Constitutional law."

On the day when O'Connell thus addressed a multitude computed by the *Nation* to consist of 750,000 persons, and which, although that number was probably an over-estimate, yet was undoubtedly an enormous gathering, the people of Clontibret in the County Monaghan held a numerous meeting to which I accepted an invitation. It was presided over by Captain Seaver of Heath Hall, a Protestant gentleman of fortune, and a convert to Repeal from Orangeism. On a rising ground at a small distance from our meeting, a party of dragoons were drawn up under the command of an officer. This species of military supervision had become rather usual about that period. The pretext was that a breach of the peace might occur between the Repealers and the anti-Repealers, requiring military intervention to suppress it. The red-coats looked lively, and were a picturesque addition to the landscape. The meetings were all perfectly peaceful; and if the soldiers were on any occasion permitted to approach within hearing of the speakers, they must—if Irish—have been heartily delighted with the doctrines announced, and with the resolutions that expressed the most fervid determination to persevere.

O'Connell sometimes alluded to the beauties of the scenery. At the Clifden meeting he said: "I love the wild and majestic scenes through which I have this day passed in coming to your meeting. Perhaps I might be justified in saying that Nature did not intend me for a politician, but that, judging from my feelings, I ought rather to have spent my life in the quiet and undisturbed admiration and enjoyment of Nature's beauty and magnificence. The scenery I have this day passed has made me think so. It filled my soul with a thrilling and undefinable sensation to behold that wild and swelling morass encompassed by cloud-capt and majestic mountains—the regions of the storm and the mist—and the quiet lake surrounded with its high and heath-covered banks, or sometimes embossed among trees, its surface scarcely disturbed by the soft and perfumed autumnal breeze, whilst the tiny waves with which it was rippled seemed to smile approbation upon us as our procession passed along its banks. I love the music of the waters, the silvery echoes of the mountain rill, and the sounds of the torrent rushing over the brow of the precipice. They seem to whisper to my soul the joys of youth, to arouse the energies of manhood, and to dictate to me a command that I could not refuse to obey—to use every energy of my soul, every power of my mind, every faculty of my being, to make our majestic yet neglected country the garden and the paradise for which Nature has so obviously designed it."

There were altogether some forty-five monster meetings, quite enough to develop the genuine sentiments of Ireland upon the Union, were any such evidence wanted.

On the 20th of October, 1843, Mr. Smith O'Brien addressed a letter to the secretary, enclosing his first subscription, and announcing his adhesion to the Repeal Association. In his letter he said :

"At this moment, after forty-three years of nominal Union, the affections of the two nations are so entirely alienated from each other, that England trusts for the maintenance of the connection, not to the attachment of the Irish people, but to the bayonets which menace our bosoms, and to the cannon which she has planted on all our strongholds."

On the 23rd of October, Conciliation Hall was formally opened. The accession of Mr. O'Brien was hailed with delight. He had long adhered to the delusive idea that justice to Ireland might be obtained from the united Parliament; but on the failure of his motion for a parliamentary inquiry into Irish grievances, was compelled to despair of any good from such a source. His motion was prefaced with a speech of great ability, fraught with extensive and accurate information as to the wrongs sustained by Ireland. He sought inquiry. As a matter of course it was refused; prosecution of the Irish leaders was resolved on, and William Smith O'Brien tendered his adhesion to the National Association.

A slight outline of his career will interest the Irish public.

He was born in October, 1803. His remote ancestors were the royal O'Briens, of whose family Brian Boroimhe was a member. He was the second son of the late Sir Edward O'Brien, Bart., of Dromoland, County Clare, and heir to the estates of his maternal grandfather, Mr. William Smith. He spent three years at Harrow School, and took his degree at Trinity College, Cambridge. In 1828 he was brought into Parliament by his father for the borough of Ennis, a close borough to which the O'Brien family and the late Lord Fitzgerald alternately possessed the nomination. He ardently supported the Catholic claims, and enrolled himself a member of the Catholic Association in the year of his return to Parliament. He did not, in the House of Commons, give a regular support to the Tory Ministry, although his father was a politician of the class called Liberal Conservatives; but after the Duke of Wellington carried Emancipation and lost the support of the ultra-Tories, Mr. O'Brien became a supporter in general of the Government —voting, however, against it upon some questions involving Constitutional principles. In 1831 he lost his seat on the dissolution which followed the defeat of the Whigs on the Reform Bill. On that measure Mr. O'Brien did not vote, being absent from London, but he voted against General Gascoigne's motion, declaring that the number and proportion of English representatives ought to continue undiminished. In 1832 he was invited to stand for Ennis on the Liberal interest, but having transferred his residence from the County Clare to the County Limerick, he declined the invitation. In 1834 he re-entered Parliament for the County of Limerick, and from that year until 1843 he generally acted with the Liberal Whigs, giving them an independent support, but opposing them whenever he deemed them in the wrong—for example, on the Jamaica question. During their tenure of office he neither asked nor received any favour for himself or his family.

Such is the outline of Mr. O'Brien's political career prior to 1843. It displays a single-minded consistency in the pursuit of political truth. His motion on behalf of Ireland was couched in the following words: "That this House will resolve itself into a committee for the purpose of taking into consideration the causes of discontent at present prevailing in Ireland, with a view to the redress of grievances, and to the establishment of a system of just and impartial government in that part of the United Kingdom."

The rejection of that motion by the House decided the mover to join the Repeal agitation. He brought to the cause great practical ability, a complete mastery of the details of public business acquired from his long experience in parliamentary committees, and an honest zeal, of which the enthusiasm was at that time tempered by a calm and accurate judgment. His descent from the proudest line in Irish History gratified the Celtic prepossessions of the people; his social position commanded respect; and his Protestant creed afforded one more proof, in addition to the many already existing, that Irish nationality is of no particular sect or persuasion; and that amongst those who own its sacred influence, the most ardent, the most useful, the most active, may be, and have been, Protestants.

On his junction with the Repeal Association, he immediately founded the parliamentary committee of that body, whose occupation was to watch and report upon all Bills affecting Ireland in their progress through Parliament. The committees of the Association were practical schools of legislation. They amassed and disseminated information on matters with which the Irish legislator ought to be familiar. The Repeal leaders devoted their labours not merely to the organising of the people, but to the equally necessary task of diffusing through the land a body of knowledge calculated to exalt and fortify the movement by enlisting the intellect of Ireland as well as her feelings in favour of Home Government.

One of the topics to which the attention of the Association was called was the project, from time to time renewed, of abolishing the Viceroyalty. Against that project the Association passed a unanimous resolution. The Viceroyalty, like every human institution, has its defects; but it is better than any executive system by which it could be replaced. Not a shadow of proof has been given that Ireland would derive any benefit from its abolition. Many of the pretexts for abolishing the office have an ugly resemblance to the pretexts for abolishing the Irish Parliament. Many of them would equally serve for abolishing our Supreme Courts of Judicature and transferring the jurisdiction of the Four Courts to Westminster Hall. We might be told about steam-rails and telegraphic wires. We might be told that the retention of a separate judicature was a mark of provincial dependence, and that we should be raised to the level of

England, and made "an integral member of the Empire" by the extinction of all that gives metropolitan rank to the capital of our country, and national character to our jurisprudence. English egotism is engrossing; and whenever a scheme for the further spoliation of Ireland is contemplated by the absorption to London of our public institutions or offices, the project of robbery is pretty certain to be represented as " making Ireland an integral part of the Empire," and exalting us to an equality with England. If the Viceroyalty were abolished, the Supreme Courts of Law and Equity would become the next objects of attack. Significant indications of this have already been given.

Some advocates of the abolition of the viceregal office have—in my opinion inconsistently—deplored the evils of Irish absenteeism. They deem it mischievous that the owners of Irish estates should be absentees; yet they are ready to make an absentee of the Irish Executive. I know no reason why any governmental acts or functions that can be performed in Ireland, should be performed out of Ireland.

The talk we hear about the jobbery, flunkeyism, and corruption engendered by the viceregal institution supplies no sound argument for abolishing the office. That talk merely means that the Executive has something to give, in the way of either place or countenance, and that for what it can give there will be applicants. The same objection may be made against every executive Government that ever existed, or that ever will exist.

The Viceroyalty marks our national distinctness, and is a practical acknowledgment that Ireland is sufficiently great to require the permanent presence of the Sovereign's representative.

The admirable regularity and effective working of the Association at this period were mainly due to the care and ability of its secretary, Mr. Ray. He conducted the multitudinous correspondence of the Association, smoothed difficulties, disentangled and arranged the most complex details of public business with a quiet, easy mastery, resulting partly from long habit, but far more from natural sagacity. His acquaintance with Irish political subjects was accurate and extensive. He had a singularly tabular mind, well stored with information, historic and statistic; and he could, at a moment's notice, produce to you any fact or detail you might require from his copious stores. Each item occupied its place in his mental repositories, duly labelled and ticketed.

An able and efficient officer of the Association, he was popular not only from his official merits, but also from his great and well-known private worth.

Mr. Ray was the originator of the Repeal Reading-rooms. He established them in several towns on his Repeal mission in 1842. The first of these rooms opened was at Newcastle, County Limerick. As the Reading-room system extended, it developed its utility in furnishing local centres to combine and permanently organise the local patriots; centres where political information could be constantly acquired; social rallying points for the provincial Repealers where the intellect was exercised and improved; where habits of morality were strengthened by the inducement afforded to the people to employ their leisure hours in mental recreation instead of sensual indulgence.

Among the gentlemen who rendered frequent and efficient assistance to O'Connell in getting up meetings, was Maurice Linehan, Esq., the able and accomplished author of a valuable "History of Limerick." A list of the meetings which Mr. Linehan contributed to organise would nearly fill a page. His exertions in this department of the popular service commenced in 1832, in which year he assisted in promoting the Repeal and anti-tithe demonstrations of Clonmel and Carrick-on-Suir. In 1837, 1838, 1843, and 1844, we find him actively engaged in a similar service at Cork, Mallow, Skibbereen, and Lismore. He was the principal organiser of the monster meeting held at Thurles in September, 1845, to petition for Repeal, and his graphic pen was frequently employed in describing for the press the popular gatherings assembled by O'Connell. Mr. Linehan may look back with honourable pride on his usual and active part in the national agitation; for he is staunch to his national principles, and as incapable as ever of comprehending how Ireland can be benefited or exalted by the robbery and degradation of the Union.

CHAPTER XXV.

MILITARY PREPARATIONS TO OPPOSE THE REPEALERS.

The King of France, with twenty thousand men,
Marched up the hill, and then marched down again.

THE autumn of 1848 was advancing to its close; three or four monster meetings yet remained to be held. Of these, the Clontarf gathering was fixed for Sunday, the 8th of

October. The Executive had hitherto looked passively at the agitation. They now resolved on a sudden demonstration of vigour. Late on the afternoon of Saturday, the 7th, a proclamation by the Viceroy, Lord de Grey, was issued from the Castle, prohibiting the intended meeting of the morrow at Clontarf. O'Connell, apprehensive of a sanguinary attack upon the people in case of their disregarding this proclamation, issued a counter-proclamation from the Corn Exchange, enjoining the Repealers to abandon their purpose of assembling. Messengers were despatched into the country in all directions to meet the people on their way to the metropolis, and to send them back to their respective homes.

Meanwhile the Government placed Dublin in a state of siege. All the guards at the barracks and at the Castle were doubled; and for the special protection of Earl de Grey from Repeal violence, a squadron of dragoons and two extra companies of foot were quartered in the Lower Castle Yard. Aldborough House was garrisoned with a regiment of infantry; at night there were patrols established through the city. The roads in the vicinity were patrolled by parties of mounted police. Three vessels in the river had their guns run out, commanding the spot where the meeting was intended to have been held. The guns at the Pigeon-House Fort were also run out so as to command Clontarf, and prepared for immediate action. The *Rhadamanthus* and the *Dee* war-steamers brought the 87th Royal Irish Fusiliers to Dublin. The 34th Regiment arrived in Dublin on Sunday morning after a stormy passage from Glasgow. As that regiment marched through the city the multitude heartily cheered them; the commanding officer mistook the cheer for a hostile indication, and ordered the men to halt and fix bayonets. The crowd cheered again. The officer was wiser the second time, and quietly marched his men to their barrack.

The 5th Dragoon Guards were stationed at Clontarf. The men were accoutred for active service—each man and horse being provisioned for twenty-four hours. The 60th Rifles were stationed in their immediate vicinity; each soldier was served with sixty rounds of ball cartridge. A brigade of the Royal Horse Artillery occupied a position near Clontarf sheds, with four six-pounders limbered and ready for immediate action. There were also the 11th Hussars and the 54th Regiment of Infantry stationed near the sheds. A monster armament was brought against a peaceful, unarmed multitude to prevent their petitioning the Legislature for the repeal of a destructive and detested statute. It is impossible not to be struck with the similarity of the means whereby the Union was carried, and those by which it is sustained. Pitt and Castlereagh corrupted and coerced. Ebrington bribed Unionists with the lure of Government patronage; De Grey brought down troops to overawe the Repealers. Pitt poured 137,000 troops into Ireland to carry the Union. Peel poured in 30,000 bayonets to preserve it.

The display of military force could not disconcert men who meditated no appeal to arms. The Tories, however, declared that the military occupation of Ireland was indispensable to preserve the connection of the countries. What a pregnant commentary on the Union! The Union which was to have fused, consolidated, identified the nations, so that they were to have no longer been "twain, but one flesh;" this consolidating Union lasts for three-and-forty years, at the end of which period (on the Tory showing) it' requires 30,000 troops to restrain one of the "consolidated" parties from breaking loose from the other! I repeat, what a pregnant commentary on the Union! It is the same at the end of eighty-five years. It will be the same as long as the Union lasts. A measure in the highest degree insulting to the national honour, abhorrent to the national sentiment, and pernicious to the national interests, can have no other security for its continuance than the overwhelming brute force of England.

Meanwhile the Repealers betrayed no relaxation of zeal or activity. The first weekly meeting of the Association after the Clontarf affair was so crowded that the committee were obliged to adjourn it to the theatre in Abbey Street. Prosecutions were threatened, and the public mind was greatly excited. On that day, and on the two following Mondays, the chair was successively occupied by John O'Connell, by myself, and Mr. John Augustus O'Neill of Bunowen Castle, who threw into his address a genuinely Irish spirit of chivalrous devotion to the cause.

Then came the prosecutions, under the management of the Attorney-General, Mr. Thomas Berry Cusack Smith, son of Baron Smith, whose support of the Union has been noticed in a former chapter of this work. At first the proceedings excited curiosity; but their dull monotony soon palled upon the public. The traversers kept up their spirits despite this monster nuisance. Amusement was given by the public perusal of fantastic, amatory, or romantic poetry in Court, from the versical department of the *Nation*. Mr. Steele was in hopes that the principal witness against him, Mr. Frederick Bond Hughes, would have been discredited by the Court and jury from the following circumstance. Steele was in the habit of writing out his speeches for the newspapers, and introducing whatever additions or changes might occur to him while the pen was in his hand. Mr. Hughes, who was employed by the Government to report the speeches of the Repealers, appeared as a witness for the prosecution of Steele, and swore to his actual delivery of a speech which contained the quotation :

> Behemoth, biggest born of earth,
> Upheaved his vastness.

Now, these words had not been delivered by Steele but had been added by him to the report of whatever he had really said. Yet Hughes swore positively to Steele's delivery of the speech as reported with the added passage about Behemoth and his vastness. Steele made an affidavit denying the delivery, and asserting that he had introduced the addition while writing out his speech for the press. But the objection to Mr. Hughes's credibility was overruled by the Court; and in candour it must be admitted that such a mistake might be made by the witness without any intentional deviation from veracity. The mistake was made the most of, and increased the unpopularity which had already attached to Mr. Hughes as a Crown witness. The owner of an itinerant equestrian troupe, whose name was Hughes, tried to turn the affair to his own account by appending to his placards and advertisements the following intimation : " N.B.—No connection with Mr. Frederick Bond Hughes " ; which disclaimer may perhaps have drawn some extra spectators to the equine show.

The trials went on slowly and wearily. One of the attorneys for the defence made a serio-comic complaint of the Court, the agents, and the defendants, who all seemed engaged in a conspiracy to deprive the trial of becoming gravity and dignity. "Heaven help me!" said this gentleman, "I have got no peace among 'em all. I want my clients to swear an affidavit—they've levanted somewhere, and aren't to be found. Well, there's a hurry-scurry after them, and at last they are discovered sitting for their pictures to some vagabond coxcomb of an artist from London. By-and-by I want

Mr. ——" (a brother solicitor) "on a very pressing matter. He's invisible—another hue-and-cry—at length he's caught in a back parlour, with his thumbs in his waistcoat pockets, strutting up and down in a dignified attitude, and looking as majestic as he can for some other grinning picture-drawing scamp. We go back to the court—the traversers are cracking their jokes among themselves in their box, and my lords are poking their necks over the desk to find out, if they can, what the d— the fun is all about. Counsellor Fitzgibbon does duty by his client, whereupon the Attorney-General jumps up and sends him a three-cocked invitation in open court to come and be shot at twelve paces."

The most brilliant speeches that enlivened the prolonged monotony of the trial were those of Sheil, who defended John O'Connell, and of Whiteside (afterwards Chief Justice), who defended Charles Gavan Duffy. A few days before the delivery of Sheil's speech some person expressed to O'Connell a hope that as it was sure to be a splendid display of eloquence it might be carefully reported. O'Connell replied with a smile, "It is in type at this moment in London." From Mr. Whiteside's speech I extract the following passage, which is important as a record of the order of men whom the ennobling influences of native legislation raised up in Ireland:

"Men have lived amongst us who approached the greatness of antiquity. The imperishable records of their eloquence may keep alive in our hearts a zeal for freedom and a love of country. The comprehensive genius of Flood —the more than mortal energy of Grattan—the splendour of Bushe—the wisdom of Saurin—the learning of Ball—the noble simplicity of Burrowes—the Demosthenic fire of Plunket, and the eloquence of Curran rushing from the heart, and which will sound in the ears of his countrymen for ever. They failed to save the ancient Constitution of Ireland—wit, learning, genius, eloquence, lost their power over the souls of men. With one great exception * our distinguished countrymen have passed away, but their memorials cannot perish with them. While the language lasts their eloquence lives, and their names will be remembered by a grateful posterity so long as genius shall be honoured and patriotism revered. The Irish people, lastly, demand that the Union shall be repealed, because, they

* Plunket, who then still lived.

say, their feelings have not been consulted nor their miseries relieved by the Imperial Parliament. Wealth has diminished, they say, amongst us; before us there is a gloomy prospect and little hope. . . . They have embraced this project of Repeal with ardour. It is their nature, where they feel strongly, to act boldly and to speak passionately."

The management of the trial by the Government officers is familiar to the public—the refusal of the caption to the traversers—the defective jury list—the shameless packing of the jury—the admission of a species of evidence against the traversers which was actually condemned as inadmissible at the very same period by the Court of Queen's Bench at Westminster*—the charge by the Lord Chief Justice against "the other side," and, finally, the wrongful imprisonment.

But the imprisonment was a great point gained for the Orangemen. No matter by what means accomplished, it was the subject of loud exaltation. The traversers were at last in jail, convicted of a "conspiracy," which conspiracy no ten rational men outside the court and jury-box believed to have any existence at all.

The exclusion of Catholics from the jury list because they were supposed to be Repealers, was defended by Sir James Graham in the following manner: "We wanted," said the right hon. baronet, "to avoid the partiality necessarily arising from preconceived opinions favourable to Repeal on the part of the jurors."

Did it occur to Sir James that there might be as strong a partiality on the opposite side, arising from the preconceived opinions of jurors adverse to Repeal?

When a man says, "Don't put Repealers into the jury-box—they will be sure to acquit," it sounds extremely like saying, "*Do* put anti-Repealers into the jury-box—they will be sure to convict."

* Viz., the admission of newspaper articles as evidence against men who never saw them.

CHAPTER XXVI.

IMPRISONMENT OF O'CONNELL AND HIS FRIENDS IN 1844.

Who helpeth not himself, Fortune disowns;
Who braves all obstacles will win i' th' end.
Success crowns perseverance—coward souls
Who shrink from work, shall never win work's guerdon.
HERBERT SMITH.

THE Orange and Tory party now had their triumph. Truly the Government had deserved success, if a reckless disregard of all decency in their vindictive pursuit could entitle them to victory.

But the verdict was obtained, no matter how; and sentence was pronounced, and there was a mighty uproar of delight in all Orangeland. The *Mail* announced that the traversers had been hurried to their prison with less *éclat* than had often attended a coal-porter's wedding. I think it was that journal that jocularly said, "O'Connell has got two feather beds conveyed from his house to the jail —one for himself, and the other, we presume, for Repeal." That Repeal could survive the incarceration of its leaders was deemed impossible. The cause was extinct; that was loudly announced; the Repeal rent would dwindle to nothing. The deluded people, having their eyes opened to the wickedness, folly, and peril of their evil ways by the well-merited punishment of their chiefs, would be scared from any further connection with the movement. They would no longer furnish the sinews of war to a set of men who could not keep their heads out of Sir Robert Peel's net. The leaders were seized; the flock would scatter. And, above all, the mischievous magic of O'Connell's legal infallibility, which so long had kept the Repealers together, would now be destroyed. The spell was dissolved; the magician would henceforth be powerless.

Such were the boasts of the anti-Repealers on O'Connell's imprisonment. Bets were laid whether the Repealers would hold their usual meeting on the following Monday. The Conservative party were firmly convinced that they would not dare to assemble.

The committee met on the evening of the day that saw O'Connell consigned to a prison. The room was overflowing, and great excitement necessarily prevailed. It was surmised that the Government would proclaim down the Association on the Monday morning, and arrest the principal leaders who were still at large. On the question being discussed as to who should occupy the chair, a post of possible danger, numerous gentlemen offered themselves; but Mr. Smith O'Brien said that as he conceived that the struggle against despotic power could perhaps be most effectively made in his person, he claimed the chief post of peril as a particular favour. It was, however, deemed more advisable that Mr. O'Brien should occupy the place usually filled by Mr. O'Connell.

Monday arrived. It soon became manifest that the Repealers were not scared by the recent prosecution. They mustered in such crowds that Conciliation Hall was filled long before the hour announced for the commencement of the day's business, and thousands who could not obtain standing room were obliged to go away. The Tory predictions did not seem likely to be realised. There was no shrinking, either among the leaders or the people.

The chair was occupied on Monday by Mr. Caleb Powell, of Clonshavoy, the Protestant representative of the County Limerick; and on Tuesday by another Protestant gentleman, Captain Seaver, of Heath Hall, near Newry. There was a sustained yet quiet energy in the proceedings. There was the most intense enthusiasm combined with the most cautious discretion. Every face expressed firm resolution to encounter all risks that might beset the pursuit of Repeal; but at the same time to play the game warily as well as firmly. The minds of men were braced and strung for a mighty effort. It was glorious to behold the crowds that filled the national hall at the moment when the thunders of the Government were directed against Ireland's nationality. The people never assumed a loftier port or a nobler attitude than when they calmly bade defiance to tyrannic power, and opposed the simple might of popular opinion to the chicanery of perverted law and the formidable array of British bayonets. The troops that filled the land, and the monster indictment, alike were unable to scare them from a course recommended by its own intrinsic justice, and endeared to their hearts by the sentiment of honourable national pride. They hailed with delight the entrance of men who were accustomed to take a prominent part in the proceedings. The roof rang again with the joyous acclamations that greeted their appearance.

The prosecution did not paralyse the contributors to the

Repeal exchequer. There was actually an inconvenient rivalry to hand in money. Each man was eager to pour into the treasury the contribution committed to his care, and thus were several hours successively occupied. The first week's receipts amounted to £2,593 18s. 2d., which sum was considerably exceeded on several subsequent occasions.

Almost immediately on O'Connell's imprisonment the several municipal Corporations of Ireland sent deputies to the metropolis; where, having been refused admission to the prison for the purpose of presenting addresses to the captives, they assembled at O'Connell's house in Merrion Square, and there agreed on a solemn declaration that Ireland required a domestic Parliament to develop her resources and secure her prosperity. This declaration, emanating not from noisy agitators, but from the very flower of the trading and mercantile community of Ireland, was necessarily calculated to produce a deep impression.

Whilst these events occurred out of doors, let us take a peep within the prison walls.

O'Connell, on the evening of his incarceration, had exclaimed: "Thank God, I am in jail for Ireland." He believed that Peel's false move tended to augment the strength of the national cause. All the prisoners dined together, and the party wore anything but a tragical air. They all enjoyed the exhilaration of spirits arising from a hope that, whatever inconveniences they might sustain, their imprisonment would accelerate the triumph of the cause that was nearest to their hearts.

They were for the first few days occupied with the bustle of fixing themselves in their new quarters. At last they settled down into something like their usual habits. Charles Gavan Duffy, the editor of the *Nation;* Doctor (afterwards Sir John) Gray, the editor of the *Freeman;* and Richard Barrett, the editor of the *Pilot,* found abundant employment in superintending their several journals. The moments unoccupied by business they devoted to study, or to taking exercise in the adjoining garden. Mr. Duffy, under the impression that the imprisonment would last a year, announced his purpose of reading through Carte's "Life of Ormond," in three folio volumes. Mr. Ray still exercised his supervision of the affairs of the Association. John O'Connell wrote his amusing and instructive Repeal Dictionary, which appeared in the weekly press, and which I believe was subsequently published in a collected form.

Steele read Kane's "Industrial Resources of Ireland," and defaced the fair pages of the work with innumerable marks of admiration. Barrett was ready for fun, frisk, joyous frolic of any sort, and more than once kept the incarcerated coterie in roars of laughter by attitudinising and grimacing in a style that would have done honour to Liston. Two of the visitors played the short-armed orator; the comic force of the pathetic passages being much enhanced by a cambric handkerchief, which the gentleman who performed the action held to the weeping eyes of the gentleman who performed the eloquence. Nearly all the prisoners contributed to the pages of a *jeu d'esprit* called the *Prison Gazette*, in which they quizzed each other and their friends with merry malice. In short, there never were prisoners who bore so lightly and joyously the hours of imprisonment, or whose deprivation of freedom was more soothed by the kind and sympathetic offices of friends.

They had access to two gardens. In one of these was a mound with a summer-house on the top. The mound they amused themselves by calling Tara Hill; the summer-house was termed Conciliation Hall. In the other garden they erected a large marquee, which they styled Mullaghmast, and in this marquee were received the numerous deputations who bore addresses to the "convicts" from the different quarters of the kingdom. I learned from a gentleman, who was present on one of these occasions, that O'Connell replied to the bearers of an address in the following words : " Tell your friends that my heart is joyful, my spirits are buoyant, my health is excellent, my hopes are high. My imprisonment is not irksome to me, for I feel and know that it will, under Providence, be the means of making our country a nation again. I am glad I am in prison. There wanted but this to my career. I have laboured for Ireland—refused office, honour, and emolument for Ireland—I have prayed and hoped and watched for Ireland—there was yet one thing wanted—that I should be in jail for Ireland. This has now been added to the rest, thanks to our enemies; and I cordially rejoice at it."

O'Connell, in the course of that day, was waited on by a party of American tourists. When they arrived, he was standing on the top of "Tara Hill." They doffed their hats and remained at the foot of the mound until desired to walk up. "You are probably more visited here," said one of them, "than if you were at large." "Yes," replied the

Liberator, "and here I cannot use the excuse of 'not at home.'"

The progress of Repeal during his imprisonment enchanted him. "The people," said he, "are behaving nobly. I was at first a little afraid, despite all my teaching, that at such a trying crisis they would have done either too much or too little—either have been stung into an outbreak, or else awed into apathy. Neither has happened. Blessed be God! the people are acting nobly. What it is to have such a people to lead!"

He rejoiced especially over the excellent training of the Repeal Association; praised the young talent called forth by the movement, bestowing particular eulogy on MacNevin and Barry.

"In the days of the Catholic Association," said he, "I used to have more trouble than I can express in keeping down mutiny. I always arrived in town about the 25th of October, and on my arrival I invariably found some jealousies, some squabbles—some fellow trying to be leader, which gave me infinite annoyance. But now all goes right—no man is jealous of any other man; each does his best for the general cause."

Speaking of his own pacific policy, he remarked that it was a curious coincidence that the Conal of Ossian should say, "My sword hangs at my side—the blade longs to shine in my hand—but I love the peace of green Erin of the streams."

The convicted patriots received numerous presents of fresh fruit and flowers. A patriotic confectioner presented them with two monster cakes. Mr. Scriber, of Westmoreland Street, sent them seven musical-boxes to cheer their imprisonment; and it is said that, immediately on the arrival of the harmonious cargo, the prisoners evinced their satisfaction with more musical zeal than taste—by setting the seven boxes all playing together.

Mr. Steele one day placed a stone, which he dignified with the name of Liach Fail, or the Stone of Destiny, on the side of the mimic Tara Hill in the garden, calling on Duffy to doff his hat in honour of the august ceremony.

With these and similar helps and devices did the prisoners try to cheat the hours of that bondage which, under every circumstance of mitigation, must ever be oppressive to men of ardent minds and active habits. One day John O'Connell made some remark on the high, gloomy prison buildings, which excluded the view of the country from the dining-room. " I am better pleased," said his father, "that the view is excluded. To see the hills, and fields, and sea-coast, and to feel that you were debarred from the freedom of walking among them, were a worse affliction than to be deprived altogether of the sight. It would tantalise too much."

But these little fits of gloom were merely passing clouds. There was great and enduring consolation in the steady progress the Repeal cause seemed to be daily making. The meetings of the Association at this time wore an eminently business-like and practical character. There was no wild, driftless rhapsodising. Men spoke to the purpose, and not at immeasurable length. Their eloquence—the more effective because compressed within reasonable limits—was alternated with the delivery of the vast remittances which showed how stedfastly the nation backed the demand for independence. The money was an index that could not be mistaken of the people's resolve. When a poor and oppressed people give their money, they are ready to give everything else—life itself, if needed—to achieve their object.

The verdict, sentence, and imprisonment failed to produce the results which had been confidently predicted by the anti-Irish gang who had hounded on Sir Robert Peel to prosecute. It was prophesied :

Firstly, that a salutary terror would be struck into the souls of the Repealers. When their leader was made amenable for his crimes to the outraged law, his followers would shrink from exposing themselves to the like penalty.

But the Repealers were not so easily terrified. They mustered at Conciliation Hall with greater energy and in larger numbers than ever.

Secondly, it was thought that if the people could not be immediately scared, their indignation at the legal outrage on their Liberator might at least goad them into a useful *émeute;* for which contingency a potent armament had been prepared. Repeal might be drowned in a river of blood.

But again—the provoking people knew better than to treat their kind friends to an *émeute.* They were not quite so reckless or impulsive as those sagacious speculators had deemed possible. Instead of taking up pikes, they thronged Conciliation Hall to supply themselves with Repeal cards.

Thirdly, there were among the Tory editors and politicians good, benevolent souls, who were sorry to see the knowing managers at the Corn Exchange gull their poor dupes out of the Repeal rent. They had said: "Shut up O'Connell, and the rent will immediately dwindle to nothing. The Irish 'treason' will lose its supplies."

But this benevolent hope was also doomed to be disappointed. For the fourteen weeks preceding the imprisonment the Repeal rent had amounted to £6,679 12s. 6d. For the fourteen weeks that O'Connell was in jail the National Treasury swelled up to £25,712 17s. 2d.

Fourthly, it was confidently promised that the imprisonment would for ever deprive O'Connell of the prestige of legal invulnerability. The people would fly from the impostor, now unmasked by the searching operation of the law.

But the people were so wickedly obtuse that they did not understand how O'Connell's reputation as a lawyer could suffer from a notoriously virulent and one-sided charge, and a verdict so battered and shattered and damaged as to lose all moral weight in the estimation of rational and unprejudiced men. They did not require any experiments in the Court of Queen's Bench to convince them that twelve hot Tories could easily be got to seize with alacrity on an opportunity of finding O'Connell guilty. The Agitator's legal prestige accordingly remained unimpaired.

Fifthly, as the glorious result of all the above sagacious speculations, Repeal would be extinct.

But Repeal turned out to possess an unexpected vitality. To the dismay and astonishment of the prophets, instead of becoming extinct, it towered aloft in new pride and strength; it expanded and fortified its influences; it assumed, to all outward appearance, an attitude of majesty and power far greater than it had previously exhibited; it daily received fresh adhesions from important recruits; it took such a grasp of the national heart that a prudent statesman might have reasonably asked himself whether the refusal of a demand so just, so righteous, so essential to Irish prosperity, and on which the desire of the people was unalterably fixed, could be persevered in without deeply imperilling the integrity of the British Empire?

So far, at least as concerned the immediate results of the imprisonment, new force was thereby imparted to the movement. The energy of former friends was increased. Our ranks were enlarged by new and valuable auxiliaries.

Baffled and discomfited by results so different from what

they had expected, the anti-Irish party began to think that it had been wiser to abstain from meddling with the Nationalists; and that, as Dr. Gray had tersely remarked, O'Connell could far better afford to remain in prison than Peel could afford to keep him there.

The prisoners had appealed from the decision of the Court of Queen's Bench to the House of Lords. Such an appeal seemed unpromising enough; the House of Lords was a foreign assembly; but the prisoners felt it a duty, not less to their country than to themselves, to try every chance, however improbable, of procuring a reversal of the unjust judgment under which they suffered. The great majority of the English judges was against them. Providentially the ultimate decision lay with five law-lords — Lyndhurst, Brougham, Cottenham, Denman, and Campbell—of whom the last-named three respected the Constitutional rights of the Queen's subjects; detested jury-packing and partisan charges; did not comprehend how a sound and legal judgment could be based on an unsound and illegal indictment; and accordingly, both on the merits of the case and on legal grounds, reversed the judgment of the Irish Court of Queen's Bench. The words of Lord Denman are too important to be omitted from a record, however brief, of the transaction; they have become historical: "If," said his lordship, "such practices as have taken place in the present instance in Ireland should continue, the trial by jury would become a mockery, a delusion, and a snare."

Three law-lords against two decided the matter in favour of the prisoners. They had been thrust into jail with vindictive haste. The ultimate Court of Appeal now decided that they should not have been in jail for an instant. The *Times*, in its dismay, made a desperate effort to extract an argument against Repeal from the decision of the Lords. Thus spoke the leading journal: "It (the decision) will teach the most anti-Saxon of the Irish people—the most vehement instigators to Repeal—the most violent denouncers of England, that the only tribunal where the strict and literal construction of the law is brought to aid the impugners and violators of law, is the highest court of that nation from which Ireland prays to be divorced—that the only place where those who have assailed England and her peerage can have justice meted, is the House of Peers in England."

The decision of the three honest law-lords taught the Irish no such thing. That there were three Constitutional law-lords out of five was sheer accident. But there was no accident in the Saxon spirit that initiated the prosecution; no accident in the anti-Irish tendencies of the Court of Queen's Bench; no accident in the Saxon hate of Ireland which denied the accused throughout the trial the ordinary privileges dictated by common justice; no accident in the fiery speed with which the accused were hurried from the courts to the jail; no accident in the decision of a large majority of the English judges, who confirmed the judgment delivered by their Irish brethren in a mode whereof the falsehood and the folly contended for predominance; no accident in the indecency with which the lay-lords were struggling to negative the reversal of judgment pronounced by the law-lords, if they had not been restrained for very shame's sake by Lord Wharncliffe.

No. These things were not accidental; and in them, each and all, did the Irish people recognise the impression of English influence. In them, and not in the lucky accident of a favourable majority (and it was the smallest possible majority) among the English law-lords, do the Irish people find the motives rationally applicable to their dealings with the Legislative Union Statute.

On the evening of the 6th of September, O'Connell and his fellow-prisoners were liberated. About ten days previously, his intimate friend, Mr. Patrick Fitzpatrick, of Eccles Street, had expressed to him his expectation that the law-lords would confirm the sentence, but that the prisoners would be liberated by the exercise of the Royal prerogative. "You must, in that event," said Mr. Fitzpatrick, "be prepared with instant securities. How large is the amount of bail required?"

O'Connell had forgotten the amount, and descended to the Governor's office to inspect the book. Mr. Fitzpatrick speedily followed, and found O'Connell laughing heartily at the personal description annexed to his name in the book: "Daniel O'Connell—complexion good." The amount of bail was £5,000 personally, and two securities at £2,500 each. "But it is idle, quite idle to talk of it," said O'Connell; "there is not the least probability—not the smallest shadow of a chance of our being set free. No, my good friend, we shall suffer our full term."*

In this conviction O'Connell continued until the evening of the 6th. Two messengers from the Corn Exchange rushed

---

* Communicated to me by Mr. Fitzpatrick.

simultaneously into the prison with the news, vociferating in such noisy rivalship that their tidings were for a long time unintelligible. At length one of them, per force of better wind, shouted his comrade out of breath, and having reached the corridor leading to O'Connell's apartments, he continued to bellow, "I'm first! I'm first! I'm first!"

"What is it all about?" demanded Mr. Barrett, who was calmly perambulating the corridor.

"Only that you're free," cried Edmond O'Hagarty (the messenger). "I'm first! I'm first! Hurrah! Where's the Liberator? I'm first!"

They rushed into a drawing-room where O'Connell was seated between two ladies, O'Hagarty in his noisy delight still shouting, "I'm first! I'm first! You're free, Liberator! Thanks be to God for that same! The judgment's reversed."

"Bah! not true; it can't be true," replied O'Connell coolly.

"But it *is* true, Liberator." And the messenger showed him the placard which had been printed in London announcing the fact. He examined it attentively, and said to Fitzpatrick: "After all, this may be true," when doubt was dispelled by the sudden appearance of the attorneys for the defence. "On the merits," were the first words of Mr. Ford, who threw his arms round O'Connell's neck and kissed him. O'Connell wore his green velvet Mullaghmast cap, and Ford wore a broad-brimmed beaver hat, oblivious in his ecstacy of the presence of the ladies. "On the merits," he triumphantly repeated; "no technicalities at all—nothing but the merits."

The news had now spread through the prison, and the other prisoners crowded to the drawing-room to learn their fate. There was a quiet sort of triumph, no boisterous joy amongst the traversers. In the course of the evening O'Connell said to my informant in a tone of deep solemnity: "Fitzpatrick, the hand of man is not in this. It is the response given by Providence to the prayers of the faithful, stedfast, pious people of Ireland."

It was near twilight when O'Connell left the prison to return to his house in Merrion Square. As he walked along the streets, the people at first gazed on him in bewildered astonishment. They could scarcely believe the evidence of their eyes. Was O'Connell indeed free? They crowded round him to ascertain the fact; the crowds augmented; and by the time he arrived at the western end of Merrion Square, his friends were obliged to form a cordon around him to avert the inconvenient pressure of the delighted multitude. When he placed his foot on his own hall-door step, to re-enter the home from which he had for three months been iniquitously exiled, the popular ecstasy became uncontrollable. Cheer after cheer rose and swelled upon the air. The people gave vent to their wild delight in vociferous acclamations; every heart beat high with pride and triumph at the liberation of their venerated leader—not by ministerial grace or royal favour, but by the strict and stern vindication of that law which had been so nefariously outraged in the trial and conviction.

O'Connell appeared on the balcony and addressed the people briefly. He exhorted them to bear their victory with moderation. Let them, he said, demonstrate their fitness to rule themselves by the spirit of conciliation and friendliness with which they should enjoy their triumph.

On the next day (Saturday, the 7th of September) the liberated patriots passed in procession through the leading streets of the metropolis. It was a scene of indescribable excitement. When opposite the door of the old Parliament House in College Green, the cavalcade halted—O'Connell rose in his triumphal car, uncovered his head, and pointed with significant emphasis to the edifice. Then arose a mighty shout from the surrounding thousands—again and again did O'Connell, looking proudly around him, repeat his significant gesture; again and again did the myriads who thronged the broad street upraise their glad voices in deafening cheers. It was like the roar of the ocean, that proud shout of a nation's triumph and a nation's hope.

On Monday, the 9th of September, the Association met; the Lord Mayor of Dublin occupied the chair. Thousands were obliged to return from the door of Conciliation Hall from the incapacity of that building to contain them. Floor, benches, galleries, all were full. The enthusiasm of O'Connell's reception was beyond the power of imagination to exaggerate.

His speech embraced many topics. He exulted in the vindication of the Constitution and of trial by jury. He showed, in reply to the cavils of the enemy, that the favourable decision of the three law-lords was a direct decision on the merits, inasmuch as the sixth and seventh counts of the monster indictment, which expressly charged

s

the traversers with conspiracy to hold meetings to intimidate —counts which contained the very essence of the prosecution —counts on which the conviction and sentence were ostentatiously justified; these sixth and seventh counts were pronounced to be bad and invalid by the English judges and the English House of Lords; although the English judges, in condemning the counts, yet sanctioned the sentence that had been based on them, by the preposterous presumption that it was not on those counts, but on some others, that the Irish Bench had rested their judgment; a presumption notoriously contradicted by the fact, and by the charges of the Irish judges themselves.

O'Connell next complimented the Whigs for their felicitous judicial appointments. He complimented Sheil, who had been harshly censured for seeming to solicit, as a matter of favour to the traversers, some concession from the Government: "I was vexed and angry with Sheil at the time, that he should have uttered any words to which the meaning could be possibly attached of soliciting a favour on my part from Sir Robert Peel. He ought to have known that I would rather have rotted in jail than condescend to accept a favour from Peel. I said from the commencement— I announced it to the world—that, come what might, there should be no compromise or shrinking. There has been none; and there is not a man of us who would not have died in jail rather than sully our hands by receiving the slightest concession from our enemies. Sheil was wrong in that instance; but he is one of those who can afford to be wrong once, for his country owes him a deep debt of gratitude. Oh! I cannot forget his past career—his glorious career! I cannot forget how he ornamented and made interesting our struggle for Emancipation. When I was going on with my dull, prosy speech, wearying the public ear with the monotony of my tones and accents, and with the continued repetition of the same facts, Sheil used to burst forth in the dazzling effulgence of intellectual glory, irradiating our cause with the coruscations of his genius and the illumination of his powerful mind."

O'Connell appealed with great force to his Protestant countrymen; exhibiting the delusive nature of the fears of those who were still timid, by referring to his past pacific policy: "What *are* you afraid of? Did we threaten? Did we menace? Did we overawe? We were strong enough to commit violence; nothing save the spirit of conciliation and love for each other could have brought us together in such multitudinous masses without violence. In the midst of a people who love me and trust me—with more power in my hands than any monarch in Europe enjoys " (here the speaker was interrupted with vehement cheering and waving of handkerchiefs), " so situated, how have I demeaned myself? But first—how did I acquire that power? I acquired it and retained it because of the conviction that every man, woman, and child feels that I would not abuse it. I have acquired it and retained it because I was congenial in opinion with the millions of my countrymen, and because they were perfectly persuaded that in the exercise of that power with which by their confidence they invested me, I would sedulously guard against the commission of any crime whatsoever. I have kept my compact, but I never could have done this without the assistance and co-operation of the Catholic clergy. They saw the jealous scrutiny with which our minutest movements were watched by our Protestant brethren; they entered unreservedly into my views—and here is all the secret of my success. They knew me—they appreciated me. They knew that I was the first apostle and founder of that sect of politicians whose cardinal doctrine is this—that the greatest and most desirable of political changes may be achieved by moral means alone, and that no human revolution is worth the effusion of one single drop of human blood. Human blood is no cement for the temple of human liberty."

Such were the leading topics of O'Connell's address on that important day. His manner and appearance corresponded well with the triumphant style of his language. Never were his spirits more elate, his step more elastic, his tone more exulting. There was a fire in his eye, an eager vivacity in his voice, and a vigour of intellect in his address, that beseemed a nation's chief disenthralled from unjust bondage, and impatient to devote his unfettered energies to the renewed battle for legislative freedom.

It needs not be told that the enthusiastic joy which animated Dublin was diffused through the whole kingdom. The glad news of the liberation was immediately telegraphed all over the land by signal fires. Cresset answered cresset; mountain and valley started into light. You gazed into the dark distance, and blaze after blaze sprang up. The red flame glowed in the sheltered hollow of the rock, and streamed in the light breeze on the hill-top. The heart and soul of the land rejoiced ; the exulting shouts of the people were borne far on the night wind ; glen, river, plain, and mountain were vocal with their triumph. Stirring sights—joyous sounds. I was in the country at the time, 150 Irish miles from Dublin. From the roof of my house on the banks of the Bandon river I looked on the national illumination. I omitted to reckon the number of fires, but I think it probable that from that one point not less than from sixty to seventy might have been counted.

Heretofore, our prospects looked well. O'Connell probably did not then know that his health had been fatally undermined by his imprisonment, and there were not yet any external indications that his strength was impaired. The reversal of the judgment established his "legal infallibility," as the enemy ironically styled his extensive and accurate knowledge of the law.

CHAPTER XXVII.

CAREER OF A ROMANTIC AGITATOR.

Bold and true,
In bonnet blue,
Who fear or falsehood never knew.
SIR WALTER SCOTT.

BEFORE tracing any farther the progress of O'Connell's agitation, I shall give a short account of the career of O'Connell's Head Pacificator, Mr. Steele.

"Honest Tom Steele," as he was usually called, was born at Derrymore, in the County Clare, in 1788. His family came from Somersetshire in the reign of Charles II. Their name was then Champion, which they changed into the name of Steele for reasons now unknown. William Champion, the lineal ancestor of the Head Pacificator, was, I believe, an officer in Monmouth's regiment. He established himself near Nenagh, in the County Tipperary. His first experiment as a settler was inauspicious, inasmuch as the Tipperary folk three times burned his house over his head, the proprietor on each occasion narrowly escaping with life. Unwilling to incur the peril of a fourth combustion, he migrated to the more pacific county of Clare, where his posterity continued to reside.

Steele received a university education at Cambridge,

where he obtained distinction for his scientific acquirements. The death of an uncle placed him in possession of his family property in Clare, just at the time when the Spanish nation was in insurrection against the tyrannical King Ferdinand VII. Steele, whose love of the cause of universal liberty has ever been associated with that total forgetfulness of self which the world calls imprudence, resolved to assist the Spanish insurgents with his hand and fortune. He was said to have fitted out and filled with arms, at his own expense, a vessel which he brought to Cadiz; but he told me that he had not committed that piece of extravagance. He accepted a commission from the Cortes, and distinguished himself by his valour in several engagements against the French, who had invaded the country as the allies of a despotic monarch in order to perpetuate the bondage of the Spanish people.*

When the struggle against despotism failed, Steele quitted Spain and returned to Ireland. He constantly attended the meetings of the Catholic Association, and watched with anxious scrutiny the words and actions of O'Connell. So soon as his judgment convinced him that O'Connell was a trustworthy leader, he immediately proclaimed his adhesion to the cause, and worked with zeal to remove those disabilities from the Catholics which he, as a Protestant, felt were disgraceful only to the party by whom they were inflicted.

Notwithstanding the military bent of Steele's ideas, and the constitutional bravery of the man, he highly appreciated the value of O'Connell's moral force system of political warfare. Seeing clearly that the wild and illegal combinations of Whitefeet, Ribbonmen, Terry-Alts, and other misguided parties assuming equally fantastic and absurd denominations, could only tend to embarrass the friends and injure the cause of rational liberty, he applied himself to the task of quelling disturbances in his native county, and of getting up arms from the misguided peasantry. There was in this occupation something peculiarly congenial to the wild and Ossianic spirit of Steele. He loved at night to traverse the mountain fastnesses of Cratloe; to watch the dark low clouds

---

* All this I stated, in concurrence with the common belief, in the first edition of this work. Steele said my account was inaccurate; but I think his correction only applied to the statement of his fitting out the vessel. But as I am not quite sure, I wish to guard the reader against accepting this part of the narrative as of undoubted verity.

sailing slowly through the heavens as he wandered along the lonely ravine by the side of the swollen brook, in whose midnight wave stars shimmered as they broke through the mists. Those scenes had for Steele a charm of magical potency, especially when associated with the function of Head Pacificator which he discharged in the midst of them. His soul thrilled with an indefinable feeling, of which fancy, poetry, and patriotism were constituent parts, as he paused to hold communings with Nature in her sombre moods—to listen to the voice of the night wind as it swept through the gloomy woods, and to catch the inspiration of the hills in his solemn, thoughtful, and imaginative, yet energetic career. He spent many a night in the cottages of the insurgent peasantry, endeavouring to reclaim them from their driftless and mischievous conspiracies. In some of these nocturnal excursions O'Connell accompanied Steele. They got up a large quantity of arms. Steele, by constant and familiar association with his peasant countrymen, convinced himself that their crimes were principally, if not wholly, the fruits of oppression; while he proudly recognised the traits of high and virtuous feeling which often appeared in their conduct. One instance of devoted heroism in five poor Terry-Alts he has often recorded.

There was a Mr. Smith who resided at Fort Fergus, and who, during the period when robberies of arms were frequent, habitually boasted that his house was so well defended that no insurgents would dare to attack it. Accordingly, the neighbouring gentry, having confidence in Smith's superior valour, entrusted the greater part of their arms to his keeping. It so chanced, however, that five Terry-Alts availed themselves one day of Mr. Smith's absence from home, entered the house, and carried off all the arms, notwithstanding that a party of constables had been left at Fort Fergus to guard them.

There was a man prosecuted for the outrage on the evidence of the constables, whose sworn testimony was so contradictory that in any ordinary case the acquittal of the accused would have been certain. It was, however, tried by a special commission; and at special commissions jurors have too frequently deemed it their duty to hang as many men as possible. The prisoner was accordingly found guilty.

On receiving the news of the verdict, the five Terry-Alts who had really taken the arms came to Steele, and said that if the innocent man who had been falsely convicted could be thereby saved, they would surrender the arms. They added that if his life could be obtained on no other terms than those of dying in his place, they would all go to Ennis and give themselves up to the jailer. But there was no occasion for this sacrifice, as the condemned man was saved on a strong application in his favour to the Government.

In 1828 the Catholics resolved on opposing every member of the Peel-Wellington Administration, whether personally hostile or friendly to their claims. That Administration pretended to make the Catholic question an open one ; at the same time contriving that all substantial power should be placed in the hands of those who opposed it. To end this delusion it was determined by the Catholics to start a candidate for Clare in opposition to Mr. Vesey Fitzgerald, who had been nominated President of the Board of Trade by the Prime Minister. O'Connell conceived the idea of standing for the county. An unemancipated Catholic, chosen by the electors as their representative, yet disqualified by law from taking his seat, would present a striking impersonation of the Catholic grievances. O'Gorman Mahon proposed, and Thomas Steele seconded, the nomination of O'Connell. The influence of this dexterous movement of the Agitator in accelerating Emancipation is now a matter of history. O'Connell presented himself at the table of the House of Commons to take his seat, but could not overleap the barrier of the Protestant oaths. Emancipation was hastily passed in the spring of 1829, and seldom had the shabbiness of personal enmity been more conspicuous than in the conduct of Sir Robert Peel, who, in admitting the Catholics to Parliament, yet excluded O'Connell as having been unduly elected. Peel was unable to forgive O'Connell for having compelled him to emancipate. The exclusion was inoperative for any political object ; it was solely the result of personal spleen, for O'Connell—as every one necessarily anticipated—was immediately re-elected by his former constituents.

In 1839 Steele addressed a letter to the King of the Belgians, requesting permission to bear arms as a volunteer in His Majesty's service. An enthusiast in all his undertakings, Steele incurred the ridicule of persons who were incapable of appreciating, or even of comprehending, the intense fidelity to Ireland by which he was actuated. His very faults were often the exaggeration of high and noble qualities. If he shared the extravagance of Don Quixote, he also partook of the Don's contempt for baseness, perfidy, and cowardice. In his language there was certainly a strong and marked peculiarity; an occasional application of strong phrases to comparatively insignificant objects; a blending of the ideal and poetic in undue proportions with the real and practical; a disposition to seek illustrations of his views from sources too recondite for ordinary comprehension. But what of all that? The man loved Ireland, and would have died for her with infinitely more pleasure than even the selfish place-hunter who sneered at his verbal eccentricities could derive from personal aggrandisement. The people of Ireland gave Steele full credit for his pure and single-hearted patriotism, and it would have been shame to them if they had not duly appreciated the qualities of unsullied honour and enthusiastic love of freedom which pre-eminently distinguished him.

If we smile at the poetic temperament of the orator who could harangue the peasantry of Connaught about the Scandinavian Edda and deduce from Icelandic mythology, for the edification of the Connemara rustics, comparisons between O'Connell's policy and the antagonistic influences of the Hrympthur and the Muspelthur; if these eccentricities evoke a passing smile, it is on the other hand impossible to deny that Steele had a vivid perception of all that was grand and beautiful in external nature, and that he could portray his impressions with force, and grace, and delicacy. Take, for example, the following descriptive passages from a pamphlet published by Steele in 1828 : *

"I passed late (it might have been about an hour after midnight) along the Shannon side; it was dark, and dreary, and stormy, in squally gusts, and frequent showers of heavy rain; the moon sometimes, but very rarely, and without showing her form, lighted the clouds with a pallid watery light, but so pale, and faint, and transitory, as in general to be perceptible for little more than a few moments between its apparition and evanishment. The night wind sometimes sighed softly and mournfully on high, around the topmasts and lifts of the topsail yards of a ship near the wharf; and sometimes the 'winde that whistleth and cryeth like doleful ghosts' did whistle and cry over the distant strand; and sometimes at irregular and capricious intervals, when the strong squalls and gusts rushed from the mountains, it moaned and howled through the round tops and blocks and

* "Practical Suggestions on the Navigation of the River Shannon, etc." By Thomas Steele, Esq. London, 1828.

condensed cordage of the shrouds. The solitude was dismal, for no one but myself was abroad by the river side. The Shannon had been swollen to a torrent by the incessant rains of the season, and the white foam on part of it faintly appeared through the darkness. The wild and dreary shrieks of some sea-gulls, or other water birds which I could not see, were the only sounds of animated nature that smote my ear in that midnight desolation. The darkness deepened almost to blackness; the rain came on and fell with violence, and plashed and pattered upon the pavement near the wharf where I was standing; and the sound of the rain, and the howling wind, and the roaring of the wide and rapid flood over its rocky bed, and the dreary shrieks of the sea-birds heard through the darkness, were sounds, at that hour, of solemn, deep, and mystic wildness. The whole scene and the hour were in accordance with the spirit of the time— mysterious, ghastly, wild. When I got home I wrote a description of it, and I said to myself while I was writing it, ''Tis a night to remember Limerick in its history.'"— (Pages 84, 85.)

Steele was a sort of political Ossian. The drifting shower, the mountain-mist, the sunbeam sparkling in the brook, the howling tempest, were all duly noted to illustrate exhortations to popular energy and perseverance. His public letters have been sometimes dated thus: "Country of Fingal;" or, "Eagle Crags, O'Connell Mountains, Shores of the Atlantic." The next specimen of his descriptive powers is of a less gloomy character than the former:

"There is a spot upon a mountain promontory in Fingal, where, in my early boyhood, external nature first burst upon my vision in beauty and sublimity—not separated, but in combination. Upon the eastern side of the solitary mountain where it shelves abruptly into the sea, and so near its summit that there was a glorious expanse of horizon, was a little fountain bursting among the rocks, and wild flowers, and sunbeams. A bee hummed over the flowers close to the fountain and its little rill; some sea-gulls wheeled and floated in the air, high above the sea that broke upon the shore; and there was a bark with white sails, holding on her course on the swelling tide.

"Whenever I call this scene to remembrance, 'pure, bright, Elysian,' it floats in my imagination like a vision of enchantment. This is the pure Elysian enchantment of external nature, without any intermixture of feelings inspired by the history of times of old. 'Canst thou loosen the bonds of Orion, or canst thou bind the sweet influences of the Pleiades?' No; and there are other sweet influences, too, that while man retains his nature never can be bound:

> There is given
> Unto the things of earth that Time hath bent
> A spirit's feeling. . . . . .
> There is a power
> And magic in the ruined battlement;

and when I stand in the ancient cathedral of Limerick and listen to the choir and the organ; when I hear the chant of the High Mass, the ringing of the mass-bell and view the incense ascending from the altar in one of their convent-chapels; when I wander through the gardens of the holy sisterhood of St. Clare, and view their figures gliding among the Gothic ruins, or when I stand within the sanctuary of their convent-chapel; when I sit upon the ancient bastion in St. Munchin's Cemetery upon a gloomy evening, and listen to the sullen sough of the wind among the dark elms over my head and the rushing flood of the Shannon that sweeps at its basement, and hear the roar of the bugles, the beat of the drum, and the voice of the trumpet within the court of the castle, I become inspired by a feeling solemn and mournful, different from that of which I am susceptible in any other place in the world; but not very unlike that with which, upon the shore of the solitary lake where he reposes, I hear the wind whisper at night in the grass around the grave of my father whom I have never seen."—(Pages 125, 126.)

How wild, how mystic, how impressive!

Steele's personal devotion to O'Connell is proverbial. Although a Protestant himself, he fitted up an apartment in his house in the County Clare as a chapel to be used for the celebration of mass whenever he should be visited by his mighty leader, as he delighted to designate O'Connell. He combined with this tribute to his political chief, his own devotion to Celtic antiquity, for the altar of the domestic chapel was a large, rude block of stone which for ages had remained in the woods, gray, moss-grown, and solitary; and which was averred by a rather vague tradition to have been used in pagan times for Druidical rites, and subsequently for the celebration of the Catholic worship in the days of the penal persecution.

Steele's declaration has often been quoted, that if

O'Connell desired him to sit on a mine about to be sprung, he would implicitly obey the mandate. This, which from other lips would be hypocritical exaggeration, was with Tom Steele the strict truth. His faith in O'Connell's integrity and wisdom was intense. He deemed his incarceration as a fellow-conspirator with O'Connell as the proudest honour of his life.

The characteristics of Steele are easily summed up. Brave as a lion, thoroughly honest and straightforward, intensely devoted to his country, incapable of thought or deed unbecoming a high-souled and chivalrous gentleman, he combined these qualities with a certain exuberant poetry of idea and of language, peculiarly liable to the criticism of the prosaic multitude. His office of Head Pacificator was conferred upon him by O'Connell in consequence of the essential services which from time to time he rendered in getting up arms from the parties whom suffering and oppression had driven into turbulence and disaffection. He repeatedly attempted, and sometimes with success, to tranquillise disturbed districts. Those who regarded the Irish movement from a distance had little or no conception of the moral authority wielded by Steele when presenting himself as O'Connell's ambassador to the turbulent inhabitants of districts where local tyranny had irritated its victims and their sympathisers into the commission of criminal acts. Steele, aided by the Catholic clergy, enjoined peace at the behest of Ireland's "mighty leader." The impressive singularity of his language would appear, on such occasions, to add force to the character assigned to him in the movement, by stamping on him an individuality peculiarly germane to the earnestness of purpose which was one of his most prominent characteristics.

When the unfortunate division between the Young Irelanders and the Old Irelanders (exasperated, I have not the least doubt, by mutual personal jealousies), rose to a height that permanently weakened the Repeal Association, Steele of course adhered to O'Connell; but he could not shut his eyes to the decline of the Liberator's influence among the people. O'Connell refused to believe that he had lost ground; and John O'Connell ignored, as long as it was possible, the diminution of his father's popularity, although Steele pressed it earnestly upon his notice.

I find, in one of Sir Bernard Burke's entertaining publications, a picturesque description of the old castle called

Craggan Tower in the County Clare, which is stated to have been a favourite haunt of Mr. Steele, on whose property it stood. " The situation of Craggan Tower," says Sir Bernard, "is romantic and striking. It stands in the centre of a fertile valley upon a bold, and in some parts almost perpendicular rock, surrounded on three sides by the deep waters of a small lake. On the west it is protected by an impassable morass, now planted with various aquatic shrubs and trees, and on the land, or northern side, by a deep cutting in the solid rock."

We are told that Steele occasionally sought the solitude of Craggan. "Lonely on its bold isolated rock, it towered over the valley, and cast its dark shadow on the peaceful lake. The goats cropped the long grass on its deserted walls, and the hoarse notes of the owl or the raven alone broke in upon the stillness of its desolation. . . . This castle, and much of the surrounding lands, were recently the property of that misguided, but noble-hearted and accomplished Irishman, Mr. Tom Steele. In the wild and gloomy recesses of this ancient fortalice he found a haunt congenial to his own disappointed feelings and blighted hopes. Neglecting the substantial comforts of his house at Cullane, with its well-wooded park and its lovely lake, he preferred, during his short visits to this part of the country, to lurk within and about this old neglected tower; he caused even some repairs to be made, and the initials of his name are to be seen on a large stone forming a portion of the northern coign of the building. It is even said that he meditated an entire restoration, but unfortunately his funds were wasted upon other objects."*

When O'Connell died, life lost all its savour for Tom Steele. His heart and soul were wrapped up in the movement of which his departed chief had been the leader. To him there seemed nothing now worth living for. The hideous visitation of famine laid waste the land he loved so well. His private means had been long since exhausted; and it is painful to record that he tried to put an end to the existence which was now become a burthen, by leaping into the Thames from one of the bridges of London. He was taken up alive, but greatly injured by his rash attempt. A benevolent Englishman, the proprietor of Peele's Coffee-house in

* " Visitation of Seats and Arms," by Sir Bernard Burke; vol. ii. pp. 183, 184. Craggan is said by Sir Bernard to have been purchased and rendered habitable by an Englishman, the Rev. John H. Ashworth.

Fleet Street, received the ill-fated agitator into his house, where he ministered with the utmost generosity and delicacy to the wants of poor Steele during the short remainder of his life. His remains were removed to Dublin, waked in Conciliation Hall, and interred near O'Connell's last resting-place in the cemetery of Glasnevin.

Steele's figure was tall and well-proportioned, and had much of a martial appearance, to which his undress blue military cap and frock-coat not a little contributed. His face was bronzed by exposure to all weathers and several climates, and the expression of his countenance was that of resolute determination.

CHAPTER XXVIII.

CONDITION OF THE REPEAL MOVEMENT AFTER THE LIBERATION OF THE PRISONERS.

"To hinder insurrection by driving away the people, and to govern peaceably by having no subjects, is an expedient that argues no great profundity in politics. To soften the obdurate, to convince the mistaken, to mollify the resentful, are worthy of a statesman; but it affords a legislator very little self-applause to consider that where there was formerly an insurrection, there is now a wilderness."—JOHNSON's *Journey to the Western Islands of Scotland.*

THE Repeal agitation appeared to advance with increased momentum for some time after the liberation of O'Connell and his fellow prisoners But in October, 1844, O'Connell published a letter of great length, in which, without absolutely committing himself to what was called Federalism, he so far seemed to sanction it as to create some fear that he might recede from the principles of 1782. Federalism may briefly be described as a system of separate local Parliaments for each island, for the regulation of their local or internal interests only; whilst the external interests of the Empire were to be controlled by an Imperial Congress sitting in London. O'Connell, by his Federalist letter, undoubtedly disturbed the confidence his followers had previously reposed in his leadership. But he speedily recanted his Federalist lapse, alleging that his letter had been merely an experiment to ascertain how far certain Northern Whigs were disposed to advance in that direction. Some of them, he said, had held out 'private promises to enrol themselves under a

Federalist flag. He had unfurled the flag, and they came not. So Federalism was discarded as inadmissible, and the Irish Constitution of 1782 was once more held forth as the great object of pursuit. There was no apparent diminution of the popular fervour. On the 30th of May, 1845—the anniversary of the imprisonment—O'Connell held a magnificent levée at the Rotunda, at which Smith O'Brien presented to him, and to his fellow "conspirators," an address in the name of the Repeal Association, breathing fidelity and pledging perseverance. The display was as impressive as it could be made by gorgeous decorations, bannered processions, and the blended order and enthusiasm of the multitudes who thronged the streets and overflowed the building. English visitors in Dublin, who were present at the levée, expressed their admiration of the noble scene, and derived from it a strong conviction that the political purpose which had given it birth originated in a permanent, deeply-fixed principle, and not in a transitory impulse.

The Agitation went on. I visited Scotland in 1842, and again in 1843, and addressed meetings of the Irish who were settled in that kingdom. They cheerfully gave me substantial support for the Repeal Association. In June, 1845, I returned to Scotland, where the Irish once more gathered round me. We had meetings in Edinburgh, Glasgow, Airdrie, Aberdeen, and Dundee. I find in the report of my speech, delivered in the City Hall of Glasgow to a crowded audience, the following passage, which I quote, because it gives a faithful picture of the Repeal confederacy in the imposing aspect it presented at that period:

"There is a portion of your address to which I have listened with unalloyed delight. It is that in which you congratulate me on the rapid advances of our cause. I reciprocate your congratulations. Yes—let us rejoice together over the triumphs we have achieved and are daily achieving. Our connexions are extended; old friends remain stanch and firm; new friends join us with enthusiasm; the Irish at home remain true to their colours; the Irish abroad, in Scotland and elsewhere—God bless them!"—(great cheering) —"the expatriated Irish all over the world have combined with the central body at Conciliation Hall in a firm and compact confederation, which has really no parallel in ancient or modern history. I repeat that our combination is unparalleled. There is not, there never has been, anything at all like it. To the eye of the philosopher and the Christian, the Irish people at home, and dispersed all over the globe, present one of the most sublime spectacles it is possible to conceive. Trampled on, despoiled, slandered ; robbed of their political privileges; assailed as they have been by the bigot, the tyrant, and the hollow friend—yet steadily advancing in the peaceful, crimeless path to freedom. Unscared by oppression, and repelling by their native sagacity all efforts to delude them, they at last have the Land of Promise full in view ; they will emerge from the land of Egypt and the house of bondage into the unfettered possession of self-government so justly due to their virtue, their sagacity, their perseverance, their unprecedented organisation. And if the world admires, as it must, the moral phenomenon of our organised countrymen all over the globe, what is the tribute due to him whose creative genius gave birth to that magnificent confederacy—who shaped and moulded the innumerable energies of scattered millions into one vast engine of resistless potency ? "

The reader will remember that at the time when those words were spoken, the description they contain was apparently borne out by the state of the Repeal agitation. In addition to local associations in every town where Irish emigrants had settled in Scotland and England, we had large contingents all over North America. We received contributions from the colonies; sometimes from Irishmen in India. The pecuniary remittances were generous and constant. The letters which accompanied the money evinced in general a perfect acquiescence in O'Connell's policy of moral force and exclusively pacific action. The wrongful imprisonment, and the judgment reversed on appeal, seemed to place the agitators on a vantage-ground higher than they would have occupied if they had been unmolested by Sir Robert Peel's Government. For Peel had done his worst against them, and failed. He had borne unwilling testimony to the formidable strength of the Repeal agitation when he said, on the 18th of April, 1845 : "I believe the Irish agitation cannot be put down by force."

As yet the public saw no symptoms of a dangerous division between Old and Young Ireland. But O'Connell's agitation had reached its culminating point. He became nervously anxious to repress all indications of a warlike spirit among his Young Ireland allies; whilst they, on the other hand, betrayed a growing inclination to preach up the lawfulness of physical resistance to the Government, of which impolitic course O'Connell anticipated no other than the worst results. I have elsewhere examined this topic of dispute at some length,* and shall not dwell farther on it in this place. Then there was the dispute about Whig patronage; whilst O'Connell maintained that the agitation of Repeal would not suffer from the appointment to office of some of his followers.† An intimate friend of O'Connell said to me at that time: "There is as great an outcry against O'Connell on the ground of Government patronage, as if he had anything to gain, or was gaining anything by it." Personally O'Connell gained nothing; but a few hundreds a year were given to two or three members of his family.

In September, 1845, Thomas Davis died after a week's illness. He was the ablest of the Young Ireland party. His death was a serious loss to the cause, for he not only possessed great information, great intellectual power, thorough honesty, and indomitable zeal, but he had also the gifts of calm temper and practical wisdom, which I have little doubt would have been exercised, had his life been prolonged, to restrain the indiscretions of the party who proclaimed him their prophet, their philosopher, and guide.

The germs of dissension were rife in our body, and were daily developing into mischievous luxuriance. Meanwhile a terrible and mysterious dispensation visited the land. The potato crop of 1845 was partially blighted. Although serious fears were entertained, yet we flattered ourselves that the visitation would be transient, and that the crop of the following year would at least be of average value.

The squabbles in the Association continued. Smith O'Brien had said with some humour: "I am neither Old Ireland nor Young Ireland; I am Middle-aged Ireland." When O'Connell, on the questions of public policy to which I have adverted, came to open warfare with the *Nation* newspaper, the organ of the Young Irelanders, O'Brien took part with the *Nation;* angry debates consumed the time of the Association, and O'Brien, with a numerous following, seceded from that body. This was in 1846.

Early in autumn it became apparent that the potato crop of 1846 would be a total failure. Famine menaced the doomed land. For a detailed and faithful account of the horrors of that famine, I refer the reader to John Mitchel's clever little book, entitled "The Last Conquest of Ireland (Perhaps)." Mr. Mitchel calls attention to the fact that

* "Personal Recollections of O'Connell," vol. ii. p. 245.
† For an account of this dispute, see the same work.

Ireland, under the political conditions that afflicted her, was exporting a larger amount of food, contemporaneously with the potato-famine, than would have sufficed to support all her inhabitants—wheat, oats, barley, pigs, and cattle. Yet there was in political circles an established idea that Ireland contained a surplus population who ought to be shipped off.

"Ireland, perhaps," says Mr. Mitchel, "was the only country in the world which had both surplus produce for export and surplus population for export—too much food for her people, and too many people for her food."

While myriads starved to death in Ireland, ships bursting with grain and laden with cattle were leaving every port for England. There would have been no need for the people to emigrate if their food did not emigrate. But the exhausting results of the Union had brought matters to a point that compelled Ireland to sell her food in order to supply the enormous money drain. The food is first taken away, and then its price is taken away also.

The horrors of the famine strongly illustrated the true nature of the Union, and the paramount need for a domestic Parliament. The potato blight was indeed the visitation of Providence; but the monstrous drain of Irish wealth, which deprived the people of a reserve to fall back upon, was the visitation of England. The drain of absentee rents, averaged at £3,000,000 annually for the forty-six years the Union had then lasted, reached £138,000,000 sterling. If we average at £1,000,000 per annum the Irish taxes exported from Ireland during the same period, the combined drain will reach £184,000,000. It is impossible to calculate with accuracy the amount of actual cash sent out of the kingdom to purchase the articles of English manufacture which, after the Union, supplanted our own. If we average the drain on this head at the very low and inadequate amount of £1,000,000 per annum,* the total loss on those three heads

---

* I have not the least doubt that it is a great deal more. An old and intelligent Dublin merchant told me that it certainly exceeded £5,000,000 per annum. But I have not access at present to data which would throw sufficient light on the question; and I prefer what I am sure is a very considerable understatement to the danger of exaggeration. We learn from the "Castlereagh Correspondence," vol. iii. pp. 483, 484, that, in 1800, the cotton trade at Belfast, Balbriggan, Dublin, and Cork, employed large numbers of people, and was stated by Mr. Hamilton of Balbriggan to retain in Ireland £250,000 per annum; and Mr. Clarke tells Lord C—— that he had expended £20,000 in setting up the cotton business at Palmerstown, County Dublin, which gave constant support to 1,000

must have amounted in 1846 to £230,000,000. Had Ireland been self-governed, the greater part of that wealth would have remained at home, furnishing a fund for industry, circulating among the people by whose labour it had been produced, forming numberless reservoirs of humble opulence, and thereby enabling the people to tide over the calamity of the potato blight. But the Union had stripped them of their means, and the only alternatives left to the perishing multitudes were the workhouse, emigration, or the grave. Yes—the potato blight was the visitation of Providence; but the famine was the visitation of England. There were advances of money from the Government to employ the people upon unproductive works. Of these the mismanagement was demoralising;* and although the amount of the advances was not more than a few pence in the pound of the vast sums England had in various ways extorted from Ireland since the Union, yet the *Times* kept up a constant outcry that Irish paupers were thrown for support on English wealth; complained that every industrious family in England had a starving Irish family mounted on their backs; proposed with characteristic jocularity (as an Irish famine was a ludicrous event) that "some Baron Munchausen should immediately plant the Emerald Isle with ten million quartern-loaf trees, and the same number of roast-beef and leg-of-mutton trees in full bearing;" and distanced all its other feats by announcing with due gravity that if it were not for the Union the Irish would not have a meal to eat.

Meanwhile the people were fast perishing. The Union had done its deadly work. There were indeed many humane and munificent persons in England who subscribed their money with princely generosity to relieve the sufferers. All honour to those noble and benevolent hearts! Money and vessels laden with food were sent by American friends. But the calamity was too great to be effectually alleviated by the efforts of individual charity, however extensive.

It is here proper to observe that the Union-plunder has been destructive not only to the material interests of this kingdom, but in many cases also to the souls of the Irish whom it forces out of their country. The Bishop of Toronto

persons—men, women, and children. These casual statements regarding one single branch of manufacture are extremely suggestive.

* For an excellent and instructive account of the advances, their purpose, and their mismanagement, see Mr. Mitchel's "Last Conquest of Ireland (Perhaps)."

addressed to the bishops of Ireland a most painful statement on this subject in May, 1864, from which I extract a few sentences: "The Germans, French, and even the Norwegians," says his lordship, "come to America, provided with the means of establishing themselves either as farmers or mechanics; but the large majority of the Irish come absolutely penniless; and hence they cannot reach the interior of the country, and are obliged to look for the cheapest lodgings in the cities; and every one knows that such places are the haunts of vice. The consequence is, they and their children are lost to morality, to society, to religion, and finally to God."

Again, his lordship says: "The number of good Irish girls who arrive at New York and the other seaboard cities is prodigious. Many of them are destitute of means and friends; they are obliged, by their poverty, to take situations wherever they can get them, and as soon as possible. Hence they fall—not an easy prey either, but after many struggles —into the thousand snares which profligate cities throw in their way. . . . It is humiliating indeed to see numbers of poor Irish girls, innocent and guileless, sitting around in those large depôts in seaport cities waiting to be hired. Men and women enter those places, and look around to find out the girl that would apparently answer their service. How many of them found the protection of the wolf is known only to God."

The Bishop of Toronto quotes the late Bishop of Charleston, Dr. England, as having estimated the number of souls lost to the Church in his own diocese, up to 1838, at 50,000. The emigration, then considerable, received a prodigious momentum from the famine and its resulting miseries, and also from the largely increased money-drain from Ireland in the shape of additional taxes, imposed by Mr. Gladstone while the national calamity still bore hard upon the people.

It is scarcely necessary to say that the famine greatly weakened political agitation. If, on the one hand, it afforded a terrible demonstration of the paramount necessity for home government, on the other hand it deprived us of the means which were indispensable to the efficiency of our efforts. O'Connell entered his seventieth year on the 6th of August, 1846. His health, which had for some time been manifestly giving way, was seriously affected by his mental anxieties. These were great and grievous. He saw with unspeakable pain the fatal division in the Repeal ranks, and his heart sank within him at the horrible affliction of the famine. In January, 1847, he quitted Ireland, and after a short sojourn in England, proceeded to the Continent *en route* to Genoa, where he died on the 15th of May.

John O'Connell still continued to administer the lingering remnant of the Repeal Association. The Young Irelanders had set up a Repeal League of their own, which seemed to monopolise what remained of the popular activity. Its meetings were addressed by Smith O'Brien, Duffy, Mitchel, and other prominent seceders. I was extremely anxious that the two bodies of Repealers should be reunited, and I explained at some length to Mr. Smith O'Brien the conditions upon which I considered such reunion possible, consistently with the honour of all parties. From O'Brien, with whom I corresponded from time to time, I had a long letter dated 31st of December, 1847, stating the conditions upon which alone he was willing to consent to the proposed reunion. One of his conditions was that the existing Association, founded by O'Connell, should be dissolved; and that both parties should concur in the formation of a new society. I knew that the Old Irelanders would not consent to this condition; and as O'Brien insisted on it as a *sine quâ non*, I did not at that time press the matter any farther.

Notwithstanding the continued pressure of terrific distress from the failure in successive years of the potato crop, the Young Irelanders persevered in the agitation of Repeal. Protestant Repeal Associations were instituted in Dublin, Drogheda, and Lurgan. There was one of these in Belfast, of which a respectable physician, Dr. Beck, was honorary secretary. It will be remembered that Mr. Sharman Crawford had at one time been an avowed Repealer, but that he opposed O'Connell's agitation when invited to join the Repeal Association. O'Connell was now dead, and Mr. Crawford returned to his earlier opinions. As the unswerving advocate of the Irish small farmer, he filled for many years a conspicuous position in Irish politics; and in the present hasty record of the various phases of the Repeal agitation, I think the following extracts from his letter to Dr. Beck are worthy of a place:

"LONDON, *July* 15*th*, 1848.

" SIR,

"I have received the communication with which you honoured me, containing the address issued by the Protestant Repeal Association of Belfast.

"I have long been of opinion that the centralisation of

Imperial legislation was unfit for Ireland; but if I had any doubt on the subject the proceedings and results of the two last sessions have been sufficient to remove them, and to raise in my mind the positive conviction that Englishmen and Scotchmen, sitting in the Imperial Legislature, have neither the knowledge nor the feelings towards Ireland necessary to qualify them for just and useful legislation; that the numerous subjects on which Parliament is required to legislate do not leave the time necessary to attend to the interests of a country in the condition of Ireland; that the same system of legislation which is applicable to the circumstances of England and Scotland is not applicable to Ireland; and an equally strong conviction that Irish Members sent to the Imperial Legislature under the present system of election, removed from the correcting control of the people, and having no real responsibility for the laws passed for Ireland, will be generally neglectful of their duties, and will not even use the powers they possess to advance the interests of their country.

"I see no remedy for this state of things other than a representative body for Ireland, elected by such a system of suffrage and laws of election as will constitute them the fair representatives of the voices and interests of the nation.

"I do not deny that contingent objections may be made to the system of two legislative bodies under the same Crown. I have stated these objections on former occasions, and with that view advocated the federative principle of connexion; but the proposition received no support, and I know it would be more strongly objected to by British representatives than the simple Repeal of the Legislative Union. But I am now of opinion that the necessity for a local legislative body has become so manifest and imperative that minor objections must be yielded. . . . So long as I thought that the system of Imperial legislation could be brought to act for practical good, I was not much inclined to agitate for a change; but that hope has now entirely vanished from my mind. I therefore feel myself bound to give up minor objections, and assent to the principle of legislative independence as acknowledged by the Constitution of 1782, subject to such modifications as would seem best suited to guard against collisions on matters of Imperial interest affecting the connexion of the two countries under an Imperial Crown.

*   *   *   *   *

"I believe that Protestant power is capable of resisting aggression from any quarter; and therefore that aggression would never be attempted unless provoked by Protestant injustice.

* * * * *

"I highly approve the sentiments contained in the published address to which your name is attached, and wishing your Association every success, I am, Sir, your obedient
"W. SHARMAN CRAWFORD.
"J. W. BECK, ESQ., M.D."

The Protestant Repealers, possessing ability, respectable position, and a powerful case, were beginning to produce a strong impression on the minds of their fellow-religionists of the humbler class. In order to counteract their progress the fanatical bellows were kept in full blast. Preachers, orators, and writers, whose idea of Christianity appeared to be confined to the duty of hating the Papists and shouting "To hell with the Pope!" now bellowed about Antichrist, romanced about apocalyptic numerals, ranted about the Inquisition, threatened that if Repeal were obtained the Papists would ride roughshod over the Protestants, and by rude and vigorous appeals addressed to the sectarian prejudices of their fellow-Protestants, succeeded in creating among them a fanatical determination to perpetuate, so far as in them lay, the servitude and spoliation of their country.

Meanwhile Smith O'Brien and his allies continued to agitate—not in O'Connell's mode. The fiery eloquence of some of the Young Irelanders had withdrawn the minds of numbers from the moral-force policy by which O'Connell had gained his victories; insomuch that Steele, a few months before O'Connell's death, had declared with poignant grief that the moral-force wand had been broken to pieces in the hand of the great magician. The sterling honour, the pure and lofty spirit, and the single-hearted patriotism of Smith O'Brien, were unquestionable. He was hurried into actions of enormous imprudence by the impulses of generous indignation. He saw the physical miseries of his countrymen; he saw the political prostration of Ireland; he saw the callous contempt with which the suffering multitudes were treated by a large class of British politicians; he saw in the want of home government the source of these horrible evils, and the sight maddened him. He, Meagher, and others, set on foot the system of local clubs. On the 20th of July, 1848, he wrote to me, exhorting me to establish clubs in all places within my reach. I did not establish clubs, which were part of a system for arming the people ; and any scheme of armed or physical resistance by a population stricken to the earth by famine, and destitute of every element of probable success, I could only regard with the deepest apprehension and the gravest sorrow. Many years later I recollect seeing in the newspapers a letter from Mr. O'Brien, in which he stated that while ready to bear his full share of the responsibilities attaching to the unfortunate events of 1848, he had received representations or promises—he did not say from whom— which, if I remember aright, were calculated to encourage hopes of a different result, but which promises were not realised.*

O'Brien had come into collision with the law. He, Meagher, Leyne, and O'Donoghue were arrested. Martin of Kilbroney, Duffy, Williams, and O'Doherty, were all in prison awaiting their trials. MacManus was also captured. The trials of O'Brien and his immediate companions took place at Clonmel, in October, 1848. Sentence of death was pronounced against him, which was afterwards commuted into banishment.

The aspect of the country was now most melancholy. Despair seemed to cast a black funeral pall over the land. The people either crowded the workhouse or took flight to America. Travel where you would, deserted and ruinous cabins met the eye on every side. You frequently met large parties of emigrants proceeding to the seaports, the exodus consisting principally of the youth and strength, the bone and sinew of the population. Every emigrant treasured up wrath in his heart against the power that forced him out of the land of his birth.

Meanwhile there was a lull in politics, and the anti-national classes flattered themselves that the people had been starved and terrified into helpless provincialism. But—to adopt a phrase employed by Mr. Aubrey de Vere upon another subject—quiescence is a very different thing from acquiescence. The national mind was never more dissatisfied.

In the summer of 1849 Queen Victoria was advised to come to Ireland. Her Majesty came, and the *Times*, of course, had a characteristic flourish on the royal visit.

* I write this from memory; I have not a copy of the letter in which O'Brien made the statement referred to.

"At this moment," said the leading journal, "the Sovereign of the Empire goes as the ambassador between two of its constituent nations to extinguish the embers of a flickering jealousy, and ratify an amnesty of attempted wrong. The Queen is at this moment the representative of English feeling and *forgiveness.*"

"Now," says DIRK HATTERAICK to GLOSSIN, "*strafe mich der deyfel!* this provokes me more than all the rest. You rob and you murder, and play the silver-cooper, or kidnapper, as you call it, a dozen times over, and then—*hagel und windsturm!* you speak to me of conscience!"

Pretty much in like manner did the *Times* talk of "English forgiveness." You destroy our Legislature—you grasp our surplus revenue—you enjoy our absentee rents—you reduce this land to pauperism, and slay its inhabitants by wholesale; and then you tell us that you *forgive* us for it all!

The *Times* showed scant respect to the Queen in representing Her Majesty as the ambassador of this astounding species of forgiveness. It was clearly irreverent to associate the Sovereign's venerated name with such a piece of jocular impertinence.

The Queen was received with the respect and courtesy due to her position and character. After staying a few days she went away.

CHAPTER XXIX.

ENGLISH POLITICIANS ON NATIONAL CLAIMS TO SELF-GOVERNMENT.

> How thrive we by the Union?
>   Look round our native land;
> In ruined trade and wealth decayed,
>   See slav'ry's surest brand.
> Our glory as a nation gone,
>   Our substance drained away,
> A wretched province trampled on,
>   Is all we've left to-day.
>   Then curse with me the Union,
>   That juggle foul and base,
>   The baneful root that bore such fruit,
>   Of ruin and disgrace.
>   *Spirit of the Nation.*

THE disturbed state of Italy, the prevalence of insurrection, the movements especially which menaced the temporal power of the Pope, elicited from statesmen and journalists in England the most fervid declarations of the right of all nations to choose their own Governments. Said Lord John Russell:

"I think with regard to this matter of states and nations regulating their own Governments, that it is not very different from that of a man in a city—say the city of Aberdeen—regulating his own house. I think we are bound to say, and we do say, and we have said, that against any interference by foreign force to prevent those peoples having their own Government, and conducting their affairs as they like, we do loudly and solemnly protest."

During the year 1860, the doctrine thus proclaimed by Lord John was preached by English journalists, who of course overlooked its manifest application to Ireland. Said the *Times:*

"That Government should be for the good of the governed, and that whenever rulers wilfully and persistently postpone the good of their subjects, either to the interest of foreign states or to abstract theories of religion or politics, *the people have a right to throw off the yoke,* are principles too often admitted and acted upon to be any longer questioned."

"Europe," said the *Daily News*, "has over and over again affirmed that one principle on which the Italian question depends, and to which the inhabitants of Central Italy appeal—the right of a people to choose its own rulers."

Another utterance of the *Times:*

"The goodness or badness of a Government should be estimated with reference, not to abstract rules, but to the opinions and feelings of the governed."

"As free Englishmen," said the *Sun*, "we assert the right of the Romans, *and of all nations*, to have governors of their own choice."

"England," said the *Times*, "has not scrupled to avow her opinion that the people of the Roman States, *like every other people*, have a right to choose their own Government, and the persons in whose hands that Government shall be placed."

Again, the *Times* told its readers that:

"The destiny of a nation ought to be determined, not by the opinions of other nations, but by the opinion of the nation itself. To decide whether they are well governed or not, or rather whether the degree of extortion, corruption, and cruelty to which they are subject is sufficient to justify armed resistance, *is for those who live under that Government* —not for those who, being exempt from its oppression, feel a sentimental or a theological interest in its continuance." *

Now here are political canons which more than sustain the demand of the Irish for a repeal of the Union. Applying to Ireland, for instance, with a slight verbal alteration, the Italian doctrine of the *Times*, the dictum of the leading journal teaches us that " the destiny of Ireland ought to be determined, not by the opinion of England, but by the opinion of the nation itself. To decide whether the Irish are well governed or not, or rather whether the amount of extortion, corruption, and cruelty to which they are subject, is sufficient to justify armed resistance, is for those who live under that Government, not for those who, being exempt from its oppression, feel a sentimental or a theological interest in its continuance."

Smith O'Brien decided that the degree of extortion, corruption, and cruelty to which his countrymen were subject, *was* sufficient to justify armed resistance. The extortion consists in an annual tribute of many millions sterling drained out of the kingdom to England. The corruption consists of bribes in the shape of Government patronage, which is employed to purchase educated men to uphold the giant wrong, or at least to be silent respecting it. The cruelty consists in the sufferings necessarily sustained by the multitude from the enormous pecuniary extortion which defrauds them of the natural fund which Providence has given for their support. Were there such a state of things in any Continental country, Earl Russell and the *Times* would of course preach the right of the oppressed to resist, and to be the sole judges not only of the necessity of resistance, but of the precise mode of resisting. But when Ireland is in question, the English friends of Continental liberty take a different view of duties and responsibilities. In the days of O'Connell's agitation the *Times* declared that even were the Union gall to Ireland, it should be maintained. And no doubt the *Times*, and all the other British sym-

* The above extracts, with many others from different authorities bearing upon Irish questions, have been collected by A. M. Sullivan, proprietor of the *National Irish National Almanack and Historical Remembrancer*, a most useful and well-compiled publication, in which the anniversaries of Irish events of personal, political, or historical importance, are substituted for the anniversaries of English and other foreign incidents, in which other almanacks abound, and in which the Irish reader cannot take much interest.

pathisers with Continental insubordination, would at any time renew that declaration.

Politics in Ireland had apparently gone to sleep. A Conservative friend said to me: "How completely politics have died out; there are no political parties now." A Protestant clergyman said, "The people only care about their turnips; they don't now care for politics." In both cases the wish was probably father of the thought; but it is true that the surface was as calm as it could be made by pinching want and by dire anxiety to obtain the bare means of existence.

During Mr. Smith O'Brien's banishment he composed a work entitled, "Thoughts on Government, by an Exile." In 1856 he was permitted to return to Ireland. He expressed great delight at beholding his native land once more. His return was hailed with hearty satisfaction by all classes of his countrymen, for his high and unsullied character and the genial kindness of his disposition had won the respect and regard of even his political opponents.

In 1860 some gentlemen who were considerably struck with the fervid enthusiasms for the Rights of Nations which glowed in the columns of the English press, considered that it was a good opportunity to take the English apostles of liberty at their word, and to put in a claim on behalf of Ireland. A Declaration was drawn up by a committee in Dublin, and circulated through Ireland for signatures. It suggested the *plébiscite*, and asserted the immortal principles of 1782. It received between 400,000 and 500,000 signatures. It was forwarded with a loyal and respectful address to the Queen, and entrusted to the care of Sir George Grey for presentation to Her Majesty. I am not aware whether Sir George Grey so much as acknowledged the receipt of the document; but at a later period he published a pamphlet in which he recommended the establishment of a State Legislature in Ireland. He had then arrived at the knowledge of the real needs of Ireland, and of the only true remedy for Irish discontent, as the following extract from his pamphlet will show:

"Give to Ireland," he says, "a State Legislature and a State Executive in Dublin; secure thereby the residence of its ablest men in the country. Open a fair field as ministers, legislators, orators, to its best and wisest men. Afford, from the same source, as would necessarily and certainly be done, occupation to Irish architects, sculptors, painters, and secure a resident aristocracy of worth, talent, and wisdom, and you will at the same time restore the wealth, trade, and commerce of Dublin and Ireland. Dumb Ireland will speak again. Half-inanimate Ireland will again awaken to national life, and breathe the breath of hope and freedom. Whilst, by again accustoming the Irish people to the management of their own affairs, and to administrative duties of the highest order, a willing people will be educated in that political knowledge which will enable them to put an end to the ills which afflict them, the causes and cure of which none can understand so well as themselves."*

Sir George goes on to say:

"Only those who have lived in populations accustomed to manage their own affairs can realise the dignity under such circumstances imparted to the mass of the people."

And undoubtedly the degrading sense of being held in the iron chains of foreign legislation effectually tends to exasperate the national mind, and to predispose the people, deprived of national self-rule, to embrace all or any means, however wild or desperate, to escape from the thraldom which is felt as a perpetual insult.

On the 4th of December, 1860, a meeting was held at the Rotunda to promote the revived movement for Repeal. The O'Donoghue, M.P., was in the chair. The Round Room was filled to inconvenience, and the meeting showed that the spirit which had animated the vast gatherings in O'Connell's day was yet alive and vigorous. Excellent speeches were made by John Francis Maguire and John Martin. One of the secretaries of the meeting was an intelligent young man named Joyce, about two or three-and-twenty years of age. I said to him: "You are so young that you cannot have had any part in O'Connell's movement; whence do you derive your Repeal principles?" "They are born with us," was his answer.

In 1864 a league was formed, chiefly by Mr. John Martin of Kilbroney, County Down, a Presbyterian gentleman, and the O'Donoghue, founded on the principles of 1782. The League published in the Irish, English, French, German, Italian, and Spanish languages a brief abstract of some of the most flagrant wrongs resulting from the Union. The French version of that document was republished in Paris at the expense of the Marquis de Nettancour.

* "The Irish Land Question," by Sir George Grey, K.C.B. London, 1869.

A League formed on the Principles of 1782.

The First Annual Report of the League was issued in February, 1865. The Second Annual Report, which was issued in February, 1866, records that, owing to a concurrence of adverse circumstances, the Irish Nationalists at home did not gather round the centre formed by Mr. Martin and The O'Donoghue, but that in Australia a generous movement in support of the League had commenced, and was still continued. The Report announces the sympathy of the Irish settlers and of the descendants of Irish settlers throughout New South Wales. The movement had spread into Queensland also. "If the Irish people at home," the document proceeds to say, "could be persuaded to declare frankly and openly the truth of their convictions and their wishes, and to present themselves before the world as a people robbed of their national right and seeking its restoration, we are confident that not only the Irish of all the Australian colonies, but the Irish of Canada and all the other American colonies, and the millions of Irish of the United States, would cordially give us their aid."

Unluckily the Irish in the United States had at that time embarked in the Fenian experiment, and their emissaries in this kingdom had succeeded in destroying to a large extent the faith of our countrymen at home in Constitutional action. Many whose feelings and principles were identical with ours, were saddened into inaction. Many were seduced by sheer desperation into the Fenian ranks. Many were led to unite not with the League, but with the National Association, inaugurated on the 29th of December, 1864, and embracing in its programme the improvement of the Land Laws, the disendowment of the State Church, and the freedom of Catholic education.

To that Association I have already adverted,* and have here only to add that for eight years previous to the date of its inauguration the disestablishment question had been persistently worked by myself and by Alderman M'Swiney, of Dublin, in connection with the English Liberation Society. My difficulty was at first to secure the joint action of the Irish Catholic prelates and the English Nonconformists. This obstacle was overcome by the influence, chiefly, of Doctor Leahy, Archbishop of Cashel, who saw that the aid of our English allies was indispensable to success. When the movement had acquired undoubted strength, Sir John Gray joined it, and gave it the valuable help of

* Chapter X., *ante*.

his advocacy in Parliament and in the *Freeman's Journal*, of which he was proprietor.

I believe that among the Irish in America there is now scarcely one who dreams of an Irish Republic. They have in general discarded from their policy the Republican element. There is not, I am certain, a single man amongst them who would not hail with delight the re-establishment of the Constitution of 1782. We have the strongest possible demonstration of the ample efficacy of that Constitution in making Ireland prosperous. Millions of the Irish at home desire its restoration beyond all other earthly objects. One of its essential conditions is the identity of the sovereign of these two islands. It would needlessly augment the difficulties in our path to introduce a project unacceptable to the great majority of the Irish at home. You have adopted a Constitutional policy—a policy which, if wisely administered, is capable of welding the Irish at home and their dispersed compatriots into one compact mass, formidable in their numbers; formidable in the truth and justice of their cause; formidable in the legal safety of their position; formidable in the magical strength of being, both in principle and in practice, thoroughly in the right. For Republicanism in America I entertain the highest respect. But whoever is conversant with the actual political condition of the various Irish parties, must know that any attempt to embody the Republican principle with a scheme to restore to Ireland self-government, bespeaks its own failure at the outset. It is simply and inevitably self-destructive.

There is an influential portion of the British press incessantly engaged in the diffusion of false and calumnious statements about Ireland. An immense circulation sends these statements to the ends of the earth. The Irish scattered over the globe could effectually repel the misrepresentations of the enemy by uniting with a central institute in Dublin in our claim of right, and in our peaceful protest against the monster wrong of 1800, so as to enlist in our behalf the public opinion of the civilised world. Such a protest and demand, made by the vast majority of the yet unexpelled Irish, backed by the support and sympathy of the Irish in Australia and Canada, and in the United States and Great Britain, " would not," says the Second Report of the League, "fail this time, provided that the Irish Nationalists bring the quality of earnest perseverance to their task, undeterred by the occasional defeats which are always incidental to the struggles for just freedom against power."

"With the examples before us," says the Report, "of Canada, the Cape, the Australian colonies, the Ionian Isles, all which States have obtained self-government . . . . we have reason to apprehend no obstinate resistance to such a movement if renewed in these times."

The American Secretary of State, Mr. Seward, expressed strong opinions on the subject of the Union. Writing in 1853, as appears by the *Boston Pilot*, he says, when describing a visit to the Irish Parliament House: "Whilst traversing its apartments, I reverted to the debate when the degenerate representatives surrendered their Parliament; and I thought that had I occupied a place there, I would have seen English armies wade in blood over my country before I would have consented to so disgraceful a Union."

Again, in the same letter, Mr. Seward says: "I confess that, overleaping all obstacles which are deemed by many well-wishers of Ireland insurmountable, I wish the Repeal of the Union. I will not believe that if relieved of that oppressive Act, she does not possess the ability to govern herself."

Mr. Seward is quite right. Ireland, after 1782, displayed an ability for self-government that resulted in great national prosperity—how and by whom overthrown the reader knows. Prior to that date the usurped power of the English Parliament had produced a state of things unfavourable to the development of Irish intellect, even among Protestants. The Catholic Irish of ability and ambition were compelled by penal laws to seek foreign fields for the exercise of their mental qualities. As to the stuff they were made of, hear the evidence of Dean Swift: "I cannot," says the Dean, "but highly esteem those gentlemen of Ireland who, with all the disadvantages of being exiles and strangers, have been able to distinguish themselves by their valour and conduct in so many parts of Europe, I think above all other nations; which ought to make the English ashamed of the reproaches they cast on the ignorance, the dulness, and the want of courage in the Irish natives; those defects, wherever they happen, arising only from the poverty and slavery they suffer from their inhuman neighbours, and the base, corrupt spirit of too many of the chief gentry."*

---

* Swift to Sir Charles Wogan, July, 1732.

Lord Macaulay, who had certainly no Irish sympathies, bore similar testimony to the fertility of Ireland in mental wealth. Speaking of the Irish whom the penal laws sent to seek their fortunes abroad, his lordship says: "There were, indeed, Irish Roman Catholics of great ability, energy, and ambition; but they were to be found everywhere except in Ireland—at Versailles and at St. Ildefonso, in the armies of Frederick and in the armies of Maria-Theresa. One exile became a marshal of France. Another became Prime Minister of Spain. . . . In his palace at Madrid he had the pleasure of being assiduously courted by the Ambassadors of George II., and of bidding defiance in high terms to the Ambassador of George III. Scattered all over Europe were to be found brave Irish generals, dexterous Irish diplomatists, Irish counts, Irish barons, Irish Knights of St. Louis and St. Leopold, of the White Eagle, and of the Golden Fleece."*

Such is Macaulay's description of the Irish Catholic intellect in exile. Of Irish Protestant intellect at home we have noble representatives in Malone, Pery, Flood, Foster, Yelverton, Grattan, Curran, Saurin, Plunket, Bushe, Goold, Butt, Whiteside, and numerous others. Our American sympathiser, Mr. Secretary Seward, does not assume too much when he states his belief that a country so prolific of high intellectual qualities possesses the ability to govern herself. Independence quickly teaches its own uses. The brave Irish generals, the dexterous Irish diplomatists, of whom Macaulay speaks, were as competent to regulate the political and military affairs of their own country as to govern the councils and lead the armies of the foreign lands where fate had placed them. The penal laws deprived Ireland of the services of her Catholic intellect. The Union deprives Ireland of the best and highest services of her intellect, both Catholic and Protestant; for it banishes the legislative body in which that intellect could find its greatest, its noblest, its most useful exercise.

In 1864 Colonel (afterwards General) Dunne, member for the Queen's County, obtained, but not without much difficulty, a committee to investigate the question of Irish taxation. It included eight English and seven Irish members. In the proceedings of the committee, as I have elsewhere remarked,† there is nothing more constantly and prominently

* "History of England," chap. xvii.
† Speech delivered at the National League, 7th November, 1865. For statements on this subject see the Appendix.

manifest than that the English members assume as an axiom that Ireland has no right to her own revenues. "England, under the convenient name of 'the Empire,' is assumed to be the rightful owner of the revenues of Ireland. England, in their view, is entitled to grasp all the Irish revenue she can lay hold of, and is not bound to refund anything. The Union is practically interpreted to be an identification of burdens and of taxes, but not of benefits or of expenditure. 'The Empire' means England when there is question of outlay, but it is held to include Ireland when there is question of taxation. The English members disregard the disparity of the two pre-Union debts, which, although it is the very pith and marrow of our case, yet forms no part of the ground on which Sir Stafford Northcote appears to have arrived at the conclusions in his report."

Yet in spite of the foregone conclusions of the English members, General Dunne succeeded in extorting an admission that Ireland is grievously and disproportionately overtaxed. The General, on this fiscal question, was an excellent and patriotic Irish agitator. His meritorious labours are appropriately mentioned in this work; for one of the standing complaints of the Repealers is the great fiscal wrong done to Ireland.

On the 17th of June, 1864, Smith O'Brien, whose health had been for some time declining, died in Wales. I need not say that his death caused heartfelt grief, not only among those who personally knew and loved him, but among the millions of his countrymen who revered him as a brave and honest man, and a true Protestant patriot. His remains reached Dublin in the *Cambria* steamer about four o'clock in the morning of the 23rd, and were met by a sorrowing crowd, who had in many instances remained up all night to be present at the arrival of the vessel. A procession was formed through the city to the Kingsbridge terminus; the number of persons who attended at that early hour were computed at 20,000. O'Brien's remains were interred at Rathronan, in the County Limerick. He had reached his sixty-first year. "Requiescat in pace."

CHAPTER XXX.

SUCCESSIVE AGITATIONS AGAINST POPULAR GRIEVANCES.

Can the depths of the ocean afford you not graves,
That you come thus to perish afar o'er the waves,
To redden and swell the wild torrents that flow
Through the valley of vengeance, the dark Aherlow?
Spirit of the Nation.

THE reader who has accompanied me thus far will have seen that ample provocatives exist in Ireland for that discontent which, when coloured by American connexion, assumes the shape of Fenianism. I have elsewhere examined the causes of the Fenian phenomenon,* which is in my judgment the direct result of the Legislative Union.

The popular discontent I regard as not only legitimate but inevitable. The Fenian attempts at redressing the national wrongs were absurd, ill-conceived, ill-contrived, treasonable, and impracticable. The National Association, which comprised all, or nearly all, the Catholic bishops and a large number of clergymen, earnestly invited the people to support it. The National League, instituted by Mr. Martin and The O'Donoghue, sent forth a similar invitation. The objects of both these societies were in a high degree popular. Yet the great body of the people held aloof, because they were destitute of confidence in the Imperial Parliament, to which the appeals for removal of wrongs were to be addressed by the two societies I have named; and because they had taken up a vague idea that conquering hosts were speedily to come from America and set all right. This idea was very prevalent, and in my intercourse with the peasantry I found it extremely difficult to dispel the illusion. A particular day would be fixed by the Fenian agents for the landing of the armament; and when the day would arrive, bringing with it no armament, another day would be named, and another, and another; successive postponements still leaving the popular credulity undiminished.

The number of signatures to petitions for disendowing the State Church amounted in 1866 to no less than 202,682. This number does not represent the whole, for many petitions were rejected in consequence of informality. The number would have been much greater if the people had confidence

* In a small pamphlet entitled, "Why is Ireland Discontented?" published by Cameron & Ferguson, Glasgow.

in the Imperial Legislature. The signatures to petitions for a change in the Land Laws amounted, during the same year, to 233,766. Such numbers, under circumstances of considerable discouragement, must be allowed to indicate great earnestness in the petitioners. Sir John Gray, M.P. for Kilkenny, took charge of the question of ecclesiastical disendowment in Parliament. Of his speech, delivered on the 11th of April, 1866, the *Times* of the next day said: "Whoever doubts the anomaly or the failure of the Irish Church, may be recommended, once for all, to peruse the speech of Sir John Gray." It is indeed a very able statement.

The Fenian organisation proceeded apace. Of course the Government had full and early information of the secret doings of the Fenians; for there never was, and never will be, an illegal conspiracy in Ireland in which spies and false brethren will not swarm. The very existence of such a conspiracy is certain to invite pretended enthusiasts, whose sole object in swearing themselves into the society is to betray its members to the Government for payment.

Pierce Nagle, Petitt, and Warner, in 1866, were mere reproductions of John Donnellan Balfe in 1848, and of Reynolds, Newell, and Armstrong in 1798. The useful though infamous services of informers placed the Viceroy, Lord Wodehouse, in possession of every detail of the conspiracy; and it is due to him to say that he used his powers not only with firmness and discretion, but with as much clemency as consisted with the performance of duties in themselves severe. He proclaimed in Parliament that Ireland had grievances to be redressed, amongst which he gave the alien State Church a prominent position. When the first batch of Fenian prisoners had been tried, convicted, and sentenced, it was fondly hoped by persons who could not see beneath the surface that Fenianism was extinguished. The Earl of Derby knew better; he said it had only been scotched, not killed. Lord Wodehouse was created Earl of Kimberley to reward him for having killed or scotched it. From his early and accurate knowledge, derived from the informers, he was able to anticipate and counteract every movement projected by the conspirators.

The English journals had for some time been amusing the world with statements that Ireland was prosperous and contented; that she had cordially accepted the Union, and had at length become sensible of its benefits. Fenianism came into awkward collision with those statements. Here was a conspiracy against English connexion, extending nobody could tell how far among the population. Persons who knew nothing about the matter imagined that it was an integral conspiracy, confined to the men who were actually enrolled in it. But in truth it was no more than a symptom of a far more extensive disease—of that national discontent inevitably flowing from the Union and its evil consequences, and of which the Fenian exhibition was merely the accident of special circumstances.

It is well to recall the solemn warnings given in 1799 and 1800 by the parliamentary friends of the Irish Constitution, that the Union necessarily tended to promote the ultimate separation of the countries.

Mr. Saurin said: "It will endanger the present happy Constitution and connexion with Great Britain."

Colonel Barry: "It will impair the connexion."

Right Hon. John Foster, Speaker of the House of Commons: "The ruinous measure of an Union—a measure calculated to disturb the harmony and threaten the existence of the Empire."——"Which, if persevered in, must threaten separation."

Mr. Saunderson: "It will endanger, perhaps dissolve, the connexion."

Lord Powerscourt (moving an amendment): "It would tend, in our opinion, more than any other cause, ultimately to a separation of this kingdom from Great Britain."

Mr. Waller: "It will weaken, if not dissolve, the connexion."

Lord Mathew: "The Union will tend more to weaken than to fortify the connexion."

Lord Cole: "The strongest abhorrence of the Union is compatible with the most unshaken attachment to the connexion."

Mr. John Claudius Beresford: "It will undermine the welfare and subvert the liberties of Ireland, and endanger the connexion."

Right Hon. W. B. Ponsonby: "I oppose the Union from an anxious desire to maintain the connexion."

Right Hon. George Ogle: "A rejection of the Union is the only mode by which the connexion can be preserved."

Mr. R. French: "The preservation of the Irish Parliament will encourage and maintain the connexion."

Mr. Gorges: "The happy communion with Great Britain is best maintained by the Constitution of 1782."

Mr. George Ponsonby: "The Parliament which so recently protected the Irish Crown is the firm and saving bond of British connexion."

Colonel Vereker: "The Union will effect the downfall of Ireland, the annihilation of her independence, and separation from British connexion."

Mr. Bushe: "Union is alienation from British connexion."

Mr. Peter Burrowes: "This Union not only menaces the connexion, but the Constitution itself."

Mr. Plunket: "This bill I oppose, not as a bill of Union, but of separation; as a bill calculated to dismember the Empire."

Mr. Grattan: "The two nations are not identified, though the Irish Legislature be absorbed; and by that absorption the feeling of one of the nations is not identified, but alienated. . . . Union is Irish alienation."

In truth, any other result than Irish alienation was out of the question. That alienation rankles and festers in the nation's heart. How could it be otherwise? The Union seems pre-eminently calculated to destroy the attachment of Irishmen to British connexion, and to render them indifferent to the conquest of their country by a foreign force. If Ireland's destiny is to be robbed, degraded, and dispeopled, Irishmen may, not unnaturally, ask what can it matter whether the robbery, the degradation, the dispeopling, are achieved by Great Britain, or by any other power?

How different the case if the Union had never been enacted! Had the policy of equal laws which Earl Fitzwilliam believed he was commissioned to effect in 1795 been fairly carried out; had the country been suffered by England to advance in the career of prosperity she enjoyed under her domestic Legislature; we should have seen her own resources expanding into national wealth and employed for the support of her own people; we should have seen, deeply rooted in the nation's heart, the loyalty that springs from national happiness and from an honourable pride in domestic institutions adapted to the people's wants and dear to their affections; we should have seen no exodus of impoverished millions from a land to which God has given plenty; we should have seen no Fenianism.

The *Times* now and then tells truth. "There is nothing," said the leading journal (30th of June, 1863), "about which we Englishmen know so little as Ireland. We are often told this, and no doubt very justly."

The connexion of the countries has now lasted well-nigh seven centuries. The Union has lasted since the year 1800. If at the end of more than two generations of legislative connexion, and seven hundred years of Imperial connexion, Englishmen avowedly know less about Ireland than about anything else, we may safely conclude that their *crassa ignorantia* is incurable. The legislation of ignorance can neither be intelligent nor beneficial.

If Fenianism includes, like every other secret society, its rascals and traitors, it has also its better representatives. Kickham, and some other enthusiasts, had respectable characters. But if Fenianism has its special hero, I would say that hero is Thomas Burke. His address to the Court after conviction was marked by calmness, earnestness, dignity, and resignation. The following passages of his eloquent speech are worth preserving:

"I, my lords, have no desire for the name of a martyr— I ask not the death of a martyr; but if it is the will of the Almighty and Omnipotent God that my devotion to the land of my birth shall be tested on the scaffold, I am willing there to die in defence of the rights of man to free government—the rights of an oppressed people to throw off the yoke of thraldom. I am an Irishman by birth; an American by adoption; by nature a lover of freedom, and an enemy to that power that holds my native land in the bonds of tyranny. It has no godly structure of self-government. Before I go any farther I have an important duty that I wish to dispose of. To my learned, talented, and eloquent counsel I offer the poor gift of thanks—the sincere and heartfelt thanks of an honest man. I offer them, too, in the name of America, the thanks of the Irish people. I know that, although I am here without a friend, without a relative —in fact, three thousand miles away from my family—I am not forgotten there. The great and generous Irish heart of America feels for, to-day sympathises with, and does not forget the man who is willing to tread the scaffold—ay, defiantly, proudly, conscious of no wrong—in defence of American principles, in defence of liberty. . . . I shall now, my lords, as no doubt you will suggest to me the propriety of doing, turn my thoughts to the objects beyond the grave. I shall now look only to that home where sorrows are at an end—where joy is eternal. I shall hope and pray that freedom may yet dawn on this poor, down-trodden country. It is my hope—it is my prayer; and the last words I shall utter will be a prayer to God for forgiveness, and a prayer for poor old Ireland. . . . True, I ask for no mercy. My present emaciated form, my constitution somewhat shattered, it is better that my life should be brought to an end than to drag out a miserable existence in the prison pens of Portland. Thus it is, my lords, I accept of the verdict. Of course, my lords, my acceptance is unnecessary. I am satisfied with it. And now I shall close. True it is, there are many feelings which actuate me at this moment—in fact, these few disconnected remarks can give no idea of what I desire to say to the Court. I have ties to bind me to life and society as strongly as any man in this court; but I can remember the blessing I received from an aged mother's lips as I left her for the last time—she speaking as the Spartan mother did: 'Go, my boy; return either with your shield or on your shield.' This consoles me; this gives me heart. I submit to my doom, and I hope that God will forgive my past sins. I hope that inasmuch as He has for 700 years preserved Ireland, notwithstanding all the tyranny to which she has been subjected, as a separate and distinct nationality, He will also assist her to retrieve her fallen fortunes, and to raise her in her beauty and her majesty—the sister of Columbia—the peer of any nation in the world."

Those are noble words, and there is not the least doubt that they give true expression to the sentiments of the Irish in America. Notwithstanding the scandal entailed on Fenianism by its swindling, peculating leaders, there is not, in the sentiments and aspirations of the great majority of Irish-American Fenians, anything sordid or degrading. They deem their country wronged, and they eagerly desire to emancipate her. The purpose is lofty and honourable, but the details of the project are preposterous and inadmissible.

Part of Burke's speech consisted of an able analysis of the evidence borne against him by two informers, Massey and Corydon. With regard to the evidence given to the Government by Corydon, a curious question was raised.

Corydon, it appeared, had been in the pay of the Government as a spy from the 16th of September, 1866. On his cross-examination by Mr. O'Loghlen he admitted that from September until the following January he continued to report to the authorities the different meetings in Liverpool; the names of the persons who attended them, including the American officers; the names of the places where the American officers could be arrested. He told them that a rising was contemplated; and twice or thrice a week he had given important written information to the police authorities in Ireland. He admitted that he was, as a Fenian, under Massey's orders. The Government, then, were aware of the intended outbreak, which they could have prevented by timely arrests. And although aware of it, yet in the Queen's Speech in February they announced themselves able to restore the Habeas Corpus Act. If they thought Corydon faith-worthy, why did they not make use of his information, commencing in September, to prevent the outbreak? Why, in the Queen's Speech, did they represent tranquillity so far settled as to authorise the restoration of the Habeas Corpus Act? On the other hand, if they thought Corydon unworthy of credit, why ask the jury to convict Burke upon his testimony? This dilemma was proposed in substance by Mr. Butt in his address to the jury, and by the editors of several journals.

At the trial of one Goulding, a Fenian, at the summer assizes of 1867 in Kerry, one of the principal witnesses for the prosecution was Head Constable Talbot, of the Irish Police force. Talbot was employed by the authorities at Dublin Castle to watch the movements of the Fenians. To effect this purpose he became an enrolled Fenian, outstripping all his Fenian *confrères* in the fervour of his Fenian enthusiasm. In his evidence at Goulding's trial he stated that such were the influence and confidence he acquired among the insurgents, "they would not hold a meeting, night or day, without him." The insurgents, he said, "took him to be the head of the whole thing," and intended to reward his zeal by appointing him Fenian Commissary-General. The London *Star* called public attention to the fact that "Government employed a policeman to become a Fenian; that the policeman joined in all the arrangements for an armed rising; and, indeed, took so leading a part in the business as to make the Fenians believe he was 'the head of the whole thing.'" The circumstance furnishes one more significant warning to the Irish people of the ruinous folly of expecting political movements of a secret and illegal character to escape the vigilance of Government.

Before the Fenian conspiracy began to attract notice, much had been said about the permanent quiet and contentment that now pervaded Ireland. True, the people were rushing out of the country; but then it was satisfactory to think they would be better off elsewhere—better off anywhere than under the wing of the foreign Parliament sitting in London. In short, British legislation had done wonders in producing tranquillity, and in substituting bullocks for men. We were now at last in the right path. But when Fenianism ruffled the surface, the supposed contentment of the people turned out to have been merely superficial. The Orange journalists were of course for shooting and hanging. Their philosophy did not contemplate the removal of grievances. Odd exhibitions of fantastic zeal diversified the monotony of Orange journalism. A young lady wrote to a newspaper, boasting of her Orange principles, her heroic indifference to danger, and her proficiency in the use of firearms. An "Old Soldier" wrote to the *Evening Mail* to make a suggestion, which I quote, partly as an amusing indication of panic, partly because it contains a touch of the picturesque: "Permit me, through your columns, to suggest that in the construction of all new police-barracks a better form for defence could hardly be selected than that of the old square towers or keeps which abound in the country, three storeys high, with galleries at each angle on the upper storey, the windows on the ground floor to be six feet at least from the ground outside, small, with iron frames and shutters, the latter with loopholes and slides; only one entrance, having on the outside a strong iron gate, inside which a short passage, say five or six feet long, closed at the inner end by a ball-proof sheet-iron door, loopholed; the side walls of the passage to be also loopholed. Four stout men in such a building might defy incendiaries, or, indeed, any attack, except by artillery. Were these barracks built on slightly rising grounds, and within signalling distance of each other, intelligence of any disturbance could, in even moderately clear weather, be conveyed to the nearest garrison town by flag signals in the daytime, and lamps or flash signals at night. For example: let each tower have a number, and if there is an attack upon No. 4 tower, he hoists a red flag in the daytime, or a red light at night, and his number. No. 3 sees it, and hoists No. 4 and the red signal, and so on until it reaches the sub-inspector, who communicates with the officer in command of the troops, and a flying column starts in the direction indicated, the tower needing assistance keeping the danger signal flying until relieved, the other towers only keeping its number without the danger signal. I merely give this as an outline of a plan which I think might be worked out with advantage and at little cost."

CHAPTER XXXI.

FORMATION OF BUTT'S HOME GOVERNMENT ASSOCIATION.

> And are not all our ties the same,
>   One sod beneath, one blue sky o'er us,
> True Irish both, in heart and name,
>   One lot, or dark or bright, before us?
> A thousand links about us wound,
>   To peace and mutual kindness urge us;
> The very seas that gird us round,
>   Speak UNION in their sleepless surges.
>
>   THOMAS DAVIS.

WHEN the Fenian conspiracy was crushed, an agitation sprang up for the disestablishment and disendowment of the Protestant State Church in Ireland. Of this agitation I have traced the progress in a previous chapter.* Many years ago the late Earl of Derby had predicted that if the anti-Irish State Church were overthrown the Repeal of the Union would necessarily follow. The prediction was natural. The temporalities of that Church, amounting to at least £700,000 per annum, formed an excellent provision for the cadets of the Protestant nobility and gentry of Ireland. The preservation of the giant fraud had been expressly guaranteed by the fifth article of the Union; and there is no doubt that in 1800 a good deal of Protestant hostility to the Union had been softened by the expectation that England would for ever maintain the lucrative ecclesiastical establishment for the benefit of her Protestant allies in this kingdom. That establishment, also, fed the sectarian arrogance of its members. It pampered their pride to see the Catholics despoiled of the ancient Catholic Church revenues, and compelled to hand over those revenues to the dominant minority. They were taught to believe that this outrage on honesty was a just homage to the spiritual superiority of the Anglican Church. A Tory acquaintance expressed their common feeling to myself, saying: "Our Church is such an excellent Church that it ought to be established."

Well, it is not wonderful that Lord Derby and many others thought that the Irish Protestants would be alienated from the Union and from England if the English Government should overthrow an institution that furnished comfortable, and in several instances enormous, incomes to their ministers,

* Chapter x.

stimulated their sectarian conceit, and of which the perpetual preservation was provided for as forming an essential and fundamental condition of the legislative Union. I concurred in Lord Derby's opinion; and its correctness was soon proved by the movement among the Irish Protestants to obtain self-government for their country. In 1868 the Orange party held a meeting at their hall in Dublin, and resolved that the disestablishment and disendowment of their Church would annul the Union, which, they said, could thenceforth be only maintained by superior physical force. On the 19th of May, 1870, a large number of Protestant and Catholic gentlemen met in the great room of the Bilton Hotel in Dublin; the names of the most prominent persons at that meeting are given in the twelfth chapter of Alexander Sullivan's interesting work, "New Ireland."* They resolved that Ireland was entitled to self-government on a federative principle, and invited their countrymen to support an agitation to obtain it. On the 1st of September, 1870, the inaugural public meeting of the Home Government Association was held in the Rotunda, and some of the speeches then delivered by Protestant gentlemen are so significant of the accuracy of Lord Derby's forecast, as well as so honourable to the speakers, that I deem it right to give the following extracts, which show the spirit by which they were animated.

Mr. William Shaw, the Protestant Member for Protestant Bandon, said:

"They could not possibly regard Ireland as a county of England. The sea, nature, Providence, had forbidden it. History was against it. For generations this war had been going on between the centralising influence of England on the one hand, and the national spirit of Ireland on the other; yet, with all England's power, she had never been able to wipe out the national aspirations of this country."

My next extract is from the speech of a man whose name is a household word in Ireland—the Rev. Joseph A. Galbraith, Fellow of the Protestant University of Trinity College; a Protestant clergyman of thoroughly national principles, whose splendid intelligence and generous heart impelled him to give to the movement for Home Government the assistance of his high character and great ability.

---

* "This," says Mr. Sullivan, "was not 'Repeal,' as O'Connell's scheme was loosely and imperfectly called. O'Connell entirely avoided defining his plan of arrangement." Mr. Sullivan is mistaken here. O'Connell defined his plan with elaborate minuteness, as I have shown in the nineteenth chapter of the present work.

"He had never," he said, "spoken in that room before, and he doubted whether his voice could reach all parts of it. But of this he was certain, that if his voice could reach as far as his heart and his affections, it would reach from the Giant's Causeway to Cape Clear, and from Ireland's Eye to the Isles of Arran. . . . He defied any man in Ireland to maintain in public the proposition that Home Rule was a bad thing in itself; no one would believe him, no one would listen to him, he would be hooted off any platform."

Mr. Galbraith quoted the memorable words of Charles James Fox, who, speaking of the Union, said: "The whole scheme went upon that false and abominable presumption that we (English) could legislate better for the Irish than they could do for themselves—a principle founded upon the most arrogant despotism and tyranny. There was not a more clear axiom in the science of politics than that man was his own natural governor, and that he ought to legislate for himself. No other being could enter into his feelings or have anything common in sympathy with his nature, and therefore the Legislature of a people must flow out of and be identified with the people themselves. It was idle to talk to Ireland of the word Union, since there could be no such thing as a real union on an equal footing between countries so disproportionate and unequal."

Old Richard Grattan, cousin of his illustrious namesake, proposed a resolution which condemned the design to force the existing system on the Irish people, " whose legitimate national aspirations it ignores or outrages." Mr. Grattan expressed his firm belief " that Ireland would prosper under native rule to a greater extent even than she had suffered under centuries of English misgovernment."

The Rev. George M'Cutchan, Protestant clergyman of Kenmare, declared that in heartily joining the Home Government Association, he desired to make Ireland

> A land of settled government,
> A land of just and old renown;
> Where freedom broadens slowly down
> From precedent to precedent.

Dr. Maunsell, proprietor of the Tory *Evening Mail*, declared that he would belie the convictions of his whole life if he did not give every assistance in his power to the movement which he hoped they were about successfully to inaugurate.

The numerous letters from persons unable to attend the meeting, invariably expressed the zealous concurrence of the writers in the object contemplated by its promoters. The cause advanced apace. On the 18th of July, 1871, the Corporation of Dublin assembled in the City Hall, to receive a deputation from the Home Government Association, consisting of the Rev. Joseph Galbraith, John Martin, M.P. for the county of Meath, and myself. The deputies were members of the three chief religious communities in Ireland —Episcopal Protestant, Presbyterian, and Catholic; and it was deemed that our appearance together, associated as brother champions of the cause of Ireland, would usefully typify that union of creeds for a national object which every one admitted would essentially conduce to success.

We rehearsed the old story. We presented the strong principles and facts of our case: the indefeasible right of the Irish nation to make their own laws, to retain their own revenues, to control their own national concerns; the misery entailed on our people by the invasion of that right; the inveterate hostility with which England, previously to 1779, had crushed out every Irish manufacture which she feared might successfully compete with her own; the prosperity which sprang up when the Irish Volunteers and Parliament, in 1782, inspired by the illustrious Grattan, flung off for a time the pernicious usurpation of the British Legislature; the criminal conspiracy of Pitt and his agents to persecute our people into insurrection in order to carry the Union; the consequent decay of manufactures, the monstrous abstraction of national wealth, the financial pillage, the public despondency, the occasional famines, the abnormal emigration, the smouldering disloyalty, the utter dislocation of the Irish social system resulting from the wicked destruction of the Irish Parliament—these things we pressed upon the notice of the metropolitan Corporation and of the country, and the example thus set in Dublin was soon followed by other municipal bodies, Town Commissioners, Boards of Guardians, County Clubs, and Farmers' Clubs. To obtain the support of an Irish constituency it now became needful in almost every case that the candidate for parliamentary representation should announce his devotion to Home Rule.

There were occasional indications that the spirit of discord would expire. Protestants of good position and intelligence gradually joined the national ranks.

The Orange processions in Monaghan, held on the 12th of July, 1872, had passed off quietly, no opposition to them having been given by the Nationalist multitude. In recognition of this tolerance, the following Notice to the Orangemen of Monaghan was issued by their Grand Master:

"DEAR BRETHREN,
"Having been informed on good authority that it is the intention of our Roman Catholic neighbours to celebrate the 15th of August by processions in different parts of the county, I now call upon all Orangemen to abstain, by word or deed, from interfering in any way with such processions. The Orangemen of Monaghan had their processions on the 12th of July, and were not interfered with in any way. Let us return the compliment.
"(Signed)   WILLIAM WOLSELY MADDEN,
"*Grand Master, Orangemen of Monaghan.*
"Co. Monaghan, 8th August, 1872."

With regard to a proposed Home Rule meeting in that county, I corresponded with a Conservative gentleman of local distinction and of large fortune in Ulster. I am not aware of his being an Orangeman; but I believe he was closely connected, either by kindred or personal friendship, with leading members of the Orange party. Not having his permission to publish his name, I do not give it. I may, however, mention that he was a deputy-lieutenant, and held the commission of the peace in four Northern counties. The following extracts from his letter, dated 10th of August, 1873, will furnish evidence that our hopes of an union between Irishmen of different parties were in progress of being realised. Speaking of a recent Home Rule meeting in an Orange district, he says:

"A large number of my men went to it from here and passed through one of the strongest Orange districts in the North, with green flags, music, etc. Throughout the day the best feeling was displayed, and I did not hear of a single instance of an uncivil word being addressed to the processionists. From some of the houses on the way jugs of milk were brought out by the Protestant party and distributed to those who had come from a distance. And I know that on a recent occasion drums were actually lent by some of the Orange lodges near Monaghan on the occasion of a Green procession."

What rational and Christian Irishman would not ardently welcome such blessed indications that the internecine rancour which so long had cursed our country was at last giving way to the influence of nationality? My correspondent continued :

"Let me add—this constitutes a very marked change for the better, and what I would really advise would be to be content with it, and not risk compromising everything in the event of ill-judged persons making foolish speeches. For instance, I am utterly opposed to mixing up the Home Rule question with collateral issues, such as Tenant Right, Denominational or Undenominational Education, etc. The ground for us to take, as it seems to me, is the simple one of obtaining the management of our own affairs, by which I have no hesitation in saying an *immense* reduction in taxation of every kind might be made in Ireland, whereby everybody would be benefited."

In this opinion I thoroughly concurred. In fact, the mixing up of collateral questions with the main national question of Home Rule, would have been a deviation from the principles on which our Association was founded. While every member was free to hold what opinion he thought proper on all other public subjects, the one, only object contemplated by the Association was the establishment of Home Rule upon a Federal basis. My correspondent concluded his letter with a statement well worth putting on record :

"The only thing," he said, "which I believe prevents the Protestant party and gentry generally from joining the movement, is the fear that out of Home Rule may arise a series of assaults upon the rights of property against which England would protect them; and these objections must be removed by the force of reasoning, and not by popular demonstrations."

Such was the judgment of an Ulster Conservative landlord; and I have not the least doubt that he was right. If popular agitation had thenceforth been constantly and *exclusively* directed to the acquisition of Home Rule, the revived sentiment of nationality would have gradually led the landlords to emulate the patriotism displayed by their grandfathers, who in 1782 had made Ireland ring from sea to sea with the declaration that no power on earth had any right to make her laws, save her own King, Lords, and Commons. Combined with the masses of their countrymen, and leading them in the pursuit of legislative independence, the landlords of Ireland would have now been the most powerful and popular aristocracy in existence. They would have defied and defeated hostility. Strong in their position as spirited guardians of our national rights, they would have saved their country, entrenched themselves in the popular heart, and effectively preserved the special interests of their order.

CHAPTER XXXII.

PUBLIC CONFERENCE ON HOME GOVERNMENT.

> God of peace, before thee
> Peaceful here we kneel,
> Humbly to implore thee
> For a nation's weal.
> Calm her sons' dissensions,
> Bid their discord cease;
> End their mad contentions—
> Hear us, God of Peace!
> *Spirit of the Nation.*

IT was resolved by the council of the Home Government Association to invite a public conference on the subject of our national claim. We believed that, as Lord Ffrench said, public opinion in England, as well as in Ireland, would be much enlightened by the proceedings of a conference which, from its composition, would possess a representative character. The requisition received the signatures of about 24,000 persons, and at the head of the signatures appeared the venerated name of John MacHale, Archbishop of Tuam. In compliance with the requisition, the Conference was convened by four gentlemen, namely, Philip Callan, M.P., William Shaw, M.P., E. R. King-Harman, and myself. We assembled in the Rotunda on the 18th of November, 1873, under the able presidency of Mr. Shaw, who at that time represented Bandon.

The first resolution was moved by the leader of the movement, Isaac Butt. The international arrangement which he advocated, proposed to restore to Ireland the exclusive right of legislation on all our domestic affairs; the revived Irish Parliament to consist, as of old, of the Sovereign, Lords, and Commons of Ireland. The power of legislating for the local or domestic concerns of this country was thus to be withdrawn from the Imperial Parliament; but that Parliament was still to retain its control of all Imperial business, and Ireland was still to send Members thither to take part in such business. Mr. Butt's speech was a masterpiece of ingenious and eloquent advocacy. For myself, I should have much preferred an arrangement resembling Grattan's Constitution of 1782; but I acquiesced in the scheme proposed by Mr. Butt and accepted by the Conference, mainly because it appeared to be more attainable than the other. He travelled over the whole ground; quoted the numerous proofs of the Irish prosperity that prevailed while Ireland was emancipated from English legislation; dissected objections; enforced the claim of right, and produced from his personal experience resistless evidence that the system of governing Ireland *ab externo* by an alien Parliament was the fruitful source of Irish disaffection—disaffection incurable while that system lasted.

The remark is trite that when Ireland claims Home Government by agitation, a large section of English politicians exclaim that what she seeks must be withheld, because nothing should be granted to clamour. On the other hand, when a lull from agitation prevails, the same politicians declare that Ireland needs no change, because she is quiet; that her contentment is demonstrated by the fact of her being at peace. What Isaac Butt thought about such peace will appear from the following passage in his opening speech. He said:

"Under our present system of government there can be no real peace in Ireland. Corruption and coercion may produce a forced and unreal stillness. True tranquillity can only spring from the contentment of the people. We never will have that contentment in the absence of free institutions —of that National Parliament which is the greatest and best of free institutions, which alone can give life and reality to all others. Ten years ago English statesmen said that Ireland was at rest. May I read for the Conference a passage which I well remember reading at the time—Conservative testimony to the character of that stillness which was called rest. . . .

"'Nearly half a century has elapsed since the cry of Justice to Ireland was a watchword through the land, and the voices of the men who then raised it are silent for ever, but still it ascends like a wail above their graves. Then it was for equal rights and liberty; now the Irish nation only asks the bare permission to exist. Nothing indicates more plainly the miserable condition of Ireland than the utter apathy with which the recent attempt to get up a Reform agitation was received. Public spirit is dead, and those who are not looking for a revolution from beyond the Atlantic, sit down in hopeless apathy, despairing of any good result from attempting to reform or move that British Parliament which has so often disappointed the country's expectations, and turned a deaf ear to her reiterated appeals for justice.'"

Having read the above passage, written by a Conservative who afterwards occupied a high judicial station, Mr. Butt proceeded:

"Is this the peace you desire for our country? A peace that is only the inaction of exhaustion and decay—an inaction that is produced by the corruption of the upper ranks, and the hopeless and sullen apathy of the masses of the people?—a peace that, even at its best, means an ignoble acquiescence in the degradation of our country—a stagnation of all political and national life—a quenching of all public spirit, and an extinction of all public opinion? It is just the peace that is created by an alien power, that, like the vampire, sucks away the life-blood of a nation, and, as it does so, lulls its victim to a ghastly repose. There was a time when Ireland seemed sinking to that fatal sleep."

Mr. Butt then traced the events that had startled the country from its slumber, and roused the alien Government from its false security. He referred to the Fenians who had dared the desperate enterprise of freeing Ireland by revolt, and then went on:

"Over a torn and distracted country, a country agitated by dissension, weakened by distrust, we raised the banner on which we emblazoned the magic words, 'Home Rule.' We raised it with feeble hand. Tremblingly, with hesitation, almost stealthily we unfurled that banner to the breeze. But wherever the legend we had emblazoned on its folds was seen the heart of the people moved to its words, and the soul of the nation felt their power and their spell."

After an impressive and animated exhortation to perseverance, Mr. Butt concluded by moving the following resolution:

"That, as the basis of the proceedings of this Conference, we declare our conviction that it is essentially necessary to the peace and prosperity of Ireland that the right of domestic legislation on all Irish affairs should be restored to our country."

The Conference lasted for four days. Its proceedings were marked by great unanimity. Mr. Kenelm Digby suggested that the re-establishment of a House of Lords in the revived Constitution of Ireland was a project not reconcilable with the democratic opinions largely prevalent in England, and to some extent also in Ireland. In these opinions he appeared to participate, but he refrained from pressing them, as the predominating sentiment of the Conference was plainly in favour of a return to the old pre-Union lines of Sovereign, Lords, and Commons. Mr. P. J. Smyth, and Mr. Martin, M.P. for Meath, concurred with me in preferring an Irish Constitution on the basis of 1782 to the Federal connexion proposed to the Conference for its adoption ; but, like myself, they yielded their individual preference to the consideration that Federalism, although in their opinion the less desirable, was apparently the more attainable solution of the international difficulty.

That excellent man and true patriot, the Rev. Joseph Galbraith, F.T.C.D., communicated to the audience the interesting fact that the celebrated Irish novelist, Charles Lever, then lately deceased, had thoroughly sympathised with the national movement. "It may not," said Mr. Galbraith, "be known to the members of this Conference, that he (Charles Lever) took a deep interest in our movement, and was from conviction and love of country a genuine Home Ruler. I hold in my hand a paper—it is labelled on the back, 'Home Rule—author's proof.' It was written and revised by Charles Lever for *Blackwood's Magazine*, but he went so far in expressing this sentiment that it was suppressed. It was too much for *Blackwood*."

At the end of the fourth day well-merited thanks were unanimously given to Mr. Shaw, the chairman of the Conference, for the tact and ability with which he had discharged the duties of his office, as well as for the zeal he had uniformly evinced in support of the national demand. Mr. Butt closed the proceedings with language appropriately solemn :

" We have passed," said he, " through four days which were a crisis in the history of Ireland, and never were days more nobly passed by a nation and a people on their trial. The moderation, the dignity, the self-control, I will say the wisdom, of these proceedings have more than answered the hopes of our friends, and more than disappointed the malignant expectations and prophecies of our enemies. Our meetings have been presided over in a manner worthy of the old Roman senate, and not a word has been uttered which any of us have need to desire to blot out from our records. In the same spirit of reverence in which in my opening words I offered up a prayer for that guidance without which all human effort is in vain—in these closing words I will say that the God of our fathers has looked down upon us. We will go forth from this under His blessing; and with that blessing the efforts originated in this Conference will achieve the liberties of our native land."

Thus ended the Conference; and we strongly hoped that the unanimity that had characterised its proceedings, the confederation of men of different religions and opposite political doctrines for a common purpose—we hoped that the example thus given would be followed through the kingdom of Ireland. We cared not for Whig or Tory—for Radical or Conservative—we only insisted upon one bond of brotherhood—a hearty acceptance of the doctrine that the Irish people should alone govern Ireland, and an honest endeavour to achieve that vital right.

CHAPTER XXXIII.

THE GENERAL ELECTION OF 1874.

"To combine classes, Roger O'Moore embraced Preston of Gormanstown, on the summit of Knocklofty, in 1641; to combine classes, Sarsfield rode from Limerick town to Galway garrison to bring back Tyrconnel; to combine classes, Henry Grattan sent the resolution in favour of Emancipation to the Convention of Dungannon."—D'ARCY M'GEE.

FOR some months the agitation proceeded through the country on the principles adopted by the Conference. Large meetings were held, with the usual display of enthusiasm. At the general election of 1874, which came suddenly on the country, fifty-nine Repeal or Home Rule members were returned to the foreign Parliament, notwithstanding the restricted electoral franchise. A larger number would have been returned if the constituencies had been better organised, or if they had been given more time for preparation. As a matter of course, our Irish claim was as unpopular in England as the restitution of stolen goods is commonly distasteful to the robber. England, by the Union, had struck her fangs into our vitals. She had grasped Ireland in her clutches, and had no inclination to relinquish her prey. Her arrogance was gratified by the control of Irish interests which the Union gave her. The power of extorting inordinate revenue from Ireland gratified her avarice. And her ancient hatred of this country was gratified by the destruction of the Irish Parliament and the degradation of Ireland from the rank of a self-governed kingdom to the condition of a tributary province. The correlative of English usurpation was Irish resentment. " Conquest," says Cardinal Manning, " does not create authority. It is only a sanguinary investiture of the person who shall bear the authority." * The Irish people felt that the Union was a conquest achieved by sanguinary crimes; and that the Power that had received the sanguinary investiture was entitled to no other obedience than superior physical force could exact.

Isaac Butt had considerable qualifications for the leadership of a popular movement. He had great eloquence, great debating power, a thorough conviction of the justice of his cause which imparted to his speeches an impressive air of earnestness. He was perfectly free from the miserable meanness of personal jealousy, which has sometimes stained the character and marred the usefulness of abler men.

On the 31st of May, 1874, he brought the Home Rule question into the House of Commons. In a speech of great power he moved, "That the House resolve itself into a Committee to consider the present parliamentary relations between Great Britain and Ireland." He said that if the Committee were granted, he would then move " That it is expedient and just to restore to the Irish nation the right and power of managing all exclusively Irish affairs in an Irish Parliament; and that provision be made at the same time for maintaining the integrity of the Empire and the connexion between the countries by reserving to the Imperial Parliament full and exclusive control over all Imperial affairs."

The debate occupied two nights. I do not attempt to summarise the arguments, for the reader of this book is already aware of the principal grounds of our demand. The Irish votes on the division stood thus: Ayes, 56; Noes, 36; giving the Home Rulers a majority of 20, so far as the Irish representation was concerned. But, of course, the British majority sustained their usurpation by overwhelming numbers.

For some time a belief prevailed in Ireland that the

* *Contemporary Review*, July, 1883.

Home Rule question, like the Catholic question of old, would become a subject of annual parliamentary discussion, gradually acquiring accessions of strength until the united action of the various sections of Irishmen should finally render resistance extremely inconvenient to the English Government. To intensify this inconvenience, it occurred to Mr. Parnell that the intervention of the Irish Members in the constant debates upon all sorts of topics could be effectively utilised. He felt that the foreign Legislature was not in any sense an Irish Legislature, except in the bare fact of having power over Ireland; which power had been acquired by the perpetration of enormous crimes. Its function was to hold down Ireland; to wring money out of Ireland; to repress the honourable sentiment of Irish nationality, and to perpetuate this degrading condition of ruinous bondage. In January, 1878, Mr. Parnell, at a Conference at the Rotunda, thus described his view of the situation, and the motives of his policy:

" Being of an active turn of body and mind myself, and having gone over to the House of Commons, I found myself kicking my heels about the House of Commons for months with nothing to do; so, consequently last session I thought that as the Government would give us nothing to do on Irish questions, it would be no harm if some of us turned our attention to English ones. We took up the Prisons Bill and one or two other English Bills—only two or three altogether —and we turned our attention to them with very good results, for everybody admits that we did improve them; though they made a great fuss about the process of improvement."

That process was denounced as being an "obstruction" to the business of Parliament. The foreign Parliament, however, was itself an obstruction to Irish prosperity; so that if Mr. Parnell's action were really obstructive, he was only obstructing the obstructor.

Mr. Bright said in the House of Commons, in 1869, that Parliament then, for the first time since the Union, displayed a sentiment of friendliness to Ireland. The hostility of sixty-nine years is thus admitted by that distinguished Englishman; but the friendly sentiments of the subsequent period have not yet been exhibited. In truth, the persistent usurpation of legislative power over Ireland is in itself a position essentially hostile to our national rights, and poisons every measure, of whatever nature, the alien Legislature may enact in our regard.

Mr. Parnell continued to practise what was called "*obstruction*" in that Parliament which had acquired its control of Ireland by the *destruction* of the Irish Parliament. It was no doubt amusing to see the enemy worried in his own stronghold; but the question remained—to what extent could the process be prudently carried? The action of Mr. Parnell and his friends was complained of as being intolerable to Englishmen; but it should have been remembered that the Union was, and is, intolerable to the enormous majority of Irishmen, and that some inconvenience in the transaction of legislative business was indeed a very small reprisal on the Power that had made havoc of Irish legislative rights and Irish prosperity.

Mr. Butt, however, disapproved of the process styled obstructive. He relied, apparently, on the force of argument to overcome the hostility of English legislators; and he condemned, sometimes in language of asperity, the more energetic policy of Mr. Parnell. From his age, from his talents, from his experience, and from his unquestionable devotion to the cause of Ireland, great deference was due to his opinion; and his feelings must have been extremely painful when he found that his followers gave strong indications of their preference for the policy which he condemned.

Still he continued to occupy the position of leader, pretty much as a Prime Minister may be said to lead in Parliament, although confronted with an active and increasing Opposition. A conference of Home Rulers, to which I have already alluded, was held at the Rotunda to consider the respective merits of the two policies. It ended in a compromise. Parnell did not wish to break up the Home Rule party, but only desired to infuse more energy into their parliamentary action. Yet Butt plainly saw that his policy did not command the assent of the people. This was a painful consciousness; it preyed severely on a mind much harassed by public cares and private anxieties. He soon formally resigned a leadership which had become scarcely more than nominal. His health gave way, and on the 5th of May, 1879, he died, sincerely lamented by all who had enjoyed his private friendship, and revered as the founder of the Home Government League even by those persons who deemed his parliamentary tactics mistaken. "Requiescat in pace."

After his death a strong disposition existed among many Home Rulers to invest Mr. William Shaw with the leadership. Mr. Shaw was a gentleman of much ability and had rendered great service to the cause by his able speeches, his liberal pecuniary subscriptions, and his able presidency of important public meetings, where his tact was conspicuously exercised. He accepted the position of leader, and in the performance of its duties he evinced the business-like capacity for which he had been previously distinguished. He retained the leadership till the 17th of May, 1880, on which day a meeting of the Home Rule members assembled at the Royal Exchange to take counsel concerning the condition of their body and its future organisation. Of course the vexed question of parliamentary "obstruction" was discussed. The result of the meeting was the enthronement of Parnell as leader of the movement by 23 votes against 18 which were given for Shaw.

And it is undeniable that the strength which Home Rule has now acquired in Parliament is the result of Parnell's parliamentary policy.

CHAPTER XXXIV.

MR. PARNELL'S QUALIFICATIONS FOR LEADERSHIP.

"It is the English people who hold Ireland."—*The Economist* (London journal).*

MR. PARNELL now became the central figure in Irish agitation. His qualities of fearlessness, energy, and perseverance obtained for him the confidence of the rural population, to whose interests he professed himself entirely devoted. His supreme indifference to the opinion of the foreign Parliament was duly appreciated by a people whose experience of its rule was an experience of chronic disaster, and who knew enough of the criminal means by which Ireland was brought under its power to regard its authority as illegitimate.

The Home Rule League was founded to agitate solely for Home Rule. By its original principles all persons were admissible to its membership—Conservatives, Liberals, Tenant Righters, Landlords—provided only that they accepted the doctrine that Ireland needed and was entitled to Self-Government, and undertook to assist the movement for its restoration. But by degrees an attack on landlordism was practically incorporated with the Home Rule agitation,

* Quoted in *Irish Times* of July 1, 1882.

and this was plainly a divergence from the programme on which many of its members had joined it. The reader has seen that there were at one time strong indications of a possible junction of the landlords with the friends of our legislative independence; a junction which of course required time to effect, but of which the progress, though slow, was pretty sure to gain momentum unless checked by an onslaught on their special interests. Looking at all Irish questions from a Home Rule standpoint, I had fondly hoped for the realisation of the late Lord Derby's prophecy, that the Repeal of the Union would follow from the disestablishment of the anti-Irish State Church. It seemed as if his lordship had prophesied correctly when Protestants of distinction assembled in a meeting where national principles were strongly expressed and loudly applauded. Our object was to combine all parties in the demand for native legislation; for it seemed unquestionable that Home Rule, if obtained by a combination of all Irishmen, would be far more valuable than Home Rule if obtained by one party of Irishmen against another. To promote that combination was the task of the Home Rule League as originally constituted; and I thought, as time went on, that Mr. Parnell should have devoted his great talents to weld, if possible, the scattered parties into a solid brotherhood of Constitutional nationalists, instead of dropping Home Rule for four years, and supplanting it with a violent agrarian agitation that drove back the landlords into the slough of West-Britonism from which they were just beginning to emerge.

No propositions can be plainer than these: first, that it is the interest of every country to retain her own income and to develop her own resources for the benefit of her own people; second, that the external control that drags away her income in large masses, overthrows her manufactures, and trains every class of her aspirants to look for promotion to a foreign source, must be ruinous alike to her national honour and to her material prosperity.

Any rational landlord must have seen these truths if he could only shake off the fears and the fetters of party and sectarian prejudice. In November, 1847, Smith O'Brien wrote to Charles Gavan Duffy:

"The tone of feeling amongst the gentry is much changed with reference to Repeal. *I hope that you will abstain from attacking the landlords as a class.* When an individual does wrong, spare him not; but do not render hostile to you a whole class—the most influential—by indiscriminate and undeserved censure."

There must, indeed, have been many of their class who had sense enough to see that it would be better for Ireland to keep at home whatever wealth the Almighty had given her, than that a powerful and jealous neighbour should rob her of the means of supporting her inhabitants. But the class were slow to move. They needed the spur of Disestablishment to force them into action. They were blind to their own interests. John Mitchel wrote to O'Brien in 1847, that if the landlords would act as Irish patriots, " they could make fair and honourable terms for themselves, and become the most powerful and popular aristocracy on earth."

That they could have become so I have not the slightest doubt. Had they taken the initiative in the Repeal agitation; had they worked it with earnestness and with the weight of their influence ; had they summoned their people to support them in demanding Ireland for the Irish ; had they earned the popular confidence by showing themselves Irishmen in heart and soul ; had they repudiated foreign legislation as a grievance and an insult ; had they lowered their rents when excessive to a just and moderate level—had they done all this, their people would have loved them as champions and protectors, would have rallied vigorously round them, and invested them with all the strength that well-earned popular support can confer.

I can see no wrong in landlordism, considered purely as an institution. I can see no wrong in the fact that one man, possessing land, lets it at a fair and honest rent to another man as tenant. But landlordism may be either a scourge or a blessing, according to the mode in which it is administered. If a numerous body of landlords extort the last farthing that can be squeezed out of the industry of their tenants ; if they hate the creed professed by their tenants and despise them for believing it ; if they uphold the pestilent system of Ireland for the English, the system that makes their country the bond-slave of another; if they practise the policy of extensive evictions ; if, in a word, they show themselves the agents of an alien power to perpetuate the degradation of their country, and to effect the oppression and expulsion of their humbler countrymen—then indeed landlordism, thus viciously administered, incurs the merited hatred not only of its victims but of all lovers of justice.

The indications of national feeling which Smith O'Brien

recognised in 1847, appeared to revive when the State Church was disestablished. I knew something of the progress of that feeling, and I hoped that the landlords and the Protestant gentry in general would gradually join our Constitutional agitation. In my opinion Mr. Parnell should not have dropped the Home Rule agitation for a moment. He should, I humbly think, have perpetually held up the Home Rule banner. He should have abstained from attacking the landlords *as a class*, and confined his agrarian policy to attacks on the rack-renters, who, unhappily, were sufficiently numerous to afford ample scope to his aggressive activity. This course would have given no alarm to the landlords who were *not* rack-renters, and would not have deterred them from standing up for Home Government. An indiscriminate onslaught against *all* rents, whether fair or unfair, was calculated to scare the whole class from any movement which assailed their means of living, and to confirm the fatal prejudice which had taught them to fancy that their best chance of protection lay in acting as an English garrison.

The land agitation soon assumed enormous proportions. It was supported by vast numbers of farmers who were in many cases sufferers from rack-renting, and who in all cases were led to believe that it would eventuate in making every tenant his own landlord.

The agitation, based on an undoubted grievance and professing to rescue the aggrieved from their oppressors, was unhappily accompanied by a multitude of crimes. For many months the newspapers contained a black record of constantly recurring murders, cruel mutilations of cattle, and destruction of property. I inferred from my conversations with peasants that the perpetrators of these outrages believed that their crimes would promote the interests of the Land League. I had hoped that Mr. Parnell, the leader of the movement, would have strongly and sternly denounced the outrages as horrible offences to Almighty God, injurious to the cause he advocated, and unspeakably disgraceful to the character of the country. He certainly pronounced them to be unnecessary; but this gentle condemnation did not prevent their frequent repetition.

The social frame was dislocated by the Union, which, together with the anti-national influences of the English Church in Ireland, and the heartless greed of individual rack-renters, operated to produce great popular discontent, proneness to conspiracy, reckless impatience of the prevalent misery, and hatred of the English connexion. There were grave faults on all sides. The anti-Irish landlords are largely responsible for the existence of the Land League. They do not like it; but they should remember that it is only a revolt—often, doubtless, criminal in its manifestations—but still a revolt, against their own criminal tyranny.

The social anarchy that overspread the land suggested to some gentlemen of military proclivities the expediency of defending their houses from attack. In a former chapter I have quoted the plan communicated by an OLD SOLDIER to the *Evening Mail*, during the alarm excited by the Fenian conspiracy. A writer who calls himself an EX-FRONTIER MAN, gives his notions on the subject of defence to the *Daily Express* of October 18th, 1881. His letter is worth quoting, as an illustration of the state of insecurity to which eighty-one years of what is called Union had brought Ireland:

" It was mentioned in the *Express* not long ago," says the EX-FRONTIER MAN, " that measures were taken to secure a flank fire from an adjacent stable along the rear, I think, of the house at New Pallas in which it was lately attempted to blow up Captain Lloyd and his party. Captain Lloyd of course knows, but the public in general do not seem to, that for the efficient defence of a building against a musketry attack (artillery is not here supposed to be in question at all) every face should be capable of being swept by the flank fire of the defenders, and this flank fire should be delivered from the main building itself. . . . A quadrilateral enclosure (not necessarily a quadrangle), be it merely a house alone, or a house and walled yard combined, can be defended by the minimum number of men, *i.e.* two."

But the writer does not quite approve of a plan which would expose the defenders to the fire of the assailants. He goes on:

"The best method of protecting them, and at the same time allowing them a full view of the outside of each adjacent wall, is by having projecting, partly circular iron, or, still better, steel turrets built into the corners of the walls, twelve or fifteen feet at least from the ground. These should stand out enough to allow three-fourths of the circle to be outside the walls, and be furnished with narrow loopholes to be closed at will by sliding iron shutters. . . . If I were building a country residence in Ireland for myself, assuredly it should be on the plan here sketched out "

The defence of Dublin Castle was deemed expedient. Cannon (nine-pounders) were planted, fronting the gates that opened on Cork Hill and Dame Street.

In 1799 the friends of the Irish Constitution issued a weekly journal styled the *Anti-Union*. In the 31st number an Address to the Irish Grand Jurors tells them that the Union, "if carried, must make perpetual hostility the wretched inheritance of your unhappy posterity."

How truly events have verified this prophecy!

When the EX-FRONTIER MAN wrote the letter from which I have made extracts, Parnell and some of his supporters had just been imprisoned under the Coercion Act. They issued, from their prison, a manifesto requiring the farmers of Ireland to withhold all rents. The call was made in the following words: "The Executive of the National Land League, forced to abandon the policy of testing the Land Act, feels bound to advise the tenant farmers of Ireland from this time forth to pay no rents under any circumstances to their landlords until the Government relinquishes the existing system of terrorism, and restores the Constitutional rights of the people." The names appended to this document were those of Mr. Parnell and six other notable Land Leaguers. The Archbishop of Cashel was shocked at the reckless anti-rent exhortation, and rose from a sick bed to condemn it. The writers apparently calculated on the general obedience of the tenant farmers to their counsel; but very many tenants tendered what they deemed fair rents to their landlords. Some allowance must be made for the natural irritation of men smarting under the infliction of imprisonment; but they might have recollected that if the Government, as they complained, put in practice a system of terrorism, the progress of the Land League had been accompanied by a system of terrorism that consisted in multitudinous outrages on life and property.

The Government appears to have discovered that no benefit was to be obtained by keeping Parnell in jail. He was accordingly released from Kilmainham on the 6th of May, 1882, and speedily resumed his career of agitation. He soon declared that he would not have taken off his coat to work the land question, unless with the ulterior view of recovering the legislative independence of Ireland. That independence is indeed indispensable to our national life, and I have already expressed my regret that he did not, *ab initio*, concentrate his great abilities on its acquisition. He has now the support of three provinces, and that of more than half Ulster, and his undoubted strength is emphasized by the rage of the Ulster West-Britons.

Meanwhile the condition of Ireland, strangled in the grip of what is termed the sister kingdom, became more and more deplorable. The newspapers constantly recorded large numbers of evictions, and the ceaseless emigration of our people. The present Earl of Derby is reported to have said that it would pay England well to advance a large sum of money—I think a quarter of a million—to be expended in shipping off as many of the Irish race as that expenditure would pay for exporting. His lordship does not think the ordinary operation of the Union drives us out of the country fast enough. Yet he, and those who partake his hostility to our people, may be consoled by the progress of depopulation as recorded by the Registrar-General. The following summary of the Registrar's report is taken from the *Daily News* of the 3rd of April, 1883:

"From the Registrar-General of Ireland's Report we get two remarkable facts—that the efficient working population of Ireland is proportionately 10 per cent. less than in England and Scotland, while the possible mothers are 20 per cent. less. Thus there are very much fewer possible mothers in Ireland than in England and Scotland, and these mothers with their husbands have a much harder task to perform. It is evident from these facts that during the next generation the population of Ireland must diminish at a very rapid rate. Even now the diminution is going on quickly. Thus we find from the Irish Registrar-General's Report for 1881 that, while the excess of births over deaths during the ten years 1871–80 averaged 43,553 per annum, the emigration averaged 62,393 per annum. There was thus a yearly loss of population of nearly 10,000 persons. But in 1881, the excess of births over deaths fell to 35,912, while the emigration rose to 78,417. There was, therefore, a decrease of population of 42,505. Last year the decrease of population exceeded 50,000. In the past two years, consequently, the loss of population exceeded 92,000. As we have already shown, the loss is likely to go on increasing in the future."

The conclusion of the *Daily News* is a striking illustration of the state of a country deprived for eighty-three years of self-government:

"It follows from all this that during the next quarter of a century the decrease in the Irish population promises to be very considerable, while it is equally evident that the paucity of effective workers must stand in the way of developing the resources of the country."

The *Daily Telegraph* of September 12th, 1884, in an article on a paper by M. Kummer, Chief of the Federal Bureau of Statistics at Berne, thus lightly refers to the decay of Ireland after eighty-four years of Union :

" Famine and misery at home, and the prospect of plenty and happiness in new countries, have drained Ireland of many among the best of her people."

Famine and misery at home ! and in a country of natural fertility! Why is this? The *Economist* supplies the answer in the sentence prefixed as a motto to this chapter:

"It is the English people who hold Ireland."

CHAPTER XXXV.

THE QUESTION OF REPEAL EXAMINED.

"Ireland is far too important in itself, and too different in many respects from Great Britain, to allow of its being ruled entirely by the Imperial Parliament. The craving for self-government has become so strong that it cannot be neglected."—RAMSAY's *Political Discourses*, p. 325. Edinburgh, 1838.

"In reality, the central system is nearly allied to despotism, as the local is to liberty; but so far as they can be distinguished, they lend a mutual assistance. As centralisation leads to despotism, so despotism to centralisation; and as love of the soil prompts to self-government, so self-government to love of the soil."—*Ibid.*, p. 343.

"It was idle to talk to Ireland of the word 'Union,' since there could be no such thing as a real Union on an equal footing between two countries so disproportionate and unequal. Could the Irish believe that in this connexion they were to have an equal voice in legislating for England as the English had in legislating for Ireland ? "—*Speech of* RIGHT HON. C. J. FOX, *at the* "*Crown and Anchor,*" 7*th May,* 1800.

I SHALL now attempt an exposition of the great question which, ever since 1800, has kept the minds of the people of Ireland in a state of chronic excitement, and which has now enlisted the solemn attention of Mr. Gladstone's Government.

There is no topic on which such utter ignorance prevails in England as on the Repeal of the Union. There is no political question that has been more systematically misrepresented by almost the whole newspaper press of that kingdom. The prevalent English notion seems to be that Repeal means all sorts of Irish turbulence and riot, mob-domination and universal anarchy; total separation from England and all her "civilising" influences, and a return to antediluvian barbarism. This notion floats vaguely through the English brain; for our British censors are in general content with denouncing our claims with fierceness, or dismissing them with scorn. An impartial examination of the merits of the case appears to be the last thing that occurs to their minds. Repeal has been assailed from the throne. Parliamentary majorities have scouted it. Ministers have declared that a civil war would be preferable to the concession of the measure. And a late reverend divine protested it ought only to be encountered with grape-shot and canister.

Yet, despite this storm of hostility, the Irish people still persevere in their demand; because they know they are in the right, and they know that the success of their just claim is vitally essential to the welfare of their country.

Ireland is sufficiently great to require the exclusive care and attention of a Legislature of her own.

Let us now examine what are the merits of the case for the Repeal of the Union, and the restoration of the Irish Parliament.

The people of Ireland seek to rescind a statute which was passed against the consent of the whole nation—Orangemen and all—and of which the operation was to extinguish their resident Parliament.

From the earliest period of the connexion of the islands under Henry II., the King's Irish subjects enjoyed a Parliament distinct from, and perfectly independent on, the Parliament of England.* Some efforts on the part of England to usurp jurisdiction over the Irish subjects in the reign of King Henry VI., elicited from the Irish Parliament, in the thirty-eighth year of that monarch's reign, a full and unequivocal declaration of its own independence.† That Parliament declared—

* " The statute 2 Richard III. chap. viii., recites as follows : " Que le *Statute de Henry Fitz-Emprice* ' (Henry II.) ' ordeine ponr la eleccion del gouvernor,' etc., had made several regulations for supplying occasional vacancies in that office; it then proceeds to amend the same. Here, therefore, we have an evidence of a purely legislative enactment of primary importance made in Ireland, arranging the executive government itself, and coeval with the supposed conquest of the kingdom."—MONCK MASON'S *Essay on the Constitution and Antiquity of Parliament in Ireland*, p. 3. Dublin, 1820.

† Leland's " History of Ireland," vol. ii. p. 42.

"That Ireland is, and always has been, incorporated within itself by ancient laws and customs, and is only to be governed by such laws as by the Lords and Commons of the land in Parliament assembled have been advised, accepted, affirmed, and proclaimed; that by custom, privilege, and franchise, there has ever been a royal seal peculiar to Ireland, to which alone the subjects are to pay obedience; that this realm hath also its constable and marshal, before whom all appeals are finally determinable; yet, as orders have of late been issued under another seal, and the subjects summoned into England to prosecute their suits before a *foreign* jurisdiction, to the great grievance of the people, and in violation of the rights and franchises of the land; they enact that for the future no persons shall be obliged by any commandment under any other seal than that of Ireland to answer any appeal or any other matter, out of said land; and that no officer to whom such commandment may come shall put the same into execution under penalty of forfeiture of goods and chattels, and 1,000 marks, half to be paid to the King, and the other half to the prosecutor; and further, that all appeals of treason in Ireland shall be determined before the constable and marshal of Ireland, and in no other place."

It is impossible to express more distinctly and unequivocally legislative independence than it is expressed in the language of the Irish Parliament, 38 Henry VI. The reader will observe also, that the statute recites and establishes the fact that our distinct independence was then no new claim, but had existed as of right from the earliest periods: in the words of the Act, "it always had been." It is as explicit on the question of final jurisdiction as Henry Grattan or Daniel O'Connell could be.

It may be objected, firstly, that the Irish Parliament of Henry VI. was the Parliament only of a portion of the Irish people—of that portion which was of English descent, and of those aboriginal Irish who had then combined with the English settlers. I reply, that if the Parliament of a part of the nation had distinct independence, it certainly did not lose that independence by extending its legislative power over the whole island. It surely did not forfeit its rights by enlarging the area of its jurisdiction. It surely did not lose its privileges because it at length embraced within its sway the whole Irish nation. If its independence was distinct and undoubted when it was only the Parliament of a part of the nation, that independence must have necessarily been fortified and strengthened when it rested on the basis of the whole Irish people. Should it be urged that the whole Irish people were never at any time represented in the Irish House of Commons, I reply that at this moment a large majority of the English people are unrepresented in the English Parliament. No argument, therefore, can be drawn from that circumstance against the right of Ireland to self-legislation which will not be equally fatal to the right of the people of England to govern themselves.

It may be objected, secondly, that the authority asserted by the Irish Parliament of Henry VI. was *de facto* set aside by the exercise of English power—by the English Act of the 6th George I. I reply that that Act was a usurpation, and can no more be validly pleaded in bar of the right of Ireland to self-government, than any other usurpation can be pleaded in bar of the rights which it invaded. We might just as well argue against the rights of the English Legislature, because they were to a great extent prostrated by Henry VIII., and encroached on by the First James and the First Charles; or against the rights of the English monarchy, because they were temporarily overthrown by Cromwell. It is sometimes weakly urged against the rights of Ireland that for centuries before the Union the Irish Government was influenced and often controlled by the English and Protestant party. It might with equal force be urged against the right of Englishmen to self-legislation, that the Government of England was for centuries in the hands of the Norman aristocracy.

We have seen the early origin and existence of Irish legislative independence. Our right, in this respect, is at least coeval with the corresponding right enjoyed by our English fellow-subjects. That right was again affirmed at intervals, and finally by the Irish Parliament in 1782, and formally recognised by the British Legislature in 1783 by the Act 23 George III. chap. xxviii. By that British Act the right of the Irish people "to be bound only by laws enacted by His Majesty and the Parliament of Ireland in all cases whatever, and to have all actions and suits at law or in equity which may be instituted in that kingdom decided in His Majesty's courts therein finally and without appeal from thence," was "declared to be established and ascertained for ever; and at no time hereafter to be questioned or questionable."

Thus was the public faith of England solemnly pledged to recognise and respect the free Constitution of Ireland.

The Object of the Union was to rob Ireland.

Before I come to that gross breach of England's public faith entitled the Union, let me quote a few authorities showing the spirit in which the friends of that measure had always contemplated it.

The great object of the Union was to rob Ireland.

So far back as 1699, Sir Richard Cox, an Irishman by birth, but a strenuous supporter of that baleful exotic entitled "the English interest in Ireland," proposed a Union in the following words: "It is your interest to unite and incorporate us with England, for by that means the English interest will always be prevalent here, and the kingdom as secure to you as Wales, or any county in England. *Your taxes will be lessened when we bear part of the burthen. . . . All our money will still centre at London;* and our trade and communication with England will be so considerable that we shall think ourselves at home when there; and where one goes thither now, then ten will go when all our business is transacted in your Parliament, to which, if we send sixty-four knights for our thirty-two counties, ten lords, and six bishops, *they may spend our money, but cannot influence your councils to your disadvantage. . . . By the Union, England will get much of our money, and abundance of our trade.*" *

I believe that no honest Englishman will read the above extract from an *Irish* writer, without a feeling of contemptuous disgust at the unprincipled servility it displays. Sir Richard Cox is the species of Irishman manufactured by English influence in Ireland.

My next proof that the Union was regarded by its friends as a machine to sqeeeze all that could be got out of Ireland, is taken from an English writer on trade, Sir Matthew Decker, who, in 1751, says: "By a Union with Ireland, the taxes of Great Britain will be lessened." †

Another English writer, Postlethwayte, in his book entitled "Britain's Commercial Interest," published in 1767, has the following passage: "By the Union, Ireland would soon be enabled *to pay a million a year towards the taxes of Great Britain. . . .* As England does already possess no inconsiderable share of the lands of Ireland, *so the Union would prove an effectual method to vest the rest in her; for, as*

---

* The above passage is extracted from the autograph correspondence of Sir Richard Cox, in pp. 89 and 90 of the printed catalogue of the Southwell Library, on sale in 1834 by Thomas Thorpe, 38, Bedford Street, Covent Garden, London.

† "Essays on Trade," p. 156.

the riches of Ireland would chiefly return to England, she continuing the seat of empire, the Irish landlords would be little better than tenants to her, for allowing them the privilege of making the best of their estates." *

Dean Tucker, an Englishman, in his proposal for an Union, says: "The inducement of being near the Parliament, the Court, the public funds, etc., would bring many more Irish families to reside here than now do. In short, whatever wealth Ireland would draw from other countries by its produce, manufactures, and happy situation, *all that would eventually centre in England.*"

Doctor Johnson, far more honest than the writers I have quoted, was equally clear-sighted as to the operation of the projected Union. "Do not make an union with us," he said to an Irish friend; "we should unite with you only to rob you. We would have robbed the Scotch if they had anything of which we could have robbed them." †

The spoliation of Ireland was too tempting to be overlooked by Pitt, whose expensive Government taxed to the utmost his financial ingenuity. He had an old grudge, too, against the Irish Parliament, having had a sharp quarrel with that assembly in 1789, respecting the amount of power with which the Prince Regent should be invested during George III.'s illness. He had also another and an older cause of enmity; for, as the editor of the *Annual Register* for 1790 tells us, "the defeat of his commercial propositions in 1785 had left an impression of resentment against the nation on the mind of the Minister." And he was influenced by a sentiment as powerful as any of these motives—namely, that hostility to Irish Constitutional liberty which had for centuries been the invariable characteristic of every English Government.

He laid his plans for the extinction of the Irish Parliament with consummate art. The reader is already aware that the construction of the Irish House of Commons, the large number of close boroughs under the exclusive influence of patrons, seemed to offer a facility for the accomplishment of his design. But even with that advantage it was not an easy matter to persuade a majority in Parliament to vote their own extinction. It was indispensable in the first place to create a state of things that should allow unrestricted operation to the two great instruments upon which Pitt relied—Terror and Corruption.

* Pages 203, 204.
† Boswell's Johnson, *ad ann.* 1779.

I have in a previous chapter sketched the policy adopted by Pitt and his Administration to produce the rebellion of 1798, without which outbreak, and the national weakness it caused, the Government never could have carried the Union.

It is needless here to repeat the details already given of the alternate excitement and depression of the hopes of the Catholics, by which dexterous policy they were kept in a state of political fever. Nor is it necessary to repeat the horrible narrative of tortures, burnings, and wholesale murders, whereby the agents of the Government goaded the people into rebellion. The reader, I presume, recollects that through the agency of the spy, Nicholas Maguan, who was a member of the rebel directory, Government had constant information, which, for about thirteen months prior to the outbreak, would have enabled them at any time to arrest the leaders, and thereby prevent the rebellion from exploding. But the outbreak of the rebellion was considered essential to the success of the Union. It was deemed advisable to scare the Protestant party into a belief that in a Union with England could they alone find protection from the sanguinary violence of the Popish population. It was also considered requisite to terrify the Catholics into thinking that in a Union with England was their only prospect of escaping from the ruthless persecution of their murderous Protestant tyrants. By thus creating an internecine enmity between the two great sections of the Irish people, it was calculated that the national strength would be totally prostrated.

The project succeeded. Troops were poured into Ireland to the number of 137,590.* Martial law was proclaimed. The Habeas Corpus Act was suspended. Sheriffs, in the interest of Government, refused to call meetings to petition against the Union.

The condition into which the Government had brought the nation may be inferred from the following testimonies.

* The Regulars were	32,281
The Militia	26,634
The Yeomanry	51,274
The English Militia	24,201
Artillery	1,500
Commissariat	1,700
Total	137,590

This table is taken from a speech of Lord Castlereagh's, prefacing a motion on military estimates, and contained in a Report of the Parliamentary Proceedings of the 18th February, 1799.

The author of the Memoir of Lord Clare, in the work entitled "Public Characters of 1798," concludes his notice in these words: "Such is now the miserable state of his (Lord Clare's) native land, that any change must be for the better: and if an Union is attended with nothing else *than a cessation of carnage*, every good man must rejoice at the prospect of it."

Lord Castlereagh flattered himself that the Catholics would deem even an Union better than the bloodthirsty system he helped to administer. On the 23rd November, 1798, he writes to William Wickham, Esq.: "There appears no indisposition" (to the Union) "on the part of the leading Catholics; on the contrary, *I believe they will consider any transfer of power from their opponents as a boon.*"

Lord Cornwallis grounds similar hopes on the same state of things. His Excellency writes to General Ross on the 15th November, 1798: "From what I learn, the present mode" (he is speaking of the Union as then projected) "is not likely to be opposed by the Catholics: *they consider any change better than the present system.*"*

Castlereagh and Cornwallis were both mistaken in expecting that the Irish Catholics could be scourged into giving their assent to the Union. "The Catholics still continue against us," writes Castlereagh to the Duke of Portland, 7th January, 1799.†

But the hope expressed that the Catholics would accept the Union as a release from sanguinary local tyranny, is frightfully significant of their wretched condition. What a state must that have been, in which the Viceroy and his secretary expect that the sufferers would consider that any change must be an improvement!

Lord Cornwallis, though determined to carry the Union, was sufficiently humane to regard with horror the ferocity of the troops. On the 1st of July, 1798, he writes to General Ross: "The violence of our friends, and their folly in endeavouring to make it a religious war, added to the ferocity of our troops *who delight in murder*, most powerfully counteract all plans of conciliation." ‡

On the 8th of July he writes to the Duke of Portland: "The Irish militia are totally without discipline; contemptible before the enemy when any serious resistance is

---

* "Cornwallis Correspondence," vol. ii. p. 436.
† "Castlereagh Correspondence," vol. ii. p. 84.
‡ "Cornwallis Correspondence," vol. ii. p. 357.

made to them; but ferocious and cruel in the extreme when any poor wretches, whether with or without arms, come within their power—in short, murder appears to be their favourite pastime."*

The success with which Pitt's policy had lashed party hatred into fury appears by the following description given by Lord Cornwallis to the Duke of Portland of the sentiments held by the leading Protestants of Ireland—the date is 8th July, 1798 : " The principal persons of this country and the members of both Houses of Parliament are in general averse to all acts of clemency; and although they do not express, and are perhaps too much heated to see, the ultimate effects which their violence must produce, would pursue measures that could only terminate in the extirpation of the greater number of the inhabitants, and in the utter destruction of the country. The words Papists and priests are for ever in their mouths, and by their unaccountable policy they would drive four-fifths of the community into irreconcileable rebellion."†

Again, Lord Cornwallis writes to General Ross on the 24th of July, 1798 : " But all this (namely, martial law) is trifling compared to the numberless murders that are hourly committed by our people without any process or examination whatever. The yeomanry are in the style of the loyalists in America, only much more numerous and powerful, and a thousand times more ferocious. These men have saved the country, but they now take the lead in rapine and murder. . . . . The conversation of the principal persons of this country all tends to encourage this system of blood; and the conversation even at my table, where you will suppose I do all I can to prevent it, always turns on hanging, shooting, burning, etc. etc. ; and if a priest has been put to death the greatest joy is expressed by the whole company. So much for Ireland and my wretched situation." ‡

Lord Cornwallis received occasional reproofs from the English Cabinet for being too lenient with the rebels. The yeomanry were chiefly Orangemen,§ and it would appear that His Excellency had been accused of unduly interfering with some of the loyal operations of that body. Against this accusation the Viceroy thus defends himself in a letter to the Duke of Portland, dated 11th of March, 1799 : " Your Grace may be assured that I shall omit no means in my

---

* "Cornwallis Correspondence," vol. ii. p. 359.
† Ibid., p. 360.   ‡ Ibid., p. 371.   § Ibid., vol. iii. p. 89.

power to encourage and animate the whole body of yeomanry to a faithful and active discharge of their duty; but I never can permit them to take advantage of their military situation to pursue their private quarrels and gratify their personal resentments, *or to rob and murder at discretion* any of their fellow-subjects whom they may think proper, on their own authority, to brand with the name of rebels." *

Lord Cornwallis had incurred the wrath of the ascendency party by attempting to restrain the Orangemen from their pastimes of robbery and murder. On the 15th of April, 1799, he gives General Ross the following sketch of the loyal amusements which he deemed it expedient to check: "You write as if you really believed that there was any foundation for all the lies and nonsensical clamour about my lenity. On my arrival in this country I put a stop to the burning of houses and murder of the inhabitants by the yeomen or any other persons who delighted in that amusement, to the flogging for the purpose of extorting confession, and to the free quarters, which comprehended universal rape and robbery throughout the country." †

To put a stop to burning, torture, murder, universal rape and robbery, was, one would suppose, if not a meritorious, at least an excusable exercise of the viceregal authority. But the Viceroy's interference with these amusements of the Orange loyalists provoked the violent indignation of their party. The celebrated champion of Protestant ascendency, Dr. Patrick Duigenan, writes to Lord Castlereagh on the 20th of December, 1798, that the lenity of Lord Cornwallis " has rendered him an object not only of disgust but of abhorrence to every loyal man with whom I have conversed since my return from England." ‡

---

* "Cornwallis Correspondence," vol. iii. p. 167.   † *Ibid.*, p. 74.
‡ "Cornwallis Correspondence," vol. ii. p. 371. That the Orange "loyalists" of our own day have lost none of their ancestral enthusiasm is shown by numerous proofs; among the rest by the riots they provoked in the town of Belfast in the autumn of 1864, which lasted for 14 days, during which nine persons were killed and 176 wounded, and a large amount of property destroyed.—(*Northern Whig*, quoted in *Cork Examiner*, 9th September, 1864.) The pretext of the Orange rioters was, that the Government had not interfered to prevent a large procession and assemblage in Dublin, met to fix a place for the site of the O'Connell Memorial. This was deemed an insult to the Orange party, who avenged their wounded sensibility by getting up an anti-Catholic riot in Belfast. Let us reverse the case, and suppose that in Belfast an Orange gathering had met to mark the ground for a statue of William III. or Dr. Cooke. What would be thought of

To a complaint from Mr. Wickham of Lord Cornwallis's lenity, Lord Castlereagh replies that exclusively of all persons tried at the assizes, Lord Cornwallis had decided personally on 400 cases; that out of 131 condemned to death 81 had been executed; and that 418 persons had been transported or banished in pursuance of the sentence of courts-martial since Lord Cornwallis had arrived in Ireland.*

Considering that the unfortunate people had been deliberately driven to rebel, the amount of capital punishment and transportation recorded by Lord Castlereagh, whose letter is dated 6th of March, 1799, might have satisfied the most exacting loyalist that the imputed clemency of the Viceroy was not excessive. But the punishment inflicted did not satisfy the cravings of "loyal" enthusiasm, unless accompanied with burning, torture, murder, universal rape and robbery.

Lord Cornwallis, who wished to rob Ireland of her Legislature with the least possible effusion of blood, was hard pressed by the sanguinary loyalists. On the 16th of November, 1799, he gives General Ross a description of his difficult position which is of great historical value, not only for the picture it affords of the state of Ireland at the period, but also for the Viceroy's distinct admission that the people had been driven into rebellion by violence and cruelty. Sir Robert Peel denied that fact in the Repeal debate of 1834. The proofs that establish its truth are numerous and conclusive. It is of some importance to include among those proofs the testimony of Lord Cornwallis. "The greatest difficulty," he writes, "which I experience is to control the violence of our loyal friends, who would, if I did not keep the strictest hand upon them, convert the system of martial law (which God knows is of itself bad enough) into a more violent and intolerable tyranny than that of Robespierre. The vilest informers are hunted out from the prisons to attack by the most barefaced perjury the lives of all who are suspected of being, or of having been, disaffected; and, indeed, every Roman Catholic of influence is in great danger. You will have seen by the addresses

---

the Catholics of Dublin if *they* had taken their revenge on the Northerns by getting up a formidable anti-Protestant riot in the metropolis, with a copious show of killed and wounded, and extensive destruction of property ?

* "Cornwallis Correspondence," vol. iii. p. 90. Lord Cornwallis assumed the reins of government on the 20th of June, 1798.

both in the north and south that my attempt to moderate *that violence and cruelty which has once driven, and which, if tolerated, must again soon drive this wretched country into rebellion,* is not reprobated by the voice of the country, although it has appeared so culpable in the eyes of the absentees." *

Of course the atrocities were not all on one side. In Madden's "Lives of the United Irishmen," the reader will find the principal outrages of the insurgents candidly recorded. Their detestable act at Scullabogue, where a number of royalist prisoners, including some Catholics, were burned to death in a barn, merits the execration of mankind.† On the 20th of June, 1798, a party of insurgents slaughtered a crowd of royalists on the bridge of Wexford —the number of the sufferers being estimated at 97 by Sir Richard Musgrave; but by Hay and other authorities at 36. At Vinegar Hill the rebels committed a massacre, the number of their victims being variously stated at 500, at 400, and at 84. And at Enniscorthy a body of insurgents murdered 14 royalists in cold blood. Lord Cornwallis also, in one of the letters from which I have made extracts, speaks of "the feeble outrages, burnings, and murders, which are still committed by the rebels, and these," he says, "serve to keep up the sanguinary disposition on our side."

Let the patriot, or the man of humanity, who shudders at the hideous scenes of carnage which Ireland then presented, bear in mind that Mr. Pitt was solemnly warned by Lord Fitzwilliam in 1795, that the policy he adopted would "raise a flame in the country that nothing short of arms would be able to keep down." But Mr. Pitt chose to disregard the Viceroy's warning. He waded to his object— the Union—through the blood of tens of thousands of the Irish people, reckless of the human lives destroyed; reckless of the national misery created; reckless of the awful guilt which he incurred; reckless of every moral impediment in the way of his grand purpose—the overthrow of that Constitution which had promoted the material prosperity of Ireland to an astonishing extent.

---

* "Cornwallis Correspondence," vol. iii. pp. 144, 145.

† At Wexford, "he (General Lake) caused the hospital that sheltered the sick and wounded of the insurgent army to be set on fire, and, horrible to relate, all the unfortunate inmates were burned to death in the flames that consumed the building."—KAVANAGH's *Insurrection of* 1798, p. 190.

When the insurrection was put down, the nation lay prostrate at the feet of the soldier. The Government deemed the presence of an irresistible military force indispensable to the success of the Union. This is avowed by Lord Castlereagh, who, referring to a project of withdrawing the British militia from Ireland, plainly intimates that with the Union in view, it would be impossible to dispense with their services. In his cold, diplomatic language, he writes to Mr. Wickham on the 22nd of November, 1798 : "Were the British militia to press their recall, there is reason to apprehend that several regiments of Fencibles, who were induced by the same public motive to offer their services in Ireland, would do the same. The alarming effect of withdrawing from this country, where the treason is rather quiescent than abandoned, the flower of its army, at a period when the King's Ministers have in contemplation a great Constitutional settlement, His Grace (the Duke of Portland) will feel. The Lord Lieutenant's opinion decidedly is, that without the force in question it would expose the King's interest in this kingdom to hazard a measure which, however valuable in its future effects, cannot fail in the discussion very seriously to agitate the public mind." And in a postscript Lord Castlereagh adds that he had communicated very fully with Lord Buckingham, by the Viceroy's direction. He says that with respect to the troops "his lordship (Buckingham) saw the importance of their service in the same point of view with the Lord Lieutenant; he went so far as to say that, in his lordship's judgment, *the event of the question of the Union is altogether dependent on their continuance.*"*

And at the very time when a large army was required to force the Union on the Irish people, Mr. Pitt assured the British House of Commons that the national mind of Ireland was in its favour.

While terror reigned throughout the kingdom, corruption soon became paramount within the walls of Parliament. In 1799 a majority of the Irish House of Commons, despite the stupendous exertions of Pitt, had negatived the Union. That Minister employed the recess in redoubling his efforts to bribe and overawe. For the latter purpose it is worthy of note that although the rebellion had been crushed, yet the military force in Ireland was increased.†

---

* "Castlereagh Correspondence," vol. ii. pp. 12, 13, 14.
† In the " Summary Report on the State of the Poor of Ireland,"

With respect to the effort to corrupt, it may suffice to say that every man who had a price was bought. No secrecy was observed upon the subject. Lord Clare, when Attorney-General, had openly said in the House of Commons, "Half-a-million, or more, were expended some years since to break an opposition; the same, or a greater sum, may be necessary now."*

To effect the Union a greater sum *was* necessary. The direct money bribes amounted to one million and a half. In the purchase of boroughs the sum of £1,275,000 was expended. Peerages, judgeships, bishoprics, commands in the army and navy, were profusely showered in reward for Union votes. There were 116 persons in the House of Commons in 1800, holding employments or pensions under Government, and some of these were English and Scotch officers introduced into nomination boroughs by the influence of Government, for the express purpose of voting away a Parliament in whose existence they had no manner of interest.

Yet, notwithstanding the gigantic efforts of the Government to stifle the national voice—notwithstanding the suspension of the Habeas Corpus Act, and the refusal of sheriffs, who had been appointed by the Government in the interest of the Union, to convene meetings of the people to oppose it—the petitions to Parliament against the measure were signed by no less than 707,000 persons, while those in its favour were signed by only 5,000.

But despite the opposition of nearly every human being in the kingdom, except the corrupt band in the pay of the Government, the measure was carried by the joint influence of military violence without, and barefaced bribery within issued in 1830, the military expenditure of several years is stated, and among others the following:

1798	.	.	.	.	£2,227,454
1799	.	.	.	.	3,246,228
1800	.	.	.	.	3,528,800
1801	.	.	.	.	4,021,783

The Union came into operation on the 1st of January, 1801, in which year it may be inferred from the foregoing figures that Pitt deemed an overwhelming military force indispensable to quell the discontent excited by his Union, and to secure the victory he had achieved over Irish Constitutional liberty.

* In "Ireland and Her Agitators," the declaration in question was inadvertently ascribed to Lord Castlereagh. It was uttered by Lord Clare, and quoted by Grattan as uttered by that nobleman in Grattan's "Answer to Lord Clare."

the walls of Parliament. Lord Castlereagh, writing on the 21st of June, 1800, to Mr. Secretary Cooke, on the necessity of keeping a particular promise of patronage, says : " It will be no secret what has been promised, and by what means the Union has been secured. Disappointment will encourage, not prevent, disclosure ; and the only effect of such a proceeding on their part will be to add the weight of their testimony to that of the anti-Unionists in proclaiming the profligacy of the means by which the measure was accomplished."*

Thus, I repeat, was the Union carried. The fraudulent and sanguinary means by which it was inflicted on the Irish people essentially vitiates the whole transaction. It was, and is, a colossal and sanguinary swindle.

It has, indeed, been said that however void and null the Union may originally have been, from the vitiating nature of the means whereby it was achieved, yet the Irish people have given subsequent validity and force to the measure by their own act in sending representatives to the Imperial Parliament. I reply that their act in so doing does not and cannot give moral validity to the Union, simply because it does not indicate free choice. True, they have sent representatives to the English Parliament, just because they had no other Parliament to send them to. Their own Legislature having been suppressed by force, no alternative remained for them except to return members to the British House of Commons. Their act indicates nothing but their reluctant and coerced adoption of a *pis aller*. They have deemed it just preferable to return members to the English senate than not to return them at all. But give them the option of an English or an Irish Parliament, and if they shall prefer the former, why then (but not till then) shall I allow that their act in returning representatives to England gives moral validity to the Union.

It has been urged that to impeach the moral validity of the Union statute is, of necessity, to impeach the legal validity of every statute passed by the United Parliament. Not so. Saurin drew the distinction with accuracy. " You may," said he, " make the Union binding as a law, but you never can make it obligatory on conscience. Resistance to it will be, in the abstract, a duty." The Union is binding as a law—as a bad, oppressive, and iniquitous law. Being

* " Memoirs and Correspondence of Lord Castlereagh," vol. iii. p. 331.

thus legally binding, the statutes enacted under its authority by the United Parliament are also legally binding.

If, however, we should admit the corollary imputed to our doctrine by the Unionists, "that the post-Union statutes are rendered legally invalid by the moral invalidity of the Union," I should turn round upon the Unionists and ask, Whose fault is that? Not ours, surely, who opposed in 1800 the enactment, and who now deprecate the continuance of the Union, the source of the statutory invalidity in question. The fault would rest with those who, by the flagitious suppression of the legislative rights of Ireland, have deprived legislation of validity, and shaken to their base the bulwarks and landmarks of civil society.

The Unionists, unable to deny the infamy of the means by which the Union was effected, allege that the means have nothing to do with the measure; that the measure may be good, although the means used to carry it were indefensible, and so on.

The means have a great deal to do with the measure. They demonstrate two important facts—firstly, the hostility of the people of Ireland to the Union, which could not be achieved without such means. No measure can be good which outrages every wish, sentiment, and principle of the people to whom it is applied. Secondly, the means used to carry the Union demonstrate that the contrivers of the measure were animated with the most deadly hostility to the Irish nation. The men who connived at torture—the men who designedly provoked a rebellion—the men who ruthlessly sacrificed the lives of thousands, and who laboured with demoniac activity to corrupt the senate—were such men our friends? Were they men from whose hands a good measure could possibly emanate? The means they employed afforded a superabundant demonstration of their animus—an animus totally incompatible with friendly intentions to Ireland. The Union was the measure of our enemies, not of our friends.* There is in this fact *primâ facie* evidence that the measure could not have been either intended or calculated to benefit Ireland.

The Union, then, being a gross outrage on Ireland's legislative rights—rights of as ancient a date as the corresponding rights of England; being, moreover, the work of our

* On the 10th of November, 1796, Earl Fitzwilliam wrote to Edmund Burke : " He (Pitt) is determined not to make friends with the Irish."—BURKE'S *Correspondence*, vol. iv. p. 359.

deadliest enemies; being achieved in shameless breach of England's national faith, pledged to us by the 23rd George III., chapter xxviii.; being achieved in defiance of our expressed national will, and by means which it is no exaggeration to term diabolical; this Union has ever since its enactment been opposed with more or less activity by the people of Ireland, who allege that its results on their social condition have been fully as disastrous as might have been expected from the nature of its origin, and the character and purpose of its authors.

They allege that the Imperial Parliament taxes Ireland much more heavily than the native Legislature did, and that the fiscal management of Ireland, resulting from the Union, is grossly dishonest and oppressive. As this part of the subject will be touched in the Appendix, I shall here content myself with a few brief statements.

At the time of the Union the British debt was about sixteen and a half times as large as the Irish debt. To impose equality of taxation on countries whose liabilities were so unequal, would have been a proposition too outrageous even for Pitt and Castlereagh to make directly. On the 5th of January, 1799, Lord Castlereagh forwarded to the Duke of Portland what he called "a short sketch that has been thrown out to feel the public sentiment on the terms" (of Union). From his lordship's sketch I take the following paragraphs:

"DEBTS AND REVENUES.

"The Exchequer of Ireland to continue separate: Great Britain to be responsible for her own debt and its reduction; Ireland to be responsible for her own debt and its reduction.

"The future expenses of Ireland in war and peace to be in a fixed ratio to the expenses of Great Britain.

"When' the revenues of Ireland shall exceed her proportion of expense, the excess to be applied to local purposes. The taxes producing the excess to be taken off." *

This sketch forms the basis of the arrangement which was subsequently incorporated in the Act of Union. I shall only remark on it at present, ·

Firstly, that the Exchequer of Ireland does *not* continue separate; that Great Britain has shuffled off the separate

* "Cornwallis Correspondence," vol. iii. pp. 32, 33.

responsibility for her own pre-Union debt and its reduction, and extorts from Ireland a contribution to the payment of the whole British annual debt-charge.

Secondly, that Lord Castlereagh took care to fix the ratio of Irish and British expenses on a false and exaggerated estimate of Ireland's relative ability. By this clever contrivance, Ireland became entangled in a technical bankruptcy in 1816, of which Great Britain took advantage to abolish separate ratios of contribution, and thereby to mortgage Ireland for the whole British debt, pre-Union as well as post-Union.

Thirdly, Lord Castlereagh promised that the excess of Irish revenue over Irish expense should be applied to local purposes in Ireland. That promise was never performed. He also promised that the taxes producing the excess should be taken off. The mode in which the Imperial Parliament has performed this promise is by increasing Irish taxation fifty-two per cent. since 1853.

Pitt and Castlereagh both said that an income tax would be the best criterion of the quota of expense each country would be able to bear.* But there was not then an income tax in Ireland. That criterion now exists. The property and income of Ireland assessed to income tax in 1869 was returned at £25,992,699. The total assessed property and income of the three kingdoms at the same date was returned at £434,803,957. By this test it appears that in 1869 Ireland had not much more than a seventeenth part of the general wealth of the three kingdoms, while the alien Parliament extorted from us nearly one-tenth part of the general Imperial taxation. The revenue of the three kingdoms for the year ending 31st March, 1870, was, including balances, £78,646,412 12s. 1½d. The Irish revenue, including balances, was at the same time £7,620,622 9s. 6½d. Yet a writer of Mr. J. R. M'Culloch's reputation talks of "the extraordinary favour shown to Ireland in respect of taxation;"† the extraordinary favour consisting in the exaction from Ireland of nearly a tenth part of the Imperial taxes out of scarcely more than a seventeenth part of the Imperial wealth. I do not impute intentional mis-statement to Mr. M'Culloch, who

---

* See "Cornwallis Correspondence" for Pitt's opinion, vol. ii. p. 457.
† "A Descriptive and Statistical Account of the British Empire," by J. R. M'Culloch, Esq. Fourth Edition, revised, vol. ii. p. 239. Longmans, London, 1854.

was probably ignorant of the whole subject on which he expressed his opinion in the words I have quoted from him.

If the Union had not been enacted, we should have long since paid off every shilling of the Irish National Debt, and we should now be one of the least taxed and most prosperous countries in Europe.

Among our greatest fiscal grievances is the absentee drain, chiefly consequent on the Union, and which is believed to have frequently reached the amount of £4,000,000 per annum.

The manufactures of Ireland, once the source of comfortable subsistence to large numbers of her people, have been prostrated by the irresistible competition of great English capitalists who drove the Irish manufacturer out of his native market when the protective influence of a native Legislature was removed. No person now contends that protective duties should be permanent. But they may be indispensable for a time, to guard manufactures in their infancy; and until manufactures acquire sufficient strength to dispense with protection.

The progress of popular liberties in Ireland after 1782 was rapid, until checked by the vigorous interference of England. Had not the Irish Legislature been destroyed, the anti-national Church Establishment would have ceased, at least so far back as 1831, to insult and oppress the Irish people.

The very fact of being governed by laws made in another country has degraded the minds of the Irish aristocracy and gentry. Use has familiarised them with national servitude; and the consequent depravation of their sentiments operates most perniciously on the interests of their country. They have lost that pride of national honour which is the best protector of a nation's prosperity.

The existence of a domestic Parliament in Ireland, enjoying the Constitution established in 1782, produced an increase of national prosperity unexceeded within the same period by any other nation on earth, despite the counteractive force of English influence, administrative corruption, and sectarian intolerance. In proof of this all-important fact we have the evidence of Pitt, Clare, Cooke (the Under-Secretary), Foster, Plunket, Grattan, Jebb (M.P. for Callan), Dillon (M.P. for Mayo), the Dublin Bankers, the Dublin Guild of Merchants, and a host of equally competent witnesses. Plunket thus described the progress of Ireland in his speech delivered 15th of January, 1800 : " Her revenues, trade, and manufactures thriving beyond the hope or the example of any other country of her extent : within these few years advancing with a rapidity astonishing even to herself."

Lord Cornwallis bears his testimony to the daily increasing wealth and prosperity of Ireland in a letter to the Duke of Portland, 28th of January, 1799 : " As the general democratic power of the State," says His Excellency, "*is increasing daily by the general wealth and prosperity*, and as the Catholics form the greater part of the democracy, their power must proportionably increase whilst the kingdoms are separate, and the Irish oligarchy stationary or declining." *

It was not to be tolerated that Ireland, with her Catholic majority, should increase in prosperity and wealth. A stop must be put to such dangerous progress by an Union.

Pitt was of course obliged to varnish his scheme with a pretext of friendship for Ireland. He admitted the prosperity of Ireland; the Union, he said, would increase her prosperity and give it stability. The Union would give Ireland the advantage of a thorough identification with the greatest and wealthiest nation in the world. The Union would cement the affections of England and Ireland by perfectly incorporating their previously separate interests, and thus consolidate the strength and security of the whole Empire.

Let us now see how far the Union has kept the promises of its author; and in this inquiry I shall avail myself of English and Tory authority.

Firstly, touching the prosperity which the Union was to have produced, take the following description from the *Times* newspaper of the 26th of June, 1845 : "The facts of Irish destitution," says the *Times*, " are ridiculously simple. They are almost too commonplace to be told. The people have not enough to eat. They are suffering a real, though an artificial famine. Nature does her duty. The land is fruitful enough. Nor can it fairly be said that man is wanting. The Irishman is disposed to work. In fact, man and nature together do produce abundantly. The island is full and overflowing with human food. But something ever interposes between the hungry mouth and the ample banquet. The famished victim of a mysterious sentence stretches out his hands to the viands which his own industry has placed before his eyes, but no sooner are they touched than they fly. A

---

* " Cornwallis Correspondence," vol. iii. p. 54.

perpetual decree of *sic vos non vobis* condemns him to toil without enjoyment. Social atrophy drains off the vital juices of the nation."

Here, then, was the realisation, in 1845, of Pitt's prediction of Irish prosperity. The potato blight had not at that time commenced. "The famished victim of a mysterious sentence stretches out his hands to the viands which his own industry has placed before his eyes, but no sooner are they touched than they fly." Yes. They fly to pay absentee rents; to pay taxes shipped to England; to pay for English manufactures which have found a market on the ruin of our own; in a word, to pay the gigantic and manifold tribute thus extracted from this kingdom by England. While Ireland possessed her free Constitution, there was no "mysterious sentence" to prevent the producer of food from enjoying the profits of his industry. Can any rational man suppose that if Ireland governed herself, we should behold a famine-stricken people inhabiting "an island full and overflowing with human food"?

Some such light appears to have broken at intervals upon even the dim vision of the *Times*, for in the beginning of September, 1845, I find in another article in that journal the following remarkable admissions: "Whilst it is the fortune —and the good fortune, we will add—of England to import annually a million quarters of foreign corn, *it is the misfortune of Ireland to export what should be the food of her own population.* From Ireland we draw a part of our daily bread. But it is evident how precarious is that dependence. This year, as appears by a return just out, we have imported very much less than in the two previous years, notwithstanding the higher prices. . . . *As Ireland may be truly considered in a perpetual state of famine*, she should rather import from foreign countries than export to us. *Her wheat, barley, and oats are the rents of absentees.*"

I pray the English reader to ponder well this testimony, in connexion with Pitt's hypocritical promises, in 1800, of blessings, and prosperity, and wealth, to be showered upon Ireland by the Union. "Ireland," says the *Times* in 1845, "may be truly considered in a perpetual state of famine." And this, it is to be observed, was before the potato disease had set in; it was in the same year in which the same journal had pronounced that Ireland "was full and overflowing with human food." Just reflect on such a condition of things—a country overflowing with food, yet its people in a perpetual state of famine! It would indeed be miraculous if Ireland were in any other state, while the means which God had given her for the support of her inhabitants were constantly wrung out of her by the Union. Well might the *Times* exclaim: "Social atrophy drains off the vital juices of the nation." That social atrophy is the want of Self-Government.

One more testimony to the realisation of Pitt's Union-prosperity promises: "We cannot," say the Irish Poor Inquiry Commissioners in their Third Report, "estimate the number of persons out of work and in distress, during thirty weeks of the year, at less than 585,000, nor the number of persons dependent on them at less than 1,800,000, making in the whole 2,385,000."

That was the state of affairs in 1836. That would *not* have been the state of affairs in 1836 if the annual produce of Ireland had not been swept off by England as fast as it was produced. That was *not* the condition of the Irish population while Ireland possessed her Constitution of 1782. Manufactures which were then rapidly growing up, would have continued to extend, and to absorb the surplus agricultural hands. The income of the country would have continued to circulate at home among the Irish people, forming innumerable little capitals. There would not have been a perpetual decree of *sic vos non vobis* condemning millions to toil without enjoyment. There would not—there could not have been 2,385,000 destitute paupers out of a population (at that time) of eight millions.

With these evidences of national misery before our eyes, it is at once ludicrous and melancholy to reflect that the pretext upon which the Imperial Parliament rejected O'Connell's motion for Repeal in 1834 was the "giant-stride prosperity of Ireland." Could there be a more conclusive proof of the transcendent ignorance of that Parliament on Irish matters, or of its total incompetence to govern Ireland for the benefit of the country? The "prosperity" of a people "in a perpetual state of famine"! Of a people whose "vital juices are drained by a social atrophy"! Of a people, more than a fourth of whom were at that very time reduced to a state of pauperism for thirty weeks in every year, and whose numbers have since then been enormously thinned by the Imperial plunder that renders their native country incapable of supporting them! Imagine legislation gravely founded on the alleged prosperity of such a people! Who can wonder that the wronged and outraged nation should try to shake loose from this *beau idéal* of legislative ignorance and impudence?

Let us next see whether Pitt's pretext that the Union would cement the affections and incorporate the interests of the countries, was in any respect better founded than his promises of Irish prosperity. On this point I shall again quote from an intelligent Tory authority. "The position of Ireland," says *Fraser's Magazine* for May, 1845, "considered as an integral portion of the British Empire, is a thing quite by itself in the history of nations. Subjects of the same Crown, governed by the same laws, represented in the same Parliament, and partakers in the same free Constitution, the Irish people are as far removed from an amalgamation with the people of England as if the breadth of Europe stood between them, and they were known to each other only by name. Moreover, the sources of alienation lie so deep—they are of such ancient date, and so continually present to the minds of both races, that up to the present moment the best endeavours of Kings, and Ministers, and Parliaments to remove them have availed nothing. . . . Attachment (using that term in its more generous sense) there is, it is to be apprehended, very little between the two countries—certainly none on the Irish side towards their English fellow-subjects."

True—perfectly true. It would indeed be most extraordinary if there were any. Men do not love the spoiler, the robber, the destroyer of their liberties. The attachment of the Irish people is not to be won by the corruption and destruction of their native Legislature, and the wholesale abstraction of their national resources. It is not to be won by the prostration of Ireland from the rank of a kingdom to that of a province; nor by the irritating and insolent intrusion of England into all their domestic concerns. The Union was a crime and a curse—a crime in its perpetration and a curse in its deadly results; and the attachment of a people is not to be won by crimes and curses. Those persons who yet cherish the preposterous fancy that the Union operates as a bond of international affection, should think of *Fraser's* evidence: "Far removed from amalgamation with the people of England." "Deep and ancient alienation of the countries." "No attachment." And is this the mutual love produced by nearly half a century of Union? I think it is much more like dismemberment. I cordially forgive *Fraser* for the nonsense he talks about Kings, and Ministers, and Parliaments trying to heal the international sore, in consideration of the testimony he bears to an important truth—namely, the tried and proved incompetence of the Union to promote good-will, or anything but alienation, between the two countries.

It is, indeed, remarkable that whilst Unionists allege that the dissolution of the Union would infallibly be followed by our total separation from Great Britain, they omit all notice of the tendency of the Union itself to produce separation, by disgusting the Irish people with a connexion whereby they are degraded and impoverished. I admit the advantage to Ireland of connexion with Great Britain; connexion under the same Crown, and with separate Parliaments. But if I deem, as I *do* deem, such a connexion greatly preferable to separation, I also deem separation greatly preferable to the Union. Connexion is a very good thing, but like many other good things it may be purchased at too high a price; and undeniably the destruction of our Parliament is too high a price to pay for British connexion.

A connexion satisfactory to Ireland would be far more likely to endure than one which is the source of perpetual irritation and ill-will. Norway and Sweden afford a happy example of two friendly nations united under the same Crown, and each enjoying its own domestic Parliament. We hear a vast quantity of grave and solemn nonsense about two co-ordinate Parliaments necessarily clashing against each other, and destroying the integrity of the Empire. The problem is practically solved by Sweden and Norway. The collision of the nations was a much more probable event if the one aroused the deadly hatred of the other by destroying her power of self-legislation. True, the overwhelming strength of one of the countries may, in a time of peace, neutralise any attempts on the part of the other to throw off the yoke. But the history of the world is not yet ended. If England does not atone for the Union-crime by restoring to Ireland her Parliament, the latter will, in all probability, be yet the sharpest thorn in her so-called sister's side.

The Unionists allege that the Union, by centralising the legislative power, consolidates and strengthens the Empire. Centralisation, up to a certain point, is indispensable for Imperial integrity and safety. But when it passes that point it becomes despotism; and despotism resembles the brazen statue with the feet of clay. Its strength is corroded, its foundations are undermined by the just dissatisfaction of those portions of the Empire that are the victims of its monopoly of power, of expenditure, and of influence. There is no permanent political health in a State whose extremities are oppressed and despoiled to augment the strength and enhance the grandeur of the centre. Such a political condition is analogous to the state of a human body affected with an overflow of blood at the head or heart, which everyone knows is a state of disease not unfrequently followed by death.

Centralisation, in the shape of Legislative Union, is the source, not of strength, but of weakness—weakness arising from alienated hearts and trampled interests. Local self-government in the several nations which collectively constitute an empire or a republic, affords the best security to the whole against foreign aggression—a security derived from the greater zeal each separate portion must necessarily have in defending those local institutions which are beneficial to each man's local interests, and entwine themselves around his best affections. On the other hand, centralisation, by rendering the inhabitants of the parts at a distance from the centre dissatisfied and discontented, necessarily weakens the outposts of the empire, and thereby renders the provinces vulnerable to the foreign invader. Men will fight better in defence of happy homes than they will in defence of hearths despoiled by the centralising tyranny. Men will fight better in defence of their liberties than they will in defence of their own bondage. They will struggle with a bolder heart and a more stalwart arm in defence of free local institutions prolific of blessings and redolent of nationality, than in support of a system that strikes down their natural rights, and brands them with national inferiority.

Among the pretexts for refusing Repeal which are used by English statesmen, it is insolently urged that English power is indispensably needed to keep a people so divided among themselves as the Irish from absolute anarchy and mutual destruction.

The direct reverse is the fact. English power has been constantly employed, not to allay but to foment our divisions, on the principle of *Divide et Impera;* and the only possible exorcist of the baleful spirit of internal discord is a resident National Legislature, in which all Irish parties would possess a proportional representation; and which would promote the numerous and varied interests which are common to Irishmen of every sect and party.

The divisions existing at the present day in Ireland are analogous to those which existed in England after the Norman Conquest. Take the following description of the latter from Thierry: "The reader," says that historian, " must imagine to himself *two countries ;* the one possessed by Normans, wealthy and exonerated from capitation and other taxes; the other, that is the Saxon, enslaved and oppressed with a land tax; the former full of spacious mansions, of walled and moated castles ; the latter covered with thatched huts and old ruined walls ; this peopled with the prosperous and idle, with soldiers and courtiers, with knights and barons—that with men miserable, and doomed to toil, with peasants and artisans. Lastly, to complete the picture, these two lands are in a manner woven into each other ; they meet at every point, and yet they are more completely separated than if there were seas between them. Each has a language of its own which is strange to the other. French is the Court language used in all the palaces, castles, and mansions, in the abbeys and monasteries, in all the residences of wealth and power ; while the ancient language of the country is only heard at the firesides of the poor and the serfs."

This description, with a few variations of detail, would accurately serve for the Ireland of our own day. How, or why was it, that from the jarring and apparently irreconcilable elements of Norman and Saxon, the great and well-combined English nation of the present day has been formed?

It was because the Conqueror placed the central Government *within*, and *not without*, the realm of England. Had England been ruled then and now by a Government seated in France, we should still see the degrading and disastrous divisions described by the historian existing in pestilent vigour. There would be the National English party, detesting the absentee Legislature ; and there would be the French or Norman party, sustaining the national evil because of some personal profit or class monopoly by which they might be bribed to support it. These parties would cordially hate each other ; and doubtless French statesmen would announce that French intervention and control were indispensably required to keep Englishmen from cutting one another's throats.

But, happily for England, all her governmental institutions were planted upon English ground. There they took root, and there they formed a nucleus around which the descendants of the Saxon, of the Norman, of the Dane, might alike forget their distinctive enmities, and blend, under the shadow of an English Legislature, into one amalgamated people.

This is just what we want in Ireland to terminate our ruinous divisions. A resident Parliament, representing all, accessible to all, and harmonising all into one great national party.

But English Whigs—especially when out of office—interpose with soft and soothing accents : "Give up Repeal, and we will give you full justice in a British Parliament. Did not King, Lords, and Commons in 1834 promise you that every just cause of complaint should be removed? Every British privilege shall be yours ; full equality of rights and franchises ; anything, everything, except an Irish Parliament in College Green."

Yes, everything is promised, except the concession of that ancient indefeasible right which is worth a thousandfold more than all the rest ; I say promised—for the intention to perform is far more than doubtful. But were that intention as sincere and honest as I believe it to be otherwise—were Whigs triumphant in both Houses with their hands full of boons, ready to bestow upon Ireland, still the political equality of Ireland with England under an incorporating Union is thoroughly impossible. It is out of the nature of things. In any distribution of members, England must always have a numerical superiority in a united Legislature, capable of defeating the legislative influence of the whole body of Irish members in questions affecting their own country. This single circumstance must necessarily render a legislative Union of equality impossible. For many years before 1829 a majority of Irish members uniformly supported Emancipation, and that measure was as uniformly rejected by the English Parliament. What equality was there in that? The Coercion Act of 1833 was passed by the London Parliament in defiance of a majority of Irish members. What equality was there in that? The income tax was imposed on Ireland in 1853 against a large majority of Irish votes. What equality was there in that? Again, it is ridiculous to expect that so long as the Union lasts, England will not always continue the residence of the Legislature. That also debars an Union of equality. The seat of Parliament is the centre of power, and will necessarily attract the absentees to London. Your "equality" would still leave Ireland afflicted with an absentee drain, which has been frequently calculated to amount to £4,000,000 per annum. So long as the Union lasts, so long will England (under the name of "the Empire") hold the purse-strings of the Irish nation. What equality is there in that? Equal rights with England under an Union! The thing, I repeat, is totally impossible. Common sense laughs to scorn the flimsy delusion.

Oh, but there is to be a fusion of England and Ireland into one nation—just as Sussex and Kent are identified with each other. This, again, is impossible. A nation, as Burke says, is not merely a geographical arrangement—it is a moral essence. The pregnant experience of the past and of the present—the experience of seven eventful centuries—demonstrates the total impracticability of fusing together the moral essences of England and Ireland. To constitute separate nationhood are required the moral, the historical, the geographical elements. By these elements the special distinctness of Ireland is as clearly marked out as is the distinctness of any other nation in the world. Kent and Sussex may amalgamate. Ireland can no more amalgamate with England than with Holland or with France. In the words of Goold, "Her patent to be a nation, not a shire, comes direct from heaven. The Almighty has, in majestic characters, signed the great charter of our independence. The great Creator of the world has given our beloved country the gigantic outlines of a kingdom. The God of nature never intended that Ireland should be a province."

So spoke Goold, as truly as eloquently. God has stamped on Ireland the indelible character of national distinctness; and the violent and unnatural efforts to counteract His manifest designs, to obliterate the features of her individuality, and to bring her people and her institutions under the control of uncongenial Britain, have resulted in unspeakable disaster and misery.

As to the Whig notion that any conceivable political ameliorations could render the Union endurable, I have already tried to show its absurdity. Name as many good laws as you please; they would surely be as attainable from an Irish Parliament as from an Imperial one. So that, whilst upon the one hand Imperial legislation can give us at best no advantage over home government, on the other hand home government possesses over Imperial the inestimable advantage of home expenditure, home sympathies, the sole control of our national resources and revenues, the exclusion of foreign hands from Irish coffers, and the residence instead of the absenteeship of the great Irish proprietors who follow in the wake of the Legislature. Imperial legislation, even under the most favouring circumstances, would still leave us under the withering influence of absenteeism, of a swindling tax drain, and of the Anglicised, anti-Irish prepossessions and prejudices of our aristocracy; whilst it could not give us one solitary good law that could not be far more readily procured from an Irish Parliament.

I shall now examine some common objections to the Repeal of the Union; availing myself of the language of Mr. Daniel Owen Maddyn, the clever and amusing but superficial author of "Ireland and its Rulers." Mr. Maddyn's arguments are in substance the same as those which have been used by English senators, journalists, and politicians in general. "England," says Mr. Maddyn, "would (in the event of Repeal) cease to be a substantive power, and Europe would be left at the mercy of Russia, France, Austria, and Prussia."

In the name of common sense, we ask, Why? What is there in Repeal to diminish the power of England? The Union at this moment fills the minds of the Irish people at home and in America with rancorous jealousy of England. Does the rancorous jealousy of some millions of the Queen's European subjects conduce to the stability of England's power? Is English power necessarily built on the depression of the Irish people? Is the strength of the Empire dependent on the weakness of one of its constituent nations? On the contrary, the national sense of intolerable wrong inflicted by England upon Ireland in the demolition of her Legislature, is more calculated to perpetuate international animosity and thereby produce Imperial weakness, than a system in which two free Parliaments should provide for the respective wants of the two countries. "A house divided against itself shall not stand;" and the Union promotes and foments the perilous division of the household.

Mr. Maddyn continues as follows: "The Irish Repealers may object that such a consummation (namely, the decrease of England's European influence) should have happened in the last century, previous to the Union, if it were likely to take place again upon its supposed dissolution. But to this and all similar arguments of the Repeal party it is a sufficient political answer to reply, that Ireland had never a free

Parliament till 1782; that within eighteen years the connexion was, three times, all but dissolved—viz., by Flood's Convention for ultra-Reform, by the difference upon the Regency Question in 1789, and by the rebellion in 1798; that Fox and Burke, while yielding to an Irish army, led by an Irish aristocracy, considered that Grattan's revolution was most calamitous to England; and that Pitt, in the very outset of his parliamentary life, resolved on the measure of an Union and the extinction of the Irish Parliament, from his sagacious foresight of the probable results of two Legislatures in one Empire."

"Ireland had never a free Parliament until 1782." This assertion is, in Mr. Maddyn's sense, unfounded. We have already seen the Irish Parliament in 1460 affirming, not only its own independence on England, but that of all previous Parliaments from the days of Henry II. In another sense, however, Mr. Maddyn is correct; that is, if he means to imply that the imperfect construction of the unreformed Irish House of Commons left it, as the English Parliament from a like cause was also left, open to corrupt Court influence. In this sense it is true that even the Irish Parliament of 1782 was not free enough; that it was not based on a representation sufficiently extensive; that too large a portion of the Lower House represented, not the people, but the patrons of boroughs. It may be said that the Irish Parliament was only the more easily managed on that account. Perhaps so. But that species of management, like all other international dishonesty, incurred the strong risk of defeating its own object; and instead of binding the two countries together in the solid, lasting bonds of full, free justice and fair play, it tended to exacerbate the victimised nation, and to create a store of rankling hatred, fraught with eventual danger to the Empire. The Repealers believe that heartfelt international amity and consequent Imperial safety can alone co-exist with a truly free and popular Irish Legislature; one which will do justice to the Irish people, and be placed beyond the reach of all corrupt management.

Let me here notice a fallacy commonly put forward by the Unionists. They say: "As long as you had a Parliament, its utility was obstructed and its members were corrupted by English influence. Therefore an Union was indispensable to correct the evils resulting from such a state of things."

It is true that the unreformed Irish Parliament was exposed to pernicious English influence. The natural and rational course would have been to get rid of that influence instead of getting rid of the Parliament. But what is the remedy of the sagacious Unionists? Why, truly, to increase the disease. That disease, they themselves allege, was the English influence then partially operating through channels of parliamentary corruption. What is their cure? To render the same mischievous influence dominant, paramount. To render it perpetual and resistless. It was, they say, pernicious, even when counteracted by the occasional virtue or the national interests of an Irish Legislature. And yet they would have us believe that it becomes innocuous when that counteractive power is extinct, and when no check exists to its detrimental operation.

I come back to Mr. Maddyn. He blunders in his assertion that within eighteen years from 1782 the connexion of the countries was three times all but dissolved. Flood's fellow-conventionists were totally incompetent to effect separation from England, even had they desired it. And a very small minority of them did desire it.* In truth, the parliamentary reform for which they struggled, would, if successful, have satisfied their utmost aspirations. It is absurd as well as false to represent their efforts to reform the Parliament as in the slightest degree endangering the connexion of the kingdoms.

It is also false that the difference upon the Regency Question in 1789 "all but dissolved the connexion of the countries." Both Parliaments concurred in their choice of the Prince of Wales as Regent during the King's illness, and thus the identity of the regal power was secured. The Irish Parliament invested the Regent with full royal prerogatives, whilst the British senate, influenced by Pitt, placed some restrictions on his powers. The party who supported the popular view in the Irish Commons were as warmly attached to British connexion as was their leader, Grattan. The theoretic danger arising from a possible difference in choosing the Regent might have easily been provided against by a law enacting that whoever at any time might be Regent in England should also be Regent in Ireland. A Bill to that effect was brought into the Irish Parliament by the Right Hon. James Fitzgerald, and—thrown out by the Government.

Mr. Maddyn's assertion that the rebellion of 1798 was n any degree ascribable to the existence of a resident

* Flood himself was one of the few conventionists who desired separation.

Parliament, is a curious instance of the slapdash hardihood with which a clever writer will sometimes lucubrate on topics he knows little or nothing about. Mr. Maddyn makes no attempt tó demonstrate any connexion between the rebellion and the residence of the senate. To attribute the rebellion to the Irish Constitution of 1782 is a monstrous falsification of history. The Government deliberately lashed, goaded, shot, tortured the people into insurrection against their intolerable tyranny, with the view of creating a condition of national paralysis which would render possible the suppression of the national Parliament.

The Irish Parliament of 1798 was eminently devoted to British connexion. Foster, in his splendid anti-Union speech of the 11th of April, 1799, boasted that that Parliament put down the insurrection. The stimulants to rebel were to be found, not in the residence of the Legislature, but in the ample provocatives administered to the people by the Government.

The convulsive throes of revolutionary France then agitated Europe. Wild spirits—chiefly Protestant—amongst the Irish middle classes, first caught the contagion of French principles and preached up rebellion in their secret conclaves, when they found it impossible to obtain the parliamentary reform which at one time would have satisfied their desires. They unfortunately found in the hearts of the Irish peasantry a soil well prepared to receive the seed they scattered. England had prepared the soil for the reception of that seed. Persecution had taught the Irish of that day to seize on any project that held out a hope of deliverance from their tyrants.

Mr. Maddyn next asserts that "The character of England would be ruined by consenting to such a measure (as the Repeal). Her reputation for sagacity and political ability would be destroyed; her fame would vanish."

It may be asked how her character and fame would suffer by the mere performance of an act of justice; which act would remove from the Empire a dangerous source of weakness—possibly of eventual disruption.

He continues: "Her material interests would share the same ruin as her moral power. As in individuals, so in nations, character is the creator of national rank and wealth in the social scale."

Undoubtedly. But again, Mr. Maddyn does not show how England's character would be compromised by simply undoing an intolerable national wrong, and by recurring to a system precisely analogous to that which she instructed her ambassador, Lord Minto, to negotiate in the instance of Sicily and Naples.

Mr. Maddyn goes on: "It (the Repeal) would rob England of a large home market for her manufactures, for of course an Irish Parliament would adopt the political economy of the national school, and pass a tariff hostile to English manufactures. In so doing, it would not merely cut off from England a large portion of her home trade, *but it would also set up a rival trader at her very side.*"

So, then, the Repeal of the Union is resisted on the express and avowed ground that it would resuscitate the manufactures of Ireland which the Union had destroyed. Pitt, to be sure, had said fine things about the marvellous increase of Irish trade and manufactures to be effected by the Union; but here we have an Unionist, and an Irishman to boot, apprehensive lest the restoration of the Irish Parliament should wake up Irish manufactures from the torpor of death, and erect the Irish trader into a rival of the Englishman.

Now, if Mr. Maddyn be right—and I am sure that he is —in suggesting in the above-quoted slavish paragraph, that the Union has operated to extinguish Irish manufactures and to throw the monopoly of the Irish market into the hands of British manufacturers, it necessarily follows that violent hostility to England must be excited in the breasts of those who feel themselves sacrificed to the competition of the English trader. Mr. Maddyn, however, startles us with the discovery that it is not in any such causes that hostility lurks, but in the Repeal; which measure, he proceeds to say, " would be creating a hostile country whose emigrants swarm in the British colonies ; all of whom would be ready to act in concert with the Irish rulers at College Green."

But he does not explain how an act of great national restitution could excite the hostility of the people whose goods it would restore to them. His notion is as irrational as it would be to suppose that you excite the enmity of your creditors by paying your debts. Their enmity would be much more probably aroused by the refusal of payment. He might have learned to think more accurately if he had read the letters addressed to the Repeal Association by Irish emigrants in America and the Colonies. Their communications overflowed with hostility to English injustice. The Irish in America at present teach a similar lesson. Mr.

Maddyn should have asked himself from which of two causes would Irish hostility to England more probably proceed—from the jealousy that crushed a Legislature, and has starved out the Irish manufacturer; or the frank and honourable, although tardy justice, that would restore the Parliament, and adopt as its motto, *suum cuique?* In truth, there is no fallacy more common than to predict, as prospective evils to result from Repeal, the very hostility and jealousy existing at the present moment, and of which the Union itself is the real cause.

The fear that the Repeal of the Union would deprive England of a profitable commercial intercourse with Ireland, is as foolish as it is unfounded. A similar fear was entertained by the British merchants who in 1776 believed that the American revolt would destroy their trade with the American colonies. But their trade, instead of being destroyed, expanded into proportions commensurate with the increased vitality and energy acquired by America from her independence. Mr. Herman Merivale, in his work on Colonisation,* asks whether the English trade with America suffered by the severance of the American colonies from England, and their establishment as a Republic?

"All the world knows," he says, "on the contrary, that the commerce between the mother country and the colony was but a peddling traffic, compared to that vast international intercourse, the greatest the world has ever known, which grew up between them when they had exchanged the tie of subjection for that of equality;" equality, which, as Mr. Merivale says in the words of a Greek poet, is "the surest bond between friends, between states, and between allies." †

Again, Mr. Goldwin Smith, advocating the concession of independence to the Colonies, contends that their trade with England would in no way suffer by the concession. "Rather," he says, "it would increase, and they would become more active producers and customers, *since independence sends life through all the veins of a nation.* The rivulet of trade which ran between England and her American Colonies before they became independent, swelled, from the moment when they became independent, to a current as mighty as the Gulf Stream flowing between shore and shore." ‡

This example should lead English merchants to inquire whether the dishonest profits derived from monopolising the

---

* Cited in "The Empire," 1863, by Goldwin Smith, p. 25.
† "The Empire," p. 25.   ‡ *Ibid.* p. 132.

manufacture markets of plundered and impoverished Ireland, would not be greatly exceeded by the commercial gain of having in Ireland a prosperous and wealthy neighbour.

Mr. Maddyn next alleges, as a result of Repeal, that "the difficulty of maintaining a standing army would be increased considerably. Even if Irish soldiers enlisted in the British ranks, upon any collision with Ireland they would probably desert, and start up against the 'Saxons.' The loyalty of a large portion of the army would be doubtful, and the vast Indian Empire, and the Colonies, would probably be left exposed for want of troops."

I might argue that here again Mr. Maddyn suggests difficulties as probably resulting from Repeal, which are a great deal more likely to result from the Union. But it needs not. English policy has hunted the human material of war out of the country. "The Celts are gone with a vengeance." "Ireland will be henceforth the fruitful mother of herds and flocks." Such have been the boasts of English politicians. Ireland is not at present a fruitful mother of recruits; and as they are not forthcoming, it is scarcely worth while to speculate on what their probable conduct would be if they were among us as of old.

Again—Mr. Maddyn fears that "The funds would be very liberally spunged, for of course Ireland, when separate, would not consent to be held responsible for debts which she never contracted."

In the name of common honesty, why should she? It is painful to contrast such slavish lucubrations as these with Pitt's hypocritical disclaimer in 1799 of all desire to grasp our financial resources for British purposes.

Let me now sum up. Ireland demands the Repeal:

1. Because self-legislation is her indefeasible right. She has never surrendered that right.

2. Because self-legislation, even though accompanied with the serious drawbacks of a most corrupt borough system and Catholic disability, conferred great and increasing prosperity on Ireland from 1782 until the Union.

3. Because the Union is the undoubted product of bloodshed and corruption, and the inherent vices of its origin send their poison through every vein of the Irish body-politic. While the people were butchered into an incapacity of effective resistance, a corrupt parliamentary majority were bribed to sell what was not theirs to sell—the

Constitution of their country.* We were robbed of our property—the Constitution—by the most infamous means—the only means, in fact, which could be employed for such a purpose; and we now demand the restoration of the stolen goods.

4. Because the destruction of our national Constitution has covered the land with decay, and has produced unspeakable suffering among its inhabitants.

5. Because Ireland is truly desirous that the integrity of the Empire should be preserved on such terms as will not involve her own degradation and the ruinous plunder of her people.

The Union imperils the integrity of the Empire by holding out the strong lure to foreign invasion which is furnished by the just discontent of Ireland. Foreign invasion were indeed an affliction of great magnitude. But the Union is also an affliction of colossal magnitude—an affliction so great that it may easily render even foreign conquest a mere question in the minds of many between one species of tyranny and another. Samson, in his thirst for vengeance, pulled down the house to crush his foes, rejoicing in the deed that overwhelmed them, even although he was himself included in their ruin. Tyranny has often merged the instinct of self-preservation in the burning desire to punish the tyrant.

But—give to the Irish people an Irish Parliament to defend, and then let the foe invade our shores—he will be met with the stout arms and intrepid hearts of a gallant people, fortified and inspired by the resistless, the ennobling influences of triumphant nationality. Give to the Irish that strong interest in repelling invasion which local institutions and domestic government alone can give them. Restore to them their national Constitution, and they will feel that they have something really worth defending. It needs no words to prove that men will fight more readily to protect a domestic Legislature that gratifies the national pride and keeps the national wealth at home, than a system of absentee legislation that is in itself an insult, that drains the country of its wealth, and beggars multitudes of its inhabitants.

British connexion with two Legislatures is preferable to separation ; but separation would be a better thing than the destruction of the Irish Parliament.

There seems no reason why Ireland should not flourish in

* "The Constitution of Ireland is the indisputable property of the nation, and not of its Parliament."—*Anti-Union*, 1799, p. 22.

a separate existence as well as Sweden, Portugal, Denmark, Holland, Belgium—countries all naturally her inferiors in the qualities and resources that entitle a nation to self-government. But there is every reason why Ireland, possessing a fertile soil, capacious estuaries, a first-rate situation for commerce, a brave and intelligent people, should find absolute and separate independence incomparably preferable to a legislative Union which cripples her powers, absorbs her resources for the benefit of England, and acts as a social and political blister—draining and irritating.

An Englishman may easily test the capacity of the Union to attach Irishmen to British connexion, by asking himself the question, whether he would submit to a political alliance with any land on earth that involved the destruction of the English Parliament, or which deprived the English nation of self-government?

It is to be deplored that England, with her ample means of securing our attachment by the simple justice of Repeal, should yet prefer to perpetuate our hostility by refusing us that justice. I am no blind anti-English bigot. For estimable individual Englishmen I entertain warm regard and deep respect. I can recognise the many claims of England to our admiration—would that she could enable me to add, our affection! In the sixteenth century my paternal ancestors were English,* and a sentiment not wholly dissimilar from filial reverence will sometimes steal over my mind when I think that for many centuries my forefathers belonged to that land, so full of glorious monuments of all that can exalt and dignify the human race, rich with memories of martial valour and pacific wisdom, famed for the splendid pre-eminence in arts and arms of her mighty sons, covered over with her stately old ancestral dwellings, adorned with majestic churches and cathedrals—the venerable records of the piety that once distinguished her inhabitants. Even an Irish Repealer may experience a momentary thrill of pride when he thinks of his remote connexion with a country possessing such claims on the world's admiration; but the sentiment is quickly banished by the wrongs that England's crimes have inflicted upon that far dearer land in which his first breath was drawn, with which his fondest affections are identified, and of which God's providence has made him a citizen.

England—England! why *will* you compel our reluctant detestation?

* They had, in a previous century, been French.

CHAPTER XXXVI.

THE GLADSTONIAN FRANCHISE—HOME RULE PROPOSED.

On the opening of Parliament in February, 1884, Her Majesty's Speech congratulated the Legislature on the improved condition of Ireland. The alleged improvement was unfortunately imperceptible to the Irish people; for a return then recently issued set forth that in the decade ending in 1881 more than half a million of acres in Ireland had gone out of cultivation; and that during that decade the decrease in cattle was 19,777, and in sheep 977,250. The outflow of the people was continuous, and the great decrease of tillage was the natural result of the exodus. The hands that had tilled the land were now in America.

During the year the Nationalist agitation was actively carried on. Mr. Gladstone had stated that there was no moral force behind the Government. Accordingly Lord Rossmore, in order to supply the Government with moral force, led bodies of armed Orangemen to attack the Nationalists. Earl Spencer was then Viceroy, and as he disapproved of the Orange idea of moral force thus exemplified, he dismissed Lord Rossmore from the magistracy. It may give the English reader some idea of the sort of intelligence which characterises Irish Tory magistrates, to learn that a large number of their body signed a declaration of sympathy with Lord Rossmore, and condemned his dismissal. They deemed that his breach of the peace did not at all disqualify him from holding the commission of the peace. There was also some talk of a subscription to console the fallen hero, but it did not take a practical shape.

During the years 1883 and 1884, the extension of the parliamentary franchise was hotly agitated. The Irish Tory leaders, conscious that they had no claim on the confidence of their countrymen, worked hard to obtain a reduction in the number of Irish parliamentary representatives. They argued that the great decrease of the relative proportion of the Irish to the British population since the Union should be accompanied by a corresponding decrease in the number of members sent by Ireland to Westminster. The Union had operated to banish vast numbers of the people by abstracting their means of support, and the great depopulation thus caused was employed as a good and sufficient argument for striking off a fifth or a fourth from our parliamentary representation. Mr. Gladstone effectively combated this project. He reminded its advocates that at a time when the Irish population bore to the British a far larger proportion than at present, they had never demanded an increase of the Irish parliamentary contingent on that account; and he would not now allow that the altered proportions afforded any reason for lessening the number of the Irish members.

The extended franchise was accompanied with a redistribution of the electoral districts. As the Tories had failed to obtain a reduction of the number of Irish members, they devoted their energies to the task of so arranging the electoral boundaries as to limit the benefit which the Nationalist electors might derive from the recent enlargement of the franchise. The mode in which the Boundaries Commissioners occasionally acted in the Tory interest may be learned from the following instance:

In Down there is a district in which the majority is Nationalist. The only mode of preventing that district from returning a Home Ruler to Parliament was to divide it among contiguous Orange and Whig districts, or to unite it in its entirety with a large Orange or Whig division with which it has no natural connexion. This last plan was adopted by the Boundaries Commissioners, although a chain of mountains separates the National from the anti-National portion of Down.*

But notwithstanding this exercise of Tory dexterity, notwithstanding also the vociferous boast that Ulster was "solid for the Union," the result of the new franchise—the power which it conferred on the people to declare their real sentiments—appeared in a Nationalist majority of the members for the Ulster constituencies. Seventeen Home Rulers were returned against sixteen Unionists; and the Home Rule majority in our northern province would have been greater if it were not for the mode in which the electoral divisions were manipulated by the Boundaries Commissioners. Two great Orange strongholds, Derry and Belfast, are now represented by Home Rulers; Derry by Mr. M'Carthy, and West Belfast by Mr. Sexton. The Nationalists have frequently expressed their desire that the political sentiments of Ulster could be tested by a *plébiscite;* confident that such a test would reveal an enormous majority

* *Nation*, 27th December, 1884.

of Home Rulers in the Ulster population. The result of the General Election gave Mr. Parnell a party of eighty-six members, of whom eighty-five were returned from Ireland, and one from Liverpool.

In the spring of 1885 the Archiepiscopal See of Dublin became vacant by the death of Cardinal M'Cabe. There were intrigues, in the interest of the English Government, to obtain the appointment of an anti-national, or unnational, successor to the deceased prelate. The Catholics of Ireland, clerical and lay, were well aware of the injury to religion which would result from the appointment of a spaniel bishop, and they consequently felt anxious to defeat the conspiracy that seemed to threaten them with such a calamity. In a previous chapter* I have briefly adverted to the question of the veto, and to the successful efforts of O'Connell in 1813 to defeat the attempt of the Government to obtain an influential voice in Irish Catholic episcopal appointments. The Government, many years ago, had tried to induce the Pope to withhold his sanction from the appointment of the late Dr. Machale to the Archiepiscopal See of Tuam; their agent, Mr. Seymour, requested his Holiness to appoint "anybody but him." The appeal was disregarded, and Dr. Machale assumed the crozier, greatly to the advantage of the cause of religion and of the kindred cause of nationality, within the sphere of his extensive jurisdiction.

The agent who is generally credited with the management of the recent attempt to provide a Castle bishop for the See of Dublin is Mr. Errington, who, for his services in that regard, has been honoured with a baronetcy. The editor of *United Ireland* published a letter which had somehow fallen into his hands, in which Mr. Errington gives an amusingly complaisant account of his own diplomacy. The reader will smile at the free-and-easy way in which this diplomatist speaks of his ability to keep the Pope "in good humour," and of the "strong pressure" on his Holiness which he claims to be able to exercise. Here is his letter to Lord Granville:

"House of Commons, 15th *of May*, 1885.

"DEAR LORD GRANVILLE,

"The Dublin Archbishopric being still undecided, I must continue to keep the Vatican in good humour about you, and keep up communication with them generally as much as possible. I am almost ashamed to trouble you

* Chap. vii.

again as you are so busy; but perhaps on Monday you would allow me to show you the letter I propose to write. This premature report about Dr. Moran will cause increased pressure to be put on the Pope, and create many fresh difficulties. The matter, therefore, must be most carefully watched, so that *the strong pressure I can still command* may be used at the right moment, and not unnecessarily (for too much pressure is quite as dangerous as too little). To effect this, constant communication with Rome is necessary.

"I am, dear Lord Granville,
"Faithfully yours,
"GEORGE ERRINGTON."

Doubtless Mr. Errington deemed this letter a masterpiece of diplomatic art. We admire the exquisite discretion with which he will relax or increase the necessary pressure on the Vatican according to circumstances; keeping his powerful forces under due control until the right moment shall arrive to spring them on the Pope! and carefully watching for that moment. Twice in his letter he suggests the importance of his constant intervention, impressing on Lord Granville the necessity of keeping up perpetual communication with Rome. In addition to his other invaluable services he has composed, or proposed, a letter doubtless calculated to bring his agency to a triumphant issue, which letter he wishes to submit to Lord Granville. But although this astucious agent could command "strong pressure," and could, as he fancied, tickle the Vatican into "good humour," yet his dexterity failed to procure the appointment of an episcopal policeman to the English Government. The Pope, conceiving that the clergy of the archdiocese were better judges than Mr. Errington or his employers of the person best fitted to rule them, wisely sanctioned their choice of Dr. Walsh, whose appointment was hailed with satisfaction by every Catholic lover of his creed and his country.

As the year advanced, there were increasing rumours that Mr. Gladstone had given favourable consideration to some measure of self-government for Ireland. What that measure was to be, what shape it should assume, to what extent it would restore the right of which Ireland was basely deprived in 1800—these were questions anxiously debated by every class of politicians. A published letter of Mr. Herbert Gladstone seemed to foreshadow a very liberal concession, and excited the alarm of the domestic enemies of Irish legislative independence. An association was formed to sustain the Union; it was styled *The Irish Loyal and Patriotic Union;* and the utterances of its orators betrayed a craven fear of the enmity of their own countrymen. At one of their meetings in October, 1885, Lord Carysfort is reported to have said that "he thought they would all admit that the minority in Ireland must look to English support if they wished to hold their own at all."

What a shameful confession! The minority in Ireland, according to the noble speaker, must have scandalously failed in their duties, since external help is needed to protect them against the people by whom they are surrounded.

Again, these friends of the legislative Union thus describe the condition of Ireland under that Union: "Life," said the Earl of Meath, "was insecure, property was insecure; individual liberty was abolished." His lordship is reported to have also said: "They must realise that they must fight for their lives and their properties at great odds."

And this in the 86th year of the Union! So that English legislation after more than three-quarters of a century has failed to rescue its Irish supporters from a state of perpetual siege. The evils of such a condition are all their own fault. Will they not ask themselves whether they would not occupy a place of strength and honour by acting as Irishmen, by leading their countrymen in the noble effort to recover domestic legislation, instead of sustaining that alien rule under which, according to their own account, their state is one of chronic terror and perpetual disaster? The weakness of the Irish minority is the direct result of their estrangement from the Irish majority. It is the direct result of their false and unnatural policy of holding down Ireland for the benefit of England. Opposed to Irish rights they are necessarily weak. They are blind to the true source of their strength—identification with the great mass of their own nation.

The increased importation of foreign corn and cattle acted against the capacity of Irish farmers to pay rent on the same scale as when prices were more remunerative. The landlords, good and bad, were in general reduced to severe difficulty. Among their difficulties was the merciless extortion of the tithe rent-charge. If the reader will turn back to the tenth chapter of this History, he will there find that the Act of 1869, which disestablished the English Church in Ireland, preserved the tithe rent-charge intact for fifty-two years from the date of a certain transaction called "purchase." I have, in that chapter, described the obstacles opposed to the ultimate expiry of the impost.

In 1883 the grievance, always oppressive, had reached an acute stage. So long as the landlords received a considerable portion of their rents, although *not* the addition to their rents intended by the Act of 1838 to cover the tithe rent-charge, they had gone on paying that tax with tolerable regularity. But the vast shrinkage of rents in 1883 deprived them, not only of the means to pay tithe rent-charge, but also, in numerous instances, of the means for the ordinary support of their families. Yet the Commissioners of Church Temporalities issue writs all over the kingdom to recover the tax from defaulting landlords, whose default had arisen from the simple fact that they had not got the money.

Where the landlord cannot contrive to meet the extortion from some other source than unpaid rents, the Commissioners place a receiver on his property to recover the arrears of tithe rent-charge which have accumulated from the great agricultural collapse, and from the consequent inability of the landlords to pay the tax. The iniquity of this procedure is increased by the fact that the tax is computed on a scale of prices for corn which cannot now be realised. Prior to Disestablishment the tithe-tax was liable to septennial revision, rising or falling with the fluctuating prices of corn as published in the *Dublin Gazette.* Shortly after Disestablishment it became pretty certain that the market value of all cereal produce would permanently fall, from the great and increasing facilities of foreign importation. Accordingly Parliament, in order to deprive the payers of tithe-tax of the benefit of the fall, passed the Act 35 and 36 Victoria, c. xc., by which the right of septennial revision is abolished, and the tax is permanently fixed on the obsolete rate of now unattainable corn prices.

Although the sole source of payment provided by the Act of 1838 has disappeared, yet the Commissioners proceed to extort the amount of the tax from whatever else they can lay their hands on. They demand the tax from non-existent means, calculated on an impossible scale of corn prices. The amount of arrears of tithe rent-charge had reached, at the commencement of this year, 1887, £204,102.

The plain statement of this grievance is a record of oppressive and impudent dishonesty. Our rulers, who did not hesitate to squander millions in unprofitable foreign wars, should not grudge whatever sum may be needed to buy out the Irish tithe rent-charge.

The Government, since 1871, have been receiving the whole income of the Disestablished Church. This must have gone a good way to recoup the Treasury for the advances made to compensate the disestablished clergy. I do not know how the account stands between the Treasury and the Commissioners ; but it seems probable that the balance yet remaining unpaid of their advances cannot be more than a third, perhaps a fourth, of the sum advanced in 1834 to compensate the West India planters for their losses by the abolition of the slave trade.

I have elsewhere remarked that West Indian negroes were not asked to pay for their emancipation from slavery ; the Irish landlords *are* forced to pay for their emancipation from State Churchism. Parliament has abolished the fund for the payment of the tithe-tax, and as a matter of plain justice it should also abolish the tax.

The fiscal accompaniments of Disestablishment have severely scourged the unlucky tithe-payers.

As time went on, public anxiety became more and more excited by Mr. Gladstone's expected proposal of Home Rule. It was known that he had formulated a scheme to be laid before Parliament, and every repealer of the Union hoped that the approaching bill would restore to Ireland—at least in a great measure—her inalienable right to make her own laws. It was encouraging to find that a statesman of vast ability and influence had discovered that the Union was a monstrous crime, and was not afraid to announce his discovery. It had been habitual with English politicians to treat it as a compact. Lord Salisbury called it a fundamental law ; bestowing that designation on a measure which broke the solemn compact by which England in 1783 stood pledged to respect the free constitution of this kingdom.

The leading principle of the Union is the subjugation and robbery of Ireland. The results are horrible disorder, chronic disloyalty, and the expulsion of millions of our people. The Union was forced on Ireland by our old hereditary foe—a foe who hated us with the accumulated venom of six centuries. We eagerly awaited Mr. Gladstone's exposition of the mode in which he proposed to deal with this great legislative crime.

On the 8th of April, 1886, Mr. Gladstone rose to place before the House and the Empire his plan for changing historical enmity into permanent friendship. His speech well sustained his reputation for splendid eloquence and argumentative power.

He reviewed the condition of Ireland since the Union; showed the total failure of coercive legislation to produce respect for law and social order; and ascribed the want of popular confidence in the administration of law in Ireland to the fact that the mainspring of law is felt by the people to be English, not Irish. To remedy this great national evil he proposed to restore to Ireland autonomy.

He insisted that the concession which he proposed would confirm Imperial unity instead of impairing it. He dwelt with much force on the examples of Sweden and Norway, governed by one king, but each country possessing its own Legislature. "And yet," he said, "with two countries so united, what has been the effect? Not discord, not convulsions, not danger to peace, not hatred, not aversion, but a constantly growing sympathy."

He also took the case of Austria and Hungary.

"At Vienna sits the Parliament of the Austrian Monarchy; at Buda-Pesth sits the Parliament of the Hungarian Crown; and that is the state of things which was established, I think, nearly twenty years ago. I ask all those who hear me whether there is one among them who doubts? Whether or not the condition of Austria be at this moment, or be not, perfectly solid, secure, and harmonious?"

Mr. Gladstone contended that these examples bore him out in asserting that the international harmony of England and Ireland would be secured, not disturbed, by the establishment in Dublin of an Irish Legislature for the conduct of both legislation and administration for Irish as distinct from Imperial affairs.

He proposed the exclusion of Irish representatives from the English Parliament. In my humble opinion, their exclusion would meet with nearly universal approval in Ireland. Our experience of the English Parliament is an experience of disaster, extortion, and coercion, and the less we have to do with it the better. Home affairs in our own Legislature would fully occupy the energies of Irish legislators. Mr. Gladstone's opponents in England insist on retaining the Irish Members at Westminster. He seems inclined to give some consideration to their views on this matter. It is possible that if still eligible to the English Parliament, Irish constituencies would seldom, if ever, send members there.

The financial arrangement proposed by Mr. Gladstone assumed an exaggerated estimate of Ireland's liability, as well as of her financial capacity. He stated that at the time of the Union it was intended that Ireland should pay 2-17ths, or in the relation of 1 to 7½, out of the total charge of the United Kingdom. This is inaccurate. The Act of Union provided that Ireland should pay 2-17ths, not of the *total* charge of the United Kingdom, but only of that portion of the charge which should remain after each country should have first provided for its own separate debt charge. The pre-Union debt of Great Britain was, in round numbers, £450,000,000, with which Ireland had nothing to do. Her own debt was then £28,000,000, for which she should of course be responsible. The 2-17ths were found to exceed the capacity of Ireland. Under their pressure she became bankrupt.

Mr. Gladstone infers from the tests of income tax and death duties that Ireland's proportional ability is one-fifteenth of the British. There are, however, other tests which lead to a different conclusion. In 1864 Mr. Chisholm, chief clerk of the Exchequer, gave twelve tests to Colonel Dunne's Committee on Irish Taxation, including the tests of income tax and probate and legacy duties. The mean of those twelve tests was one Irish to twenty-five British; representing, so far as they go, Irish wealth as being only one-twenty-fifth part of British wealth.* These, and all other questions affecting our comparative financial ability, would have received minute examination if Mr. Gladstone's Bill had reached the stage of committee. But it did not reach that stage. On the second reading it was defeated by a majority of thirty.

Among the Unionist orators was Mr. Goschen, who implored the House to remember that they were only life trustees, and to reject a measure that would maim the Constitution. He did not reflect that the Irish Parliament who were bribed to enact the Union were only life trustees, and that their crime did not merely maim, but did suppress the Irish Constitution.

Mr. Gladstone's effort was a noble one. He tried to restore to Ireland the unquestionable right of every nation to govern herself, and thereby to extinguish the hostility inevitably generated by the denial of that right. Shortly after the introduction of his Home Rule Bill I addressed to

* See p. 131 of *Essays on Ireland*, by W. J. O'N. Daunt. Gill, Dublin.

him a letter which he was good enough to say that he read "with singular interest," and from which the following is an extract:

"It seems to me clear that a settlement of the Irish claim, in order to be satisfactory and permanent, should be as large and liberal as can consist with Imperial integrity. If it were practicable to follow the model afforded by the Austrian-Hungarian settlement, it would be the best mode of terminating the troublesome Irish difficulty. That settlement secures Hungarian loyalty to the Sovereign of the Empire by the free concession of their national rights to the Hungarian nation. The sense of national dignity—of dignity free from all infringement—the pride of honour gratified by analogy of condition with the greater kingdom, is in itself a potent guarantee of loyalty to the monarch under whom it is enjoyed. The attachment of Ireland to the Empire would be rendered firm and stable by her sense that her place in that Empire was honourable, not dependent; that her Parliament was co-ordinate, not subordinate.

"I observe that Lord Hampden and others have recommended the present Home Rule scheme to English acceptance on the express ground that it gives Ireland so little—less, his lordship says—than the colonies possess. 'Half measures,' said Sir Walter Scott, 'do but linger out the feud'; and Grattan, on a memorable occasion, said that 'the liberty withheld would poison the good communicated.'"

After the defeat of Mr. Gladstone's Bill, Parliament was dissolved, and the new election resulted in an English majority against Home Rule. Scotland, Ireland, and Wales had each returned majorities in its favour; but England turned the scale the other way by a majority on the whole of one hundred and ten. Mr. Gladstone resigned the seals of office, and Lord Salisbury became Premier. This result was hailed with rapture by the Tory and other anti-Irish parties.

The modes in which the exultant foes of Home Rule displayed their joy were characteristic and significant. The Protestant Archbishop of Armagh, Doctor Knox, issued to his clergy a form of thanksgiving for Gladstone's defeat to be used in their churches, which throws clear light on the anomalous position in Ireland of the garrison Church. The prelate thus directs his clergy to address the Almighty:

"We bless Thy holy name that it has pleased Thee to deliver us from those great and imminent dangers wherewith we were encompassed. We acknowledge it is of Thy goodness alone that we were not delivered over as a prey to those who sought the dismemberment of the Empire *and the overthrow of Thy true religion.*"

This prelate is a leading officer of the institution which calls itself the *Irish* Church, and which has existed in Ireland for more than three centuries. Here, according to his lordship, we have the soi-disant "Irish" Church afraid, at the end of three centuries, to trust itself to the Irish people ! It has failed, during that long period, to acquire their confidence, and his lordship apprehends that, unless supported by the legislative Union, he and his co-religionists would be delivered over as a prey to their enemies. He informs the Almighty that the "true" (*i.e.* the Protestant) religion is only protected from overthrow by an Act of Parliament—namely, the Act which in 1800 destroyed the Irish Constitution. What a ludicrous confession of impotence ! His lordship's feverish dreams—unreal as regards any danger to himself or his Church—very clearly indicate the anti-Irish spirit of that institution.

While Archbishop Knox's satisfaction at the defeat of Mr. Gladstone's Home Rule Bill evaporated in a thanksgiving address to the Almighty, the triumph of the Orange party was displayed in a more practical manner. They certainly needed no fresh stimulant to outrage ; but Lord Randolph Churchill visited Ulster to encourage their military spirit. Colonel Waring had informed them that "deeds, not words," were now required, and Lord Randolph, in a burst of poetic fervour, exhorted them to put their chivalry in action :

> "The combat deepens. On, ye brave,
> Who rush to glory or the grave.
> Wave, Ulster, all your banners wave,
> And charge with all your chivalry."

This spirited exhortation was followed by one of the periodical outbursts of Orange enthusiasm which distinguish Belfast. Houses were wrecked and looted, lives were lost, a large party of Catholic schoolgirls returning from a holiday excursion were dragged and hustled about the streets; in short, the Orange banners waved over the city, Orange chivalry had charged schoolgirls as well as other obnoxious individuals, and it seemed indisputable that Orange heroism was pledged to resist the "dismemberment of the Empire," and to protect true religion with a zeal as fervid as that of their archbishop—although exhibited in a more energetic manner.

Lord Aberdeen as Viceroy. 367

On the 10th of February, 1886, the Earl of Aberdeen was sworn in as Viceroy. The Irish public knew that His Excellency fully sympathised with the national desire for Home Rule, and that he supported Mr. Gladstone's project. This knowledge necessarily rendered His Excellency the most popular Viceroy we had seen since the days of Earl Fitzwilliam;. and the feeling that Government was prepared to concede autonomy to Ireland produced its natural result in the pacification of the country. The popularity of the Viceroy was reflected back upon the Sovereign whom he represented. Go where he would, he was greeted with a hearty welcome by the people, for the people believed that he was their friend, and in that belief they were not mistaken. The defeat of the Gladstone Government necessarily terminated Lord Aberdeen's viceroyalty. He departed on the 3rd of August, followed to the water's edge by sorrowing crowds—as Earl Fitzwilliam had been in 1795, when recalled by the sinister policy of Pitt.

Mr. Gladstone looks on the defeat of Home Rule as merely temporary, and thinks that the English electorate will get rid of the ignorant prejudice which caused them to oppose it at the last General Election.

Meanwhile, a Coercion Act has been passed, which will have no more efficacy in repressing the Irish demand for Home Rule than had the numerous Coercion Acts with which we have been accommodated since the Union by the English Parliament.

Lord Salisbury acknowledges that the existing relations of England and Ireland have not conciliated Irish affection. Speaking on the 12th of June, 1886, at a meeting of the Hertfordshire Conservative Association, his lordship is reported to have said:

" Are we good friends with the population of Ireland ? (Cries of 'No.') I deeply regret that there should be any doubt upon that question, but only three days ago I heard a Minister of the Crown, the Minister who was leading the House of Lords, say that the larger proportion of Irish people hated us. I deeply regret that such a phrase could be used, and that it could be used with truth."

Now, the two kingdoms have been more or less connected for seven hundred years; and if Irish alienation is still alive and vigorous, Lord Salisbury might discover its source in a series of continuous aggressions on every Irish interest, culminating in that worst crime of all, the destruction of the

Irish Parliament, and the consequent misery, the famines, the Coercion Acts—the expulsion of our people in great numbers, and the unconcealed desire to get rid of them. In all these things a source of alienation can be easily found; and the mode by which hatred can be easily replaced by international friendship is equally patent to any intelligent inquirer. It is simply to give Ireland her own.

The Union was achieved by force, and it is upheld by force. It has not any moral validity.

"Had the Union," says Mr. Gladstone, "constituted morally a valid covenant, the Irish nation would have been morally bound by it; and, in the event of its proving to be injurious to them, their claims to relief could only have been urged on general grounds, such as are applicable in any contested case of legislative improvement.

"Or, had the Union not been a compact morally binding at the time, it might nevertheless have become such, as Mr. G. Smith has justly shown, by subsequent ratification.

"But neither of these cases has occurred. Instead of arguing what in truth requires no argument, I have put into the witness-box two determined opponents, and I take my stand on their declaration that the Union Acts, which were in the nature of a Treaty, *were absolutely wanting in the conditions which alone could give them moral validity.*"

In saying this, Mr. Gladstone substantially corroborates the often quoted words of Saurin: "You may make the Union binding as a law, but you can never make it obligatory on conscience. It will be obeyed as long as England is strong, but resistance to it will be in the abstract a duty, and the exhibition of that resistance will be a mere question of prudence."

We were robbed of our Constitution, and England has no more moral right to withhold it from us than the burglar or highwayman has to retain stolen property. England has hitherto withheld it by superior force; but there is every hope that her national conscience is awaking to the justice and necessity of restoration. I will here repeat the opinion I have already expressed—that the larger, the more generous, the more ample the concession, the more potent and durable will be its efficacy in cementing international friendship.

The financial part of the coming settlement will form an important subject of inquiry. Mr. Robert Giffen, Secretary to the Statistical Department of the Board of Trade, does not partake of the idea that Ireland is able to contribute very largely to imperial expenses. I shall conclude by quoting from that gentleman the following brief statements :

"In the assessments to income tax the proportion is 1 to 17; viz. United Kingdom (including Ireland), £629,000,000 sterling; Ireland, £37,000,000 sterling. This is more than 5 per cent., but not very much more. *And there is reason to believe that Ireland is more strictly valued than Great Britain, and that it is overvalued.*"

Mr. Giffen also says: "Ireland as a poor country is disproportionately taxed, although the taxes of the United Kingdom are technically indiscriminate."

One more quotation :

"Ireland, while constituting only about a twentieth part of the United Kingdom in resources, nevertheless pays a tenth or eleventh of the taxes. Ireland ought to pay about £3,500,000, and it pays nearly £7,000,000."

The benefit of Home Rule to Ireland will largely depend on a just and honest financial arrangement.

MISCELLANEOUS APPENDIX.

THE FINANCIAL GRIEVANCES OF IRELAND.

ONE of the worst evils entailed upon Ireland by the destruction of her native Parliament, is the great injustice with which the English Parliament has treated her in matters of finance. The pecuniary loss sustained on this head is enormous, and to state it in all its details would demand a large volume. I only propose at present to bring before the reader a few leading facts of our case.

Firstly, it is to be borne in mind that at the time of the Union the National Debt of Ireland was, in round numbers, 28 millions sterling. At the same time the National Debt of Great Britain amounted, in round numbers, to 450 millions. It was plain that whereas the British debt was more than sixteen times as large as the Irish debt, there could be no plausible pretext for subjecting Ireland to as high a rate of taxation as Great Britain. Accordingly, Lord Castlereagh, the leader of the Unionists in the Irish House of Commons, promised that Ireland never should have any concern with the pre-Union debt of Great Britain, and that the financial terms of the Union should not only protect Ireland from excessive or unfair taxation, but should also secure to her the exclusive benefit of any surplus Irish revenue that might remain after defraying the public expenses as set forth in the Union statute.

The financial terms were as follows :

I. Ireland was, as I have said, to be protected from any liability on account of the British National Debt contracted prior to the Union.

II. The separate debt of each country being first provided for by a separate charge, Ireland was then to contribute two-seventeenths towards the joint or common expenditure of the United Kingdom for twenty years; after which her contribution was to be made proportionate to her ability, as ascertained at stated periods of revision by certain tests specified in the Act.

III. Ireland was not only promised that she never should have any concern with the then existing British debt, but she was also assured that her taxation should not be raised to the standard of Great Britain until the following conditions should occur:

1. That the two debts should come to bear to each other the proportion of fifteen parts for Great Britain to two parts for Ireland; and
2. That the respective circumstances of the two countries should admit of uniform taxation.

The proportion of two parts for Ireland to fifteen parts for Great Britain was strongly protested against by Mr. Foster, the Speaker of the Irish House of Commons, and by the other opponents of the Union. Proofs were given that the load thus imposed on Ireland exceeded her capacity. The anti-Union members of the House of Lords entered on their journals a protest containing a careful and able calculation of the comparative taxable ability of the two countries. They contended, with justice, that the ability of Ireland, instead of being two-seventeenths, or 1 to $7\frac{1}{2}$, was no greater than 1 to 13. But the patriots reasoned and protested in vain. The ratio of 1 for Ireland to $7\frac{1}{2}$ for Great Britain, became law along with the Act of Union in which it was incorporated.

The predictions of Mr. Foster and his friends were soon verified. They had spoken truly when they alleged that Ireland was overloaded by the Union proportions. When the general taxation of the Empire was augmented by the prolonged and increasing expenses of the war, she broke down beneath the enormous burden, and recourse was had to a system of disproportionate borrowing on her credit, in order to make good the deficiencies of her revenue. The borrowings with which she was charged exceeded immensely the comparative ratio of her taxable ability, even as that ratio was stated by Lord Castlereagh and by the Union Act. Lord Castlereagh had stated her ability to bear to the ability of Great Britain the proportion of 1 to 7½. But the post-Union borrowings on Irish account by the Imperial Government were to the contemporaneous British borrowings in the much higher ratio of about 1 to 3½. Here are the figures:

Year.	British Debt.	Ann. Charge.	Irish Debt.	Ann. Charge.
	£	£	£	£
5th Jan. 1801.	450,504,984	17,718,851	28,545,134	1,244,463
5th Jan. 1817.	734,522,104	28,238,416	112,704,773	4,104,514

Parliamentary Paper, No. 35 of 1819.*

Thus, while the Imperial Parliament less than doubled the British debt, they quadrupled the Irish debt. By this management the Irish debt, which in 1801 had been to the British as 1 to 16, was forced up to bear to the British debt the ratio of 1 to 7½. This was the proportion required by the Act of Union as a condition of subjecting Ireland to indiscriminate taxation with Great Britain — a condition equally impudent and iniquitous. Ireland was to be loaded with inordinate debt; and then this debt was to be made the pretext for raising her taxation to the high British standard, and thereby rendering her contributory to the pre-Union debt of Great Britain.

* By another Parliamentary Paper, No. 256 of 1824, signed by J. C. Herries, Secretary of the Treasury, the debts as they stood in 1801 are thus stated—

British Funded ... ... £420,305,944.
Irish Funded ... ... 26,841,219.

By adding the Unfunded Debts to these amounts, Great Britain is brought up, in round numbers, to 446 millions, and Ireland to 28 millions. The difference between the two returns is unimportant, as its effect on the proportions is infinitesimal. This return makes the Irish debt charge less than it appears in that of 1819.

By way of softening down the glaring dishonesty of such a proposition, Lord Castlereagh said that the two debts might be brought to bear to each other the prescribed proportions, partly by the increase of the Irish debt, but partly also by the decrease of the British. To which Mr. Foster thus answered on the 15th March, 1800:

"The monstrous absurdity you would force down our throats is, that Ireland's increase of poverty, as shown by her increase of debt, and England's increase of wealth, as shown by diminution of debt, are to bring them to an equality of condition, so as to be able to bear an equality of taxation."

But bad as this was, the former and worse alternative was what really befel. The given ratio was reached solely by the increase of the Irish debt, without any decrease of the British.

The following declarations of prominent statesmen in the United Parliament, attest the nature and extent of the fiscal dishonesty of which the Union made Ireland the victim.

On the 20th of June, 1804 (four years after the Union had passed), Mr. Foster observed that, whereas in 1794 the Irish debt did not exceed $2\frac{1}{2}$ millions, it had in 1803 risen to 43 millions; and that during the current year it was increased to nearly 53 millions.

In the discussion on the Irish Budget in 1804 (for up to 1817 the Irish and British Exchequers continued separate) Mr. James Fitzgerald observed that "it was obvious that Ireland could not discharge her share of the unequal contract entered into for her; and of course that England should ultimately pay all." And seeing that the "unequal contract" was forced upon Ireland by British bribes and British bayonets, it was no more than just that England should ultimately pay all. But it will appear by-and-by that this equitable liability is not recognised by modern English statesmen.

On the 19th of March, 1811, Mr. Parnell adverted to what he termed the main cause of the increase of the Irish debt, and the failure in the produce of the Irish taxes. "The ratio of the contribution of Ireland to the general expenditure fixed by the noble lord" (Castlereagh) "was that cause. In this his lordship was mistaken; and that," continued Mr. Parnell, "was the source of all those evils and embarrassments that oppressed the country. Ireland had been paying a greater proportion than she ought to have done."

On the 20th of May, 1811, Sir John Newport said, in a

debate on the Irish Budget: "The revenues of Ireland have made no progress adequate to her debt. *No instance had occurred within the last three years in which the separate charge of Ireland amounted to within one million of the joint charge.* This was one effect of the rate of contribution fixed at the Union, which, so long as it was acted on, would render the payment of the debt impossible."

On the 11th of June, 1813, Mr. Wellesley Pole said that when the Union proportions were settled, the Imperial expenditure was only twenty-five millions, whereas it now was seventy-two millions. He added that it never could have been expected that Ireland would be able to pay two-seventeenths of so large a sum as seventy-two millions.*

On the 20th of May, 1816, Mr. Vesey Fitzgerald, in proposing the consolidation of the two Exchequers, said:

"You contracted with Ireland for an expenditure she could not meet; your own share of which you could not meet but by sacrifices unexampled; by exertions, the tension of which England only could have borne. Ireland had been led to hope that her expenditure would have been less than before she was united with you. In the fifteen years preceding the Union it amounted to 41 millions, but in the fifteen years of Union it swelled to 148 millions. The increase of her revenue would have more than discharged, without the aid of loans, an expenditure greater than that of the fifteen years preceding 1801."

This is tantamount to an admission that a domestic Parliament would have preserved us from the insolvency in which we were involved by the Union rate of contribution.

The Parliamentary Committee of 1815 which recommended the consolidation of the English and Irish Exchequers, admitted that the two-seventeenths were "a burden which experience had proved to be too great."—(Fourth Report, published 1815, sessional number 214.)

Mr. Leslie Foster said that "taxation in Ireland had been carried to its *ne plus ultra.*" On the 21st April, 1818, Mr. Plunket, speaking to a motion of Mr. Shaw's on the window tax, said: "Ireland certainly had not paid the two-seventeenths stipulated for at the time of the Union; and for

---

* The words here ascribed to Mr. W. Pole were probably inaccurately reported. Ireland was not required by the Union statute to raise two-seventeenths of the whole Imperial revenue; but only of that portion of the revenue which remained after each country hould have first provided for its own separate debt-charge.

the plainest of all possible reasons, because she could not; because a burden utterly disproportioned to her strength had been imposed on her."

In 1822 the late Right Hon. Henry Goulburn, when speaking to a motion of Sir John Newport, said: "The Union contribution of two-seventeenths for Ireland is now admitted on all hands to have been more than she was able to bear." And in 1830 the late Marquis of Lansdowne referred in the House of Lords to the incapacity of Ireland to bear the load that had been imposed on her.

And it was precisely because of her incapacity that Pitt and Castlereagh imposed the load upon her. Their financial game was this: Her debt in 1801 was, as already remarked, less than a sixteenth part of the debt of Great Britain, and it was determined to bring her under British burdens without giving her the compensation to which she was entitled on the score of her greatly smaller liabilities. Instead of compensation, the Union statesmen hit off the idea of getting her heavily into debt by imposing on her a ratio of taxation beyond her ability to meet; and then, so soon as this fictitious debt should reach a given point, it was to be made a condition of abolishing separate quotas of contribution, and of taxing both countries indiscriminately. A more audacious fraud was never perpetrated; and it is a circumstance much to be deplored that Mr. Gladstone, in 1853, should appeal to it as authorising his additions to Irish taxation.

In 1816 was passed the Act for consolidating the British and Irish Exchequers. It is the 56th Geo. III., chap. xcviii. It became operative on the 1st of January, 1817. The pretext for passing it was to relieve Ireland from the unjust load imposed upon her by the Union rate of contribution, and from the unpaid excess of so-called "Irish" debt which had rendered her insolvent, and which was the inevitable result of the fraudulent Union ratio. Great Britain was to assume that excess; or, speaking more accurately, it was to be transferred from the separate Irish account to the general Imperial account.

It is here to be noted that the excess of so-called Irish debt which existed in 1816 is commonly spoken of by British politicians, and also by some ignorant Irish ones, as if it were really and justly Irish debt, creating on the part of Ireland an equitable liability, from which Great Britain generously relieved her by passing the Consolidation Act, and thereby taking on herself the liability in question. Nothing can be more false than this view of the matter. Firstly, the excess of "Irish" debt arose from a rate of contribution admittedly unjust. Ireland was overcharged by the Union proportion of two-seventeenths. To the exact extent of the Irish overcharge was Great Britain undercharged. If Ireland were taxed too much, Great Britain was to the same extent necessarily charged too little. The injustice of the two-seventeenths is clearly admitted by the statesmen I have quoted. The unpaid excess of debt arising out of that unjust proportion, is not properly Irish debt at all, but British.

Secondly, it appears if possible more plain that the excess of debt thus created was really British, though nominally Irish, when we consider that the Act of Union that contained the unjust fiscal ratio in which that excess originated, was forced upon Ireland by English power against the all but universal will of the Irish people, and by means of which it is utterly impossible to exaggerate the wickedness. Let us suppose a parallel case between two private persons. If A, by violence and fraud, coerces recalcitrant B into submitting to a fiscal burden beyond his ability, and which finally renders B insolvent, will any one contend that A, who forced the burden on reluctant and resisting B, is not the person morally liable to the whole extent of the excess which his victim proves unable to discharge?

So it was between England and Ireland. Yet statesmen and publicists have talked about the generosity of Great Britain in taking on herself the load of *Irish* debt!

The opponents of the Union were justly afraid that the balance, or surplus, of Irish taxes which should remain after defraying the public expenses of Ireland, would be carried out of the country by the English Government. In order to quiet this fear a clause was inserted in the 7th article of the Union, enacting that Ireland should have the sole and exclusive benefit of all her surplus taxes in any one of five modes pointed out in the clause; and moreover that the taxes producing the surplus should be taken off. This provision looked well. But its authors had taken effectual means to prevent Ireland from deriving any benefit from it by the dexterous contrivance of making her "contract" (to borrow the words of Mr. Vesey Fitzgerald) "for an expenditure she could not meet." If she could not even meet the expenditure forced on her, *à fortiori* she could not have a surplus. Thus, while a formal clause apparently secured to her the use of her own money, that clause was cleverly accompanied with fiscal conditions that rendered it worthless.

The Parliamentary Committee of 1815, as well as individual members, had, as we have seen, proclaimed that the Union ratio imposed on Ireland was beyond her ability. In 1816 the Consolidation Act passed, uniting the two Exchequers. Honesty would suggest that if the former rate of Irish contribution were condemned as unjustly high, a new and lower rate should now be substituted for it. But then a separate ratio for Ireland, fairly proportioned to her ability, might leave to Ireland a separate surplus revenue. Nay, when the public expenditure should fall to the low peace level, even the two-seventeenths, although certainly beyond the true Irish proportion, might possibly leave an Irish surplus, which surplus, under the 7th article of the Union, should be appropriated exclusively to Irish uses. This would never do. It would not consist with the English idea about Irish matters, that Ireland should retain the use of her own revenues. A special Irish surplus must, therefore, be rendered impossible. Accordingly the Imperial Parliament, by the 56th George III., chap. xcviii., abolished the Union ratio of two-seventeenths *without substituting any other*. When Ireland ceased to have a special ratio, she technically ceased to have a special surplus. Thus again was the Union guarantee that Irish surplus revenue should be applied to the sole benefit of Ireland, rendered null by dishonest legislation.

The bankruptcy of Ireland in 1816, brought about by the Union ratio of two-seventeenths and by Imperial management, was turned to account in that year by the English power that produced it. The substitution of an indiscriminate system of taxation for fixed international proportions, mortgaged Ireland for the pre-Union debt of Great Britain, a debt she had no part in contracting, and from which the Act of Union professes to protect her, but to the annual interest of which she is forced to contribute a portion of payment.

The transactions of 1816 were again turned to account by Mr. Gladstone, who, in 1853, justified the Irish income tax by pleading that in 1816 Great Britain had assumed the unpaid excess of what was termed "Irish Debt." But that excess was admitted to have originated in a fiscal injustice. Mr. Gladstone, therefore, deems that the removal of an admittedly unjust load, creates a right to impose another load in place of the one taken off. In other words, if you undo an avowed wrong, you are thereby entitled to inflict an equivalent wrong on the aggrieved party.

The Irish witnesses underwent a very hostile cross-examination from the English members of Colonel Dunne's Committee on Irish Taxation in 1864. Setting aside the multitude of details, many of them irrelevant, into which the inquiry diverged, the following facts stand unshaken, and should become familiar to every man in Ireland:

1. The British debt was in 1801 about 16 times as large as the Irish debt.

2. It was promised by the authors of the Union, and the promise was embodied in the 7th article, that as Ireland had no part in contracting that debt, so she should be for ever preserved from all concern with its principal or interest.

3. In order to give effect to this promise, Great Britain should be separately taxed to the extent of her separate pre-Union debt-charge, less the pre-Union debt-charge of Ireland. This would make the separate taxation of Great Britain about £15,000,000 per annum; whereas her separate taxation is only between three and four millions.

4. Ireland has never received from Great Britain one farthing by way of compensation or equivalent for being thus subjected to the pre-Union British debt.

5. By the fifth clause of the 7th article of the Union, Ireland, as I have already said, was promised the benefit of her own surplus taxes. She has never, during the eighty-five years of Union, received one farthing in virtue of that clause. Her taxes, after defraying her public domestic expenses, have been uniformly abstracted by England; and the clause that professes to secure to Ireland the use of them has been rendered a dead letter by the parliamentary management I have described.

6. The amount of Irish revenue annually drawn from this kingdom is a very large item in the general pecuniary drain. The late Mr. Dillon, in his able report adopted by the Dublin Corporation, compiled from the Finance Accounts, shows that the Irish taxes expended out of Ireland in the year 1860 amounted to £4,095,453; and that in 1861 they amounted to £3,970,715.

7. From the tone of some of the English members of Colonel Dunne's Committee, when examining the witnesses on Irish taxation, it seems clear that those gentlemen had not the slightest idea that any separate British liability

existed. And I cannot discover the faintest trace that Messieurs Lowe, Stanhope, Northcote, and Hankey recognised the right of Ireland to the separate use of her own surplus. They seemed to be thoroughly imbued with the truly English notion that Irish taxes, if expended for Irish purposes, would be unfairly withheld from their rightful English owners.

All this financial injustice is the inevitable result of losing the protection of an Irish Legislature. The species of connexion that exists between Ireland and England is designed and adapted to draw off Irish wealth to England without any return. Before closing this part of my subject, I desire once more to impress upon the reader the important fact that we are entitled to a great equivalent for having been subjected to the heavy pre-Union British liabilities, and that up to this hour the equivalent has been withheld. This fact should be always kept in view.

We should also keep in view the essential rascality of the fiscal trick by which Ireland was brought under English liabilities. The Union Act provided that whenever the Irish debt should be forced up to bear to the British debt the proportion of 1 to $7\frac{1}{2}$, the United Parliament should then be entitled to abolish separate quotas, and to tax both countries indiscriminately. The authors of the Union took care that the Irish debt should be thus forced up, by the villainous device of over-estimating our relative taxable ability. This overcharge, as its authors intended, necessarily resulted in enormous borrowing on Irish credit to make good the deficiencies of Irish revenue. Thus was a fictitious "debt" trumped up against us; and the fraud was made the condition of imposing excessive taxation on our country.

I have hitherto considered the abstraction of money from Ireland with reference to its injustice. I shall add a few words on the inability of Ireland to endure the drain of her means, and on the effect of that drain upon her people.

It has been said that the capacity of Ireland to pay taxes on the British scale is demonstrated by the fact of her paying them. It would be about as rational to infer the capacity of an individual for disbursement from the fact of his being robbed. True, Ireland has paid; but at what cost of popular suffering? High taxes are indeed wrung out of her; but that they are disproportioned to her strength is shown by the evanishment of her people. The pecuniary resources that should employ and support the labouring population and large numbers of small traders are drawn out of the country in a variety of ways; and millions of our people, despoiled of their natural and legitimate sources of support, have been forced in self-defence to fly to foreign lands. It must be remembered that excessive taxation is only one mode out of many in which England contrives to get hold of the money of Ireland. There are also the rents remitted to the absentee owners of Irish estates; which rents, if we average them at 3 millions per annum for the eighty-five years of the Union, amount to 255 millions sterling. There is the money withdrawn for the parliamentary expenses of passing railway Bills, and other Bills of private companies; as also for appeals from Ireland to the foreign House of Lords, which, if it were not for the Union, would be spent in Dublin. There is the money withdrawn in the commercial profits of banks and insurance companies whose head-quarters are in London. There is the money sent out of the country to purchase those articles of English manufacture that obtained possession of the Irish market on the ruin of our own manufacture. There was, until lately, the money spent in London by Irish law-students, whom an absurd and degrading practice, now removed, compelled to pass a certain number of their terms at an English Inn of Court. There is the interest of loans remitted from Ireland to English money-lenders. Wealth begets wealth, and the causes that impoverished Ireland and enriched England have placed the lenders of money in the latter country. It is of course no grievance to an Irish borrower to obtain an advance from an English lender. But it is a national calamity that Ireland should be so drained of her wealth that the capital whence the advances are made should be sought across the water, involving, in the interest paid thereon, a large addition to the absentee drain. I believe that up to this present year 1885, 400 millions sterling are a very low estimate of the actual cash extorted from Ireland in the modes I have enumerated; and it must be kept in mind that we lose not merely the enormous sums that are abstracted, but also the domestic profit that would arise from their expenditure in the land that produced them.

How is it possible that the annual production of a country thus circumstanced can ever accumulate into national capital? Capital is said by M'Culloch to consist of produce saved from immediate consumption. To employ an illustration familiar to my rural readers, a farmer's wife whose cream is regularly skimmed and carried off by a free-and-easy neighbour, may as well hope for a good supply of butter from her dairy, as Ireland can hope for an adequate growth of national capital when so large an amount of her annual income is incessantly carried off by England.

Can anyone wonder that a country thus cruelly despoiled should lose in recent years three millions of its inhabitants?* Or that, when visited by famine in 1846, the plundered nation, deprived by the Union of the power of self-support, should have become the recipient of the world's alms? All this monstrous spoliation is styled "the identification of the two islands"; "the unity of their interests"; and we are told that it makes Ireland "an integral part of the Empire." Our money is taken, our people are driven to emigrate, and we are paid off with this sort of talk. The Union of England and Ireland was compared by Lord Byron to the union of a shark with its prey. In its present operation it degrades, defrauds, and depopulates Ireland.

General Dunne's Committee issued their Report on Irish Taxation on the 1st June, 1865. General Dunne refused to sign it, very justly conceiving that it did not present a fair statement of the question. He had submitted to the committee a draft report in which the fiscal case of Ireland was very ably stated. This was rejected, and the committee, by a small majority (which included one Irish member, Sir George Colthurst), adopted a report which had been drawn up by Sir Stafford Northcote.

A question had been discussed, whether, according to the terms of the Union, a separate debt might have been created for Ireland to supplement the annual deficiencies of her contribution. On this point Sir Stafford Northcote says: "It is obvious that if a separate debt could not be created, Ireland might have been required to make good, year by year, her contribution of two-seventeenths to the joint expenditure of the whole kingdom."

Yes—but only until 1820; at which period, according to the Act of Union, there was to be a revision of the proportions. Sir Stafford ignores the revision, and argues as if the two-seventeenths were to have been perpetual. He admits (p. vi. of Report) that "experience proved that the resources

* Population in 1841, 8,196,597, as per census; population in 1885, not quite 5,000,000.

of Ireland were not sufficient to meet it" (viz. the contribution of two-seventeenths). Yet he argues throughout as if Ireland were justly and equitably liable to a load admittedly beyond her resources. The power reserved in the Act of Union to revise the proportions clearly indicates that they might have been miscalculated, and that if so, the error should be rectified. Sir Stafford admits the fact of the miscalculation; yet his reasoning assumes that this admitted overcharge constituted, in point of equity, a debt fairly binding on Ireland.

In 1817 the English and Irish Exchequers were amalgamated, and Ireland was thereby swindled out of the protection she might have derived from a just revision of the proportions. "Had that amalgamation not taken place," says Sir Stafford, "and had the system of raising revenue which prevailed from 1801 to 1816 been continued, the Irish separate debt would have continued to increase till the country might have been crushed by it."—(Page viii.)

Again Sir Stafford ignores the provision for revising the proportions in 1820. One would think he had not seen it; and yet he copies at full length the section of the Act that contains it.

The following admissions are worth extracting: " Since 1845," says Sir Stafford, "the share which Great Britain has had in the remission of Imperial taxation has been proportionally much larger than that which Ireland has had; and the additions made to the Imperial taxation of Ireland have been proportionally heavier than those made to the taxation of Great Britain, while at the same time it cannot be doubted that Great Britain has derived a larger measure of advantage than Ireland from the repeal of the Corn Laws, as a compensation for which the boon was originally given by Sir Robert Peel.

"It is not surprising that the large increase which your committee have noticed in the general taxation since 1845 should have given rise to complaint. Nor is it surprising that louder complaints should have been made by Ireland than by other parts of the United Kingdom. The pressure of taxation will be felt most by the weakest part of the community; and as the average wealth of the Irish taxpayers is less than the average wealth of the English taxpayers, the ability of Ireland to bear heavy taxation is evidently less than the ability of England. Mr. Senior, whose evidence upon the position of Ireland will be found very suggestive, remarks that the taxation of England is both the heaviest and the lightest in Europe—the heaviest as regards the amount raised, the lightest as regards the ability to bear that amount; but that in the case of Ireland it is heavy both as regards the amount and as regards the ability of the contributor; and he adds that England is the most lightly taxed, and Ireland the most heavily taxed country in Europe, although both are nominally liable to equal taxation."—(Pages x., xi.)

But Sir Stafford says that if Irish taxation were specially reduced on the score of Irish poverty, the poorer parts of Great Britain might claim reduction of taxes on similar grounds. On the first publication in the newspapers of Sir Stafford's Report, I addressed to the National League a letter, from which I take the following passage: "When Colonel Dunne claims that, in conformity with Union promises, Irish fiscal burdens should be lessened to the admittedly small ratio of Irish fiscal ability, he is told that the same claim of reduction might as fairly be set up by any distressed portion of Great Britain—say, for instance, Wiltshire. And this shallow excuse is given by able men! Pray, look at the disparity between the cases they seek to assimilate. Wiltshire never had a distinct and separate debt. Wiltshire cannot show, as Ireland can, that it was ever promised exemption from the old British debt. It cannot show, as Ireland can, that it was ever promised the local and exclusive expenditure of its own surplus revenue. In these important respects it stands in a totally different position from Ireland. On the direct contrary Wiltshire is morally, politically, and geographically, an integral member of that country which promised to secure to Ireland exemption from pre-Union British burthens, and the exclusive use of Irish surplus revenue. It is therefore absurd to pretend that Wiltshire has as good a right—or any right—to make for herself claims such as we put forward. Wiltshire, being an integral part of Britain, is herself a party to the British promise given to Ireland. She stands in the position of promis*er*; Ireland occupies that of promis*ee*. It is a shallow and discreditable juggle to pretend that an identity of position exists between parties who stand in directly opposite relations to each other."

I conclude this section of the Appendix with the following quotation from a speech delivered by Henry Grattan in 1800: "Rely on it that Ireland, like every enslaved country, will ultimately be compelled to pay for her own subjugation. Robbery and taxes ever follow conquest; the country that loses her liberty loses her revenues."

THE REGENCY QUESTION.

Among the difficulties most commonly paraded by those persons who can see nothing but mischief in the Repeal of the Union, one of the most prominent is the possible difference of the two Parliaments on the question of selecting a Regent. Mr. Sharman Crawford, in his anti-Repeal letters of 1841, copying his predecessors, insisted strongly on the perils (and no man denies them) which would follow from such a diversity. The Repealers, however, propose that the possibility of dissension on this point should be extinguished, by leaving the appointment of the Regent exclusively in the hands of the British Ministry and Parliament. To this proposal Mr. Crawford objected: "That it would surrender the independence of the Irish Parliament on that vital point."

I quote the following passage from my reply to Mr. Crawford: "I do not see how the independence of the Irish Parliament would be one whit more compromised by the *ipso facto* identity of the Regent, than it would be by the *ipso facto* identity of the Sovereign; and I never yet heard that this latter identity was deemed incompatible with the parliamentary independence of Ireland. In fact, the identity of the Regent would seem to follow as a necessary consequence from the principle of the law that requires the identity of the monarch.

"Mr. Crawford terms the Regency question 'a vital point.' So it is—vital to the Imperial connexion of the kingdoms; and it is therefore that we Repealers, being ardent friends of the connexion, are desirous to incorporate with the Constitution a provision for the identity of the Regent. But the question of the Regent's person, however important to the connexion of the countries, is a matter of very inferior importance as affecting the general welfare and everyday comfort of the people—the administration of justice—the prosperity of trade, of manufactures, of commerce. These are the matters of really vital importance to the people—matters which require all the care of a resident, well-constructed, popular Parliament. Give the people of Ireland such a Parliament as this, and they can well afford to leave to a British Ministry the selection of the Regent's person."

JOHN O'CONNELL ON THE COMPARATIVE COMFORT OF THE IRISH
PEOPLE BEFORE AND AFTER THE UNION.

John O'Connell, to show the greater comfort enjoyed by the Irish people before the Union than in 1843, wrote as follows: "A return has recently appeared in all the papers, of the number of sheep and horned cattle at Ballinasloe every year since 1790 to the present time. I extract from it the following:

Years.	Sheep.	Horned Cattle.
1799	77,900	9,900
1835	62,400	8,500
1842	76,800	14,300

"Now, by a parliamentary report of 1834, and the Irish Railway Report, I find that our whole export of sheep the first of the above years was only 800—and in the second was 125,000. What became of the 77,100 surplus sheep in the former year, as well as the sheep at other fairs? They were eaten at home. Where did the people get money to buy them? The money of the country was spent in the country. .... As to oxen, 14,000 went away in 1799, and 98,000 in 1835; yet, if we test the produce of all Ireland in the former year by the amount at Ballinasloe Fair—no bad criterion, I believe—she had for sale more in that year than in 1835, and consumed the surplus over her export. . . . Her export in 1799 was only one-seventh of what it was in 1835."

JUDGE (AFTERWARDS LORD) O'HAGAN ON THE SEPARATE IRISH
JUDICATURE.*

"We may labour, in all proper cases, to assimilate the laws of the three kingdoms, giving for that purpose from every district what light and help we can reciprocally furnish; but we should maintain for all the integrity of their independent judicatures, in the assurance that they will not the less enjoy the benefits of a common code, if it do not aim to subordinate any one to any other of them, or unduly exalt a part at the expense of exhaustion and depression to the rest. . . . . For Ireland, at least, it is essential to maintain a high judiciary and an educated bar, if she would preserve anything

* From his Address at the Social Science Congress at Belfast, September, 1867.

of the informed opinion, the productive energy, and the public spirit, without which a people stagnates and sinks into contempt."

PITT'S INSINCERITY IN REGARD TO THE CATHOLICS SEEN THROUGH BY THE DUBLIN OPPOSITION.

Cooke writes to Castlereagh from Dublin Castle, 23rd February, 1801:

"The Opposition here are angry and chagrined at Mr. Pitt's taking up the Catholics: they say, however, it is a humbug on his part, and that he does not fairly mean to do his utmost in the question, and that, after making a mock battle, he will come into power again, and leave them in the lurch."

This intentional fraud against the Catholics was charged on the Government by Plunket, who said in the Irish House of Commons, on the 15th January, 1800: "You held out hopes to the Catholic body which were never intended to be gratified; regardless of the disappointment, and indignation, and eventual rebellion, which you might kindle."—PLUNKET'S *Speeches*, Duffy's edition, p. 70.

IRISH PEERS' PROTEST AGAINST THE UNION, 13TH JUNE, 1800.

"Because the argument made use of in favour of the Union, namely, that the sense of the people of Ireland is in its favour, we know to be untrue; and as the Ministers have declared that they would not press the measure against the sense of the people, and as the people have pronounced decidedly, and under all difficulties, their judgment against it, we have, together with the sense of the country, the authority of the Minister to enter our Protest against the project of Union; *against the yoke which it imposes, the dishonour which it inflicts, the disqualification passed upon the peerage, the stigma thereby branded on the realm, the disproportionate principle of expense it introduces, the means employed to effect it, the discontents it has excited, against all these, and the fatal consequences they may produce, we have endeavoured to interpose our votes, and failing, we transmit to after times our names in solemn protest in behalf of the parliamentary constitution of this realm*, the liberty which it secured, the trade which it protected, the connexion which it preserved, and the Constitution which it supplied and fortified. This we feel ourselves called upon to do in support of our characters, our honours, and whatever is left to us worthy to be transmitted to our posterity.

"(Signed) LEINSTER, ARRAN, MOUNTCASHEL, FARNHAM, BELMORE, MASSY, STRANGFORD, GRANARD, LUDLOW, MOIRA, WILLIAM, Bishop of Down and Connor, RICHARD, Bishop of Waterford and Lismore, POWERSCOURT, DE VESCI, CHARLEMONT, KINGSTON, RIVERSDALE, MEATH, LISMORE, SUNDERLIN."

HOW THE QUEEN MIGHT ANNUL THE UNION WITHOUT THE INTERVENTION OF THE IMPERIAL PARLIAMENT.

O'Connell suggested the following mode of reviving the Parliament of Ireland:

"Let it be recollected," he wrote, "that in the judgment of our present Lord Chancellor,* who is keeper (in Ireland) of Her Majesty's conscience, the Union was in itself a NULLITY; that is his precise expression—it was his solemn judgment—and he is bound by it.

"The Queen, therefore, might be advised to act in either of these two ways:

"*Firstly*, she may call together in Dublin, by intimation or invitation, the 105 members now representing Irish constituencies. More than forty of them (that is, more than sufficient to make a House) would certainly attend any royal summons, however informal. And Her Majesty might easily bring together a sufficient number of the Irish peers. And thus, with the assent of Her Majesty an ordinance might be enacted adopting the plan we have suggested for reconstructing the Irish Parliament, and authorising the issuing of writs or summonses accordingly.

"The Parliament, when met under such writs or summonses, would have no difficulty in enacting laws, with the assent of the Queen, sanctioning their own appointment, and confirmatory of their own legislative powers.

"*Secondly*,—Let it be recollected that it was originally the exclusive prerogative of the Crown to issue to such places as it thought fit, writs for the election of members of Parliament; and this prerogative continued to be exercised down to the reign of Queen Anne. The familiar fact of the creation

* Lord Plunket.

in Ireland, by King James I., of no less than forty boroughs in a single day—boroughs that from that time continued to send members to Parliament until the Union—proves in the strongest way the power to exercise (as it also shows the abuse of) this prerogative.

"Now, there is no Act of Parliament in Ireland taking away that prerogative from the Crown. It therefore continues to exist, unimpeached and undiminished; and Her Majesty might be advised at once to issue writs to all the counties, and to the several towns named in our proposed plan; and then she may either bring together, or create, a sufficient number of Irish peers to constitute the Irish Parliament.

"It is quite true that the proposal we suggest is one intended to be enacted by the united Parliament; but we are not thereby prevented from pointing out other means (such as the two modes above described) for obtaining that same object. To each of such modes there are abundant technical and legal objections. But we believe there is no constitutional difficulty in the way.

"The Constitution of these realms is suited to meet every emergency; and the most irregular proceedings of Parliament have been sanctioned, and become the law of the land. For instance, in the year 1399, the Parliament dethroned Richard II., the legitimate monarch, and conferred the crown upon Henry IV., who had no kind of title to that crown. Nor was he even heir of succession to Richard. This Parliamentary Act regulated the succession of the crown for three generations, and several of the statutes passed during that interval are binding at the present day.

"Again: the Parliament, in the instance of Edward IV., assumed the like power of disposing of the crown; taking it away from the House of Lancaster and conferring it on that of York.

"Again: the case of Henry VII. is yet stronger. The Parliament in 1485, after the Battle of Bosworth, gave him a legal title to the crown; although he had no other title than that most irregular law. It is true he afterwards married the heiress of the House of York; but he took especial care, and indeed the most distinct modes, of disavowing any title as derived from her. And Her Majesty, whose title is so indisputable, derives that title as one of his descendants.

"But the strongest instance remains behind. It is the

case of King William III., of 'glorious, pious, and immortal memory.' The Convention Parliament at the Revolution, without any king at all, dethroned the reigning and then legitimate monarch, James II.

"They used the word 'abdicate,' but a word is nothing. The actual fact is that they dethroned King James and enthroned King William, who had no species of claim to be King—who had no kind of legal right to be King of England, as he was, not only during his wife's lifetime, but for some years after her decease. He had, we repeat, no other right, save that excellent and efficient one, of a most irregular Act of Parliament.

"No persons can be more thoroughly convinced than we are, that a most legitimate right to the crown was acquired by the transactions of the Revolution of 1688; we are quite certain that a perfect title was made out by those transactions. And our allegiance to our most gracious Sovereign, whom may God long preserve, is much enhanced by the principles which were involved in, and sanctioned by, the Revolution.

"But what a host of legal and technical objections were and may be raised against each and all of the precedents which we have thus cited, including the glorious Revolution itself! We venture to assert that none greater could be stated to either of the modes of repealing the Union we have suggested—no, nor by any means so great.

"20th May, 1840."

CONTRAST BETWEEN ORANGE AND CATHOLIC CORPORATORS.

In 1793, the partial Emancipation Act rendered Catholics eligible to municipal Corporations. But as the corporators were not compelled to elect them, the eligibility conferred by law was worthless. In the forty-eight years that elapsed from 1793 until the Corporate Reform Act of 1841, only two Catholics were admitted into the Dublin Corporation. In the reformed Corporation Catholics are a majority, and it is instructive to contrast their conduct with that of their Orange predecessors. Between the years 1843 and 1881 inclusive, the new corporation, with a predominating Catholic element, elected a Protestant Lord Mayor seventeen times. I give the names of the Protestant chief magistrates: George Roe, 1843; John L. Arabin, 1845; Benjamin Lee Guinness, 1851; Robt. Kinahan, 1853; Joseph Boyce, 1855; Richard Atkinson, 1857; James Lambert,

1859; Richard Atkinson (his second election), 1861; Hon. J. P. Vereker, 1863; Sir John Barrington, 1865; William Lane Joynt, 1867; Edward Purdon, 1870; Robert G. Durden, 1872; Maurice Brooks, 1874; Sir George Owens, 1876; Sir John Barrington (his second election), 1879; George Moyers, 1881.

In addition to the above instances of the Catholic spirit òf fair play in the election of the metropolitan chief magistrate, I subjoin the names of the following Protestants, elected to positions of trust by the Dublin Corporation:

High Sheriff for 1878, Hon. J. P. Vereker; High Sheriff for 1881, Sir George Owens; The City Treasurer, Thomas Fry, J.P.; City Engineer and Borough Surveyor, Park Neville; Assistant-Engineer, Spenser Harty; Superintendent Medical Officer of Health and City Analyst, Charles Cameron, M.D.; Overseer of Waterworks, Mervyn Crofton; Superintendent of Fire Brigade, Captain Ingram; Assistant-Superintendent, Lieutenant Boyle.

DECLARATIONS OF WAR AND PEACE.

These declarations, in the event of Home Rule being acquired, must of course rest, as they did before the Union, in the prerogative of the Sovereign, advised by the English Cabinet and Parliament. But the Irish Parliament, as before the Union, should have the exclusive power to determine the amount to be contributed by Ireland to military expenses.

INCLUSION OF IRELAND IN IMPERIAL COUNCILS.

Certain English politicians seem averse to the exclusion of Irishmen from the consideration of Imperial questions. Lady Florence Dixie, who has written many admirable letters in advocacy of Home Rule for Ireland, suggests the following arrangement:

"I go on the assumption that the Imperial Parliament at Westminster as at present composed will continue to represent Imperial interests, *in which case* regarding Ireland as a distinct kingdom from Great Britain, I hold that an Irish Parliament should be equally composed of a House of Lords and a House of Commons. When matters purely British require settlement, let Westminster legislate thereon; and when matters purely Irish require settlement, let College Green legislate thereon. But in Imperial matters the 'ayes' of *both* Parliaments should count for, and the 'noes' of *both* count against, any measure under discussion; so that in Imperial matters the two Parliaments would be as one.

"Having said so much, I am bound to add, however, that I am one of those who yearn for and eagerly expect the day on which Imperial Federation shall be accomplished. I would like to see Parliaments in England, Ireland, Scotland, and Wales, each severally empowered to legislate on matters purely connected with themselves, while sending delegates or representatives to a Central Imperial Assembly at Westminster, at which should also assemble the delegates or representatives of all our Colonial Legislatures throughout the world. It appears to me that this would be the first real Imperial Parliament that we should have ever seen, and when the growing necessity for Imperial Federation is daily becoming more urgent, an arrangement of this sort would seem to be the only workable method possible. We *must* keep pace with Progress, it is no use hanging back. What was good in 1860 is no good in 1880, and what was good in 1880 will be antediluvian and utterly impossible in 1900. The only custom that I think will long outlive the century of nineteen hundred, is *Home Rule*. True unity can only be assured by allowing nations to manage their own affairs, while many states, nay, the whole universe could be made one by convening to one Central Assembly the chosen representatives or Imperial M.P.s of the different Legislatures of the World."

A LETTER TO HIS HOLINESS POPE LEO XIII.

By W. J. O'Neill Daunt.

Mr. O'Neill Daunt has addressed the following letter to his Holiness the Pope:

Most Holy Father,

I trust that your Holiness will pardon a humble Irish Catholic for placing before you his thoughts on a subject which appears to him of essential interest to the Catholic religion in Ireland.

It is rumoured that the English Government desire to effect some arrangement with your Holiness by which they expect to obtain control over, or influence in, the appointment of the Irish bishops. Of course, I know not the particulars of the rumoured proposals; but I do know that on various occasions in past years it has been the strong desire of that Government to acquire an influence in our episcopal appointments; and it is more than probable that they are now, as formerly, actuated by the same desire.

In view of any attempt on their part in this direction, it is desirable to consider their historical and political relations with the Irish people.

It would be wrong, in this retrospect, to refer to the sanguinary efforts in former centuries to crush Catholicity out of existence, if we did not find an anti-Irish and anti-Catholic spirit operative at the present day—its exhibition modified, of course, in accordance with the modern policy, which effects by an economic process what was formerly effected by violence.

In Elizabeth's reign the Reformation was sought to be propagated in Ireland by "fines, imprisonment, tortures, and death; unscrupulously employed by the ecclesiastical as well as civil agents in that alleged Reformation."*

King James I. confiscated six whole counties in the province of Ulster, supplanting the native Catholics with Scotch and English Protestants. His Majesty said: "Root out Papists, plant Ireland with Puritans, and then secure it."

The reigns of King James and of his son, King Charles I., were marked by the confiscation of the estates of the Irish proprietors, and by a systematic endeavour to uproot the Catholic religion. Yet the Irish were loyal to King Charles, for they deemed his tyranny more endurable than the tyranny of the antagonist power that overthrew his throne and brought him to the scaffold. The extermination of the whole Irish race, including the Catholic descendants of the old English settlers, was the favourite object of the English Parliament of the period.

When King Charles was beheaded, the reins of State were assumed by the usurper Cromwell. His rule was marked by the massacres of the Irish he committed at Drogheda and at Wexford, and by the vast confiscations of Irish estates whose owners had been loyal to the late unhappy king. He died in 1658.

In 1660 Charles II. was restored. During his reign the public exercise of the Catholic religion was permitted; but the Cromwellian confiscations of Irish landed property were, with few exceptions, confirmed.

Charles died in 1685, and his brother James, by whom he was succeeded, incurred the hostility of so large a portion of his English subjects that, after a short reign of scarcely four years, he was forced to abdicate his crown. He took refuge in France, whence in 1689 he sailed for Ireland, in the hope of striking a blow for the recovery of his throne. The fortunes of war were against him, and his ill-starred campaign was closed by another flight to France.

The garrison and people of Limerick stood out to the last for King James. William of Orange, James's victorious son-in-law and rival, who had previously besieged Limerick without success, renewed his attack on that city on the 25th of August, 1691. The siege was protracted for several weeks; and after a prolonged struggle, in which both sides displayed great bravery, the city surrendered to William's

---

* These are the words of the Rev. Maziere Brady in his Preface to "State Papers."

general, Ginckle, on the terms known as the Treaty of Limerick.

By that treaty William undertook that the Catholics should enjoy the free and unmolested exercise of their religion; that all the inhabitants 'of the counties of Limerick, Cork, Clare, Kerry, and Mayo who had fought for King James should possess their estates and practise their callings and professions undisturbed. The only oath they were required to take was the oath of allegiance to William and Mary.

Not one article of that treaty was observed. Acts were passed to violate every one of its articles; to reduce the Catholics who still retained land to the alternative of surrendering their terrritorial rights or renouncing their faith; and to disqualify all Catholics from practising their callings and professions. The Irish Parliament of the period was largely composed of Protestants who held confiscated estates. William had confiscated one million and sixty thousand acres, and the holders of those and of previous forfeitures conceived that their best security against any possible resumption was to crush the Catholics to the dust. The atrocious laws that effected this purpose constitute what is called the Penal Code.

But while those laws contiuued to operate, the English Government was incessantly employed in active efforts, legislative and administrative, to paralyse every Irish interest, commercial, manufacturing, agricultural, and even pastoral. This persistent and powerful hostility was destructive to the interests of the Irish Protestants, and as years went on the imperative necessity of self-defence against English aggression produced in the Protestant mind a sentiment of Irish nationality. The mere fact of legislating at home also necessarily generated an attachment to their own country, and it is most worthy of especial note that in proportion as national principles advanced among the Protestants, in the same proportion did their sectarian animosity to Catholics decline.

In December, 1775, Henry Grattan entered the Irish Parliament. A Protestant himself, he worked through his long and glorious life to remove the restrictions under which his Catholic countrymen laboured. He spurned the insolent claim of the English Parliament to usurp legislative power over Ireland. Under his influence and that of his colleagues one after another of the penal shackles was removed from the

Catholics in 1778, 1779, 1782, and 1793 ; and there cannot be a doubt that if the Irish Parliament had continued to exist it would in a very few years have restored the Catholics to full political equality. Influenced by Grattan, it had asserted its legislative independence in 1782 ; and England, by the voices of her King, Lords, and Commons, had pledged herself to respect that independence for all future time. The Protestant feeling towards Catholics had in general lost much of its ancient acerbity, and all things seemed tending to the final extinction of old feuds, and the amalgamation of Irishmen of all creeds in one great national fraternity.

But Ireland would in that case have become strong and prosperous ; and in order to keep her weak and powerless, Pitt, the potent English Minister, resolved to check the growing fusion of her inhabitants, to revive the internecine hatreds that were gradually passing away, and to inflame those hatreds to a pitch of sanguinary fury. To effect this purpose his agents in Ireland commenced a persecution of the people which may be truly described as diabolical. The persecution accomplished the purpose of its authors: the people were driven to rebel in 1798, and the outrages on both sides which necessarily accompanied such an outbreak effectually realised the design of the Government in renewing the rancorous hatreds of classes, and in affording a pretext for covering Ireland with a large army of occupation. Under terror of that army in the country, and by the employment of enormous bribery in Parliament, the Union—rejected in 1799—was in 1800 forced on the prostrate and unfortunate country. It was a crime of the blackest turpitude. To achieve it cost some millions of money, and the sacrifice of many thousand lives.

Such, holy Father, were the hideous methods by which the Irish Parliament was destroyed, and by which the English Parliament obtained legislative power over Ireland. Pitt had pretended that the Union should be followed by Catholic Emancipation, but he subsequently told King George III. that he never would obtrude the Catholic question on his Majesty's notice. Twenty-nine years later the measure was conceded ; but the concession would not then have been made if O'Connell had not convinced the vernment that the alternative was civil war.

Eighty-seven years have passed since the Irish Parliament was destroyed by the means I have described. The long interval presents a sad record of turbulence generated by popular misery; enormous abstraction of Irish revenue, public and private, by dishonest taxation and by absenteeism; decay of Irish manufacturing interests; periodical famines; our population diminished by more than three millions, partly by deaths from famine, partly by the emigration of our people from their country, which the Union had stripped of the means of supporting them. I do not know the exact proportion of Protestant and Catholic emigrants at present; but I know that in the decade ending in 1870 thirty-six Catholics had emigrated for one Episcopalian Protestant, and nineteen Catholics for one Presbyterian. To get rid of the Irish race has been the traditionary policy of English Governments for centuries. In ruder ages the object was effected by massacre; in our more civilised period it is effected by a process that goes far to render Ireland uninhabitable.

Home Rule, which we have persistently sought since the date of the Union, simply means that the Irish nation should retain the control of their own special concerns. It means the retention in Ireland of the gifts, material and intellectual, which God has bestowed on our country, and the development of those gifts for the benefit of the Irish people. The Union, on the contrary, means that the products of Ireland, material and intellectual, should be utilised, not for her own benefit, but for the benefit of England.

Whatever we have lost there is one possession which the mass of our nation have retained—fidelity to the Catholic Church, of which your Holiness is the visible head. With the mass of our nation the sentiments of Irish nationality and of Catholic fidelity are so thoroughly interwoven that any attempt to sever them would be a most dangerous experiment. It is our earnest desire that the necessary ecclesiastical intercourse between your Holiness and the Irish Catholics, clerical and lay, should be direct and intimate, and undisturbed by the intervention, direct or indirect, of the English Government. With the dark record of that Government and of its policy to Ireland, there could be no surer way to deprive the Irish hierarchy of the confidence of the Irish Catholics than to allow the English Ministry any voice or influence in Irish ecclesiastical appointments. And it needs not be said that religion would sustain a heavy blow from such a deadly severance of our bishops and their flocks.

In all I have now written there is not one word inconsistent with our loyalty to Queen Victoria. We object to the rule in Ireland of the London Parliament, knowing the infamous means by which that rule was acquired and the horrible consequences which for eighty-seven years it has produced. We are loyal to Her Majesty, not as Queen of England but as Queen of Ireland, and we loyally desire that Queen Victoria should govern her Irish subjects through an Irish Ministry and an Irish Parliament. To this I will only add that the Irish Catholics heartily, fervently, disclaim all desire for political ascendency in our restored Constitution; being firmly convinced that the peace, prosperity, and stability of the Irish State can best be promoted by the perfect political equality of all classes of religionists.

In conclusion, permit me, most Holy Father, in this year of your Jubilee, to lay at your feet the homage of my congratulations and filial devotion. I implore your Holiness's apostolic benediction upon my declining years, as also upon all the individuals of my family and household. I pray the Almighty to prosper and protect your Holiness; and I pray Him also to preserve the Irish Church from the fatal taint of English Governmental interference. I beg to subscribe myself of your Holiness the deeply respectful and devoted servant,

W. J. O'N. DAUNT.

Kilcascan, Co. Cork, 17th June, 1887.

THE END.

INDEX.

ABERDEEN, Lord, Viceroy	367
Achill, its inhabitants slandered	127
Agitation—how conducted by O'Connell	57
American Irish—their sentiments	62, 63
Aggressive fanaticism	125, 126, 129
Aristocracy of the 18th century	1, 2, 3
Anti-Irish State Church—its origin	93
How introduced and propagated	94, 95
Guaranteed by the Union	96
Its income	97
Pleas for upholding it examined	102—114
Its social and political results	121
Anti-tithe agitation	124
Association for Repeal founded	192
BAGENAL OF DUNLECKNY—his social habits	5, 6
Bankruptcy of Ireland in 1816—how produced	336
Butt, Isaac—in the Corporation debate	230
In the Home Rule Conference	305—311
His death	311
CASTLEREAGH—tries in vain to bribe Carew	1
His financial "sketch"	335
He buys the Presbyterians	116, 228
Catholics—how affected by the penal laws	2
Catholicity—sectarian attacks on	54, 56, 61, 120
Catholic Volunteers in 1782	3, 4
Catholic Emancipation promised to follow the Union	15
Clare, Earl of—his shameless declaration of bribery	332
He is used and despised by Pitt	28
His death	29
Clontarf—projected meeting at, prevented by the Government	241
Conference on Home Rule	304
Carrick-on-Suir—its historical castle	202
Cabins of labouring families described	213, 214
Condition of Ireland anomalous	216
Castletown-Kinneigh—evictions at	170, 171
Conciliation Hall opened	237
Connorville entered by soldiers	132
Chartism	156
"Chartist Christian Church"	157
Coercion Act	163

Index.

Corporation of Dublin—adopts Repeal in 1843, and again in 1871 ... 228—301
Cornwallis, Marquis, attests the sanguinary anarchy resulting from Pitt's policy 326, 327
Crawford, Sharman—his political changes ... 206

DAVIS, THOMAS—his character, his death ... 272
Dangan—inhabited by Roger O'Connor ... 133
Burned ... 133
Depopulation of Ireland, ancient and modern ... 62, 65
Deputation of Repealers to the Dublin Corporation ... 301
Disestablishment of the anti-Irish Church ... 98, 101
Death of O'Connell ... 276

EGAN family, plot against their lives ... 82, 89
Elective Franchise, anecdotes of 152, 176
Evictions at Castletown-Kinneigh 170, 171
Exclusion of Repealers from office ... 205
Expansion of Repeal movement ... 199, 207, 212
Extermination of the People ... 62, 65
Errington's diplomacy ... 359

FAMINE—its miseries intensified by the Union 273, 275
Farnham, Lord—his polemical crusade ... 54 (note).
Fenianism ... 291
Franchise, Elective—anecdotes of 152, 176
Federalism broached by O'Connell ... 269

GEORGE IV. reluctant to pass Emancipation ... 89
Grattan, Henry—his last words in the Irish Parliament ... 44
Grattan, Richard, on Home Rule ... 300
Galbraith, Rev. Joseph A., on Home Rule ... 300—307
Grey, Sir George, on a Statutory Parliament 283, 284

HAMILTON, Rev. Mr.—his plot to hang the Egans ... 81, 87
Hall, Mr. S. C.—his letter on Achill ... 127
His appreciation of the inhabitants ... 127 (note).
Home Rule indispensable to national life ... 217

IMPRISONMENT of O'Connell ... 247

KEOGH, JOHN, O'Connell's predecessor as a Catholic agitator ... 57

LAND agitation ... 313
Landlords—how they might have saved themselves 314, 360
Landlord—an Ulster Conservative Landlord on Home Rule 302
Life of the Repealers in prison 249, 251
Liberation of the Repeal prisoners 255, 256
Letter from the Author to the Pope ... 391

MILITARY preparations against the proposed Clontarf meeting ... 241
M——y, Lord—his financial expedients ... 32, 33
Maguan, the spy ... 25
Magistrates—exuberant loyalty of ... 78, 81

Index. 399

Monster meetings 234
Montgomery, Martin—his anti-Repeal book 234

NATION newspaper founded in 1842 219
Nationality—What is it? 217, 218
Night on the Shannon side 264
Norbury, Lord—his administration of justice... 20

ORANGE faction—their hostility to temperance 201
Orange amusements ... ... 326—328
Orange Repealers 52
Orange and Catholic corporators compared 53, 388
O'Connell opposes the veto 67
   His definition of Repeal 196, 197
   He opposes the Union 90
   His speech in 1834 178
   His speech in 1843 228
O'Connor, Arthur—an honest politician 131
O'Connor, Roger—his military projects 131
   His imprisonment 132
O'Connor, Feargus—career of 133
   His election for the County Cork... 135
   His election for Nottingham 161
   His death 162
Obstruction v. Destruction 162
O'Brien, Smith—his career 238
   His *émeute* 279
   His death 289

PARNELL, his parliamentary tactics 310
   His personal qualities 312
   His imprisonment 317
   His release 317
Parliament of Ireland—its faults, its merits 36, 38
   Its early origin ... ... 320 (note).
Parson, an eccentric 168
Poetry of the *Nation* 221, 222, 223
Prosecution of the Repealers ... ... 244—246
Protest of Irish Peers against the Union 385
Protestant Repealers 278

QUAKER—opposition to a rector's demand by a Friend ... 102
Queen—visit of Her Majesty to Ireland—comment of the
   Times thereon 279, 280

"RIGBY"—his modest assurance; his political adventure ... 68, 73
Regency question 383
Repeal debate in 1834—speeches of O'Connell, Spring
   Rice, etc. 177
Revival of Irish Parliament by royal prerogative 386
Rebellion of 1798, designedly provoked by the Government 15
Repeal Association founded 192
Repeal defined by O'Connell 199
Repeal prisoners liberated 255, 256
Rossmore, Lord—his notion of moral force 356

SLANDER clothed in pious language 128
Spies in the Fenian camp ... ... 291—296
Sympathy of English politicians with foreign nationalities... 281
Separation predicted as ultimately resulting from the
   Union 292, 293
Steele—career of 260
Scotland visited 270

TAXATION of Ireland excessive 216, 335, 369
Tennent, Emerson—his anti-national servility 123
   His absurdity 183
Torture inflicted on the people to goad them into rebellion... 16—19
Terry-Alts 261, 262

UNION—how produced 10, 13, 15, 22, 25
   Productive of disloyalty 40, 42, 44, 62
   Its success dependent on military force 242, 331
   Foments international rancour 39, 341
   Parliamentary opponents of 40

VETO—opposed by O'Connell 67
Visits to Scotland 270
Viceroyalty—its abolition unanimously opposed by the
   Repeal Association 239

WAR VESSELS—how employed on the Irish coast 125
Webb—his anti-tithe plea 102

CHARLES DICKENS AND EVANS, CRYSTAL PALACE PRESS.

www.ingramcontent.com/pod-product-compliance
Lightning Source LLC
Chambersburg PA
CBHW050849300426
44111CB00010B/1191